Ideas of the Liberal Party

The House of Commons, 1833 by Sir George Hayter, oil on canvas, 1833–1843: © National Portrait Gallery, London.

Ideas of the Liberal Party

Perceptions, Agendas and Liberal Politics in
the House of Commons, 1832–52

by
Joseph Coohill

Wiley-Blackwell
For
The Parliamentary History Yearbook Trust

© 2011 The Parliamentary History Yearbook Trust
Wiley-Blackwell is now part of John Wiley & Sons

Registered Office
John Wiley & Sons Ltd, The Atrium, Southern Gate, Chichester, West Sussex, PO19 8SQ, United Kingdom

Editorial Offices
350 Main Street, Malden, MA 02148-5020, USA
9600 Garsington Road, Oxford, OX4 2DQ, UK
The Atrium, Southern Gate, Chichester, West Sussex, PO19 8SQ, UK

For details of our global editorial offices, for customer services, and for information about how to apply for permission to reuse the copyright material in this book please see our website at www.wiley.com/wiley-blackwell.

The right of Joseph Coohill to be identified as the author of the editorial material in this work has been asserted in accordance with the Copyright, Designs and Patents Act 1988.

Wiley also publishes its books in a variety of electronic formats. Some content that appears in print may not be available in electronic books.

Library of Congress Cataloging-in-Publication Data
Library of Congress Cataloging-in-Publication data is available for this book

A catalogue record for this title is available from the British Library
Set in 10/12pt Bembo
by Toppan Best-set Premedia Limited
Printed and bound in Singapore
by Hó Printing Pte Ltd

1   2011

CONTENTS

Parliamentary History: Texts & Studies

ACKNOWLEDGMENTS

This book began as a doctoral thesis, and I am grateful to the Faculty of Modern History at the University of Oxford, and to the rector and fellows of Lincoln College for their support during that stage of my work. Financial assistance for the archival travel required for this book was generously provided by the Graduate Research Fund of Lincoln College, the Research Support Committee of the Royal Historical Society and the Committee for Graduate Studies in the Faculty of Modern History. I am also very grateful for an Overseas Research Award from the Committee of Vice-Chancellors and Principals of the United Kingdom. I was very fortunate to have been supervised by the late Dr Angus Macintyre, Mr W.E.S. Thomas and Dr John Stevenson. Most of all, however, I was given excellent supervision by Professor David Eastwood, who rescued me after the death of Dr Macintyre, and kept me afloat in the following years. The bracing criticism of Drs Angus Hawkins and Peter Mandler during the examination of the thesis was not only necessary, but vital in helping me conceive how the thesis could be transformed into a scholarly monograph.

The staff at the record offices and archives listed in the Bibliography were universally helpful and enthusiastic. The Le Marchant family kindly deposited the papers of Sir Denis Le Marchant at Parliamentary Archives for me to consult. Mr W.E.S. Thomas generously allowed me to make copies of his transcribed collection of the correspondence of Joseph Parkes. Paul Seaward at the History of Parliament Trust very kindly supplied me with electronic copies of the House of Commons Division Lists.

I am grateful to the Board of Trustees of the Parliamentary History Yearbook Trust for funding the publication of this monograph, as well as for permission to reproduce some of the material from my two articles in the journal *Parliamentary History*, which appears in Chapters 1 and 2 of this book. These articles are: 'Parliamentary Guides, Political Identity and the Presentation of Modern Politics, 1832–1846', *Parliamentary History*, xx (2003), 263–84; and 'The "Liberal Brigade": Ideas of Co-operation between Liberal MPs in 1835', *Parliamentary History*, xxiv (2005), 231–46.

Duquesne University provided a presidential scholarship to give me time to do some of the additional research and writing required to update and revise the text. I am grateful to Christine Pollock in the Office of Research for her assistance in applying for grants and further funding. My colleagues in the History Department have been uncommonly understanding of my research struggles during the past few years. Theresa Raab helped with much of the editing of the text. I could not have completed the index without the immense and timely help of Professor Patricia Trutty-Coohill.

I owe a great debt to Dr John Powell, who insisted that I transform the thesis into a monograph. The anonymous referees for the *Parliamentary History: Texts & Studies* series provided much-needed criticism, and Dr Clyve Jones and Professor Stephen Taylor were highly supportive in seeing the book through to publication. Anne Rickard provided excellent copy-editing, and was very patient with my slow responses.

Professionally, I have no greater friend and confidant than Dr Philip Salmon. As doctoral students, we worked on the same period, shared resources, travelled to archives together, and aired our ideas and interpretative challenges in a seemingly endless number of conversations in a divergent number of settings. In subsequent years, he has provided more advice, help, criticism and opportunities for discussing the 'Age of Reform' than I had any right to expect. It should be a friendship of mutual benefit, but it is so over-balanced in favour of his contributions to my work that I will never be able to bring the scales back into line. My only hope is that he does not mind overly much.

I wish to dedicate this book to my young son, Christopher. I doubt the subject of this book will ever capture his attention, but perhaps some day he will understand that, without him, professional accomplishments are meaningless.

2011   Joseph Coohill

NOTES ON THE TEXT

In this work, capital letters are used to refer to the 'party' labels given to MPs in *Dod's Parliamentary Companion*, which are explained in detail in Chapter 1. Lower-case letters are used to refer to the more general use of the terms 'conservative', 'liberal', 'radical', 'reformer' and 'whig'; e.g. 'Joseph Hume, Radical MP for Middlesex, held radical and utilitarian opinions regarding state institutions'. Except when starting a sentence, 'Liberal' with a capital 'L' is only used to refer to 'Liberal' MPs within the 'Liberal Party'; 'liberal' is used in its more general, that is, ideological, sense. Throughout the text, therefore, non-conservative MPs may be referred to collectively as 'liberals', although this has been kept to a minimum to avoid potential confusion with the Liberal Party subgroup of 'Liberals'. 'Liberal Party' refers to the 'Liberal', 'Radical', 'Reformer', 'Repealer' and 'Whig' coalition of MPs in the house of commons; 'Conservative Party' refers to the party of 'Conservative' and 'Tory' MPs, both as described in *Dod*. Exceptions to this rule are, of course, when making direct quotations from correspondence and other sources where I have used the original capitalisation.

The transcriptions of the Parkes correspondence kindly lent to me by William Thomas are, in the first instance, cited as 'transcribed by W.E.S. Thomas', and thereafter as 'Parkes (WEST)'. The citing of these transcriptions is not to be confused with my own work in the Parkes collection at the University College London Manuscripts Room, referenced as such.

All references to Hansard's *Parliamentary Debates* are from the third series.

The house of commons divisions analysed here were taken from the official House of Commons Division Lists, *The Times* and Hansard. There are two major exceptions: official division lists were not compiled before 1836; and *The Times* often did not list MPs' names in their division lists, simply giving the division number totals. In these exceptional cases, I have omitted citing the official division lists and *The Times*. Whenever the evidence was available, I have included division tellers and pairs in my analyses. As such, the division numbers in the text do not necessarily agree with any one source. For instance, the official division lists do not include pairs but, on particularly important divisions, Hansard and *The Times* did. My desire was to gauge voting behaviour as an expression of opinion. That is the justification for including pairs, even though they did not, technically, vote through the division lobbies.

In footnotes, full citations for each work are given at the first appearance in every chapter. Subsequent citations use short titles.

ABBREVIATIONS

BIHR	*Bulletin of the Institute of Historical Research*
BL	British Library, London
Bodl.	Bodleian Library, Oxford
Dod	*Dod's Parliamentary Companion*
EHR	*English Historical Review*
f., ff.	folio, folios
HJ	*Historical Journal*
HPC	*History of Parliament, The House of Commons*
MP	member of parliament
MS, MSS	manuscript, manuscripts
ODNB	*Oxford Dictionary of National Biography*
PA	Parliamentary Archives
Parkes (WEST)	Joseph Parkes Papers, transcribed by W.E.S. Thomas
RO	Record Office
TNA	The National Archives, Kew
TRHS	*Transactions of the Royal Historical Society*
UL	University Library

LIST OF FIGURES AND TABLES

Figures

Tables

Introduction

Ideas of the Liberal Party offers a fresh analysis of a much-explored topic and era. Liberal governments and members of parliament in the 1832 to 1852 period have attracted no small number of historians, who have analysed them in several different ways, and shown that the years after the passage of the 1832 Reform Act carried many divergent messages and meanings. Some historians have argued that the Reform Act did not radically alter the nature and organisation of British politics and power, and that it was essentially a conservative measure designed to preserve elite power. This would have seemed to many contemporaries a misinterpretation. For them, the Reform Act provided a handy marker for a break from the past, and a myth that could be used to project a new political world, defined nationally with Westminster at its centre.[1] One of the most important aspects of this newly perceived political world was the emergence of the Liberal Party between 1832 and 1852, prompted by the conditions created by the Act.[2] The Whig government of 1830 had presented its reform bills as popular (although not 'democratic') measures, and liberal and reforming politicians were to benefit from the Act's final passage. Starting in 1832, liberal governments dominated British politics, partly because of the gains for reform-minded MPs in the 1832 election;[3] and partly because, on the surface at least, 'liberal' had lost some of its more radical and jacobin overtones, and by the late 1830s had become a respectable political label.[4] This dominance was to last until 1886, with liberal governments in power for roughly 42 of those 54 years.[5] But using the term 'dominance' might imply that liberals of this period were a unified, tightly knit governing force which retained popular support and kept the conservatives out of office through sophisticated organisation and a convincing and coherent ideology. This was not

---

[1] In the vast literature on the effects of the Reform Act and its interpretations, see the following recent works: J.A. Phillips and C. Wetherell, 'The Great Reform Act and the Political Modernization of England', *American Historical Review*, c (1995), 411–36; M. Brock, *The Great Reform Act* (1973); T.A. Jenkins, *Parliament, Party and Politics in Victorian Britain* (Manchester, 1996); P.J. Salmon, *Electoral Reform at Work: Local Politics and National Parties, 1832–1841* (Woodbridge, 1996); *Rethinking the Age of Reform: Britain 1780–1850*, ed. A. Burns and J. Innes (Cambridge, 2007). For the importance of the differences in the Scottish Reform Act and Scottish reform movements, see G. Pentland, *Radicalism, Reform, and National Identity in Scotland, 1820–1833* (Woodbridge, 2008).

[2] J.P. Parry, *The Rise and Fall of Liberal Government in Victorian Britain* (New Haven, CT, 1993), 72–3.

[3] C. Seymour, *Electoral Reform in England and Wales: The Development and Operation of the Parliamentary Franchise 1832–1885* (New Haven, CT, 1915), 99–102.

[4] C.H. Chambers, *Phases of Party* (1872), 63–4; W.H.D. Adams, *English Party Leaders and English Parties: From Walpole to Peel; Including a Review of the Political History of the Last One Hundred and Fifty Years* (1878); T. O'Brien, *A Glance at Parties* (1844); W. Atkinson, *The Spirit of the Magna Carta: Or Universal Representation, the Genius of the British Constitution* (1841). See also Parry, *Rise and Fall of Liberal Government*, 1–3; P. Jupp, *The Governing of Britain, 1688–1848: The Executive, Parliament, and the People* (2006), 191–202; C. Alington, *Twenty Years: Being a Study in the Development of the Party System between 1815 & 1835* (Oxford, 1921); D.E.D. Beales, *The Political Parties of Nineteenth-Century Britain* (1971).

[5] See Parry, *Rise and Fall of Liberal Government*, 1, for a similar argument, and one that includes the political philosophy of liberalism in addition to liberal politics and politicians. See also J. Bourne, *British Politics 1832–1885* (Oxford, 1994).

the case. The MPs who will be defined here as 'the Liberal Party' were neither organised in the way 20th-century parties were, nor were their political ideas uniform. It is not surprising, therefore, that this group of liberals (the loose coalition of Whigs, Reformers, Liberals, Radicals and Irish Repealers) has not generally been perceived as constituting an early Liberal Party.[6] Despite the recent work done on pre-Gladstonian liberalism, there exists a general conception that Whigs, Reformers, Liberals, Radicals and Repealers stumbled through the 1830s, 1840s and early 1850s, working together only temporarily, and bickering among themselves as often as they opposed the tories and conservatives in the house of commons. The Liberal Party, so the traditional argument goes, was not formed until 1859, at a meeting at Willis's Rooms in London, where Peelites, Liberals and Radicals agreed to work together to oppose Conservative policy.[7] This book attempts to change that impression in ways that have not previously been explored. The historiography of the Liberal Party before Gladstone has largely focused on the ideology and behaviour of party leaders, the drama of high politics in government during this period, and popular politics in the localities. What are missing, though, are studies of conceptions of the Liberal Party, what it meant to contemporaries and how it was formed through a combination of self-perception and political language, presentation and adherence to new conceptions of liberal politics. *Ideas of the Liberal Party* attempts to be such a study.

With a few exceptions, recent historians have generally moved away from a structuralist, Namierite and Gashian approach to the politics of the 1832–52 period, and have focused on more conceptual and ideological underpinnings to the rough and tumble of daily political affairs. In the pages of scholarly journals, and between the covers of monographs, 'whiggism', 'liberalism', 'religion', 'evangelicalism' and 'liberal value system' have replaced explanations of political 'systems', administrative analyses and biographically based studies of cabinet figures. At the same time, the names of Brent, Hilton, Mandler, Parry and Taylor have replaced those of Gash, Hanham, Moore and Aspinall in seminar discussions and in reviews. It would, however, be unfair to characterise the contributions of Gash, Hanham, Moore and Aspinall as blinkered analyses of political structures and personalities, with no thought given to the ideological dimension of politics and the ways in which trends in thinking passed among groups of political men. But, 'structure' was the fundamental concern for all four, whether they were interested in party organisation, elections and the workings of whatever political machines operated at the time, as were Gash, Hanham and Moore, or with biographies of the highest of high political players, cabinet members and party leaders, as was Aspinall.[8] Indeed, in many ways, the most complete study of the early

---

[6] See 'Notes on the Text' for explanations on how these terms are used.

[7] See A. Hawkins, *British Party Politics 1852–1886* (1998), 311; R.K. Webb, *Modern England from the Eighteenth Century to the Present* (1980), 316. This perception also holds sway in popular conceptions of Victorian history. Most textbooks, reference works and popular literature follow this interpretation, from J. Gardiner and N. Wenborn's *The History Today Companion to British History* (1995), 467, to the party propaganda from the modern-day Liberal Democrats on the Internet (www.libdems.org.uk).

[8] This is not to argue that biographical political analysis is a thing of the past. The recent contributions of Leslie Mitchell and E.A. Smith are testimony to its continuing validity. See L.G. Mitchell, *Lord Melbourne, 1779–1848* (Oxford, 1997); E.A. Smith, *Lord Grey, 1764–1845* (Oxford, 1990). For Aspinall, Gash, Hanham and Moore, see A. Aspinall, 'English Party Organization in the Early Nineteenth Century', *EHR*, xli (1926), 389–411; A. Aspinall, *Three Nineteenth Century Diaries* (1949); N. Gash, *Politics in the Age of Peel: A Study in the Technique of Parliamentary Representation 1830–1850* (1953); N. Gash, *Reaction and Reconstruction in English Politics,*

19th-century liberals was for some time Donald Southgate's *Passing of the Whigs*, which also focused on personalities in a somewhat biographical way.[9]

It would also be unfair to claim that those more recent historians interested in elections and party structures, notably Frank O'Gorman, John Phillips and Philip Salmon, have not put forward fresh and sensitive analyses of political and electoral structures. Their contributions have been vital to a new understanding of the reformed political world, and have shown in great depth how significant the details of elections and party management have been for larger ideas about political participation in an emerging democracy.[10]

The bulk of work in the past few decades, however, has examined the less structural aspects mentioned above. For the early 19th-century liberals, Richard Brent has provided an analysis that details the ideological background to the type of political liberalism that became dominant in the 1832–52 period. His *Liberal Anglican Politics* is a study of 'the distinctively religious outlook' of the whig governments of the 1830s, which he terms 'liberal anglicanism'. This liberal anglicanism was a product of the change in whig thinking from Foxite constitutionalism, which stressed an opening of the mechanics of the constitution, to an ideal of constitutional moralism, which emphasized the moral and instructive value of national institutions, including the constitution, the church of England and parliament. Partly forged in the tutorial rooms of liberal theologians at Oxford and Cambridge, liberal anglicanism had a great deal to do with the eventual attachment of dissenting sentiment to the Liberal Party post-1832.[11] Boyd Hilton has also argued vigorously for the foregrounding of religion in analyses of political life in the first half of the 19th century. His *Age of Atonement* challenges interpretations of economic change in this period that stress the secular (indeed, almost mechanistic) nature of that change. Public ideas of political and economic improvement betrayed more private reflections of salvation and atonement, with God's work on earth being partly in the hands of political and social leaders.[12] Conceptual and intellectual elements of liberal politics have also been emphasized by Peter Mandler, who has concentrated on two such aspects in the early 19th century: whiggism and aristocratic styles of governance. Both, he argues, were reasserted in the 1830s and 1840s to create a government of well-

[8] *(continued)* *1832–1852* (Oxford, 1965); H.J. Hanham, *Elections and Party Management: Politics in the Time of Disraeli and Gladstone* (1959); D.C. Moore, *The Politics of Deference: A Study of the Mid-Nineteenth Century English Political System* (Hassocks, 1976).

[9] D. Southgate, *The Passing of the Whigs 1832–1886* (1962).

[10] Phillips and Wetherell, 'The Great Reform Act'; J.A. Phillips, *The Great Reform Bill in the Boroughs: English Electoral Behaviour, 1818–1841* (Oxford, 1987); J.A. Phillips, 'Popular Politics in Unreformed England', *Journal of Modern History*, lii (1980), 599–625; J.A. Phillips, 'Parliamentary Parties and Municipal Politics: 1835 and the Party System', in *Computing Parliamentary History, George III to Victoria*, ed. J.A. Phillips (Edinburgh, 1994), 48–85; J.A. Philips and C. Wetherell, 'The Great Reform Bill of 1832 and the Rise of Partisanship', *Journal of Modern History*, lxiii (1991), 621–46; Salmon, *Electoral Reform at Work*; F. O'Gorman, *The Emergence of the British Two-Party System, 1760–1832* (New York, 1982); F. O'Gorman, *Voters, Patrons, and Parties: The Unreformed Electoral System of Hanoverian England 1734–1832* (Oxford, 1989); F. O'Gorman, 'Electoral Deference in "Unreformed" England: 1760–1832', *Journal of Modern History*, lvi (1984), 391–429; F. O'Gorman, 'Party Politics in the Early Nineteenth Century', *EHR*, cii (1987), 63–84; F. O'Gorman, 'Campaign Rituals and Ceremonies: The Social Meaning of Elections in England 1780–1860', *Past & Present*, no. 135 (1992), 79–115.

[11] R. Brent, *Liberal Anglican Politics: Whiggery, Religion, and Reform, 1830–1841* (Oxford, 1987), 1–7, 15–16, 25–37, 52–3, 63.

[12] B. Hilton, *The Age of Atonement: The Influence of Evangelicalism on Social and Economic Thought, 1785–1865* (Oxford, 1998), introduction.

connected elites with a deep sense of national responsibility, and a corresponding willingness to respond to external pressure for reform. Mandler's ideas challenge the traditional notion that the 1830s and 1840s saw the rise of a new liberalism which replaced the older tory and whig styles of politics. The whiggish idea that parliament was a national and guiding institution, and not simply a utilitarian mechanics' shop for correcting administrative faults, held sway until the 1850s, he argues, by which time liberalism had adopted much of whig thinking, had become more relevant to the post-chartist age, before eventually replacing aristocratic whiggism as a style of governance.[13] More recently, William Hay has shown the historical importance of the Whigs in the eventual emergence of the Liberal Party. Concentrating on the centrality of Henry Brougham as the leading figure in the Whig revival of the early 19th century, Hay stresses his building of alliances with non-tory provincial interests and his aggressive parliamentary tactics which, in effect, 'modernised' the Whigs and may have laid down templates for party strategy as the 1820s and the 1830s progressed.[14] For Hay, the Whigs of the 1820s and 1830s became a dynamic force with broader appeal because of the attachment to, and eventual championing of, the cause of reform. It was whiggism that led 'a more effective centre-left coalition before 1880 than the Labour Party from the 1920s'.[15] It was the Whigs' ideal of government, 'that responsiveness to public opinion and reconciling competing interests with the framework of law', which allied provincial and metropolitan reformers (whom Hay terms 'Liberals') to the Whigs, forming the liberal coalition that would dominate government for most of the 19th century.[16] This dominance of the government benches is, of course, a major theme of Jonathan Parry's essential work on liberalism and the Liberal Party in the 19th century.[17] Like Hay, Parry also sees the late 18th-century Whigs and their younger generation as those who laid the foundation for the 19th-century party. He argues that, to these Whigs, 'fidelity to party spirit was the best guarantee of honourable and principled behaviour', a fidelity maintained by the post-1832 Liberals trying to maintain the proper balance between 'elite authority and orderly popular participation'.[18]

At the radical end of the liberal political spectrum, similar arguments for the close connection between ideology and political action have been put forward by Miles Taylor. His 'reform party', a group of Radicals and Reformers who acted somewhat independently of, and sometimes in opposition to, liberal governments in the 1840s, provided a strong link between liberal and reform-minded electors in the country and MPs in parliament. By making themselves the conduits for petitions, and the mouthpieces for reform within the house of commons, these MPs provided what they saw as a necessary aggravation for liberal ministers, pushing them to pay attention to popular demands for

[13] P. Mandler, *Aristocratic Government in the Age of Reform: Whigs and Liberals, 1830–1852* (Oxford, 1990), 1–4, 280.

[14] W.A. Hay, *The Whig Revival, 1808–1830* (2005), 2–3.

[15] Hay, *Whig Revival*, 176.

[16] Hay, *Whig Revival*, 178. See also Michael Ledger-Lomas, 'The Character of Pitt the Younger and Party Politics, 1830–1860', *HJ*, xlvii (2004), 642–3, for intriguing arguments about how the Whigs used the recent past and Pitt the Younger's supposed bad character, in party propaganda and tactics.

[17] In addition to his *Rise and Fall of Liberal Government*, see J.P. Parry, *Democracy and Religion: Gladstone and the Liberal Party, 1867–1875* (Cambridge, 1986); J.P. Parry, *The Politics of Patriotism: English Liberalism, National Identity, and Europe, 1830–1886* (Cambridge, 2006).

[18] Parry, *Politics of Patriotism*, 34.

things such as the ballot and free trade. Although they would not desert the liberal cause during times of crisis in the house of commons, they considered themselves in the vanguard of reform.[19]

Where Brent, Mandler and Taylor view liberal anglicans, whigs and radicals, Parry sees a relatively cohesive Liberal Party, reasonably confident in its own political ideology to call itself such, and guided by a 'liberal value-system', a broad code of beliefs 'concerned mainly with questions of morals, economy, and efficiency'.[20] Parry has been the dominant historian of 19th-century liberalism and the Liberal Party. His early emphasis on religion in his *Democracy and Religion* has been broadened out to analyse this value system, which included a belief in the supremacy of parliament over the crown, anti-clericalism and general reform of the church of England, the belief that Irish problems had been caused by tory misgovernance, and a desire to redress the worst grievances of dissenters.[21] Further, liberalism meant inclusive government, but also a culture whereby groups of the governed, no matter how incompatible their ideas might be with other groups, accepted the rule of parliamentary law above that of their own particular interests.[22] Most recently, Parry's *Politics of Patriotism* shows how and why European affairs had a major impact on the development and 'rhythms' of 19th-century liberal politics, particularly those issues that arose after 1852.[23] He re-emphasises the liberal value system outlined in *The Rise and Fall of Liberal Government*, but shows how liberal reaction to European affairs solidified that value system, with an increased belief in the constitutional and legal superiority of English liberty and self-government over continental systems. Along with the international dimension of the liberal conviction regarding free trade, low taxes and moral and educational improvement, the continued discussion of, and comparison with, other European governing ideologies were woven together by liberal leaders 'in order to fashion a political agenda'.[24] Parry does not, however, argue that the fashioning of this political agenda was without its difficulties. His first two chapters show quite convincingly that the rhetoric used in forging this agenda created divisions between liberals, and that there were liberals who distrusted this agenda-mongering as pure party politics, more designed to gain or maintain power over the conservatives than to further high ideals.[25] As will be shown here in Chapter 8, this tension was clear between the free trade liberals (the majority of the party) and the liberal protectionists.

So far, the emphasis here has been on relatively recent work concerned with liberals in the 1832–52 period, but a book that analyses ideas of the Liberal Party must take into account John Vincent's seminal *Formation of the Liberal Party*, which has influenced more than one generation of historians. Vincent argued that the Victorian Liberal Party was 'a coalition of convenience, not the instrument of a creed',[26] and that its pre-1859 origins lay in the constituencies, and not at Westminster.[27] I will argue, especially in Chapter 3, that

---

[19] M. Taylor, *The Decline of British Radicalism, 1847–1860* (Oxford, 1995), 6–7, 9–10, 19.

[20] Parry, *Rise and Fall of Liberal Government*, 14.

[21] Parry, *Democracy and Religion*; Parry, *Rise and Fall of Liberal Government*, 14–20.

[22] Parry, *Rise and Fall of Liberal Government*, 3.

[23] Parry, *Politics of Patriotism*, 1–2.

[24] Parry, *Politics of Patriotism*, 35.

[25] Parry, *Politics of Patriotism*, 36–7.

[26] J.R. Vincent, *The Formation of the British Liberal Party, 1857–1868* (1966), 258.

[27] Vincent, *Formation of the British Liberal Party*, xv, xxx–xxi, 82, 258.

this was an overstatement, and that there was a strong sense of Liberal Party commitment in London, and especially in the house of commons. But this is not an anti-Vincent work, for he has provided us with some very significant ideas about the Liberal Party that will find support at various points. In the first instance, there is his belief that the christian dimension of liberalism, however difficult to define exactly, was a fundamental force driving liberal politics.[28] Examples of this will be analysed in Chapters 5, 6 and 7. But perhaps his most important contributions were to show that the notion of being liberal meant, to a great degree, a strong belief in 'manliness', by which he meant personal independence and self-support;[29] and the argument that the Liberal Party filled the power vacuum created by the decline in aristocratic rule.[30] *Ideas of the Liberal Party* shows that both of these important aspects of liberal politics and the nature of the Liberal Party were as present in the 1830s and 1840s as they were in the 1860s and 1870s.

It is the purpose of this book, therefore, to show that a coherent and recognizable Liberal Party existed before 1860, that central party organisation was remarkably distinct given the ad hoc nature of politics in this period, that Liberal Party MPs were a self-defined and relatively disciplined group of politicians sharing a broad sense of liberal politics and, more importantly, that they were willing to use the full scope of that politics to justify their parliamentary action to all concerned. While accepting that the liberals cannot be called a party in the 20th- and 21st-century sense of the word, this book argues that conceptions of the Liberal Party in the 1830s and 1840s were strong enough to define them as a party in line with contemporary meanings in the first half of the 19th century. There were many 'ideas of the Liberal Party'. Some MPs thought it was a party of convenience, an anti-tory coalition whose purpose was to ensure the success of reform measures in parliament and little else.[31] Others thought that it held a higher purpose, that a strong attachment to liberal politics meant that they were bound to act together with other liberals, even in support of measures they would otherwise oppose.[32]

The central argument here, however, is that there were such ideas of the Liberal Party, and that, however loose the coalition of Liberal Party MPs proved to be in terms of divisions and parliamentary behaviour, their own ideas of the party were enough to keep it together. In many ways, this was the party's greatest strength, and the reason it did not fracture over divisive issues such as church rates and free trade. Liberal protectionists, for instance, did not hive off and join Lord George Bentinck and the other tories who abandoned Peel, because they felt that their ideas of the party and their belief in liberal politics were strong enough to hold them together.[33] That a major split in the party did occur in 1886 over Irish home rule implies that the pre-Gladstonian Liberal Party was more durable than its later-century version. Edward Cardwell, secretary of state for war in Gladstone's first administration, was misreading his own party history, therefore, when he said that the liberals were only an ad hoc group that came together on specific issues,

---

[28] Vincent, *Formation of the British Liberal Party*, xvi–xvii.

[29] Vincent, *Formation of the British Liberal Party*, xiv.

[30] Vincent, *Formation of the British Liberal Party*, xii–xiii.

[31] Many Radicals, some Reformers and some Repealers held this idea of the Liberal Party. It is outlined in more detail in Chapter 4, and in Part 2.

[32] This is perhaps most clear in the parliamentary action over Maynooth. See Chapter 7.

[33] See Chapter 8.

and that 'the only man who could have kept together the so-called party, formed from such materials, for so long a time, was Gladstone'.[34]

Despite the protestations of Ian Newbould, 'party' was not a far-fetched concept for contemporaries in the reform period.[35] It was certainly not alien to Gladstone, who saw the 1830s and 1840s as a time when 'party connection [was] in its "normal state" . . . [i.e.] compact and organized'.[36] The difference between parties and factions had been codified at least since 1830, when the anonymous author of the pamphlet, *Parties and Factions in England at the Accession of William IV*, defined party as 'the union of individuals agreeing in principle, and cooperating for the public good', while faction was 'the union of persons by accident, and acting together for their own advantage'.[37] Thomas Spring-Rice, Whig MP for Cambridge and chancellor of the exchequer in Melbourne's 1835–41 government, argued that parliamentary government required 'two great and leading divisions' in the house of commons.[38] And twice in the 1840s, Lord John Russell asserted the strength of party. In 1841, he said that the Liberal Party was 'a vivacious animal',[39] and when describing the likely difficulties the Conservatives were about to face after repealing the corn laws, said: 'the tory party must be very strong if it bears such a shame as it is about to have. But English parties are immortal, though like the constitution, they are oft doomed to death'.[40]

The conceptions of party in the reform period have, however, not received adequate attention from historians. The exception to this is Angus Hawkins' ' "Parliamentary Government" and Victorian Political Parties', in the *English Historical Review*, in which the perceived constitutional role of parties between 1830 and 1880 is analysed. He argues that the previous ways in which parties have been studied (organisational, definitional, electoral and social) have overlooked their constitutional context and their relation to parliamentary government. Parties solved several constitutional dilemmas during this period, according to Hawkins. They functioned to forestall the abuse of power by either the monarchy or the people, helped ensure stable ministries and provided a smooth transition between administrations. All this was accomplished in Victorian Britain because parties were loose enough to avoid becoming solidified oligarchies.[41] The Liberal Party

---

[34] Quoted in T.A. Jenkins, *Gladstone, Whiggery, and the Liberal Party, 1874–1886* (Oxford, 1988), 39–40.

[35] I. Newbould, *Whiggery and Reform, 1830–1841: The Politics of Government* (1990), 8–9, 73, 138. See also I. Newbould, 'Whiggery and the Growth of Party 1830–1841: Organization and the Challenge of Reform', *Parliamentary History*, iv (1985), 137–56; I. Newbould, 'The Emergence of a Two-Party System in England from 1830 to 1841: Roll Call and Reconsideration', *Parliaments, Estates, and Representation*, v (1985), 25–31; I. Newbould, 'William IV and the Dismissal of the Whigs, 1834', *Canadian Journal of History*, xi (1976), 311–30.

[36] BL, Gladstone Papers, Add. MS 44475, f. 173: W.E. Gladstone, 'Party as It Was and Is', unpublished article, 1855.

[37] *Parties and Factions in England at the Accession of William IV* (1830), 1.

[38] T. Spring-Rice, 'The Present State and Conduct of Parties', *Edinburgh Review*, cxliii (1840), 277.

[39] PA, Le Marchant Papers: Russell to Sir Denis Le Marchant, 29 Nov. 1841. See also Staffordshire RO, Anson Papers, D615/P(P)/3/11: M.T. Bass to T.W. Anson, 4 Jan. 1840.

[40] PA, Le Marchant Papers: Russell to Le Marchant, 6 June 1841.

[41] A. Hawkins, ' "Parliamentary Government" and Political Parties, c.1830–1880', *EHR*, civ (1989), 640–3; Hawkins, *British Party Politics*, *passim*, but especially introduction and 312. See also O'Gorman, *Emergence of the British Two-Party System*, viii–xi; R.W. Davis, *Political Change and Continuity, 1760–1885: A Buckinghamshire Study* (1972), 102; G.H. Le May, *The Victorian Constitution* (1979), 59; P.M. Gurowich, 'Party and Independence in the Early and Mid-Victorian House of Commons: Aspects of Political Theory and Practice 1832–68, Considered with Special Reference to the Period 1852–68', University of Cambridge PhD, 1986, introduction; D.E.D.

fulfilled these roles, naturally, but in this book I wish to take Hawkins' approach in a different direction, by analysing the ideas of the Liberal Party among its members, and supporting constituents, rather than concentrating on the work of constitutional scholars.

Liberalism and liberals were to be found outside what I will define as the Liberal Party, but this is hardly surprising. Peel, after all, famously referred to his offer of increasing the Maynooth grant as being made in a 'friendly and liberal spirit'.[42] And, according to the pamphleteer with the pen name 'Gabriel Goodfellow', 'All people like to be thought liberal; everybody is afraid of being called illiberal. Hence the motley crowds which agglomerate together to form the aggregate of liberals; many of whom deprecate the extremes of liberalism, as much as the most prudent conservatives, or even the most tenacious tories'.[43]

The Liberal Party was able to exist in this general atmosphere of liberality without becoming permanently fragmented over individual issues because its members were willing to allow a degree of disagreement within their ranks. Liberal Party belief in civil and religious liberty, according to Spring-Rice, inevitably led to 'differences, though not necessarily oppositions of opinion'.[44] Being in the Liberal Party, he argued, required 'a candid and wise toleration' of differing views. This was the basis of the stability of the liberal politics that is described and analysed in Chapter 2 and Part 2 of this book. What Parry has described as 'a liberal value-system', and what I argue in Chapter 2 is more accurately termed 'a liberal politics', provided a series of points around which Liberal Party MPs could have varying specific opinions while staying within the same ideological constellation. Simply put, these were what George Anson described in an election speech in May 1835: 'I am inclined to believe that my political principles do not require any lengthy explanation: to improve institutions, and to secure to all the blessings of liberty'.[45]

The other vital element in ideas of the Liberal Party was, not surprisingly, the way those ideas were expressed in political language. David Eastwood has argued that although political language is 'both imprecise and artificial', it is 'central to the political process', and that 'the dynamism of a given political system is reflected in organic transformations in the political language it employs'.[46] There is large agreement to be found here. The ways in which political language expressed ideas of the Liberal Party are discussed throughout the book, but especially in Chapters 1 and 3, and in Part 2. Part of this, naturally, focuses on the labels that were used by liberals to describe themselves and that others used to describe them. From the polemical Goodfellow and his *Book of Liberals*, mentioned above, to the hagiographic *Saunders' Portraits and Memoirs of Eminent*

[41] (*continued*) Beales, 'Parliamentary Parties and the "Independent" Member, 1810–1860', in *Ideas and Institutions of Victorian Britain, Essays in Honour of George Kitson Clark*, ed. R. Robson (1967), 183–206; H. Berrington, 'A Back-Bench MP in the Eighteenth-Century: Sir James Lowther of Whitehaven', *Parliamentary History*, i (1983), 79–83; D. Close, 'The Formation of the Two-Party Alignment in the House of Commons between 1832 and 1840', *EHR*, lxxxiv (1969), 257–77; V. Cromwell, 'The Losing of the Initiative by the House of Commons, 1780–1914', *TRHS*, 5th ser., xviii (1968), 1–17.

[42] Hansard, *Parl. Debs*, lxxix, col. 193 (3 Apr. 1845).

[43] 'Gabriel Goodfellow', *The Book of Liberals: A Book for Liberals and Anti-Liberals; Being a Looking-Glass for the Former, and an Eye-Glass (or Spy-Glass) for the Latter* (1849).

[44] Spring-Rice, 'Present State and Conduct of Parties', 282.

[45] Staffordshire RO, Littleton Papers, *Staffordshire Advertiser*, 9 May 1835.

[46] D. Eastwood, 'Robert Southey and the Meaning of Patriotism', *Journal of British Studies*, iii (1992), 265–6.

Living Political Reformers, to the seemingly mundane parliamentary guides discussed in Chapter 1, convenient labels were attached to MPs in an attempt to convey quick explanations of political stances, intended to fill the reader's mind with a complete picture of ideology and political action.[47] It is no surprise, therefore, that, when the duke of Newcastle suggested that the label 'Whig' be abandoned by the 1830s, Lord John Russell argued for its retention based simply on the idea that 'The term Whig has the convenience of expressing in one syllable what Conservative Liberal expresses in seven'.[48] And the problem of strict pedigrees for liberals became less of a problem as the 1830s and 1840s progressed, because, in J.W. Burrow's admirable sentence, 'It is at least reassuring that, after the early decades of the nineteenth century, liberals were self-proclaimed as such, without the need for anachronistic rebaptism'.[49] Chapter 1 shows exactly when this happened for Liberal Party MPs.

These, then, are the approaches I have chosen to take in examining ideas of the Liberal Party. The methodology has been to focus mainly on Liberal Party backbenchers, their manuscript collections, and their expressions of liberal politics and ideas of the Liberal Party in a variety of sources, especially Hansard (a generally underused source), electioneering material and private correspondence, as well as their voting behaviour in the house of commons. Since the book examines liberal political language closely, extensive quotation has been necessary. This is based on the argument, made at several points, that liberal terms and liberal political language were not incidental in correspondence and debates. Rather, they were central. I have consulted the majority of known manuscript collections in English archives of liberal backbenchers who sat between 1832 and 1852.[50] *Ideas of the Liberal Party*, therefore, is the first one of its kind, that is, the first to pay adequate attention to the political middle rank.[51] In doing so, it counters the glib assertion of John Vincent and A.B. Cooke that there is a general 'lack of interesting political papers left by the lesser gods of politics'.[52] Indeed, backbench manuscript collections have proved rich and rewarding for those willing to mine them. They not only provide excellent source material for the issues discussed here, but for much else, especially local politics. Further, party leaders have been so well discussed elsewhere that a concentration on backbenchers is refreshing, if nothing else. The press has not been used extensively, and only appears to add particularly salient illumination at various points. A major exception to this is the heavy use of a different type of political press, the parliamentary guides, such as *Dod's Parliamentary Companion*, which makes up much of Chapters 1 and 2. Again, this is the first comprehensive examination both of the

---

[47] 'Gabriel Goodfellow', *Book of Liberals*, v–vii; *Saunders' Portraits and Memoirs of Eminent Living Political Reformers* (1840). Saunders lists finality Whigs and impatient Radicals, and many in between, under his umbrella of 'Reformers', including Grey and Melbourne, as well as Joseph Hume and John Arthur Roebuck. See also *Parties and Factions*, 12–50.

[48] S. Walpole, *The Life of Lord John Russell* (2 vols, 1889), ii, 156; Southgate, *Passing of the Whigs*, 237; J.W. Burrow, *Whigs and Liberals: Continuity and Change in English Political Thought* (Oxford, 1988), 12.

[49] Burrow, *Whigs and Liberals*, 4.

[50] The exception to this was the Monteagle Papers in the National Library of Ireland.

[51] Philip Salmon did this to a certain degree in his *Electoral Reform at Work*, but his purposes were different. He was not focusing solely on the Liberal Party, and his book ends at 1841.

[52] A.B. Cooke and J.R. Vincent, *The Governing Passion: Cabinet Government and Party Politics in Britain 1885–86* (Brighton, 1974), 160.

information contained in *Dod*, and also the larger questions about what its purpose was and how Liberal Party MPs used it to define themselves and present their liberal politics.[53]

Part 1, 'The Self-Perception, Construction and Presentation of a Liberal Party and a Liberal Politics in the House of Commons 1832–52', may be considered a study of the 'structural' ideas of the Liberal Party, focusing on 'Liberal Terms and Liberal Labels' (Chapter 1), 'Liberal Politics in the Constituencies and the House of Commons' (Chapter 2), 'Liberal Party Control' (Chapter 3) and 'Ideas of Co-operation among Liberal Groups' (Chapter 4). These chapters lay the groundwork for the main arguments in the book. Part 2, 'Liberal Agendas in Conflict and Consensus: Ideas, Issues, Language and Behaviour among Liberal Party MPs 1832–52', may be considered as a series of case studies of some of the important parliamentary issues that helped define, and were defined by, liberal politics. The chapters examine appropriation of Church of Ireland revenues (5), church rates (6), Maynooth (7) and free trade (8). They are in no way intended to be comprehensive examinations of the issues involved, but instead are necessarily surveys. They do, however, provide strong analyses of liberal politics and, consequently, ideas of the Liberal Party.

---

[53] The only other study that relied heavily on the use of *Dod's Parliamentary Companion* was W.O. Aydelotte, 'Voting Patterns in the British House of Commons in the 1840s', *Comparative Studies in Society and History*, v (1962–3), 134–63, but Aydelotte used it as part of his quantification of voting behaviour, not as it is used here.

Part 1: The Self-Perception, Construction and Presentation of a Liberal Party and a Liberal Politics in the House of Commons 1832–52

Chapter 1. Liberal Terms and Liberal Labels

The political terms that were used to describe MPs in the 1832–52 period are a primary concern of this book. An analysis of the ideas of the Liberal Party and how those ideas were expressed through political language and political structures must take into account the basic terms that were used as shorthand to convey the meaning and scope of political ideologies. This chapter will discuss party labelling among non-Conservative MPs in terms of perception, construction and presentation. From 1832 to 1846, the Liberal Party was a heterogeneous group of 'Liberals', 'Radicals', 'Reformers', 'Repealers' and 'Whigs'. The increase in the use of the term 'Liberal', however, and its eventual dominance by 1847, shows that conceptions of a Liberal Party were becoming more homogeneous in the 1832–52 period. The changes in party terms were a significant factor in the increasing willingness of non-Conservative MPs to consider themselves members of the same political party, however loose in formal organisation.

After a brief discussion of the terms 'Liberal', 'Party' and 'Liberal Party', this chapter examines the uses of various Liberal Party terms and labels from a variety of sources. It then focuses on party terms in *Dod's Parliamentary Companion*, which became a standard guide to parliament in the 19th century. This detailed analysis brings to light the changes in political perception mentioned above, and provides a strong foundation for the discussions of Liberal Party politics in the following chapters.

A major block to understanding early Victorian politics is, paradoxically, the existence of a political vocabulary that is in common with the early 21st century. 'Parties', 'leaders', 'whips', 'agents', 'elections', 'canvassing' and many other terms are still in use in contemporary Britain. This fact would, on the surface, seem to facilitate understanding. But the existence of common terms does not necessarily relate to the existence of common meanings from that century to this.[1] Most political words in the early 19th century usually meant something rather less than they do now, or at least party language did not imply strong organisations, quick to punish independently minded MPs. As long as it is understood that most of these terms had quite different meanings in the first half of the 19th century, then they can be used with confidence.[2] Therefore, a brief explanation of the most important terms in this book is in order, so that the later sections of this chapter may be more readily understood.

---

[1] For similar arguments, see N. Gash, *Politics in the Age of Peel: A Study in the Technique of Parliamentary Representation 1830–1850* (1953), ix.

[2] Although, for the most part, party terms in the 19th century carried less weight than they do now, this was not universally true. The 19th-century election agent was far more powerful than his early 21st-century counterpart. As Philip Salmon has shown through his important work on registration, agents may have been the most important men in early 19th-century British electoral politics. Canvassing, similarly, was more important then than it is now. See P.J. Salmon, *Electoral Reform at Work: Local Politics and National Parties, 1832–1841* (Woodbridge, 1996), 63–77, 92–116, 142–4.

'Liberal'

In the sense of having certain political opinions and behaving in certain ways politically, 'liberal' has been in use in Britain since the 1820s, and stood for someone who believed in institutional reform as a fundamental political creed.[3] But it was after 1832 that it took on greater meaning and brought with it greater expectations, particularly those with a 'party' dimension. Candidates were asked to stand for election on 'liberal principles' or with 'liberal opinions' and responded by repeating those same phrases back to electors.[4] For example, Lord Shrewsbury worried about 'two liberal candidates' going up against each other in Staffordshire in 1832.[5] Local reform associations pleaded with MPs, candidates and local liberals to find and support 'liberal' men for elections.[6] And in terms of candidates, 'Liberal' and 'Reformer' were often used interchangeably. In a printed circular dated 15 September 1837, the central committee of the new North Riding Liberal Registration Association wrote to William Wentworth-Fitzwilliam, Whig MP for Yorkshire North Riding, proposing a meeting the following month to secure a stronger alliance among liberals: 'Are the Liberal Electors thus to slumber in apathy, and suffer their political existence to be annihilated? We confidently answer No! and earnestly call upon every true Reformer within the Riding, to become a member of a condensed and organized Reformer Registering Association'.[7]

'Party'

Before the rise of the caucus and mass political participation in the late 19th century and early 20th century, parties rarely exhibited many of the trappings with which we associate them in subsequent periods, particularly in the 20th century. There were no party conferences, no manifestos in the contemporary sense of the term, little 'party'

[3] For a discussion of how 'liberal' came into British political discourse, see H. Fyfe, *The British Liberal Party* (1928), 11; Sir I. Jennings, *Party Politics: The Growth of Parties* (2 vols, Cambridge, 1961), 68; B. Hill, *The Early Parties and Politics in Britain, 1688–1832* (1996), chs 5, 6; W. Lyon Blease, *A Short History of English Liberalism* (1913), 65–71; R.B. McCallum, *The Liberal Party from Earl Grey to Asquith* (1963), 27; D. Haury, *The Origins of the Liberal Party and Liberal Imperialism: The Career of Charles Buller, 1806–1848* (1987), 8–9. See also Sir G.C. Lewis, *Remarks on the Use and Abuse of Some Political Terms* (1832).

[4] See, for example, Bodl., Barham Papers: John Barham, 4 Jan. 1832, and Richard Wilson to Barham, 30 July 1834; Bodl., Dashwood Papers, MS DD Dashwood: Election Address of Sir George Henry Dashwood, 13 Feb. 1837; North Yorkshire County RO, Wyvill MSS, ZFW, m. 1699, frames 005237–005238: Christopher Croft to Marmaduke Wyvill; R.S. Ferguson, *Cumberland and Westmorland MPs from the Restoration to the Reform Bill of 1867* (1871), 262–76. See also R. Hannay, *History of the Representation of England* (1831); *The House of Commons Elected According to the Provisions of the Reform Act, to Serve in the Eleventh Imperial Parliament* (1833).

[5] Staffordshire RO, Anson Papers, D615P(P)/1/19: Lord Shrewsbury to Thomas William Anson, 1st Earl Lichfield, 12 June 1832.

[6] See, for example, Durham County RO, Bowes Papers, D/St/C1/16/263: Reform Association poster, 20 May 1835; Essex RO, Barrett-Leonard Papers, D/DL/O44/1: South Essex Reform Association handbill, 13 Dec. 1841.

[7] Sheffield Archives, Wentworth-Fitzwilliam Papers, H/168: printed circular from the North Riding Liberal Registration Association, 15 Sept. 1837. See also Lincolnshire Archives Office, D'Eyncourt Papers, 2TDE/H/64/51: Gainsborough Reform Festival: Report of the Speeches. B. Elvins, 'The Roots of the Liberal Party in Cornwall', *Parliamentary History*, xxiv (2005), 295–315, gives a number of excellent examples of candidates and electors using 'liberal', 'reform' and 'reformer' essentially as synonyms.

selection of candidates, far less substantial central funding of campaigns, and no such thing as 'losing the party whip', in the 'being cast into the political wilderness' sense of the phrase. On the other hand, there were party labels, used variously and with slightly different meanings, but all employed in general political discourse, and certainly accepted as party *labels*. There was also a degree of central party control and funding of elections, a perception of a party press with some newspaper leader sections acting more or less as party organs, and a reasonable expectation among leaders that party MPs would support them in vital divisions and questions of confidence.[8] So, it is a mixed bag, and once the anachronistic expectations for defining parties in the 19th century are removed from consideration, it becomes quite clear that there was a well understood idea of 'party' in this period. For instance, although disavowing the negative aspects of party connection (job-hunting, sycophancy and the like), John Barham, Whig MP for Kendal, was very happy to be approached by the Westmorland election committee in 1834 as 'the only man to keep the party together'.[9] And as a way of showing that party could mean something more practical than just a formation of political opinion, J. Hennaway, an elector in North Devon, wrote to his Whig MP, James Buller, in 1839 that 'The course of events of late years has very increasingly convinced me of the importance of strengthening the Conservative Party in the House of Commons, and unfortunately for me, you are not on that side'.[10]

There are many examples of other uses of 'party' in this period: 'the opposite party' is common in election correspondence;[11] 'the zeal of the liberal party' was praised in Stroud in 1832;[12] and Richard Bethell, Liberal candidate in Aylesbury, mixed contemporary notions of party with classical language when he used 'the liberal party' and 'the liberal phalanx' synonymously in 1852.[13]

So, 'party' was clearly a well used term, and historians have not found difficulty with the fact that, *as a word*, it was heavily used in the early 19th century. The difficulty arises when trying to distinguish the different shades of meaning from the 21st-century use of the term. Frank O'Gorman, among others, has shown how strong party language was in the 50 years before the Reform Act.[14] Arthur Aspinall, who focused on language and on structural labels, has shown that much of what would become party organisational ideas by 1852 were already in place by 1800.[15] Richard Davis, using Buckinghamshire as a case study, makes a very convincing argument that two 'modern' parties existed there from

[8] See A. Aspinall, 'English Party Organization in the Early Nineteenth Century', *EHR*, xli (1926), 389–411; A. Aspinall, *Three Nineteenth Century Diaries* (1949); Gash, *Politics in the Age of Peel*; N. Gash, *Reaction and Reconstruction in English Politics, 1832–1852* (Oxford, 1965); H.J. Hanham, *Elections and Party Management: Politics in the Time of Disraeli and Gladstone* (Hassocks, 1978); F. O'Gorman, *The Emergence of the British Two-Party System, 1760–1832* (New York, 1982); Salmon, *Electoral Reform at Work*.
[9] Bodl., Barham Papers: Richard Wilson to John Barham, 15 July 1834.
[10] Devon RO, Buller Papers, 2065M/SS/2/10: J. Hennaway to James Buller, 28 Feb. 1839.
[11] Cheshire RO, Richard Grosvenor Papers, 12/11: Major Sweetenham to Lord Richard Grosvenor, 23 Sept. 1832.
[12] Gloucestershire RO, Hyett Papers, D6/F32, f. 53: G.P. Scrope to William Henry Hyett, 15 Dec. 1832.
[13] Buckinghamshire RO, Tindal Papers: Richard Bethell's address to the electors of Aylesbury, 17 June 1852.
[14] F. O'Gorman, *Voters, Patrons, and Parties: The Unreformed Electoral System of Hanoverian England 1734–1832* (Oxford, 1989), introduction; O'Gorman, *Emergence of the British Two-Party System*, esp. ix–xi. For an introduction to parties before the 1832 Reform Act, see Hill, *Early Parties and Politics, passim*.
[15] Aspinall, 'English Party Organization', 389.

the 1820s, and John Phillips has done the same, albeit more quantitatively, in his work on five English boroughs from 1818 to 1841.[16] As long, therefore, as the limitations in application of the term 'party' and in the strength of parties are accepted, there seems to be little doubt that some sort of party system was in operation between the first two reform acts.[17]

'Liberal Party'

'Liberal' and 'Party' used in conjunction as 'Liberal Party' was also not uncommon in political discourse in the reform era, starting in 1830. From the constituency level, up to national discourse, 'Liberal Party' became increasingly applied to the collection of Whigs and Reformers who were pushing for parliamentary reform. This was evident both in private correspondence and public statements. 'Liberal interest', 'Liberal cause' and 'Liberal Party' were used almost interchangeably between 1830 and 1835,[18] but it was in 1834 and 1835 that the phrase took hold.[19] In 1834, Lord Brougham warned Grey that 'all the Liberal Party' would oppose the king bringing in Wellington and Peel.[20] Lord Althorp often referred to 'the Liberal Party in the House of Commons',[21] and was reputedly the first person to 'speak regularly of the "Liberal party" with a capital "L" '.[22] Joseph Parkes, the main Liberal Party electioneering agent, used the phrase constantly in his correspondence with Lord Durham.[23] E.J. Stanley used it in his whip on the Speakership contest in May 1839.[24] Parkes again urged 'Liberal Party' candidates in 1840 not to resort to treating and bribery because 'two can play at that game; and for our 1/- the Tories always find 2/6d',[25] and that 'it is the evil of our Liberal Party that we are necessarily sectional in political opinions, whereas the Tories run in one groove'.[26]

---

[16] R.W. Davis, *Political Change and Continuity, 1760–1885: A Buckinghamshire Study* (1972), 102; J.A. Phillips, *The Great Reform Bill in the Boroughs: English Electoral Behaviour, 1818–1841* (Oxford, 1987), 52–3.

[17] Gash, *Politics in the Age of Peel*, xviii–xix. See I. Newbould, 'Whiggery and the Growth of Party 1830–1841: Organization and the Challenge of Reform', *Parliamentary History*, iv (1985), 137–8, for how he disagrees.

[18] Elvins, 'Roots of the Liberal Party'; Ferguson, *Cumberland and Westmorland MPs*, 262–3.

[19] Newbould, 'Whiggery and the Growth of Party', 140; Gloucestershire RO, Hyett Papers, D6/F 32, f. 53: G.P. Scrope to W.H. Hyett, 15 Dec. 1832.

[20] Gash, *Reaction and Reconstruction*, 165, n. 3.

[21] National Library of Ireland, Monteagle Papers, 13, 379: Althorp to Spring-Rice, 18 Jan. 1835.

[22] E.A. Wasson, *Whig Renaissance: Lord Althorp and the Whig Party 1782–1845* (New York, 1987), 342.

[23] For instance, see Lambton Estate Office, Lambton MSS: Joseph Parkes to Lord Durham, 21 July 1835, transcribed by W.E.S. Thomas, hereafter cited as Parkes (WEST).

[24] Lincolnshire Archives Office, D'Eyncourt Papers, TDE/H1/123: E.J. Stanley whip to MPs, [no date] May 1839.

[25] UCL MSS Room, Parkes Papers: Parkes to E.J. Stanley, 28 Dec. 1840.

[26] Staffordshire RO, Littleton Papers, D260M/F/5/27/14, f. 67: Parkes to E.J. Littleton, 28 Dec. 1840. See also J.P. Parry, *The Rise and Fall of Liberal Government in Victorian Britain* (New Haven, CT, 1993), 353; G.L. Bernstein, 'The Origins of Liberal Politics, 1830–1874', *Journal of British Studies*, xxviii (1989), 76–9; Phillips, *Great Reform Bill*, 47; B. Fontana, 'Whigs and Liberals: The Edinburgh Review and the "Liberal Movement" in Nineteenth-Century Britain', in *Victorian Liberalism: Nineteenth-Century Political Thought and Practice*, ed. R. Bellamy (1990), 42–57.

Ian Newbould is the major critic of this reading of the reform period. He sees the Whig-Liberal party as too dependent on Peel for support against the Radicals, without a community of purpose or central organisation, and far too loose in ideology and action to be termed a party until the next political generation (the late 1850s).[27] But most other recent studies have tended to disagree. Rather than dating the emergence of an identifiable party from the late 1850s, as was most famously argued by John Vincent,[28] historians have generally argued that Foxite whiggism and liberal toryism merged in the two decades after the Great Reform Act to form a new type of liberalism based on the ideas of popular and cheap reforming government.[29] Further, the more mechanistic aspects of the reformed political world, mainly electoral registration and the redistribution of parliamentary seats, brought with them a need for a new type of conception of party to go along with the new liberalism. This was also the view of the political writer C.H. Chambers, who, looking back from 1872, wrote:

> The Liberal party may be said to have its rise, as a technical section of the country, from the time of the Reform Bill of 1832. They in point of fact mean that body of men who, whether originally Whigs, or converts from the Conservative side, either had all along advocated Liberal principles, or on the other hand, were convinced that there was no real danger of a Jacobinical rising against property of a revolutionary nature, were open to the consideration of reform at home.[30]

It is clear, then, that these terms were in use during the 1830s and 1840s, and that many people spoke about a 'Liberal Party' with the confidence that they would be understood. The detailed examination of party labelling that follows builds on this introduction.

Self-Perception and Party Labelling in the House of Commons

Joseph Parkes often identified the various sections of the Liberal Party as 'real Reformers, and Whigs or Semi-Liberals'.[31] Most party leaders defined the Liberal Party as made up of Whigs, Liberals and Radicals, often labelling individual members. In an undated memorandum from late 1832, Sir Denis Le Marchant, another central party manager, informed Lord Brougham of the members of the new parliament, and their party affiliations. Each member was given a three- or four-line summary including descriptions of land holdings, parentage and birth connections, statements of character and sometimes a party statement. These party statements included:

---

[27] I. Newbould, *Whiggery and Reform, 1830–1841: The Politics of Government* (1990), 8–23.

[28] J.R. Vincent, *The Formation of the British Liberal Party, 1857–1868* (1966).

[29] P. Mandler, *Aristocratic Government in the Age of Reform: Whigs and Liberals 1830–1852* (Oxford, 1990), introduction; Parry, *Rise and Fall of Liberal Government*, introduction and part I; M. Taylor, *The Decline of British Radicalism, 1847–1860* (Oxford, 1995), 6–7, and chs 1–2; and B. Hilton, 'Peel: A Re-appraisal', *HJ*, xxii (1979), 585–614.

[30] C.H. Chambers, *Phases of Party* (1872), 63.

[31] Parkes (WEST): Parkes to Charles Tennyson D'Eyncourt, 31 Jan. 1835.

H. Handley[32] – formerly tory, but has for some years been becoming a whig; Brigstock[33] – once a tory, but for the last 10 years a whig; Buller[34] . . . has always been a whig . . . an excellent member; Sir E. Wilmot[35] – a moderate liberal; Roebuck[36] – a protégé of Hume's[37] & a radical; Fielden[38] – was a tory but is liberalized; Poulter[39] – was a violent tory, now a violent radical; Goring[40] – a moderate liberal.[41]

Party labelling was also common among gallery reporters and the political press. In his 1836 *Random Recollections of the House of Commons*, one of the very few detailed descriptions of the politics and daily practice of MPs in the 1830s, James Grant provided sketches of members under the labels:

> The Tory Party – Late Members
> The Tory Party – Present Members
> The Neutral Party [Stanley, Graham, F.G. Young, Robinson and Walter]
> The Liberal Party – Late Members
> Members of the Government
> Metropolitan Members
> The Country Liberal Party
> The Irish Liberal Members
> Literary Members
> Religious Members
> New Members.[42]

Grant used various non-party classifications ('Literary Members', 'Religious Members', 'Metropolitan Members' and 'New Members'), perhaps in order to make *Random Recollections* more interesting to a broader readership.[43] But by 1838, he had abandoned this idea and divided MPs more strictly into parties in his volume, *The British Senate*, which continued the 'insider's' discussion of the house of commons. In this volume he simply divided the Commons into liberals and conservatives, and sorted them by country, the only exception being that he had a section on 'Government Members'.[44]

[32] Reformer MP for Lincolnshire. The political labels given in footnotes are those that appear in the relevant volume of *Dod's Parliamentary Companion* for the year in question.

[33] Reformer MP for Somersetshire East.

[34] Le Marchant could be referring to: Charles Buller, Whig MP for Liskeard; James Wentworth Buller, Whig MP for Exeter; or Edward Buller, Whig MP for Staffordshire North.

[35] Reformer MP for Warwickshire.

[36] Radical MP for Bath.

[37] Radical MP for Middlesex.

[38] Radical MP for Oldham.

[39] Reformer MP for Shaftesbury.

[40] Whig MP for Shoreham.

[41] UCL MSS Room, Brougham Papers, undated memorandum [1832/3]: Sir Denis Le Marchant to Lord Brougham.

[42] J. Grant, *Random Recollections of the House of Commons from the Year 1830 to the Close of 1835, including Personal Sketches of the Leading Members of All Parties, by One of No Party* (1836), vii.

[43] *The Literary Companion to Parliament*, ed. Christopher Silvester (1996), xxii, 83.

[44] J. Grant, *The British Senate in 1838* (2 vols, 1838), table of contents and *passim*.

The constituencies were no exception in party labelling. W. Thompson, a Gloucestershire liberal election agent, described Charles Fox, a possible candidate for the Stroud seat in 1835, as 'a steady liberal Whig'.[45] And in a Somerset election poster from 1837, Sir Thomas Lethbridge's wavering stand on the corn laws was lampooned by providing a sliding scale of party affiliation based on the price of wheat.

Price per Bushel	Politics
5s.	STARVATION, Annuities & Interest sweeping the whole Rental.
5s, 6d.	Radical Demagogue.
6s.	Radical.
6s, 6d.	Radical Whig.
7s.	Whig.
7s, 6d.	Vibrating, a Critical & Difficult Period.
8s.	Half Tory.
8s, 6d.	Tory.
9s.	Violent Tory.
9s, 6d.	Red Hot Church, and King, and no Popery Man.
10s.	The Rental will now enable you to keep a more splendid establishment; vote with Ministers upon every measure, right or wrong, particularly if there be a Coronet in View.[46]

But these types of party labelling in correspondence, parliamentary memoirs and electioneering were inconsistently applied and subject to the prejudices of partisans. More reliable, or at least more consistent, were the ways in which contemporary parliamentary guides labelled MPs.

Party and Parliamentary Guides

One of the most significant consequences of the Reform Act was that it helped to create, or at least provided a starting point for, new ideas of the nature of parliament and how it should be presented to the public. This may be seen in the growth of parliamentary guides aimed not only at a market of political journalists and other interested Londoners, but also at a wider political public.[47] One significant area of research that has been overlooked is the proliferation of political guides and parliamentary compendiums after the passage of the 1832 Reform Act. Like newspapers, journals and reviews, these handy little books played a meaningful role in presenting parliament and politicians to the political public, crafting political perceptions and public opinion, and perhaps, in small but important ways, they maintained a type of public sphere that proved necessary to early 19th-century politics, and particularly to the application of reform and ideas of progress that helped boost the heyday of the

[45] Gloucestershire RO, Hyett Papers, D6/F32, f. 83: W. Thompson to W.H. Hyett, 19 Dec. 1834. Fox later sat as a Liberal MP for Tower Hamlets from 1841 to 1847.

[46] Somerset RO, Sanford Papers, DD/SF, 4552, item 1: undated election poster (1837 was the only time Lethbridge was a candidate for Bridgwater in Somerset).

[47] Until more research is done, we can only speculate on the readership of these guides. But the way they were written certainly implies that they were not intended solely for use inside parliament and Whitehall.

British political press after the repeal of Stamp Duty in 1855. Further, the fact that the majority of these guides strove for accuracy, completeness and lack of bias makes them a small but important part of a reference print culture that had accelerated in development during the 18th century.[48] This chapter introduces the importance of parliamentary guides into the historiography of the early 19th century, which should add to our understanding of political communication, and especially our understanding of the early Liberal Party, during that period. It does this specifically by analysing a range of published parliamentary lists and guides, and previously unknown archival material related to the dominant guide, *Dod's Parliamentary Companion*. The question of political identities is central to understanding how these parliamentary guides helped construct modern politics in Britain. Variously called 'party terms', 'political opinions' and 'political pledges', these expressions of identity with ideologies and political groupings were both strong and flexible. MPs and editors of parliamentary guides massaged the language of political identity and, in doing so, took an active, rather than a passive, role in deciding how politicians and parliament were presented to the political public.[49] One of the most significant changes in the British political world after the passage of the 1832 Reform Act took place outside Westminster. The imperatives of the reformed system placed a higher premium on dialogue between MPs and electors, and on MPs' self-construction for the political public.[50] Among other things, this was shown in the growth in the number of new parliamentary guides, and the ways in which they explained and presented parliament in the 'age of reform'.[51] In the introduction to the 1834 volume of *The Pocket Parliamentary Companion*, the editors wrote:

> the compilation of the work was undertaken from a conviction that the memorable change in the constitution of the Legislature effected in 1832, imparted such ascendancy to local influence, that it became a matter of importance, and at the same time of difficulty, to acquire clear, correct, and full information respecting the stations, family connections, pursuits, political principles, and general character of the representative body.[52]

---

[48] For biographical dictionaries and their place in reference print culture, see I. Rivers, 'Biographical Dictionaries and Their Uses from Bayle to Chalmers', in *Books and Their Readers in Eighteenth-Century England: New Essays*, ed. I. Rivers (2001), 135–69.

[49] This article concentrates on political identity in the house of commons only. Parliamentary guides in the 19th century generally did not discuss political opinions and party leanings of members of the house of lords, preferring to present their family connections.

[50] See Salmon, *Electoral Reform at Work*, for the importance of electoral registration in the strengthening of local and national party politics. This is also echoed by Phillips, *Great Reform Bill*. Further evidence of the new importance placed on MPs and the public may be seen in B.S. Trinder's *A Victorian MP and His Constituents* (Banbury, 1969).

[51] For issues raised by the idea of an 'age of reform', see D. Eastwood, 'The Age of Uncertainty: Britain in the Early-Nineteenth Century', *TRHS*, 6th ser., viii (1998), 91–115; Mandler, *Aristocratic Government*.

[52] Yale Univ., Beinecke Library, Osborn Collection, d 50, i, f. 18: flysheet from *The Parliamentary Pocket Companion*, 1834, in 'Autobiography of Five Hundred Members of Parliament, Being a Collection of Letters and Returned Schedules Received by Charles R Dodd, during the First Four Reformed Parliaments, viz. from 1832 to December 1842 and Constituting Materials for Compiling the Successive Editions of The Parliamentary Pocket Companion, London, December 1842, Collected by RPD [Robert Phipps Dod, the son of Charles R. Dod]' (hereafter Dod Papers).

Table 1.1: *Constituency/Alphabetical Arrangement of Parliamentary Lists and Guides in the Bodleian Library*

Year range	Constituency arrangement	Alphabetical arrangement	Total
1614–1831	117 (81.8%)	26 (18.2%)	143 (100%)
1832–95	9 (32%)	19 (68%)	28 (100%)

Parliamentary guides predated 1832, of course. For most of the 17th and 18th centuries, these were simple lists of MPs, arranged by constituency, such as the 1614 *List of the Names of Knights, Citizens and Burgesses, and Barons of the Cinque Ports, Retained to Serve in the Parliament Summoned to Meet at Westminster*. These lists generally did not include any further information than the constituencies and names of MPs. Sometimes they had overt political agendas, such as: 1643's *List of Members of Both Houses of Parliament, that were Forcibly Secluded by the Army*; 1660's *Mystery of the Good Old Cause Briefly Unfolded: In a Catalogue of Such Members of the Late Long Parliament, that Held Places, both Civil and Military, Contrary to the Self-Denying Ordinance of April 3, 1645*; 1715's *Collection of White and Black Lists, or, a View of those Gentlemen who have Given Their Votes in Parliament For and Against the Protestant Religion, and Succession, and the Trade and Liberties of Their Country; ever since the Glorious Revolution to the Happy Accession of King George*; and 1798's *List of the Members . . . who Voted for the Third Reading of the Assessed Taxes Multiplication Bill*.[53] And, of course, John Wade's multiple editions of *The Black Book* usually included descriptions of MPs, especially those that Wade thought tainted by old corruption.[54]

Significantly, however, such lists and polemics privilege the constituency over the MP almost universally. If the collection of Oxford's Bodleian Library may be used as a representative sample, significant changes can be detected. The vast majority of pre-1832 lists of MPs are arranged by constituency. After 1832, lists and parliamentary guides change the focus to the MPs themselves, arranging their publications alphabetically. Table 1.1 shows this clearly.

This, however, was not an immediate change. It appears that the alphabetical arrangement started to increase in use from the 1810s. Conclusions based on these changes will always be tentative, of course, owing to the use of a specific collection as a sample, but the transformation appears too significant to ignore. Perhaps this indicates increased attention on MPs outside their own constituencies, and this may mean the start of interest in individual MPs as national figures. While there had been printed lists of members of both houses of parliament in the past, after 1832 a new type of guide appeared – pocket-sized, clear and readable, and often elucidating biographical information about MPs, descriptions of the nature of parliamentary procedure and even

---

[53] These examples come from the general collection of the Bodleian Library in the University of Oxford.

[54] J. Wade, *The Black Book; or, Corruption Unmasked!* (1820). See also J. Wade, *Political Dictionary; or, Pocket Companion* (1821); *New Parliament: An Appendix to the Black Book* (1826); *The Extraordinary Black Book* (1831); *Appendix to the Black Book: An Exposition of the Principles and Practices of the Reform Ministry and Parliament* (1835). For more on Wade, see K. Gilmartin, *Print Politics: The Press and Radical Opposition in Early Nineteenth-Century England* (Cambridge, 2005), esp. ch. 1; P. Harling, *The Waning of 'Old Corruption': The Politics of Economical Reform in Britain, 1779–1846* (Oxford, 1996).

architectural drawings of the old Palace of Westminster and of the temporary building arrangements after the fire of 1834.[55]

There were many of these, and they had varying levels of success. It is exceedingly difficult to find complete runs of any of these titles, and most seem to have ceased publication within one or two years. *Vacher's Parliamentary Companion* began publication in 1833, and by 1837 was revising its lists of MPs and peers monthly. It was small and thin, pamphlet-width, and often contained interesting flyleaf inserts in the beginning (including, for 1847, facsimile autographs of Victoria and the cabinet). *Vacher's* listed members of both Houses, and had alphabetical and constituency lists of MPs. There were no party labels, biographical sketches or constituency summaries, but it was useful nonetheless, because it was updated to reflect by-elections and other changes.[56] Henry Stooks Smith's *Parliaments of England* listed election results by constituency, using party labels T(ory), W(hig) and R(adical or Reformer). While there was no explanation of these party terms, Smith did give election results for each constituency, and allocated party labels from 1774.[57] *The Reformed Parliament* was a flysheet, published in six numbers in 1833 only, and gave very brief descriptions of MPs and their politics. Radical in tone, it listed MPs as Whigs, moderate Whigs, Reformers, Moderate Reformers and Conservatives. Radicals were simply indicated by listing their opinions. Repealers were listed as Reformers who supported repeal of the Union.[58] *Webb's List of Members of the House of Commons Elected December 1832* was a list of MPs by constituency, with an alphabetical list attached, giving addresses; there were no biographical details or party labels.[59] *The Parliamentary Indicator* was a pocket guide to the 1835 house of commons, arranged by constituency, with the returned members listed beneath each constituency name. There were brief sketches of their lives, especially family connections, and their politics. Party labels were rare, and political opinions were meant to be gleaned from the reports of voting behaviour on important issues listed.[60] *The Parliamentary Test Book for 1835* was a small, thin, paperback guide to the house of commons, with MPs listed alphabetically, including some biographical details. The party labels used were only Reformer and Conservative but, importantly, they are the first thing that appears in an MP's entry. It reprinted edited extracts from electioneering statements (posters, addresses, newspaper reports) of MPs, and their votes in the 'two last Sessions on the Ballot, Duration of Parliaments, Repeal of the Malt Tax, revision of the Pension List, removal of the Bishops

---

[55] The exact composition of the house of commons during this period will not be discussed here. See, instead, E.A. Wasson, 'The House of Commons, 1660–1945: Parliamentary Families and the Political Elite', *EHR*, cvi (1991), 635–51; S.F. Woolley, 'The Personnel of the Parliament of 1833', *EHR*, liii (1938), 240–62; J.A. Thomas, *The House of Commons 1832–1901: A Study of Its Economic and Functional Character* (Cardiff, 1939); P. Salmon, 'The House of Commons, 1801–1911,' in *A Short History of Parliament*, ed. C. Jones (2009), 249–70.

[56] *Vacher's Parliamentary Companion* (1833–). Other interesting flyleaf inserts include a 'Plan for the Temporary Houses of Parliament' (1835), a plan of the ancient Palace of Westminster (1836) and a 'Fac-simile Writ of Election, 19 Edw 1 (AD 1290)' commanding representatives to come to London to meet in parliament (1837).

[57] H.S. Smith, *The Parliaments of England, from 1st George I, to the Present Time* (3 vols, 1844). See also D. Southgate, *The Passing of the Whigs 1832–1886* (1962), 38.

[58] *The Reformed Parliament: Biographical Sketches of All the Members of the House of Commons; Their Political Principles; Places of Residence, &c., &c.* (1833).

[59] *Webb's List of the Members of the House of Commons Elected December 1832* (1833).

[60] *The Parliamentary Indicator* (1835). *The Indicator* seems to have ceased publication after 1835.

from the House of Lords, the right of Parliament to deal with Church Property, extinction of Tithes, and claims of Dissenters'. Dedicated 'To the Electors of Great Britain and Ireland', it saw its role as a recorder of pledges so that legislators could be held to account.[61] The following is a sample entry:

> Mullins, Hon Frederick William [gives residences] (Kerry, County)
>
> Reformer. – "I cannot support a government founded upon the principles contained in Sir Robert Peel's address." *Times*, Jan. 22. Voted against the property tax; for the removal of the Jewish disabilities, short parliaments, and Dissenters to graduate at universities.
>
> Cousin to Lord Ventry.

Peel's entry contains the whole Tamworth statement. Another publication, *The Assembled Commons*, appeared in at least 1836 and 1837, and listed MPs alphabetically. There were short biographies, and descriptions of political opinions. Party labels were not used consistently, although most MPs were listed as voting with the Whigs or Tories ('Conservative' was not generally used).[62] Mosse's *Parliamentary Guide* was a pocket-sized guide to both houses of the 1837 parliament. For the house of commons, there was first a constituency guide, followed by a biographical, alphabetical section on MPs. Mosse divided the house of commons between Whigs and Conservatives only. There were no Radical, Reformer or Repealer labels. The entries also gave some description of their political opinions and behaviour, and votes on the Reform Bill, the Speakership, Church Rates (no date) and Municipal Corporations Bill. A sample entry looked like this:

> Poulter, John Sayer. 3 Parl. [how many parliaments he had served in] (Shaftesbury.) Whig.
>
> A barrister; gdson of the late Right Rev. Dr. Brownlow North, Bp. of Winchester. Introduced a bill for the better observance of the Sabbath in the session of 1834 and 1835. S★, C.R.★, M.C.★. [votes in divisions] 5, King's Bench Walk; The Close, Winchester.[63]

Crosby's General Political Reference Book was a compendium of electoral results from the early 18th century to 1837. Candidates were listed after 1831 as W[hig], C[onservative] or R[adical]. It was compiled alphabetically by constituency with country headings. At the end, however, there was a list of MPs alphabetically in two columns headed 'Whigs' and 'Conservatives'. The 1839 volume, re-titled *Crosby's Parliamentary Record*, was the same, except that it reproduced famous electoral speeches.[64] William Warlock's *The House of Commons: As Elected to the Fourteenth Parliament of the United Kingdom* was a biographi-

[61] *The Parliamentary Test Book, for 1835: A Political Guide to the Sentiments Individually Expressed, and the Pledges Given, at the Late General Election, by Each of the 658 Members of the Second Reformed House of Commons* (1835), iii–iv.

[62] *The Assembled Commons, 1837: An Account of Each Member of Parliament* (1837).

[63] R.B. Mosse, *The Parliamentary Guide: A Concise Biography of the Members of Both Houses of Parliament, Their Connexions, etc.* (1837).

[64] G. Crosby, *Crosby's General Political Reference Book* (Leeds, 1838); *Crosby's Parliamentary Record* (Leeds, 1839).

cal guide to the 1841 house of commons, arranged by constituency, which listed the results of the election, gave the name of the MP, his votes on the Sugar Duties, Ministerial Confidence and the Address to the Throne, biographical details, political opinions and sometimes a party label – 'reformer', 'radical Reformer', 'liberal', 'whig' and 'conservative' were used.[65] The *Parliamentary Manual for the Year 1838* was a list of MPs by constituency with no party labels. There was an alphabetical list, but it was just for reference to the constituency list.[66] *A Manual of Queen Victoria's Second Parliament* was a detailed electoral report for 1841, without biographical details. It divided the house of commons into liberals and conservatives, although it called the liberals 'reformers' when it referred back to the parliaments of 1831 and 1833.[67] Charles Lewis' *The Four Reformed Parliaments* was a study of the parliaments elected from 1832 to 1841, by constituency, showing the results of the elections. The party labels 'Liberal' and 'Conservative' were used for all MPs, and there was a summary chart in the back showing the relative numbers of each for each parliament.[68]

One guide eventually emerged as the leader by the late 1830s. *Dod's Parliamentary Companion* was started by Charles R. Dod, a parliamentary journalist for *The Times*, who clearly saw an opportunity for a pocket-sized yet comprehensive guide to parliament.[69] Originally titled *The Pocket Parliamentary Companion*, it was soon changed to *The Parliamentary Companion*, but eventually it was just called *Dod* by virtually everyone who used it. It became so well established as an 'official' guide to parliament that anonymous spoof editions were published in the 1880s.[70] Apart from *Vacher's, Dod* is the only such guide to survive to the present day, and is now titled *Dod's Parliamentary Companion*.[71] Among other things, *Dod* was made up of alphabetical entries of MPs 'compiled from official documents, and from the personal communication of members of both houses'.[72] Although there was a constituency section of *Dod* giving the results of the previous election, the most heavily used section was the 'List of Members of the House of Commons, Their Professions, Offices, Political Principles, and Pledges, with Notices of Their Public Lives, &c'. It is significant that *Dod*, unlike some other contemporary guides (and most such lists before reform), chose to list MPs alphabetically by name rather than constituency.[73] It stuck to this format, and it obviously became the standard guide. This

[65] W.A. Warwick, *The House of Commons: As Elected to the Fourteenth Parliament of the United Kingdom, being the Second of Victoria* (1841).
[66] *Parliamentary Manual for the Year 1838* (1838).
[67] *A Manual of Queen Victoria's Second Parliament* (1841).
[68] C.E. Lewis, *The Four Reformed Parliaments 1832–1842* (1842).
[69] For Charles R. Dod, his career and other work, see the author's entry in *ODNB*, xvi, 381–2.
[70] See *The Popular Dod*, ed. 'Tommy' (1884). This contained little 'biographies' of MPs, written satirically. It was called by the *Sporting Times* 'Ultra-Radical, but very clever', although *The Examiner* said: 'No political bias is distinguished, Radicals and Conservatives alike falling victims'. Some entries are in verse.
[71] It will be called *Dod's Parliamentary Companion* or *Dod* throughout this book.
[72] *Dod's Parliamentary Companion*, title page for 1833 and subsequent years to 1852. The volumes also included a similar section for peers in the house of lords, a compendium of election results for the most recent election and a brief guide to parliamentary procedure.
[73] Most pre-1832 guides were arranged by constituency, not by MP. For example, see *A Biographical List of the House of Commons, Elected in October 1812* (1813). There are two exceptions. Joshua Wilson's *A Biographical Index to the Present House of Commons* (1806–8) is a massive work, some 625 pages long. It gives long biographies of MPs, emphasizing family connections. The descriptions range from four paragraphs to 17 pages (for Fox). Wilson also included an appendix of important divisions and a list of seats alphabetically by

seems to indicate that there was, after 1832, a new type of interest in the house of commons, centred around individual MPs themselves, rather than around them as constituency members.[74] A *Dod* entry included the MP's name, constituency and, where relevant and available, address(es), club(s), biographical information, business or military careers, local political and judicial offices, ministerial career, electoral history, a party 'label' (see below for a fuller discussion of this crucial aspect), a list of political opinions, and votes in divisions. For instance, a typical entry from the 1838 volume reads:

Marshall, William. (*Carlisle*)

Eld. s. of John Marshall, esq. of Headingley, in the co. of York, an extensive linen manufacturer at Leeds and Shrewsbury, and in 1826 member for Yorksh.; br. of John Marshall, jun. esq., late member for Leeds. B. 1796; m. 1828, Georgiana Christiana, 7th d. of George Hibbert, esq. of Munden, Hertfordshire. A Radical Reformer; is in favour of triennial Parliaments, the ballot, "an extension and equitable division of the suffrage," the removal of all restrictions which fetter trade, and the reform of the Church Establishment. Sat for Leominster and for Petersfield before the Reform Act. For 4; agt. 1, 2, 6, 7. – 41, *Upper Grosvenor-st.: Reform Club; Patterdale Hall, Westmoreland*.[75]

It has generally been assumed among historians that these entries, if not entirely self-composed, represented a good degree of self-description. This appears to be a historiographical assumption based on the phrase on the title page which said that the entries were derived 'from the personal communication of members of both houses'.[76]

---

[73] (*continued*) constituency. Like *Dod's Parliamentary Companion*, which is analysed in detail below, the main section was arranged alphabetically by MP. Unlike *Dod*, it is very thick, and certainly not pocket-sized. *A Key to Both Houses of Parliament* (published in February 1832) was a comprehensive guide to both houses of parliament, with MPs listed by constituency, and a bare-bones description of occupation, residences and family connections, but no party labels. Like Wilson, it was very thick, running to some 700 pages.

[74] I do not wish to make too much of this because it would be very difficult to prove, but the change seems so complete after 1832 that there must have been a shift in what was expected in the presentation of parliament.

[75] *Dod's Parliamentary Companion* (1838), 140. 'For 4' refers to his vote in favour of 'Russell's motion on Irish Church Temporalities (2nd April) [1835]'; 'agt. 1, 2, 6, 7' refers to his votes against '1. Election of Speaker (1835).–2. Address in reply to the Speech from the Throne, on the 24th of Feb. 1835.– 6. Motion of Sir Wm. Follett to protect from the operation of the Corporation Bill those freemen whose rights had been secured under the Reform Act.–7. Sir Robert Peel's motion to divide into two Bills the measure of Ministers relating to the Irish Church. [both 1835]'. These are some of the important divisions that Dod used as indicators of political opinion.

[76] See Taylor, *Decline of British Radicalism*, 24; T.A. Jenkins, *The Liberal Ascendancy 1830–1886* (1994), 9–10; W. Arnstein, 'The Religious Issue in Mid-Victorian Politics: A Note on a Neglected Source', *Albion*, vi (1974), 134–9; and esp. P.M. Gurowich, 'Party and Independence in the Early and Mid-Victorian House of Commons: Aspects of Political Theory and Practice 1832–1868, Considered with Special Reference to the Period 1852–1868', University of Cambridge PhD, 1986, pp. 53–65, for the assumption that *Dod* entries were largely self-composed. I am very grateful to the current editor of *Dod's Parliamentary Companion*, Michael Bedford, for his generous help and advice on these matters. *Dod* passed through a variety of publishers after the death of the second editor, Robert Phipps Dod (son of Charles, see also *ODNB*), and it appears that only the Yale collection has survived. I am also grateful to the staff of the Historical Manuscripts Commission, the Guildhall Library and St Bride's Printing Library for their help in my quest for records on *Dod* and its various publishers.

There is no reference in the secondary literature to the Dod Papers in the Osborne Collection at Yale University's Beinecke Library, which I have been able to exploit.[77] In the late 1970s, Yale acquired a collection put together by Roger Phipps Dod (Charles' son, and the later editor of the *Parliamentary Companion*), which the younger Dod called an 'Autobiography of Five Hundred Members of Parliament Being a Collection of Letters and Returned Schedules Received by Charles R. Dodd [*sic*] during the first four Reformed Parliaments . . . and constituting Materials for Compiling the Successive Editions of The Parliamentary Pocket Companion'.[78] This three-volume manuscript collection contains letters between the editors of *Dod* and MPs (or their agents), and the forms that *Dod* used to compile MPs' entries.[79]

Far from having solely antiquarian interest, these manuscripts show how illuminating a seemingly mundane set of printer's documents can be. In the act of condensing their political opinions and events in their political lives for *Dod*'s editors, these MPs were becoming fully part of the language of the reformed political world, using labels and shorthand to convey fuller ideologies. This political shorthand shows that the post-1832 political culture obviously traded in such easy summaries. This is not to argue, of course, that political labels and political shorthand did not exist before 1832 ('whigs' and 'tories' are obvious examples), but that a new language that included 'conservative', 'liberal', 'reformer' and 'radical' was being set into the political consciousness, partly through the proliferation of parliamentary guides such as *Dod*, and that this process of labelling went on to a far greater extent in terms of professionalism and in presenting parliament to the political public.[80] The process by which these political identities were expressed through *Dod* provides new material for interpreting the post-1832 political world. As shown above, before 1832, guides to parliament mainly listed MPs by constituency, and party labels or expressions of political opinion were very rare. After 1832, the focus of these parliamentary guides shifted from the constituencies to the members themselves (partly shown through the alphabetical listing), and to the opinions and ideologies they wished to present. Since *Dod* and other guides are such good examples of this change in focus, perhaps this adds weight to the argument that 1832 represents the start of modern party politics in Britain.[81]

[77] J. Coohill, 'Parliamentary Guides, Political Identity, and the Presentation of Modern Politics, 1832–1846', *Parliamentary History*, xxii (2003), 263–84.

[78] S. Parks, 'The Osborn Collection: A Sixth Biennial Report', *Yale University Library Gazette*, liv (1980), 125. Charles Dod briefly changed the spelling of his surname to 'Dodd' in the early 1840s.

[79] *Dod* relied on letter correspondence for the 1833–5 volumes, and began sending out forms for compilation of the 1836 volume.

[80] As a label in *Dod*, 'whig' lasted well into the reform period, but was overtaken by 'reformer' as the label of preference for non-conservative MPs in 1835, and both were overtaken by 'liberal' in 1844. There were 194 'whigs' in the 1833 volume of *Dod* and 53 in 1852. Only two 'liberals' appeared in 1833, but there were 179 by 1852. 'Tory' was a very rare label in the *Companion*, never appearing more than a handful of times in each volume.

[81] For the recent debate on this issue, see Newbould, *Whiggery and Reform*, 8–9, 73, 138; A. Hawkins, ' "Parliamentary Government" and Victorian Political Parties, c.1830–1880', *EHR*, civ (1989), 640–3; A. Hawkins, *British Party Politics 1852–1886* (1998), *passim*, but esp. introduction and p. 312; O'Gorman, *Emergence of the British Two-Party System*; Phillips, *The Great Reform Bill*; J.A. Phillips and C. Wetherell, 'The Great Reform Act and the Political Modernization of England', *American Historical Review*, c (1995), 411–36; Jenkins, *Liberal Ascendancy*; Parry, *Rise and Fall of Liberal Government*; Salmon, *Electoral Reform at Work*.

In its early years, the editors of *Dod* (mainly Charles R. Dod and a few assistants) wrote to MPs, asking them to reply by letter, giving the details that the editors would like to have for the forthcoming volume of the *Parliamentary Companion*. These letters, signed by Charles Dod and sent from 13 Ave Maria Lane, London, asked for:

1st Town & Country Residences
2nd Parentage & Connexions
3rd Date of Birth
4th When married & to whose Daughter
5th Profession (if any)
6th Offices, Directorships, &c (if any)
7th Leading events of political life
8th Works written (if any)
9th Political Opinions & Pledges
10th Places for which previously elected.[82]

MPs, their agents or secretaries replied, giving as much information from these categories as they desired, usually giving more attention to family connections than any other information. Some simply sent in a printed address or poster from the previous election in order to provide information on their political lives.[83] MPs also responded in various ways to the request from *Dod*, some of them being quite modest. Phillip Courtenay, Conservative MP for Bridgwater 1837–41, wrote that he did not think his biographical details could 'be of any use of entertainment to the Public, but if it will be of advantage to you, you are welcome to the following particulars'.[84] Generally, MPs seem to have responded to Charles Dod's request happily.

After the 1835 election, Dod decided to use forms (sometimes called 'schedules') to gain the information needed for the *Parliamentary Companion*. There is no indication of why this change was thought necessary, but perhaps it made the compilation of data easier. In addition to the information he had requested in his letters, Dod added 'Church Patronage', 'Club', 'University Honors' and 'Other Particulars'.[85] There are very few forms from notable MPs and cabinet members in the Yale Collection, but a few stand out.[86] Benjamin Disraeli, although still a young MP when he

---

[82] Dod Papers, i, f. 3.

[83] For the use of an election poster, see Thomas Acland's reply of 7 July 1837, Dod Papers, i, f. 23. See Dod Papers, i, ff. 349–50 for an example of a reply from a third party.

[84] Dod Papers, i, f. 209.

[85] Dod Papers, i, ff. 11, 19.

[86] This, of course, does not necessarily mean that famous MPs and cabinet members did not take the time to respond to Dod's inquiries, but the general absence of letters and forms from such people may indicate that they did not reply and that Dod garnered their information from other sources. In fact, in an early letter, Charles Dod wrote: 'If you should already have supplied similar information to Debrett's or any other Peerage or Baronetage, or to Burke's History of the Commoners of Great Britain, a reference to these Works will save you the trouble of a detailed reply'. Dod Papers, i, f. 3. Further, given the general disdain felt towards journalists at the time, it is not surprising that some MPs did not bother to send their information. See L. O'Boyle, 'The Image of the Journalist in France, Germany, and England, 1815–1848', *Comparative Studies in Society and History*, x (1967–8), 290–317.

completed his *Dod* form in 1837, is one of the notable items in the collection. His form reads:

Name: Benjamin D'Israeli

Town and Country Residences: Down Street, Piccadilly; & Bradenham, Bucks

Parentage and Connexions: Eldest son of I. D'Israeli Esq, F.R.S., D.C.L of Bradenham House in the County of Bucks

Date of Birth: 1806

When Married, and to whose Daughter: [blank]

Profession: [blank]

Offices, Directorship, Church Patronage, &c: A Magistrate for the Cy. of Bucks.

Leading events of political life: [blank]

Works written: Author of "Vivian Grey" "Contarini Fleming" & various other works of fiction; of "A Vindication of the English Constitution" addressed to Lord Lyndhurst, & reputed author of "The Gallomania"; "The Letters of Runnymede" "The Spirit of Whiggism" &c &c

Political opinions and pledges: [blank]

Places for which previously elected: [blank]

Club: Carlton Club &c &c

Number of Votes in favor at the Election of 1837: W. Lewis 772 Disraeli 668 Col Thompson 518.[87]

Like a few other MPs, Disraeli did not emphasize his political opinions, preferring to concentrate on his parentage and his literary career.[88] Most MPs, however, paid great attention to the 'Political opinions and pledges' and the 'Leading events of political life' sections of their *Dod* forms. Thomas Acland, Bart, MP for North Devon, initially wrote that he was 'generally conservative' on his 1837 form, but went back and changed it to 'generally & decidedly conservative'.[89] In the 'Leading events in political life' section, William Forbes, MP for Stirlingshire, wrote 'Always Conservative'.[90]

The word 'party' was also an important part of some MPs' replies. Charles Adderley, MP for North Staffordshire, wrote that he 'adopts the Conservative Party as the only one based on national & constitutional principles'.[91] But ideas of independence from party were also evident, although not nearly as common. In his 1838 form, Edward Fellowes,

---

[87] Dod Papers, i, f. 300. It is not clear why Disraeli gives his birth year as 1806, when it was 1804. It is also not clear why he reports the results of the 1837 election inaccurately, although not wildly off the mark. Dod's *Electoral Facts* lists the results thus: Wyndham Lewis (Cons.) 782, Benjamin Disraeli (Cons.) 668, Lt-Col. T.P. Thompson (Lib.) 559 and T. Erskine Perry (Lib.) 25.

[88] The extensive list of Disraeli's literary works is in stark contrast to Thomas Babington Macaulay's modest reply in 1836, which listed only 'some articles in the Edinburgh Review'. 1836 was, of course, before his first books were published, but was well into the period when he was a major contributor to the *Edinburgh Review*. See Dod Papers, ii, f. 729.

[89] Dod Papers, i, f. 21.

[90] Dod Papers, ii, f. 447.

[91] Dod Papers, i, f. 33.

MP for Huntingdonshire, wrote that he was 'Conservative but pledged to no party',[92] and David Sombrè, elected for Sudbury in 1841, listed himself as 'Independent', which *Dod* edited as 'Of "independent" politics'.[93] Finally, some MPs were unhappy with the idea of 'pledges' requested on the form. William Astell, MP for Bedfordshire, made perhaps the simplest protest against this idea when he crossed out 'and pledges' on his form.[94]

Further evidence for the likelihood that entries in these parliamentary guides were at least partly self-composed may be found in the *Parliamentary Test Book*, where the editors appealed for 'Communications, with *corrections*, from Honourable Members or others capable of giving information'.[95] Further, R.B. Mosse advertised the direct nature of his communication with MPs thus: 'To ensure the accuracy of the details, the greatest care and diligence have been used by the Compiler in collecting and arranging various valuable communications, of which a great portion has proceeded from Members themselves, in either House of Parliament'.[96]

Dod is important, therefore, because of the direct nature of the entries, and because of the use of party labels. Because it became the predominant guide to parliament, because it lasted throughout this period, and because the editors had no obvious political bias, a detailed analysis of *Dod's Parliamentary Companion* is an excellent way to examine MPs' self-conceptions of party and politics in the 19th century.

The Editing of Political Identity

Expressions of political identity, attachment to political principles and willingness to use party labels were an important aspect of parliamentary guides, and *Dod* in particular. It is here that the Dod Papers at Yale provide some of the most significant means for reinterpreting the reform period. In some ways, the collection shows how accurately editors of such parliamentary guides tried to summarize the political opinions of MPs. As will be seen below, the majority of entries in *Dod* were exact and literal transcriptions of what MPs had expressed in their letters and forms. In other ways, however, this new material sheds light on how important editing was to the presentation of politics, since there were several ways in which *Dod* editors changed MPs' entries before they went to press.

Once the replies had been received from MPs, *Dod*'s editors began the process of preparing them for publication. In the early years, Charles Dod wrote in pencil on the letters sent to him, giving instructions to his compositors and asking them to follow up on confusing points.[97] Sometimes there was a great deal of editing needed to fit an MP's information into the short space used for entries in the *Companion*. In 1837, Reginald Blewitt, Reformer MP for Monmouth, sent in a 690-word narrative of his life, which

---

[92] Dod Papers, ii, f. 423.

[93] Dod Papers, iii, f. 1001; *Dod's Parliamentary Companion* (1841), 201.

[94] Dod Papers, i, f. 53. Other examples include Acland's entry, discussed above, which reads in full as 'generally & decidedly conservative – *but no pledges*', Dod Papers, i, f. 21.

[95] *Parliamentary Test Book*, i.

[96] Mosse, *Parliamentary Guide*, iv.

[97] Dod Papers, iii, f. 903.

the *Dod* editors pared down to a 139-word entry, but this extensive editing was atypical.[98] Most MPs sent in relatively brief information, and this went into the *Companion* with varying degrees of editing, often relying on quotation marks to give an air of authenticity.[99]

The editing of political opinions and statements was perhaps the most significant aspect of the process. Some care was apparently taken to ensure that these were correct. For instance, Richard Bellew, MP for Louth, sent in a letter in 1833, listing a number of political stances, but leaving off the question of repeal of the Union. *Dod*'s editors apparently thought that he had pledged himself for repeal, and one editor wrote to another at the bottom of the letter: 'See our own account and his letter. *Can we drop* the pledge about repeal? We can put it in the past tense. Would it not be well to ask him specifically (by letter) whether the birth, marriage, and pledge be not correct?'[100] Apparently, Bellew was asked for clarification, and he replied on 9 November 1833, saying: 'as to the Question of Repeal of the Union I did not give any pledge on the subject'.[101] *Dod*'s editors did not change most political statements, but there were certain cases where a great deal of editing took place, including removing strong partisan language. John Ellis, MP for Newry, did not use a form in 1837, but sent in a letter, in which he said that he:

> was returned by a considerable Majority in opposition to Mr D.C. Brady the late member for Newry. Acrimony & party spirit no where prevailed more than in the recent election for this borough which, being the key to the north of Ireland, was considered by the Conservative Party as a signal triumph of their principles – Priestly bigotry, the profanation of the altar, followed up by bloodshed, & the other invariable excesses to which a resort to such means gives rise fearfully embittered the struggle.[102]

Dod's editors replaced this with: 'Is a Conservative, and has been returned for the borough by the Protestant interest, in opposition to Mr. Brady, the late Member'.[103]

Although 'party' was not listed on the form for MPs to fill in, it is clear that *Dod* thought 'political opinions' and 'party' to be near synonyms at least. In the introduction to the house of commons section of the *Dod* volumes for 1833–40, there is an explanatory section for the political statements used in the MPs' entries.

> In the summary of opinions attached to each Member's name in the following list, there will be found terms of frequent occurrence, which, in the opinion of some readers, may appear to require explanation ... all terms expressive of any set of political principles, are used in the best and most respectful sense.

[98] Dod Papers, i, ff. 147–8; *Dod's Parliamentary Companion* (1838), 83.

[99] For instance, in his form for the 1838 volume, George William Wood, MP for Kendal, wrote: 'a Whig of the School of Charles James Fox & consequently a friend of civil and religious liberty'. In the printed *Companion*, it appears as 'Professes himself "a Whig of the school of Charles James Fox, and consequently a friend of civil and religious liberty" '. Dod Papers, iii, f. 1153.

[100] Dod Papers, i, ff. 107–8.

[101] Dod Papers, i, ff. 111–12.

[102] Dod Papers, ii, ff. 393–4.

[103] Dod Papers, ii, ff. 393–4; *Dod's Parliamentary Companion* (1838), 106.

They are not called 'party labels' or 'party terms' in this introduction, but Joseph Hume's 1833 entry contains the following sentence: 'He is said by the Anti-Slavery Society, to be opposed to the mitigation of the slave system described in our explanation of Party Terms'.[104] The party terms and explanations in the 1833 introduction were these:

> *Administration*, Members of the. The individual political opinions of persons forming a part of the Government have not been given, it being presumed that its different Members will generally act in concert.
>
> *Conservatives* are gentlemen who take an opposite view of the Reform Bill from that entertained by its promoters.
>
> *Radical Reformers.* Gentlemen who think the Reform act falls as much too short of the necessary of expedient extension, as the Conservatives think it exceeds that boundary.
>
> *Reformer.* This term is applied to all who have supported, or who approve of, the Reform Act, but think that its principle might with advantage be carried further.
>
> *Repealers* are Irish Radical Reformers in favour of a repeal of the Union, and advocates of all measures enumerated in Mr. O'Connell's pledges (which see). Where they have differed from, or fall short of, the opinions entertained by that gentleman, particulars have been generally given.
>
> *Whig* has been applied to gentlemen who are willing *generally* to give Ministers their confidence for future. [From 1835–40 this read: *Whig* has been applied to gentlemen who are willing *generally* to give Ministers their confidence to such a ministry as that of Earl Grey or Viscount Melbourne.]

This introductory explanation was abandoned in 1841, indicating that such an explanation was no longer needed, and that party labels were well understood.

The editing of these party statements sometimes took place in highly significant ways for the question of the nature of politics in this period. In some cases, this type of editing took the simple form of adding an obvious political opinion or party statement to an MP's entry. Disraeli, for instance, left this space blank in the form reproduced above, but *Dod*'s editors added 'Of Conservative politics' in the eventual volume of the *Companion*.[105] In other cases, this type of editing was more intrusive, changing an MP's entry so that it fitted in better with the list of political opinions in other MPs' entries. In a letter for the 1833 or 1835 volume, John Bowring, MP for Kilmarnock, wrote that his 'political opinions are those which have been called philosophical radicalism', but *Dod*'s editors changed this to 'Radical Reformer'.[106] 'Radical Reformer' was used for many other radicals in the house of commons, whereas 'philosophical radical' never appeared in the *Companion*. This shows that, along with other parliamentary guides, *Dod* forced some MPs' political statements into a handful of acceptable categories for the post-1832 period.[107]

---

[104] *Dod's Parliamentary Companion* (1833), 127.

[105] *Dod's Parliamentary Companion* (1838), 100–1.

[106] Dod Papers, i, f. 165.

[107] For a discussion of other parliamentary guides of this period, and a more extensive argument on this point, see J. Coohill, 'Ideas of the Liberal Party: Perceptions, Agendas, and Liberal Politics in the House of Commons, 1832–1852', University of Oxford PhD, 1998, ch. 1.

If we look at Dod's editing process in greater detail, many significant things stand out. In the following analysis, there are eight general types of editing of MPs' political statements in the time it took to transfer them from the letters and forms written by each MP or his agent, and the entry's appearance in a *Dod* volume. These are:

1. an exact and literal transcription of what the MP had written;
2. minor editing of the statement (usually shortening it), but retaining its basic ideas;
3. significant editing, usually in the form of watering down or summarizing a political opinion;
4. major editing, which changed an opinion or party (but not from one side of the House to the other, that is, not from a reform stance to a conservative stance);
5. holding over an MP's statement from a previous volume, even though that MP had changed it in a subsequent form;
6. a complete (and polar) change of opinion or party affiliation;
7. the addition of a statement that does not appear in the MP's original communication; and
8. the removal of a statement from an MP's original letter or form.

Table 1.2 shows the distribution of types of editing in the 450 MPs represented in the Dod Papers at Yale.

Exact and literal transcriptions speak for themselves, but it is important to note the high number of instances of this type, which confirms that *Dod*'s editors tried to maintain their promise to be faithful to their advertised use of 'personal communication of members'. The other types of editing require some further explanation and analysis, however. Of course, many of these changes might have been the result of *Dod*'s editors using information from other sources, but it is perhaps significant that they chose to avoid the easy option of exact and literal transcription in these cases, and instead inserted other wordings. And it is perhaps too much to ask for editors and compilers under the pressure of deadlines to be completely consistent, but the changes that were made (although a minority of total instances) provide useful insights into political understanding during this period.

Table 1.2: *Distribution of Editing Changes in Dod's Parliamentary Companion, Comparing the Yale Collection with the Relevant Printed Volumes*

Type of editing	Number	Percentage of all editing
Exact and literal transcriptions	273	60.66
Minor editing	66	14.66
Significant editing	15	3.33
Major editing	13	2.88
Holdover from previous edition	44	9.77
Complete change	0	0
Addition of statement or label	36	8
Removal of statement or label	3	0.7
Total	450	100

Minor editing changes are also fairly easy to understand at face value, but they contain some interesting nuances. Thomas Balfour, MP for Nairn, Orkney and Shetland, listed himself as 'Conservative' on his 1835 form, which was then changed to 'of Conservative principles' in the 1836 volume.[108] J. Temple Leader, MP for Bridgwater, labelled himself a 'decided Reformer' in 1835, which was changed to 'a Reformer' in the 1836 volume.[109] Henry Wilson, MP for Suffolk West, used the phrase 'Temperate Reformer' in 1835 but *Dod* re-christened him 'A Moderate Reformer'.[110]

Significant editing changes show *Dod*'s editors inserting more of their own understanding of political opinion and political identity into MPs' entries. This often took the form of summarizing political principles, such as changing David Barclay's 'in favour of liberal reform' to 'a Reformer'.[111] This might seem a slight change, but better understanding of the subtleties of usage during this period shows that someone might have considered himself in favour of liberal reform without going so far as to describe himself as a Reformer with a capital 'R'. This implied an attachment to a well-defined group within the liberal side of the house of commons.[112] In Barclay's case, there is no evidence that he objected to this, but it is probably too difficult to determine whether he would have done so.[113] Robert Pulsford also had changes made to his entry – the addition of a specific political stance that he did not write on his form. He 'promised to vote for liberal measures', which was changed to a description of him being 'a Liberal, in favour of the ballot'.[114] On the conservative side of the House, there were other significant changes in description, especially considering that *Dod* prided itself on the accuracy of its communication with MPs. Joseph Planta, MP for Hastings, described himself as a 'Tory' on his 1837 form, which was changed to 'is a firm Conservative' when it appeared in the 1838 volume.[115] *Dod* seems to have preferred the more modern 'conservative' over the older 'tory', at least as far as the changes made to the entries for Evelyn Shirley, MP for Monaghan, and Arthur Trevor, MP for Durham, make clear.[116]

The 'major editing' listed in Table 1.2 shows even more intervention on behalf of the editors. In response to *Dod*'s call for information, Walter Campbell, MP for Argyllshire, wrote that he had 'always supported the liberal party in the House of Commons', which *Dod* changed to 'A Reformer'.[117] Martin Blake described himself as 'of liberal and independent political principles' in 1833, but appeared as a 'Reformer' in the 1833 volume, and as a 'Repealer' in the 1834 volume.[118] William Copeland, MP for Coleraine,

---

[108] Dod Papers, i, f. 77.

[109] Dod Papers, ii, f. 691.

[110] Dod Papers, iii, ff. 1145–6.

[111] Dod Papers, i, f. 81. Barclay was MP for Sunderland, 1835–7 and 1841–7.

[112] For further discussion, see Coohill, 'Ideas of the Liberal Party', chs 1–2.

[113] As with all these cases, the relatively small and incomplete nature of the Dod collection at Yale means that there can be no definitive proof of MPs' further communications on their entries. Although there are some letters complaining of the formatting and language used, the absence of evidence for other MPs is not evidence of absence.

[114] Dod Papers, iii, f. 911.

[115] Dod Papers, iii, f. 877.

[116] For Shirley, see Dod Papers, iii, f. 989; for Trevor, see Dod Papers, iii, f. 1067.

[117] Dod Papers, i, f. 209: Walter Frederick Campbell to Charles R. Dod, 14 Feb. 1835.

[118] Dod Papers, i, f. 139.

and Lord William Lennox, MP for Lynn Regis (also known as King's Lynn), both described themselves as 'Reformers' (in Lennox's case, 'a thorough Reformer'), but were transmogrified into 'Whigs' by *Dod*, which, as any contemporary would have told you, was not necessarily the same thing.[119] Further evidence of the bluntness that *Dod* applied to distinctions on the liberal side of the house of commons is supplied by E.R.C. Sheldon, MP for South Warwickshire, who listed himself as a 'Liberal' on his 1835 form, but became 'A Reformer' in the printed entry.[120] Similarly, George Traill, MP for Caithness, wrote 'Reformer' on his form, but became 'A Liberal'.[121] The degree of synonymity that *Dod* seems to have assumed provides a good deal of support for the argument that, however loose the coalition of non-conservatives may have been during the reform period, there was a general understanding that they agreed on certain important political principles, even if this understanding was mainly a journalistic one.

Perhaps the most interesting category that illuminates general understanding of political opinions and political terms is the 'holdover' one. This comprises instances when an MP's political statement in a letter or on a form was ignored (for whatever reason) in favour of duplicating the entry that appeared in previous annual editions. As can be seen from Table 1.2, this was the third most common form of deviation from what MPs wrote on their forms. Sir Andrew Agnew, Bart, MP for Wigtonshire, completed the 'Political Opinions' section of his 1836 form thus: 'Declared in address to his constituents, attachment to constitution in church and state'.[122] But the 1837 edition of *Dod* continued to print his 1833 description, 'Of Whig principles, inclining to Conservatism'. Albert Conyngham, MP for Canterbury, wrote in an 1835 letter that his 'political opinions are strongly biassed [*sic*] in favour of reform', and listed himself as a 'Reformer' on his form from that same year.[123] *Dod*, however, continued to describe him as 'Of Whig principles', a holdover from his 1833 entry. William Gore, MP for Sligo, stated that he was 'unpledged to all but support of Constitution in Church and State', which *Dod* (not surprisingly) found to be consistent with his 1833 label 'Conservative'.[124] W. Hughes Hughes, MP for Oxford, insisted for the 1834 volume that he was 'thoroughly independent in politics and votes as frequently with one party as the other'.[125] *Dod* preferred to keep him 'A Reformer', as he had been listed in 1833. Generally speaking, these holdover instances did not jar strongly with the broad political outlook of the MPs involved. George Scrope, MP for Stroud, listed in 1835 that he 'has generally voted with the Whigs', but *Dod* kept the 1833 version, 'a moderate Reformer'.[126] And Henry Winnington, MP for Worcestershire West, claimed that he was a 'steady supporter of measures of comprehensive reform' (1835), but appeared as 'A Whig', as he had since the 1833 volume.[127]

---

[119] For Copeland, see Dod Papers, i, f. 293. For Lennox, see Dod Papers, ii, f. 703.

[120] Dod Papers, iii, f. 987.

[121] Dod Papers, iii, f. 1065. Neither Sheldon nor Traill fit into the 'holdover' category.

[122] Dod Papers, i, f. 35.

[123] Dod Papers, i, ff. 267–9.

[124] Dod Papers, ii, f. 499.

[125] Dod Papers, ii, ff. 621–7.

[126] Dod Papers, iii, ff. 973–5.

[127] Dod Papers, iii, f. 1147.

These holdovers become much more interesting and significant for gradual changes in political language, however, when we look at the use of 'liberal' and 'liberal party'. Not surprisingly, in the immediate aftermath of 1832, many supporters of the Reform Act labelled themselves 'reformers'. Indeed, *Dod's* editors used support of, and opposition to, the Reform Act as part of their definition of political principles in the early editions.[128] But within the next few years, and certainly before 1841, a number of them changed the political part of their entries to include liberal and liberal party language. Their entries in the printed editions of *Dod*, however, held over their details from the 1833 and 1834 editions (including the distinction 'whig'). Peter Ainsworth, MP for Bolton, listed 'liberal opinions' on his 1835 form, but continued to appear in the *Companion* as 'A Reformer' subsequently.[129] The earl of Belfast, MP for County Antrim, wrote that his political principles and opinions were 'liberal' on his 1836 form, but he continued to appear as 'a Moderate Reformer, inclining to Conservatism' in the printed volume.[130] Colonel George Anson, MP for Stoke-upon-Trent, listed 'liberal opinions' on his 1836 form, but appeared as having 'Whig principles' in the 1837 volume.[131] Martin Blake, MP for Galway, wrote that he was 'of liberal and independent political principles' in 1833, but his printed entry listed him as a 'Reformer', and in 1834 he was a 'Repealer'.[132] Walter Campbell, MP for Argyllshire, said that he had 'always supported the liberal party in the House of Commons' on his 1835 form, but remained 'A Reformer' and had never appeared as a supporter of the liberal party by the time he left the House in 1841.[133] Thomas Kemp listed himself as a 'Liberal' in 1835, but was described as 'of Whig principles' until he left the House in 1837.[134] James Kennedy bragged in 1833 that there was 'no member whose name is to be found more consistently in the lists of divisions & always in advance of liberal principles'.[135] He, however, remained 'of Whig principles' in the *Companion* until 1835, when he became a 'Radical Reformer'. And William Tooke, MP for Truro, wrote in an 1835 letter that he had 'ever professed and advocated liberal principles', and on his 1836 form described his political opinions as 'uniformly adhering to liberal principles'.[136] His 'Reformer' designation, however, continued in the 1837 volume (the last in his parliamentary career). Table 1.3 shows all those MPs in the Yale collection who changed their designation to include liberal language, but whose printed entries retained older designations.

There may have been several reasons for holding over an MP's political statements from a previous edition. The simplicity and cost savings of keeping the entry the same cannot be ignored. But it may also have been the case with the liberals above that *Dod's* editors did not see much difference between the various non-conservative political identities expressed, and simply assumed that their readers would not misunderstand those MPs' fundamental political opinions. It is also clear and significant, however, that *Dod* did not keep up with changing political identity during this crucial period in the

[128] See *Dod's* own explanation of political identities, above.
[129] Dod Papers, i, f. 37.
[130] Dod Papers, i, f. 103.
[131] Dod Papers, i, f. 47.
[132] Dod Papers, i, f. 139.
[133] Dod Papers, i, f. 209.
[134] Dod Papers, ii, f. 665.
[135] Dod Papers, ii, f. 667.
[136] Dod Papers, iii, ff. 1057–9.

Table 1.3: *Holdover Statements for 'Liberal' MPs in Dod's Parliamentary Companion*

MP	Political principles in manuscript	Political principles in printed volume	Lasted until*	Reason for change
P. Ainsworth	liberal opinions (1835)	A Reformer	1847	no change, left House
Sir George Anson	liberal opinions (1836)	Of Whig principles	1852	no change, left House
Earl of Belfast	liberal (1835)	a Moderate Reformer, inclining to Conservatism	1838	no change, left House
Martin Joseph Blake	of liberal and independent political principles (1833)	Reformer (1833) Repealer (1834)	1857	no change, left House
William Blamire	a liberal on every point (1835)	A Reformer	1837	no change, left House
Henry Lytton Bulmer	generally liberal (1835)	Radical Reformer	1837	no change, left House
Walter Frederick Campbell	has always supported the liberal party in the house of commons (1835)	A Reformer	1841	no change, left House
Fitzstephen French	Liberal (1835)	Of Whig principles	1852	continued to sit after 1852
Daniel Whittle Harvey	liberal Reformer (1835)	An ultra Radical Reformer	1840	no change, left House
John Jervis	Liberal (1835)	A Radical Reformer	1850	no change, left House
Sir John Vander Bempde Johnstone	professes liberal opinions (1835)	Reformer	1836	no change, left House (returned as a 'Conservative' in 1841)

Name				
Thomas Reid Kemp	Liberal (1835)	Is of Whig principles	1837	no change, left House
James Kennedy	always in advance of liberal principles (1833)	Of Whig principles	1835	no change, left House
John George Brabazon Ponsonby	liberal opinions (1835)	Of Whig principles	1844	no change, left House
John Rundle	my opinions are liberal (1835)	A Reformer	1843	no change, left House
E.R.C. Sheldon	Liberal (1835)	A Reformer	1837	no change, left House
William Thompson	Liberal political opinions (1835)	A Reformer	1840	changed to 'Conservative' in 1841
William Tooke	has ever professed and advocated liberal principles (1835); uniformly adhering to liberal principles (1836)	A Reformer	1837	no change, left House
William Turner	liberal (1835)	A Reformer	1840	no change, left House

* This date refers to the last year in which the MP appeared in a *Dod* volume, which may not be the same date that they ceased to sit in the house of commons. My research has not yet extended beyond 1852, except in the case of a few MPs. Therefore, MPs who sat in the House after that date may be listed as not having changed from pre-1852 designations.

construction of modern British politics. Many MPs had obviously adopted liberal language in their self-descriptions in the early and mid 1830s, but *Dod* waited until the 1840s to reflect that change. In *Dod's* printed volumes, use of liberal language increased throughout the 1830s, but it did not overtake 'Reformer' as a political identity until the 1843 volume, and 'Liberal' did not dominate the reform-minded side of the Commons until after the 1847 election.[137] If the editors had paid more attention to the changes in liberal language in the 1830s, a very different picture of the nature of political parties in this period might have emerged.

Instances when *Dod's* editors added a political opinion or party label were less frequent, but no less interesting. Samuel Crompton, MP for Thirsk, sent no political opinions, but he appeared as 'a moderate Reformer' in the 1833 volume of *Dod*.[138] Disraeli, similarly, did not list political opinions or party identification on his 1837 form, but was characterised as 'of Conservative politics' in the 1838 volume.[139] And William Clayton, MP for Marlow, wrote in 1833: 'I am returned to Parliament by a numerous constituency free from all Political Pledges, and consequently Independent; I am also completely independent of all party in the House'.[140] But *Dod* listed him as a 'moderate Reformer' in the 1834 volume, which lasted until 1837, when he was changed to a 'Reformer'.

The removal of a political opinion or party label was perhaps stranger and less understandable, given *Dod's* advertisement of direct communication with MPs. John Entwisle, MP for Rochdale, considered himself 'a consistent Tory' in 1835, which did not appear in his printed entry.[141] Thomas Gill, MP for Plymouth, wrote in 1841 that he was 'a Supporter of liberal Principles', but this was edited out by the time his printed entry appeared,[142] as was James Stewart's 'Reformer' designation in 1837.[143]

Accuracy and Criticism

Another significant aspect of the Yale collection of Dod Papers is that it shows the extent to which MPs cared about the accuracy of their entries in parliamentary guides. They wrote to *Dod's* editors, asking for corrections in all the categories. Although firm conclusions cannot be drawn from what evidence remains in the Yale collection, it is certainly true that marriage and family connections make up the bulk of correction notices in these volumes. On 19 April 1833, Edward Stewart, MP for Wigtown District, wrote to correct the statement that he was the son of the earl of Galloway, and to say that he was Galloway's nephew.[144] Marriage mistakes were also spotted, including dates of marriage. Villiers Hatton, Liberal MP for Wexford, wrote on 6 August 1841 that his marriage was in 1817, not 1816, as it stated in the *Parliamentary Companion*. 'The mistake was of no importance

[137] Coohill, 'Ideas of the Liberal Party', 32–40.
[138] Dod Papers, i, ff. 307–8.
[139] Dod Papers, i, f. 335.
[140] Dod Papers, ii, ff. 247–9.
[141] Dod Papers, ii, f. 403.
[142] Dod Papers, ii, ff. 479–81.
[143] Dod Papers, iii, f. 1017. Stewart was MP for Honiton.
[144] Dod Papers, iii, f. 1019.

itself', he wrote, 'but ladies are sensitive in these matters'.[145] Perhaps the most extensive set of errors on family matters came in the entry for John Calcraft, Conservative (later Palmerstonian Liberal) MP for Wareham. His brother, Granby, wrote in to complain that *Dod* had wrongly stated the MP's parentage, profession, family seat, political opinions and the number of livings for which he was a patron.[146] Apart from Calcraft's conservatism and Bellew's statement about repeal of the Union (discussed above), corrections of political opinions and party labels are not generally evident in the Yale collection. Again, while no firm conclusions may be drawn from this 'absence of evidence', it may imply that political statements in *Dod* were generally accurate.

This does not mean that MPs were universally content with *Dod* or other parliamentary guides. Some of the contempt in which journalists were held during this period may be apparent from the criticism directed at *Dod*'s editors. Thomas Turner, MP for Leicestershire South, wrote:

> Tho' I am not very willing to enter into the particulars you ask, yet as others have done so, and as you will doubtless enter some incorrect statement if I do not, I must consent . . . I have entered into these particulars, which you may curtail as you please that you may not rely on any incorrect statement given in various other books.[147]

Richard Heathcote, MP for Stoke-upon-Trent, wrote on 25 January 1835 complaining about 'great inaccuracy' in the *Companion*, and insisted that they substitute a new entry for the flawed one.[148] On the other hand, Sir William Clayton, Bart, MP for Marlow, wrote in 1837 to say that *Dod* was 'certainly the most accurate of any of those which are in circulation'.[149]

Liberal Party Labels in Dod

We may now look at how often these terms occurred on the liberal side of the House, which gives us, for the first time, a remarkable opportunity to see the complexity of the Liberal Party, and the increasing reliance on the term 'Liberal'. A variety of party terms were used in *Dod*. The literal labels ranged from the simple 'Whig' to the more complex (and possibly contradictory) 'Reformer, Whig, inclining to Radicalism' for Benjamin Lester, MP for Poole 1812–35. But they can reasonably be grouped under the terms 'Administration', 'Liberal', 'Liberal-Conservative',[150] 'Radical', 'Reformer', 'Repealer' and 'Whig'. Table 1.4 shows the literal terms used, and the groups into which they have been summarized in the analyses that follow.

Table 1.5 shows the number of summary group labels that appeared in *Dod* from 1833 to 1852. Liberal-Conservatives have been left out of Table 1.5 and Figure 1.1 because they were all identified as sitting with the Conservatives.

---

[145] Dod Papers, ii, ff. 567–8. See also Dod Papers, i, ff. 111–12, where Richard Bellew informs *Dod* that his wife had been dead several years, and that he should not be listed as married.

[146] Dod Papers, i, ff. 205–6, no letter date.

[147] Dod Papers, iii, f. 1079, no letter date.

[148] Dod Papers, i, f. 573.

[149] Dod Papers, i, f. 256.

[150] Most 'Liberal-Conservatives' sat on the Conservative side of the House, but have been included here for comparative purposes.

Table 1.4: *Explanation of the Use of Dod Party Labels*

Literal terms	Summary group
Whig	Whig
moderate Whig	
Whig; inclining to Conservatism	
Whig and Reformer	
Reformer	Reformer
moderate Reformer	
moderate Reformer, inclining to Conservatism	
Constitutional Reformer	
Conservative Reformer★	
thorough-going Reformer	
Radical Reformer	Radical
Whig, inclining to Radicalism	
Reformer, inclining to Radicalism	
Reformer, Whig, inclining to Radicalism	
Radical	
Administration	Administration★★
Repealer	Repealer
Radical Reformer and Repealer	
Liberal Repealer	
Liberal and Repealer	
Liberal	Liberal
Liberal-Whig	
liberal Whig	
None listed	None listed★★★
liberal Conservative	Liberal Conservative
Liberal, but Conservative	
Liberal-Conservative	

★ 'Moderate Reformer', 'moderate Reformer, inclining to Conservatism', 'Constitutional Reformer' and 'Conservative Reformer' usually referred to the more conservative-minded MPs on the liberal side of the House. Some of them drifted to the Conservative Party by 1837. See R. Stewart, *The Foundation of the Conservative Party 1830–1867* (1978), 370–5. See also Chapter 4 of this book.

★★ Not all members of administrations are listed literally as such, but some have their offices listed. I have labelled those 'Administration'.

★★★ Not all Liberal Party MPs have an exact and literal party term in *Dod*, even though their entries may go on to list obviously liberal (usually radical) political statements. If this was the case 'None listed' was used. All MPs in the database on which this analysis is based certainly were on the liberal side of the House (or could be called anti-Conservatives or anti-Tories). The database, which contains much other information, was compiled and checked not only from *Dod's Parliamentary Companion*, but also *Dod's Electoral Facts*, the other parliamentary guides discussed above, and *Who's Who of British Members of Parliament*, ed. M. Stenton and S. Lee (4 vols, Hassocks, 1976), i, ii.

Table 1.5: *Number of Appearances of Dod Summary Labels 1833–52*★

1833–9

Party label	1833	1834	1835	1836	1837	1838	1839
Administration	23	26	3	25	23	20	21
None listed	30	26	25	20	21	25	28
Radical	40	41	40	43	42	35	36
Reformer	145	147	165	150	147	113	107
Repealer	33	33	23	26	24	22	23
Liberal	2	1	0	2	3	35	36
Whig	194	190	124	111	115	95	89

1840–6

Party label	1840	1841	1842	1843	1844	1845	1846
Administration	18	9	2	2	2	1	1
None listed	29	27	40	41	31	31	30
Radical	34	29	27	26	27	27	27
Reformer	105	76	69	64	64	6	59
Repealer	22	17	17	16	17	73	18
Liberal	36	61	63	62	75	76	77
Whig	90	70	68	67	63	61	61

1847–52

Party label	1847	1847NP	1848	1849	1850	1851	1852
Administration	2	2	2	3	3	3	1
None listed	26	23	23	21	20	20	20
Radical	26	22	21	18	18	16	16
Reformer	57	37	38	37	37	37	35
Repealer	21	19	22	20	18	17	16
Liberal	86	166	168	172	172	176	179
Whig	60	49	51	52	52	52	53

★ Parry has listed Dod labels for 1838, 1843 and 1847, but chose the different summary categories: 'Whig', 'moderate Reformer', 'Reformer', 'Radical Reformer', 'Liberal', 'Repealer', 'Other' and 'No Entry' (my 'None listed'). The figures presented here, therefore, will not agree with his. See Parry, *Rise and Fall of Liberal Government*, 167. The same applies to Miles Taylor's table of Liberal Party labels in 1847, 1852, 1857 and 1859. See Taylor, *Decline of British Radicalism*, 24. See also Jenkins, *Liberal Ascendancy*, 45–6.

Note: After the 1847 election, *Dod* was issued in a second edition, entitled '1847 New Parliament', hence the 1847NP column above.

There are several things of significance that may be deduced from Tables 1.4 and 1.5. The first is to note that, if there had been a completely organised and regimented Liberal Party, there would not be so many different labels on the liberal side of the House. Liberal Party MPs used many different labels, while the other side of the House stuck to 'Conservative' (and, very rarely, 'Tory'). Second is the degree of change in labels among individual MPs. While it may be inferred from the data presented in Tables 1.4 and 1.5 that many MPs must have retained 'Whig', 'Reformer' and 'Radical' even after 1847, when the number of 'Liberal' labels jumps dramatically (see Figure 1.1 below), it is not very clear because the figures in Table 1.5 are compilations of the individual years. If we look at individual MPs, and trace their parliamentary careers through *Dod*, we find a remarkably high level of survival of original party labels. Of the 883 MPs on the liberal side of the House who had entries in the annual *Dod* volumes from 1833 to 1852, 731 made no change in their label from their first entry to their last. This was the overwhelming majority – 82.7%. There were 152 who did change, only 17.3%. The change to 'Liberal' from other party labels was 54, 6.1% of the total 883, and 35.5% of those 152 who did change. The other changes were scattered around the label spectrum. Of the 81 MPs who had entries in 1833 and 1852 (and who, it can be implied, are more or less all those who sat either for most of the period or sat in 1833 and in 1852), 25 made no change, 30.8% of the total. The changes to 'Liberal' among this long-serving group were 30, 37% of the total, which was made up of 11 Whigs, 14 Reformers, three Radicals and one Repealer. This shows the remarkable tenacity of the first label that an MP applied to himself. Some examples might illuminate these changes and non-changes.

Sir Robert Price, Bart, MP for Herefordshire 1833–41, and for Hereford City 1845–57, sat through most of the period as a Whig.

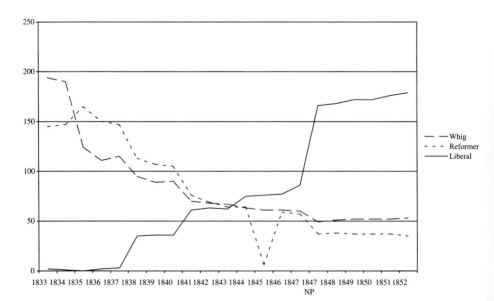

Figure 1.1: *Whigs, Reformers and Liberals in the House of Commons 1833–52*

1833 = Whig	1846 = Whig
1834 = Whig	1847 = Whig
1835 = Whig	1847NP = Whig
1836 = Whig	1848 = Whig
1837 = Whig	1849 = Whig
1838 = Whig	1850 = Whig
1839 = Whig	1851 = Whig
1840 = Whig	1852 = Whig
. . .	

Richard Montesquieu, MP for Louth, sat through most of the period as a Reformer.

1833 = Reformer	1847NP = Reformer
1834 = Reformer	1848 = Reformer
1835 = Reformer	1849 = Reformer
1836 = Reformer	1850 = Reformer
1837 = Reformer	1851 = Reformer
1838 = Reformer	1852 = Reformer
1839 = Reformer	
1840 = Reformer	
. . .	

While Henry Tufnell, MP for Ipswich in 1837, and for Devonport from 1840 to 1854, changed three times.

1838 = Reformer	1847 = Liberal
1841 = Whig	1847NP = Liberal
1842 = Whig	1848 = Liberal
1843 = Whig	1849 = Liberal
1844 = Liberal	1850 = Liberal
1845 = Liberal	1851 = Liberal
1846 = Liberal	1852 = Liberal[151]

And Sir Henry Barron, MP for Waterford City 1832–41 and 1848–52, changed from Repealer to Liberal when he returned to the House.

1833 = Repealer	1849 = Liberal
1834 = Repealer	1850 = Liberal
1835 = Repealer	1851 = Liberal
1836 = Repealer	1852 = Liberal
1837 = Repealer	
1838 = Repealer	
1839 = Repealer	
1840 = Repealer	
. . .	

[151] As with most MPs who came in for short periods (often because of by-elections or because they were unseated after an electoral petition was declared valid) the *Dod* entry appears in the following year. So, Tufnell was elected in 1837, appeared in the 1838 volume, but was subsequently unseated on petition.

Many works stress that, in the 1830s and 1840s, 'Whigs' and other liberal groups gradually abandoned these terms and adopted 'Liberal'.[152] And Miles Taylor has argued:

> In the first *Parliamentary Companion* of the Reformed Parliament of 1833, there was no mention of liberals − only 'whigs', 'reformers', and 'radicals'. But by 1859 there was only a small rump of around 20 MPs who clung to this original terminology of the 1830s, and all other MPs identified themselves as liberals. Precisely when the shift from one form of party identification to another took place is impossible to pinpoint, and certainly there is no indication that it was in 1846–47, or even during the 1850s.[153]

In the first place, there were two mentions of 'liberal' in the 1833 volume of *Dod* (Joshua Scholefield and J.G. Shaw-Lefevre). Second, it is quite clear from my analysis that the major shift to 'Liberal' took place exactly after the 1847 election, with *Dod*'s 1847 New Parliament volume. While 'Liberal' overtook 'Reformer' as the main Liberal Party label in 1844 (just as Reformer had overtaken Whig in 1835), Figure 1.1 shows a dramatic change to 'Liberal' after the 1847 election.

This graph clearly shows that 'Liberal' rose steadily throughout the late 1830s and early 1840s before dominating from 1847 to 1852. This may be explained partly by the influx of new MPs in the 1847 election, who chose 'Liberal' rather than any other label to describe their party politics (this is the most probable conclusion given the tenacity with which MPs stuck to their original labels as described above). It may also have been the case that the editor of the *Parliamentary Companion* chose to use 'Liberal' more often as a party label when faced with MPs who were reluctant to label themselves. But this is unlikely because the numbers of Liberal Party MPs who had no party label in their entries (the numbers reflected as 'None listed' in Tables 1.4 and 1.5 and Figure 1.1) did not drop sharply after 1847. What is clearly shown, therefore, is the increasing legitimacy of 'Liberal' as both a party label and an expression of political opinion. Further, the use of 'Liberal' and 'Conservative' only (as opposed to 'whig', 'reformer' and 'tory', for instance) in many other parliamentary guides shows increasing use of two-party language, with the two parties being 'Liberal' and 'Conservative'. Further, although labels sometimes changed within the Liberal Party, there were *no* MPs between 1833 and 1852 who listed themselves as 'Independents' or men of 'No Party', and very few who implied such concepts in their biographical entries.[154] Most broadly and significantly, however, the *self*-perception among MPs that these labels were valid and presented exactly what

---

[152] There are many examples of this, ranging from a relatively specialised little volume for A level and GCSE students, D. Watts, *Whigs, Radicals, and Liberals 1815–1914* (1995), chs 1, 3, to texts for university students, T.A. Jenkins, *Parliament, Party and Politics in Victorian Britain* (Manchester, 1996), ch. 2; Jenkins, *Liberal Ascendancy*, introduction and ch. 1, and for general readers, Michael Bentley, *Politics without Democracy 1815–1914* (Oxford, 1984), 95–107, among many others.

[153] Taylor, *Decline of British Radicalism*, 24. Taylor's statement about the lack of 'liberal' in 1833 is all the more surprising since one of the two MPs, Joshua Scholefield, MP for Birmingham, was a member of what Taylor has defined as the Reform Party. Scholefield was listed as a 'liberal' in 1833 and 1834, before switching to 'Radical Reformer'.

[154] In *Dod* there were only four of these among the Liberal Party. The strongest example was Sir P. Hesketh Fleetwood, MP for Preston 1832–47, whose entry reads: 'Was elected, in 1832, without giving pledges, in consequence of his character in the town and neighbourhood. Has no connection with any political party. Is a moderate Reformer'. And even he dropped 'has no connection with any political party' in his 1840 entry.

they wanted to the political public indicates that there were current ideas of a Liberal Party. We see now that it was not only a strong concept among MPs, but that it was the preferred way those MPs liked to be presented.[155]

In the 1830s and 1840s, therefore, languages of political description among non-conservatives became less heterogeneous. Even in the 1830s, when political language was not as monochrome as it would become in the 1840s, MPs were happy to be called 'Liberal' and in the 'Liberal Party'. Further, although 'Liberal Party' was a sort of secondary label in the 1830s, by the 1840s it became the dominant one. Earlier in this chapter, party terms and labels were defined as shorthand used to convey the meaning and scope of political ideologies. We have seen here how prevalent and strict the application of 'Liberal' was by the late 1840s and early 1850s. Chapter 2 will show how the expanded shorthand was presented, and will begin the discussion of the scope and meaning of liberal politics during this period.

---

[155] See also *Parliamentary Manual 1838*, iii–v, 46–60.

Chapter 2. Liberal Politics in the Constituencies and the House of Commons

The previous chapter established the increased use and acceptance of the liberal terms and labels used to describe the political stances of Liberal Party MPs between 1833 and 1852. It did not, however, put flesh on the skeleton of such brief descriptions, and did not show the extent of liberal opinion, or the specific ideas of liberal politics. This chapter introduces the nature of liberal politics in the reform period and shows how it was presented to the political public in the house of commons and the constituencies. Jonathan Parry has termed this the 'liberal value-system'.[1] 'Liberal value-system', however, implies more than political ideology, and strays too close to ideas of moral constrictions on behaviour for the purposes of this book. 'Liberal politics' is perhaps a better phrase to describe the range of political opinions among Liberal Party MPs because it fixes reasonable limits on meaning and, more importantly, as this chapter will show, it places emphasis on politics, and the new ways in which MPs presented their opinions on issues of the day. The strong attachment that Liberal Party MPs placed on the *political*, as opposed to ideological, aspects of important issues (i.e., the ways in which they should be addressed in terms of governance and practical reform), comes to light very clearly through such an examination. This is not to argue that a liberal value system did not exist, or that there was no moral dimension to being liberal with a small 'l', but that the new terms of reference brought about by changes during the reform period were, for Liberal Party MPs at least, mainly expressed as a political creed.

Until recently, the expression of political opinions through public and private electioneering material during the Age of Reform has been somewhat under-explored.[2] The exceptions to this are, of course, Peel's 1834 Tamworth Manifesto and Russell's famous letter of 1845 to his London constituents on free trade. Election addresses to constituents, set speeches and posters provide valuable insights into how political ideologies were constructed and presented. This public aspect of liberal electioneering is discussed in the first section of this chapter. Private opinion and reflections in diaries and letters between ordinary MPs, constituents and party leaders have also not been examined fully, and provide the basis for the analysis in the second section. Public political statements made through parliamentary guides are considered in the final section of the chapter.

---

[1] J.P. Parry, *The Rise and Fall of Liberal Government in Victorian Britain* (New Haven, CT, 1993), 14–17.

[2] In his *Politics and the People*, James Vernon uses some of this material, but prefers illustrations, architecture, statuary and other forms of political expression to support his arguments. See J. Vernon, *Politics and the People: A Study in English Political Culture, c.1815–1867* (Cambridge, 1993), esp. chs 3, 5. More significantly and recently, Hannah Barker and David Vincent have shown the value of election broadsides in *Language, Print and Electoral Politics 1790–1832: Newcastle-under-Lyme Broadsides*, ed. H. Barker and D. Vincent (Woodbridge, 2001).

One of the most important and convincing arguments made by Barker and Vincent is that electioneering language in the pre-1832 era is shown to be 'multilayered' because of the 'diverse . . . composition and intended audiences' of the broadsides they have mined. 'From low ballads to high political argument', the forms of pre-reform electioneering were highly sophisticated, both in terms of their production and the subtle ways in which their producers (candidates and agents) understood the nature of their political audiences.[3] This chapter argues that this continued after 1832. It also shows that electioneering materials and statements expressed a greater degree of adherence to the general and specific aspects of liberal politics among Liberal Party MPs than before 1832. Further, the degree to which these public statements cohered with more private sentiments shows more accurately the attachment to a political belief system. This section will examine both these aspects, and will provide interesting connections and comparisons with the way liberal politics was being expressed within the house of commons. Liberal Party MPs routinely used their electioneering material to express the full agenda on which their candidature was based. Rather than use bland and broad ideological terms only, Liberal Party MPs listed at length and in detail where they stood on most major issues of the day, and often reproduced records of voting in division lobbies to bolster their support among liberal electors. This agenda-mongering was one of the major differences between conservative and liberal candidates in most constituencies. If we look at a representative sample of political expressions in the constituencies, chronologically, with examples from most of the Liberal Party 'subgroups',[4] we see a recognizable coherence around liberal politics.[5]

The Whig MP for Stroud, William Hyett, neatly summarized the importance of the 1832 Reform Act when he addressed his constituents after the December election, and 'congratulat[ed] them on their political birth-day, of which he wished them many happy returns'.[6] His moderate whig stance in the election of 1832 was further characterised by his support for replacing the corn laws with a low fixed duty, general retrenchment, 'an end . . . to Colonial Slavery as expeditiously as is consistent with justice to the planter, and the welfare of the slave' and 'a compulsory and liberal commutation of Tithe'.[7] His election committee printed 1,000 cards to be handed out while canvassing, containing the simple message: 'Hyett and Reform'. And, although no advocate of the ballot, Hyett, who was one

---

[3] *Language, Print and Electoral Politics*, ed. Barker and Vincent, xxxiv–xxxvii.

[4] Since this work concentrated on archives in England, very few examples of political statements from Repealers are available.

[5] One frustrating element of research with backbenchers' manuscript collections is that the 1840s and early 1850s are not quite as well represented as the 1830s in terms of surviving documents of the type discussed here. This probably does not mean that 'agenda-mongering' had settled down to a more sedate pace in the 1840s, however, because the examples that do survive tend to indicate the same depth of feeling among MPs, as well as hint at the continued existence of this sort of electioneering activity. Essential guides to the elections discussed in this book are J. Acland, *The Imperial Poll Book of All Elections from the Passing of the Reform Act in 1832 to the End of 1864* (1869); *MacCalmont's Parliamentary Poll Book: British Election Results 1832–1918*, ed. J.R. Vincent and M. Stenton (Brighton, 1971); *British Parliamentary Election Results 1832–1885*, ed. F.W.S. Craig (1977); F.W.S. Craig, *Chronology of British Parliamentary By-elections, 1833–1885* (Chichester, 1977).

[6] Gloucestershire RO, Hyett Papers: Report from the *Gloucester Record*, 15 Dec. 1832.

[7] Gloucestershire RO, Hyett Papers: Report from the *Gloucester Journal*, 8 Dec. 1832.

of the most conservative Whigs, ordered that one of his election banners contain the motto 'Hyett and Purity of Elections'.[8] Other Whigs characterised themselves similarly. William Battie-Wrightson, Whig candidate for Northallerton in 1832, told his electors:

> My principles with regard to Reform, lead naturally to liberal opinions upon other subjects. To the present system of Corn Laws I am decidedly opposed, but I am friendly to a moderate duty for purpose of protection to the farmer, and revenue to the state. I look to a reduction of taxation as fast as the revenue will bear it. A complete change in the tythe [*sic*] system, shall have my decided support . . . [as well as] . . . the abolition of slavery.[9]

Charles Wood, Whig candidate for Halifax in 1832, chose to report to his constituents by listing what he had voted for in the previous parliament, when he was MP for Wareham. This is an early example of the length and detail of expression of a liberal political agenda. Wood made sure that both his principles and his parliamentary behaviour were presented directly.

> Acting steadily on the Principles which I profess, I have voted: For the Extension of Religious Liberty to the Dissenter and to the Catholic; For the speedy Extinction of Negro Slavery; In favour of Civil Liberty, both at Home and Abroad. I have voted for the Relaxation of Monopolies;- The Extinction of the Tythe-System in Ireland;- The Freedom of the Press;- The Relief of the Productive Industry of the Country from undue Taxation;- The Reduction of Pensions and Salaries;- Good and Cheap Government;- And lastly; For the best and certain means of obtaining each and all of these Objects,- For the Extension of Political Rights amongst the Independent and Intelligent Classes of the Community.[10]

John Benjamin Smith, Liberal MP for Stirling and president of the Manchester Chamber of Commerce, projected the broad sweep of liberal politics from 1832 to 1852, when he said in July 1832:

> The Reform Bill I consider to be an instrument in the hands of the people by which to obtain and secure good government, that is, the greatest happiness of the greatest number.
>
> I will support the ministry plan for the abolition of Church Rates, and the right of Ireland, as an integral part of the Empire, to equal laws and institutions.
>
> I have ever been the earnest and unflinching opponent of the Corn Laws.
>
> I will earnestly enforce all practical retrenchments, the abolition of unmerited pensions, and the most severe economy in the expenditure of public money.
>
> Above all, I will support the moral and intellectual education of the people, as the foremost security of national liberty and happiness.

[8] Gloucestershire RO, Hyett Papers, D6/F33, f. 7.

[9] West Yorkshire Archive Service, Battie-Wrightson Papers, BW/P/16: printed electoral address, 16 July 1832.

[10] Univ. of York, Borthwick Institute of Historical Research, Halifax Papers: printed electoral address, 12 June 1832.

Convinced that the welfare and . . . interests of mankind are promoted by friendly intercourse with all nations, I shall ever be the advocate of peace and free trade.[11]

Sir George Dashwood, candidate for Buckinghamshire in 1832, defined himself as a Reformer based on his support for: economy and retrenchment in public expenditure; the abolition of slavery and of monopolies; reform in the church of England; the 'extension of knowledge by education'; 'prompt and cheap justice'; and a reduction in the number of capital crimes.[12] John Fielden, in what became typical Radical fashion, was very extensive when he set out his agenda for the 1832 election, concentrating on annual parliaments and the ballot, but going further to say that he thought the burden of taxation was too great, due to 'iniquitous and ruinous wars', and that:

I would vote for the abolition of tithes, of all sinecures and pensions not merited by well known public services, the repeal of assessed taxes, and the taxes on malt, hops, and soap, and these having been repealed, I would support a total abolition of the corn laws. I would also support any inquiry into the debt, with a view to securing its equitable extinction. I am opposed to all injurious monopolies, a friend to civil & religious liberty, and adverse to slavery in every shape.[13]

The overwhelming victory for reformers in the December 1832 election did little to change the habit of agenda-mongering, at least partly because the dismissal of the Whig ministry in 1834 caused great consternation among liberal electors, and became part of the language of addresses and posters. The 1834–5 period saw the beginnings of a more constant use of 'liberal' as an umbrella term for all non-tory candidates. Indeed liberal candidates used 'the tory bogey' as propaganda during the election of 1835, as well as arguing that the dismissal was unconstitutional and the election unnecessary.[14] Charles Tynte, Whig MP for Somerset, listed his votes on an election poster in late 1834, running to 32 items, and including:

For publishing the votes of members . . . For the protection of the ballot . . . Repeal of the house and window tax . . . Against the Repeal of the Corn Laws . . . For Triennial Parliaments . . . For Abolition of Slavery . . . For Admission of Dissenters to the Universities . . . For the Total Abolition of Church Rates . . . For Reform of the Irish Church.[15]

In an almost exact duplication, Edward Sanford, Whig MP for West Somerset, listed his votes in the 1832–4 sessions, which were less extensive than Tynte's, but contained many of the same items: 'Against the Repeal of the Corn Laws . . . For the Abolition of

[11] Manchester Central Library Archive, John Benjamin Smith Papers, MS 923.2 S336, item 8: election poster, 19 July 1832.

[12] Bodl., Dashwood Papers, MS DD Dashwood, G.1.1: election poster, 29 July 1832. See also *Buckingham-shire Gazette and Bedford Chronicle*, 21 July 1832, in the Dashwood Papers.

[13] Univ. of Manchester, John Rylands Library, Fielden Papers, FDN/1/2/2, item 1: election poster, 1 July 1832.

[14] D. Close, 'The General Elections of 1835 and 1837 in England and Wales', University of Oxford PhD, 1967, pp. 92–5.

[15] Somerset RO, Sanford Papers, DD/SF, 4552, item 12: election poster, 22 Dec. 1834.

Slavery . . . For Shortening the Duration of Parliaments . . . For Admission of Dissenters to the Universities . . . For the Relief of Dissenters from Church Rates . . . For Reform of the Irish Church'.[16]

George Anson, who had been Whig MP for Great Yarmouth until January 1835, used the standard shorthand for liberal politics, 'reform and liberty', in an attempt to gain the South Staffordshire seat in May 1835 after E.J. Littleton had been made Lord Hatherton, and declared: 'I shall ever continue the consistent advocate of those liberal principles of Government which have now been permanently secured to us, through that second charter of our liberties, the Reform Act'.[17]

Although wishing that the cause of reform could have been pushed further in the honeymoon after the passage of the Reform Act, many Reformers argued that the Whig ministry had served the country well, and should not have been treated so harshly by the king in November 1834, when he dismissed the government (see Chapter 4). In a poster headed 'What Have the Whigs Done?', Reformers in Yorkshire wrote: 'It has often been asked, What has the Late Government done for The People?', and answered the question at length, listing what they saw as Whig successes: 'the REFORM BILL . . . [and] . . . taken off TAXES, laid on by the TORIES, to the annual amount of SIX MILLIONS'. The other successes it listed were the following:

THE IRISH CHURCH placed on a very satisfactory footing by the Abolition of several useless Bishoprics, and adding to the Salaries of the inferior Clergy. The IRISH CHURCH CESS wholly abolished. The BANK CHARTER moved to a very liberal system . . . EAST INDIA MONOPOLY destroyed . . . and, above all, the ABOLITION OF NEGRO SLAVERY.

And in the most significant part, the poster finished by saying: 'we are reformers – not whigs, but let us do the Whigs justice'.[18] William Ord, candidate for Newcastle-upon-Tyne, also railed against the 1834 dismissal, and told his constituents that he would support further franchise reform and the ballot if they were proved necessary, as well as being in favour of appropriation, church rate abolition, the abolition of the corn laws and, he promised strongly, strict opposition to what he saw as an unjustly appointed Tory administration.[19]

Only some of the stricter Radicals, like Charles D'Eyncourt, bemoaned the lack of further reform, and called for a more radical house of commons. A printed address to his electors showed how much he wanted to be seen to be pushing for more radical measures.

The Parliaments in which, by your favor [*sic*], I have sat since the Reform Act, have disappointed the hopes of the Nation. After a long career of Public service – after having shared in all your Labours to obtain the means of Reform, I participated deeply in your feelings when we found those means ineffectual; and I had the

[16] Somerset RO, Sanford Papers, DD/SF, 4552, item 24: election poster, 22 Dec. 1834.

[17] Staffordshire RO, Littleton Papers: *Staffordshire Advertiser*, 9 May 1835. See also Bodl., Barham Papers: the electoral address of John Barham, 27 Dec. 1834.

[18] West Yorkshire Archive Service, Battie-Wrightson Papers, BW/P/20: election poster, no date [1834/5].

[19] Northumberland RO, Ord Papers, NRO 324/A.69: electoral addresses of 18 Dec. and 22 Dec. 1834.

additional pain of discovering that the party struggle even to maintain a Government with liberal disposition, necessarily limited in useful efforts on the part of your representatives to that object.[20]

The 1837 election saw much of the same sort of language, especially that of repeating the Whig government's reform successes, and implying that liberal candidates were entitled to their constituents' suffrage on the basis of gratitude. Robert Slaney, moderate Whig candidate for Shrewsbury, told his constituents that he looked back 'with pride and pleasure' in voting for parliamentary reform, removal of religious disabilities and the abolition of slavery. He went on to say that further reform, especially the abolition of the house of lords and the disestablishment of the church of England, would fall on deaf ears with him.[21] Edward Sanford in West Somerset also focused on the government's reforms in appealing to his constituents, noting that they were 'most conducive to the Permanent preservation of our National Institutions of Church and State'.[22]

At the end of July, Charles Wood addressed a crowd in Halifax, pushing the idea of a continuation of Whig government on the basis of past reform success, and the implication that Whig hands were the only safe ones on the reform tiller.

> Bear me out in securing a large and Liberal majority, that the cause of reform may advance, from day to day, surely and steadily; and every session will add something to that given to the people; and will make us, under our young and liberal Queen, a prosperous, a united, and a loyal people (cheers).[23]

And Sir George Dashwood appealed to the newly christened groups of 'liberal' electors, displaying the new language of politics in the constituencies, by using the older, pre-Reform language of balanced representation for counties. An election poster of his from 1837 shows how quickly the liberal label had been adapted to this form of electioneering, and how important candidates thought using such language in repetition was.

> Electors of Bucks! A Tory Candidate has been named to Represent you; A Candidate on the Liberal Side will be offered to you this day, at the hustings!!! One Party now monopolizes the Representation of the County; it is for you to decide whether you will increase the power of that Party by giving your Votes to their Candidate, or whether you will Assert Your Independence By Electing a Man of Liberal Political Opinions. Considering it an imperative duty not to allow the liberal portion of the County Constituency to remain as it now is, totally unrepresented, without publicly protesting against the evil, or attempting to remove it, we have determined to nominate George Henry Dashwood, Esq. of West Wycombe Park, as A Fit and Proper Person to Represent you in Parliament. We confidently expect that you will do your duty as Independent Men, and shew your gratitude to him for his exertions in your

[20] Lambeth Archives Department, Minet Library, D'Eyncourt Papers, IV/3/80: election poster, no date [1834/5].

[21] Shropshire Records and Research Centre, Slaney Papers: election poster, 28 June 1837.

[22] Somerset RO, Sanford Papers, DD/SF, 4552, item 29: election poster, 26 June 1837.

[23] Univ. of York, Borthwick Institute, Halifax Papers: *The Halifax and Huddersfield Express and Weekly Advertiser*, 29 July 1837.

Cause, by making every effort in your power to place him once more in the House of Commons, as the Liberal Member for Bucks.[24]

By 1841, however, appeals to past reform triumphs were less common, although the highlights of the Reform Act and the abolition of slavery were sometimes used. The new decade saw an increased interest in pushing the ideas of institutional reform and civil and religious liberty, in even more specific ways. Trade issues, not surprisingly, became more apparent in electioneering material. The Liberal candidate for Leeds, William Aldam, allied himself with the Radical Joseph Hume in the contest, and combined posters for both candidates appeared often. 'Electors of Leeds', one announced, 'Jocelyn and Beckett are identified with monopoly, extravagance and abuse, Hume and Aldam are identified with free trade, economy, and reform'.[25] But Aldam often modified his free trade stance when on his own, arguing for eventual free trade after a moderate fixed duty and for changes in the sugar and timber duties, but not their abolition. Further, he expanded his agenda to include 'staunch' support of 'religious liberty', as well as the abolition of church rates, mild support for the ballot, national education, broader suffrage and retrenchment.[26] And George Dashwood in Wycombe continued his Reformer stance, stressing repeal of the corn laws, a modification of the poor law and some increased freedom of voting.[27]

As the 1840s progressed, a new electioneering pattern emerged. Whigs were more inclined to general statements in their electioneering material while Liberals, Reformers and Radicals listed specific votes and pledges for future behaviour in the house of commons. Hugh Grosvenor, Whig MP for Chester, simply said in a speech that he 'trusted that he had done his best by the votes he had given to promote the interests of his constituency, and that in the situation in which their confidence had recently placed him, he had [done so] honestly and faithfully in the discharge of the duties of their representative'.[28] Lord Dudley Stuart, the Liberal candidate for Marylebone, however, listed his past parliamentary votes in detail from 1832 onwards, and promised his constituents that he was in favour of 'Local Government, The Repeal of the Window Tax, Extension of the suffrage to lodgers, Vote by Ballot, Free Trade, Abolishing Flogging in the Army and Navy, Abolishing the Game Laws. And is Against All Interference by Poor Law Commissions or other Centralized Boards'.[29]

Radicals continued to list their agendas in full in electioneering material, as well as discussing what type of MP they had been, which was part of the radical idea of responsive representation almost to the point of being a delegate. Thomas Thompson spent a great deal of time in speeches reminding his constituents of his twice-weekly reports from the house of commons, and that they were the only reports of their kind.[30] Thompson was one of the few MPs who made it even easier for his constituents to

---

[24] Bodl., Dashwood Papers, G.1.2., MS DD Dashwood: election poster, 13 Feb. 1837.

[25] Doncaster Archives Department, Aldam Papers: election poster, [no date] 1841.

[26] Doncaster Archives Department, Aldam Papers: election poster, 28 May 1841.

[27] L.J. Ashford, *The History of the Borough of High Wycombe from Its Origins to 1880* (1960), 282–5.

[28] Cheshire RO, Hugh Lupus Grosvenor Papers, *Chester Courant*, 4 Aug. 1847.

[29] West Sussex RO, John Abel Smith Papers, Add. MS 22,478: election poster for Lord Dudley Stuart, [no date] 1847.

[30] Univ. of Hull, Brynmor Jones Library, Thompson Papers, DTH/3/9.

know where he stood on various issues. He distributed pocket-sized election cards on which were printed a summary of his liberal politics. Surrounding a large central message of 'Thompson and Liberty' were flags with 'Plenty & Peace' and 'Trade & Commerce'. A farmer and a sailor held up the flags, and were seated on pedestals which were engraved with: 'the people', 'less taxation & more economy; knowledge & the press; freedom & happiness all over the world; the rights of conscience; no impressment, no flogging'.[31]

Liberal candidates and MPs became more interesting in the 1840s, however, when they took stances on free trade, and the corn laws especially, that were quite different from the bulk of the party. While there were, of course, many Radicals calling for immediate abolition of the corn laws and other duties, the bulk of the Liberal Party took a moderate free trade stance, arguing for a transitional period with a moderate fixed duty, followed by eventual abolition. There was, however, a group of Liberal Party MPs, usually from agricultural counties, who might be termed 'Liberal Protectionists'. As we shall see in more detail in Chapter 8, these Liberal Party MPs voted against the abolition of the corn laws in the early 1840s, although some were convinced to support their repeal in 1846. Further, until 1846, many Liberal Party MPs listed specific free trade measures that they supported. The post-repeal world, however, became a 'free trade' world at least in the sense that the phrase itself appeared more often, and usually in place of listing support for specific trade measures. After 1846, the liberal rhetoric changed to place free trade at its centre.[32] John Bowes, Reformer MP for South Durham, showed both aspects of this in a printed address to his constituents as early as 1841. He referred specifically to his opposition to the repeal of the corn laws, and said:

> Under these circumstances, differing from the great body of that Party with which I act, on a question brought forward as a main feature of its policy, it would have been, I can assure you, more agreeable to my feelings that I, not again have the honour of representing you.[33]

Bowes was willing to withdraw himself from candidature over his opposition to what he saw as an increasingly central Liberal Party policy on trade. His supporters refused this offer, and he represented the county until 1847, but this clearly shows the importance of free trade as a party issue. By 1852, the policy had become solid. Faced with an admittedly weak Conservative attempt to revive protection in 1851, the Liberal Party fought the 1852 election mainly on trade issues. Sir Francis Crossley, Liberal candidate for Halifax in 1852, told his constituents: 'those principles of Free Trade, for which so many of us have struggled, are now in jeopardy; – that, in the next parliament, they must be reversed or finally secured; – and that their permanent maintenance renders a hearty union of true, honest and ardent, Free Traders indispensable'.[34]

And on 7 April 1852, Charles Wood, contesting the seat with Crossley, called for party unity. It was, he said, 'the imperative duty of all Free Traders to unite in the most

---

[31] Univ. of Hull, Brynmor Jones Library, Thompson Papers, DTH/3/8.

[32] Parry, *Rise and Fall of Liberal Government*, 167–8.

[33] Durham County RO, Bowes Papers, D/St/C1/16/279: election poster, 8 June 1841.

[34] Univ. of York, Borthwick Institute, Halifax Papers: election poster for Sir Francis Crossley, 2 Apr. 1852.

determined resistance to the proposed attempt to counteract the beneficial effects of the act of 1846, in whichever shape it may be brought forward'.[35]

Liberal MPs, therefore, had little difficulty in wearing their liberal agenda on their sleeves. This sort of public expression shows how much liberal politics was seen as essential for public electioneering. How it matched more private expression will be examined next.

Appeals and Correspondence: Private Expression of Liberal Politics

At least as important as the prepared and publicly presented expressions of liberal politics was the use of more private means of communication to transmit the expectations of constituents as well as concerns about liberal electioneering between MPs, and between MPs and their agents and electoral committees. This section will examine liberal politics as shown in the diaries of backbench MPs, in correspondence between MPs, in appeals from individual constituents, in communications from constituent groups and in correspondence and communications between MPs and their electoral agents and committees. The most significant finding about the private aspect of liberal electioneering was, as will be shown here, how closely it mirrored its public expression.

The most private way MPs discussed liberal issues and concerns was in their diaries or journals. While many kept such things on a regular basis, they generally used them only as a way to record correspondence, and as a general aide-memoire of their movements during the year. In other words, they used them much as they are used today in the business world. Discursive diary entries are rare, and even when MPs recorded their political thoughts, it was often to make notes for a speech in the house of commons or their constituencies.[36] In addition to the diary entries used in other chapters in this book, three examples of electioneering and concern over liberal issues show how important this agenda building had become even in the 1830s. In a journal entry dated 'July 1837', Robert Slaney, Whig MP for Shrewsbury, wrote about the 1837 election:

> We had scarcely been in the Country a week when intelligence arrived for our King's illness. After lingering some time his death followed. This necessarily called for a speedy dissolution of parliament. Called for by the Liberal party in Shrewsbury I gave an address expressing my firm attachment to gradual & reasonable reform, but my fixed determination to oppose attacks on the Church & the House of Peers. . . . After a most active & fatiguing canvass . . . we entered into the contest, the result of which was the return [of] me & Mr Jenkins as Members. My brother came down & gave me his best aid. The result of the general election throughout the Kingdom is to shew a certain reaction against Radical opinions, & somewhat against the Ministers, who are in some sort identified with every body of their usual supporters.[37]

---

[35] Univ. of York, Borthwick Institute, Halifax Papers: election poster for Charles Wood, 7 Apr. 1852.

[36] For example, see *The Parliamentary Diaries of Sir John Trelawny, 1858–1865*, ed. T.A. Jenkins (Camden Society, 4th ser., xl, 1990), 2–3.

[37] Shropshire Records and Research Centre, Slaney Papers: diary entry, [no date] July 1837.

Another moderate Whig, John Abel Smith in Chichester, was equally worried about overly radical opinions taking command of the debate in the house of commons, especially on the ballot. In a diary entry dated 'Feby 1838', he outlined his reasons for voting for the ballot and showed the thinking behind those who supported it only reservedly:

> The debate on the ballot is over and I have voted for it. If I had been told this two years since I would not have believed it & tho' in voting for it now I have listened only to my own conscientious conviction, I have acted under a strong sense of the disagreeable consequences to myself. I am not satisfied or happy. I do not feel one jot more friendly to the principle of [the] ballot than I did five years since. I hate the secrecy & concealment & like the open & avowed responsibility attendant upon open voting. I am unable to combat the arguments to those who deny the efficiency of the ballot for the purposes of concealment & its probable effect on the country. But on [the] other hand there is this strong and to me overwhelming consideration. That I know by my own experience & the cordence [*sic*] of my own senses that the little voter in Towns & the small tenants & 40s freeholders in counties cannot vote as they like, if it was right to extend the franchise under the Reform Bill it is right to give them protection in the exercise of this franchise. I cannot get over this & it was in obedience to this feeling that I voted for the Ballot. I wonder how many who did so with as heavy a heart as I did. I hope that the final result of all this push for [the] ballot and the large division of tonight will be some compromise – either that public opinion will be moved to secure to the voter real freedom of action, or else that on concession of the ballot there may be raising of the qualification.[38]

This willingness to maintain a political principle, yet vary its application in practice, and especially when considered necessary, was one of the most striking aspects of liberal politics in this period. Not only did MPs use this as a justification for voting for the ballot, they often used it when treating Ireland as a 'special case', which is shown in Chapters 5 and 7. Finally, an entry from Lord Hatherton's diary shows very clearly that not all MPs were convinced that the electorate were paying attention to the liberal agenda. He wrote in a diary entry of 26 June 1841 that his son, Edward, canvassed Walsall for the Whig candidate Robert Scott, and that 'Edward complains of the almost universal ignorance of the Electors of public interests. The greatest flight of reasoning the majority take is of this sort "Well, Trade is very bad. We've tried these Ministers a long time. I think we had better try another set" '.[39]

MPs, naturally, wrote to each other, but less of this correspondence survives. And while they usually discussed electioneering tactics, sometimes they discussed issues in a way that displayed how strongly they felt attached to liberal politics. On 11 May 1835, Robert Slaney wrote to Lord Hatherton: 'it is a matter of satisfaction to me that I was enabled to vote throughout the last few years with you & other liberal men, in the three great questions (which are now settled); of the Slave Trade Abolition, Religious Toleration &

---

[38] West Sussex RO, John Abel Smith Papers, Add. MS 22,341: diary entry, [no date] Feb. 1838.

[39] Staffordshire RO, Littleton Papers, D2260M/F/5/26/22.

Reform'.[40] Although John Abel Smith reluctantly voted for the ballot in 1838, he was not always willing to do so. In 1835, the radical candidate John Cobbett (son of William Cobbett) complained to John Fielden, Radical MP for Oldham, that Smith's influence in Chichester would never be broken without the ballot:

> I hope you saw my address to the electors of Chichester . . . I found, as is found almost everywhere, that there is no chance for any like us but through the means of the ballot, so, if you do not give us that, I shall not be member for Chichester even under another dissolution . . . The tradesmen of Chichester are all disgusted with Smith, but they are overawed by the influence that has set to work upon them, and they loudly call for the ballot.[41]

A striking example of the concerns over divisions in the Liberal Party, and over the difficulty of maintaining a liberal government, were distinctly expressed by Henry Bulwer, Radical MP for Coventry, when he wrote to fellow Radical Richard Potter, MP for Wigan, on the state of party politics and the difficulties of getting liberal measures passed through the house of commons. Like many Liberal Party MPs, even Radicals, Bulwer appealed for unity, and stressed that voting against the party was not to be done lightly:

> the nature of public affairs is such, more especially in agitated times, that you could never get or expect to get a number of persons to unite together for the carrying of more than one or two principle questions.

> I have voted against this government on one or two occasions but I have done so most unwillingly, I allow it, because I think we are thereby not behaving handsomely to them.

> We encouraged them by our votes and our conduct to come into office; we knew they could only do so by certain compromises amongst themselves. That was the necessity attendant upon the formation of the ministry, which necessity I think we are bound to conform ourselves to – unless we prefer the alternative. There may undoubtedly be occasions where private feeling of honor [*sic*] may induce us to take a different course, but these should be very rare and extraordinary, at least so I think.

> For only consider! You know as well as I do that many among the government there are persons who, on a variety of subjects – flogging in the army, or triennial parliaments, or vote by ballot, differ amongst themselves.[42]

As the 1840s began, questions of trade took precedence in this correspondence. Russell wrote to Sir Denis Le Marchant, one of the Whig grandees who helped control party matters from London, surprised that the Liberal Party lost the West Riding of Yorkshire in the 1841 election: 'This West Riding defeat exceeds all other losses. If Leeds is not for

---

[40] Staffordshire RO, Littleton Papers, D260/M/F/5/27/11/65: Robert Slaney to Lord Hatherton, 11 May 1835.

[41] Univ. of Manchester, John Rylands Library, Fielden Papers, FDN/2/1/item 3: John Morgan Cobbett to John Fielden, 20 Jan. 1835.

[42] Norfolk RO, Henry Bulwer Papers, BUL 1/6/29a: Henry Lytton Bulwer to Richard Potter, 23 Apr. 1836.

free trade, how should any other place?'[43] Edward Horsman, Whig MP for Cocker-mouth, wrote to Russell in 1846 that, when Russell came to form a government, he must include Cobden in his cabinet, not just because of the new free trade-dominated political world that repeal of the corn laws had helped to create, but because of the respect he commanded.[44]

Throughout the 1832–52 period, individual constituents wrote to their MP for many reasons: patronage, mainly, but also to express satisfaction or dissatisfaction concerning his conduct in the House, as well as requesting him to state his position on issues or to vote a certain way. MPs generally returned the correspondence, often detailing their votes on specific measures in the house of commons. In addition to the constituent correspondence displayed in Part 2, there are several examples of individual constituents writing to MPs, and revealing their ideas about liberal issues in the process. In a letter dated 1 December 1834, J. Kiernan, a Lambeth constituent, wrote to Charles D'Eyncourt: 'the open and undisguised manifestation of your sentiments as well as your Votes on what you think vital Questions of reform, particularly as to the Church, the Ballot & short parliaments, command my respect and esteem, as I believe they do of all real reformers'.[45]

Responding to a similar letter from a constituent worrying about how well he would be received in the constituency, Henry Parnell, Whig MP for Dundee, was careful to stress exactly what he had voted for in the House, and how well he thought it would be received:

> I beg the opportunity of mentioning that during the sixteen months which passed between my election in 1833 & the close of the last session, I voted for the following measures. 1st The Repeal of the Septennial Act. 2nd The Vote by Ballot. 3rd The revision of the Pension List. 4th The Abolition of Military Flogging. 5th The Abolition of Impressment. 6th The Application of the Surplus Revenues of the Church of Ireland to national objects. & 7th the reduction of the Military & Naval establishments. The general principles which governed my conduct with respect to these measures would have led me to support several other reforms, towards which the public mind has been anxiously directed, whenever brought forward.[46]

This echoed the public debate between J.B. Smith and James Heald in the 1852 Stockport election, where they traded blows in posters and pamphlets over the question of who had voted more often in divisions in the house of commons.[47] Constituents were also sometimes upset when they saw MPs acting in what they considered to be an overly partisan manner. Although Sir William Ffolkes' constituent Robert Hankinson generally supported Ffolkes' voting behaviour in the Commons, he disdained the action of liberal MPs over the 1835 Speakership contest: 'Sir C.M.S. [Charles Manners Sutton, the

---

[43] PA, Le Marchant Papers: Russell to Le Marchant, 10 July 1841.

[44] Buckinghamshire RO, Horsman Papers, D/RA/A/3E/13: Edward Horsman to Russell, 22 June 1846.

[45] Lambeth Archives Department, Minet Library, D'Eyncourt Papers, IV/3/18: J. Kiernan to Charles Tennyson D'Eyncourt, 1 Dec. 1834.

[46] Southampton UL, Broadlands Archives Trust, Henry Parnell Papers, bundle 15, item 24: Henry Brooke Parnell to Alexander Kay, 15 Dec. 1834.

[47] Manchester Central Library Archive, John Benjamin Smith Papers, MS 923.2 S332, items 30–2: election posters and pamphlets, 3–6 July 1852.

Speaker ousted in 1835] is no friend of mine . . . but this appears to me a mere party manoeuvre, and, if I mistake not your political character and conduct has been adherence to principle and not to partisanship'.[48]

In 1838, T. Hammond, constituent of William Wilshere, Liberal MP for Great Yarmouth, wrote to express his thanks for Wilshere opposing the Sabbath Bill, which, he said, would have damaged the local fishing industry.[49] Another good example of vote monitoring by a constituent was when James Kingdom, in reply to a written canvass, wrote to his MP Charles D'Eyncourt: 'the votes uniformly given by you in the House of Commons as well as the sentiments expressed in your printed circulars . . . so mainly concurred with my own opinions as would certainly induce me to aid your cause'.[50]

Constituents also banded together to express satisfaction or regret at an MP's voting in the house of commons, or to request a statement on an issue or to urge a specific vote. In March 1834, 'the Free Burgesses and other Electors of Newcastle' met and carried a vote of censure against Sir Matthew Ridley, Whig MP for Newcastle-upon-Tyne, and John Hodgson, Reformer MP for Newcastle-upon-Tyne, for their votes against an inquiry into the Pension List: 'This meeting . . . deem the vote of the members for this town against the motion . . . for enquiry into the Pension list as the very acme and height of Political impropriety, and, in consequence, [deem] Sir M.W. Ridley and Mr Hodgson as no longer worthy of the confidence of their constituents'.[51]

In 1836, in a stringent and radical address to Henry Parnell, Whig MP for Dundee, the 'non-electors of Dundee' wrote on a number of reform issues, and excoriated Parnell for what they saw as his weak support of reform measures. The issues they addressed included: church establishment reform and abolition of church rates; appropriation of surplus revenues of the church of Ireland; shorter parliaments; and peerage reform (leading to the abolition of the house of lords).[52] In the south-west, both the 'Liberal Electors of Weymouth' and the 'Youths of Weymouth' praised Thomas Buxton (Whig MP for Weymouth) upon his retirement and, in addition to recognizing his famous work in the anti-slavery cause, lauded 'his unwearied exertions in the cause of Civil & Religious Liberty'.[53] Similarly, John Fielden was asked to attend a meeting on the Ten Hours Bill in 1836, where his constituents were also 'to testify our gratitude for the past and our confidence in [y]our future services'.[54] And as we have seen earlier, the trade and corn law issues of the 1840s formed much of the communication between constituent

[48] Norfolk RO, Ffolkes Papers, NRS 8740/21/D/4: Robert Hankinson to Sir William Ffolkes, Whig MP for West Norfolk, 18 Feb. 1835.

[49] Hertfordshire RO, Wilshere Papers, D/EX 14/7: T. Hammond to William Wilshere, 23 Mar. 1838.

[50] Lincolnshire Archives Office, D'Eyncourt Papers H/19/25: James Kingdom to Charles Tennyson D'Eyncourt, 21 July 1847. See also P.J. Salmon, *Electoral Reform at Work: Local Politics and National Parties, 1832–1841* (Woodbridge, 1996), 140–2.

[51] Northumberland RO, Ridley Papers, ZRI, 25/62: newspaper clippings (titles and dates removed) reporting the meeting of 10 Mar. 1834.

[52] Southampton UL, Broadlands Archives Trust, Parnell Papers, bundle 15, item 24: 'Non-electors of Dundee' to Henry Brooke Parnell, 12 Nov. 1836.

[53] Bodl., Rhodes House Library, Buxton Papers, MS Britain Emp. s444, iii, 128: tributes to Thomas Fowell Buxton, transcriptions of the inscriptions on a candelabrum (from the Liberal Electors of Weymouth) and a silver box (from the Youths of Weymouth).

[54] Univ. of Manchester, John Rylands Library, Fielden Papers, FDN/1/2/1, item 18: W.S. Slataire to John Fielden, 21 Dec. 1836.

groups and their MPs. The 'Non-electors of the Borough of Great Yarmouth', in a typical example of political participation by the un-enfranchised, petitioned William Wilshere to vote for Charles Villiers' corn law abolition motion in 1844:

> [The] Non-Electors of the Borough of Great Yarmouth, . . . greatly interested in the prosperity of its Trade and Commerce, believing that the existing Corn Laws have been instrumental in causing the distress which now prevails amongst all classes of the community, and thinking that the Electors of this Borough, in forwarding to you a requisition relative to Mr. Villiers' motion, are performing a duty which they owe themselves as a constituent Body, and to us as Men, whose welfare depend on their political integrity, beg leave most respectfully to submit, that you will promote the cause of justice, humanity, and mercy, by voting for the abolition of the corn laws.[55]

Similarly, 'a committee consisting of members of the various Protestant Nonconforming denominations' wrote to Thomas Thompson, Radical MP for Bradford, asking him: 'In the event of your being returned to Parliament, would you vote for the separation of church and state, or, would you give your support to measures and proceedings having a direct tendency to effect this object, and would you resist all attempts to support any religious sect?'[56] By modern standards, T.P. Thompson would be considered the most conscientious of MPs. He wrote twice-weekly reports of the goings on in the house of commons for two or three newspapers in Hull.[57] But by far the most common and significant type of communication that displayed the importance and strength of liberal politics was that between MPs and their agents and election committees. It was here, out of the light of public statements, that we see how much MPs were concerned about liberal issues, and whether they thought they were vital to electoral success. These generally took two forms: an individual agent's correspondence with an MP or candidate, and a 'liberal' or 'reform' election group or committee appealing to an MP or candidate to stand on liberal principles. In 1832, Thomas Spring-Rice received an appeal from John Barber, liberal election agent in Wolverhampton:

> Sir, the Reform Bill will give to this place a right of returning two members, and the majority of electors, are I think desirous of electing two gentlemen, whose talents are highly respectable, and whose political sentiments are free and liberal . . . Should you have any leaning toward this place, and will write me your views on the Slave Trade, Corn Laws, and Free Trade in general, I should be obliged . . . I am of opinion that any individual who is not an advocate of liberal measures, who would not strive to remove monopolys [*sic*] of every description, would have but little chance of being returned for this place, – the slave trade, the East India trade, and the corn laws will be used as tests.[58]

---

[55] Norfolk RO, Wilshere Papers, Y/L15/21: petition from the Non-Electors of the Borough of Great Yarmouth to William Wilshere, dated 'February 1844'.

[56] Univ. of Hull, Brynmor Jones Library, Thompson Papers, DTH/3/29: James Hanson to Thomas Perronet Thompson, 6 May 1847.

[57] Univ. of Hull, Brynmor Jones Library, Thompson Papers, DTH: press cuttings for 1848–9; see also L.G. Johnson, *General T. Perronet Thompson 1783–1869: His Military, Literary and Political Campaigns* (1957), 201.

[58] National Library of Ireland, Monteagle Papers, 13,372, folder 1, items 1 and 4: John Barber to Thomas Spring-Rice, 2 June 1832.

Agents often asked MPs to approach other MPs to press for action on certain bills and measures. John Barham, Whig MP for Kendal, often received such requests from his agent, Edward Wakefield. On 15 March 1834, for example, Wakefield sent him a letter with very detailed local objections to William Brougham's Registry of Titles Deed Bill and asked him to ask Brougham to obviate their objections.[59] William Tancred in Banbury used to ask his agent for constituency advice on certain issues, particularly those on which he had no opinion. On 23 July 1844, he asked for guidance on the broad gauge/narrow gauge railway dispute. He was indifferent, but used the issue to please his constituents.[60]

Finally, election committees very commonly asked candidates and MPs to stand for election based on important aspects of liberal politics. A few examples of this include the following. The Banbury Reform Committee wrote to Tancred on 18 June 1832, asking him to represent the borough, but insisting that he support the repeal of the Septennial Act, the Malt Tax and other taxes on business, the abolition of all unwarranted sinecures and pensions, economy in public spending, and the abolition of slavery.[61] John Barham was asked for similar assurances on parliamentary reform and the abolition of slavery before the Kendal and Westmorland Freeholders selected him as their candidate.[62] The secretary of the Marylebone Reform Electoral Sub-committee wrote to Henry Bulwer, reporting that a resolution at a meeting of 150 vestrymen of Marylebone had requested that he stand for the seat in 1834 based on 'the following principles viz: shorter duration of Parliaments, vote by ballot, and a thorough reform of all abuses in church and state'.[63] And in December 1840, John Fielden replied in detail to Leeds Parliamentary Reform Association that he was a safe friend of an extensive reform agenda.

> I am an advocate for much more extensive measures of reform, viz. – the extension of the suffrage to all male persons of sound mind, not infants, and not incapacitated by crime[,] and Annual elections of members to serve in parliament as well as the taking of votes at elections by ballot. My objects in supporting these measures of reform are amongst other things to obtain a repeal of the New Poor Law – a law which is subversive of local government and in its operation harsh, cruel and unjust towards the poor – a repeal of the duties on malt hops & soap – a repeal of the Corn laws and a reduction of the hours of labour in factories to at most 10 hours a day.[64]

Agents, of course, wrote to potential candidates, asking if they would stand for a constituency, often using the language of liberal politics. In a letter dated 14 June 1841, Christopher Croft, a Richmond liberal agent, wrote to Marmaduke Wyvill, asking him to stand for Richmond. The other liberal candidate was going to be John Dundas, and Croft wrote:

[59] Bodl., Barham Papers: Edward Wakefield to John Barham, 15 Mar. 1834. William Brougham was MP for Southwark 1831–5.

[60] B.S. Trinder, *A Victorian MP and His Constituents* (Banbury, 1969), 15.

[61] Trinder, *Victorian MP*, xii–xiii.

[62] Bodl., Barham Papers: Kendal and Westmorland Freeholders to John Barham, 28 July 1832; see also Richard Wilson to John Barham, 28 July 1832.

[63] Norfolk RO, Bulwer Papers, BUL 1/6/17: 18 Dec. 1834.

[64] Univ. of Manchester, John Rylands Library, Fielden Papers, FDN/1/2/1/items 54 and 62: John Fielden to the Leeds Parliamentary Reform Association, 19 Dec. 1840; see also FDN/1/2/1/item 24, Fielden to the Committee of Inhabitants of Finsbury, 12 Dec. 1837.

and it now remains for the liberal party to select a gentleman of known liberal and free trade principles as his colleague in the ensuing Parliament.

. . . By such a union of the liberal party in your favour as we anticipate I do not think that there would be any opposition to your election, and if you wish for any further information before giving an answer to this proposition respecting the requisition I have no doubt that a deputation would readily wait upon you.[65]

In this section we have seen that the new liberal politics operated in both public and private ways in the constituencies. More importantly, however, public and private were strongly linked. Liberal Party MPs were rarely inconsistent in their public and private expressions. Further, constituents were clearly consistent in pressing candidates to adhere to their ideas of liberal politics. And from what we will see in the next section, the ways in which MPs wished their liberal politics to be presented to the political public were much the same.

Public Presentation: Liberal Politics in the House of Commons

Part 2 of this book examines aspects of liberal politics by analysing them as parliamentary issues, debates and votes. This section of Chapter 2 will show how MPs presented their ideas on important issues in another way. In addition to presenting themselves and their political opinions to electors and fellow politicians, as discussed in the previous section, MPs had an opportunity to display their stances and ideologies to the political public in their entries in *Dod's Parliamentary Companion*. While there were many different things that made up an entry in *Dod* (including electoral, personal, professional and family information), what is of most interest here is the 'parliamentary political statement' – a concise summary of political beliefs and opinions on specific contemporary issues. If we look again at the 1838 entry of William Marshall, Radical MP for Carlisle, we may see the differences between the types of information conveyed. The 'parliamentary political statement' is highlighted in bold.

Marshall, William. (*Carlisle*)

Eld. s. of John Marshall, esq. of Headingley, in the co. of York, an extensive linen manufacturer at Leeds and Shrewsbury, and in 1826 member for Yorksh.; br. of John Marshall, jun. esq., late member for Leeds. B. 1796; m. 1828, Georgiana Christiana, 7th d. of George Hibbert, esq. of Munden, Hertfordshire. A Radical Reformer; **is in favour of triennial Parliaments, the ballot, 'an extension and equitable division of the suffrage,' the removal of all restrictions which fetter trade, and the reform of the Church Establishment.** Sat for Leominster and for

---

[65] North Yorkshire County RO, Wyvill Papers, ZFW, microfilm 1699, frames 005237–8: Christopher Croft to Marmaduke Wyvill, 12 June 1841. Wyvill responded that he did not want to stand for election (frames 005240–1).

Petersfield before the Reform Act. For 4; agt. 1, 2, 6, 7. – 41, *Upper Grosvenor-st.: Reform Club; Patterdale Hall, Westmoreland.*[66]

These parliamentary political statements provide an excellent opportunity to examine political attitudes that may not have been reflected in other sources, such as correspondence, house of commons division lists and other standard political material. Further, parliamentary political statements in *Dod's Parliamentary Companion* are important for analysing opinion among backbenchers, because so few actually left manuscript collections to consult. Some entries displayed opinions for future parliamentary action ('is pledged to vote for the ballot'), some displayed parliamentary action in the present ('generally supports Ministers') and others reported on past parliamentary behaviour ('voted for the Reform Act'). In addition to listing opinions on the major issues of the day, these statements displayed when MPs championed unpopular issues, justified parliamentary votes or even when they had axes to grind. Most entries were short, along the lines of Marshall's above, with fewer than five issues listed generally. A few were quite long (O'Connell's runs to nearly a full page for the years 1833–40). These statements, therefore, provide an excellent opportunity to examine liberal politics as it operated in the house of commons, and as MPs wished it to be presented to the political public. Tables 2.1 to 2.12 below show the number of issues listed by Liberal Party MPs in their parliamentary political statements for each year. Many MPs had no such statement, and those are listed under 'None'. For the rest, the numbers indicate *each* time a statement occurs, and so one MP's statements might be enumerated across the categories. They are divided into the general headings 'Parliamentary and Elective', 'Church', 'Corn Laws and Trade', 'Taxes and Expenditure', 'Ireland', 'Social Legislation', 'Voting History', 'Misc.' and 'Slavery' (which applied mainly to the 1833 volume). The statements which do not have 'Support', 'Opposed', 'In Favour of' and other modifying phrases indicate support for the issue. 'Cheap Government', under Taxes and Expenditure in Table 2.4, therefore, means that the MP who used that statement was in favour of cheap government. As far as space would allow, the exact wording of statements has been given. *Dod* entries tended to change very little in the years between elections, and so I have chosen the following years as examples. 1833 was the first year of the Reformed Parliament, 1837 represents the midpoint in the 1833–41 governments, 1841 represents the end of those Whig governments, 1847 marks the end of Peel's reign, the 1847 New Parliament volume shows the beginning of a new Whig government as well as the volume that represented the large increase in the use of the party label 'Liberal' (see Chapter 1), and 1852 was the final year of that government and the close of the chronological scope of this book.

The dominant category in Liberal Party *Dod* parliamentary political statements was made up of issues related to parliament and elections, but some of the summaries require

[66] *Dod's Parliamentary Companion*, 140. 'For 4' refers to his vote in favour of 'Russell's motion on Irish Church Temporalities (2nd April) [1835]'; 'agt. 1, 2, 6, 7, refers to his votes against '1. Election of Speaker (1835).–2. Address in reply to the Speech from the Throne, on the 24th of Feb. 1835.–6. Motion of Sir Wm. Follett to protect from the operation of the Corporation Bill those freemen whose rights had been secured under the Reform Act.–7. Sir Robert Peel's motion to divide into two Bills the measure of Ministers relating to the Irish Church [both 1835]'. These are some of the important divisions that Dod used as indicators of political opinion. See also R. Byrne, *The Parliamentary Vote-Book: Containing Such Divisions of the House of Commons in the Session of 1846* (1847).

clarification. Of these, the ballot dominated. In Table 2.1, 'Ballot – Strong Support' reflects the number of instances of statements committing Liberal Party MPs to the ballot, such as 'pledged to vote for the ballot', or 'an advocate of the ballot'. 'Ballot – Mild Support' refers to statements that indicated reluctant support for the ballot, usually if other attempts to protect voters had failed, such as 'will support the ballot if necessary to protect the voter'. 'Shorter Parliaments' includes statements calling directly for 'shorter parliaments', 'the repeal of the Septennial Act' and in favour of 'triennial parliaments'. 'Franchise Extension' covers statements related to the franchise that do not fall into the more strictly defined categories of 'Universal Suffrage' and 'Household Suffrage'. 'Constituent Recall' is one of the most interesting statements, made generally by Radicals. It refers to statements such as 'is pledged to resign his seat whenever a majority of his constituents disapprove of his parliamentary conduct'. Among the more interesting of parliamentary and elective statements is the sole listing of 'Parliamentary Reform' in 1852 by George Scobell, Liberal MP for Bath 1851–7. While other Liberal Party MPs had been willing to specify their desired reforms, Scobell summarized institutional reform in this way.

Church and religious issues were also expressed in *Dod*. Although few of them require explanation, there are some important trends in political thinking reflected in these categories. Worries over endowment of the catholic church, and general concessions to catholics, do not appear until the 1847 New Parliament volume, soon after the Tractarian crisis and the Maynooth controversy of 1845 (see Chapter 7). Other issues seem to dwindle in importance by 1852, such as calls for general reform of the church of England, the abolition of church rates and the abolition of tithes.

Corn laws and trade statements are also largely self-explanatory. Like church and religious issues, they display some interesting changes in political presentation. Members of the Anti-Corn Law League were keen to list their membership even after the corn laws had been repealed in 1846, but the decline in the Free Trade Club can also be seen in its disappearance in the 1847 New Parliament and 1852 volumes.

Taxes and expenditure statements show the detail of their political opinions that Liberal Party MPs wished to be displayed. While the range of opposition to specific taxes is quite broad, we can see that several, such as the 'Taxes on Knowledge', attracted much opposition. Further, many Liberal Party MPs favoured a property tax in lieu of the assessed taxes.

Irish issues were also common in *Dod*, and not only the preserve of Repealer MPs. 'Repeal of the Union – Strong Support' indicates those MPs pledged to vote for repeal. 'Mild Support' reflects statements such as 'will support the Repeal of the Union, if justice not be done to Ireland'. Again, *Dod* statements reflect current political issues, as shown in the appearance of land and tenant issues in the late 1840s and early 1850s, as well as two statements concerning the famine after 1847.

Social issues appeared infrequently in *Dod*, with education being the most often cited. The number of statements increased between 1833 and 1852, but this was only partly explained by the attention that the 1846 government's education plans attracted. Other issues such as opposition to the poor laws and the beginnings of interest in civic life (and shown in the 'Health of Towns' and 'Public Walks in Cities' statements) appeared late in the period. Still, the relatively small number of social statements compared with the other categories is striking.

Table 2.1: Parliamentary and Elective Statements in Dod

Statement	1833	1837	1841	1847	1847NP	1852
Parliamentary Reform						1
General Reform	4	3	4	4	2	2
Ballot – Strong Support	106	119	70	59	59	64
Ballot – Mild Support	12	4	4	4	3	3
Ballot – Opposed	5	19	6	5	6	3
Shorter Parliaments – Strong Support	13	101	49	36	38	36
Shorter Parliaments – Mild Support	1	1	0	0	0	0
Shorter Parliaments – Opposed	2	16	5	4	2	2
Franchise Extension – Support	5	10	14	11	12	20
Franchise Extension – Opposed		1	2	2	3	1
Universal Suffrage – Support	1	0	0	1	4	3
Household Suffrage – Support	3	0	0	1	4	4
Ministerial Support	26	0	0	0	0	0
Not Generally a Supporter of Ministers	1	0	0	0	0	0
Votes Generally, but not always, with the Whigs	1	0	0	0	0	0
Strong Supporter of Whig Government		1	1	0	0	0
Generally Supported Lords Melbourne and Grey		1	0	0	0	0
Cordial to/Friendly to/Inclined to Support Lord Melbourne's Administration		2	4	2	0	0
Supporter of Lord John Russell					8	9
Generally Supported Recent Measures of Peel					2	0
No Confidence in/Uncompromising Opposition to a Peel/Tory Administration		1	3	2	1	1
Consistently Supported Mr Hume in Divisions	1	0	0	0	0	0
Bishops Removed from the House of Lords – Support	6	14	7	6	5	5
Bishops Removed from the House of Lords – Opposed	1	0	0	0	0	0
Peers Voting by Proxy – Opposed	1	0	0	0	0	0
Objects to the House Sitting After Midnight		1	0	0	0	0
Payment of MPs				1	1	1
Property Qualification of MPs – Abolition of				1	1	0
Constituent Recall	9	11	7	4	2	1
Will Resign if Sent Abroad	1	0	0	0	0	0
Preserve the Constitution of 1688	1	0	0	0	0	0
Nomination Boroughs – Opposed		1	0	0	0	0
Member of the Reform Association		1	0	0	0	0
Birmingham Political Union – Member of			1	1	1	1
People's Charter – Supporter of					2	2
Civil and Religious Liberty – Advancement of		1	1	1	2	6
Founder of East Somerset Registration Society					1	1
Parliamentary and Elective statements – total number of appearances	200	308	178	145	159	166

Voting history reflects statements made by Liberal Party MPs about their past votes in divisions in the house of commons (except those regarding the corn laws, which appear in corn laws and trade). This category shows how important it was for Liberal Party MPs to display their past voting behaviour as well as their pledges for future parliamentary action. It details, among other things, the strong hold that the Reform Act had on political consciousness throughout this period. As with their statements in political

Table 2.2: *Church and Religion Statements in Dod*

Statement	1833	1837	1841	1847	1847NP	1852
General Reform of Establishment	19	17	9	9	7	6
Church Establishment – Support	1	1	1	0	2	3
Church Establishment – Support with Reform				1	1	0
Church Establishment – Opposed					1	2
Church Rate Abolition	11	7	5	5	2	4
Church Rate Reform – Supported	6	6	3	3	2	3
Church Rate Reform – Opposed		1	0	0	0	0
Dissenters Rights – Support		6	1	1	4	3
Dissenters Rights – Opposed		0	0	0	0	0
Dissenters Admitted to Universities – Support		1	3	3	3	3
Dissenters Admitted to Universities – Opposed		1	0	0	0	0
Catholic Disabilities, Removal of						1
Grants to Roman Catholics – Opposed					1	1
Concessions for Catholic Education – In Favour					1	1
Ecclesiastical Titles Bill – Opposed						1
Removal of Jewish Disabilities		1	0	0	0	0
Religious Restrictions – Opposed	1	0	0	0	0	0
Tithe Abolition	24	18	9	9	4	2
Tithe Commutation	4	3	1	1	1	1
Tithes in Hands of Clergy in Control of Legislature	1	1	1	1	1	1
Tithes in Hands of Laymen are Private Property	1	1	1	1	1	1
Endowment of Roman Catholic Clergy – Support					1	1
Endowment of Roman Catholic Clergy – Opposed					29	33
Further Religious Endowments – Opposed					7	12
All Religious Endowments – Opposed					20	14
Endowment of All Religious Bodies or None					1	1
Voluntary Principle – In Favour of				1	1	1
Appropriate Church Lands for Original Purposes	2	1	1	1	1	1
Appropriate Property Lands for National Utility	1	5	3	2	2	1
More Equal Distribution of Church Property	1	1	1	1	0	0
Building of Churches at National Expense – Opposed			1	1	0	0
Bishops Having Large Revenues – Opposed	1	1	1	1	1	1
Bishops' Incomes Equalised	2	1	0	0	0	0
Creation of New Bishops – Opposed					1	0
Prevent Clergy from Secular Pursuits	2	1	0	0	0	0
Clergy Elected by Parishioners	1	3	2	1	1	1
Clergy, Reduce Numbers of		0	0	0	0	0
Clergy Removed from Magistracy	1	1	0	0	0	0
Clergy Salaries, More Equitable Distribution of	1	0	0	0	1	1
Pluralities Abolished	1	3	1	1	1	1
Lay Patronage Opposed	1	1	0	0	0	0
Voluntary Church Assoc. in Scotland – Opposed	1	0	0	0	0	0
Church of Scotland, Abrogation of Patronage in	1	0	0	0	0	0
Clergy Elected by Parishioners in Scotland	1	0	0	0	0	0
Private Patronage Abolished	1	1	1	0	0	0
Religious Liberty in its Full Extent				1	1	1
Member of Religious Party in the House of Commons	1	0	0	0	0	0
Moved Sabbath Observance Committee	1	1	0	0	0	0
Church – total number of appearances	88	84	45	44	99	102

Table 2.3: *Corn Laws and Trade Statements in Dod*

Statement	1833	1837	1841	1847	1847NP	1852
Corn Laws – Repeal	20	22	10	0	0	0
Corn Laws – Revision	19	12	5	1	0	0
Corn Laws – Fixed Duty	21	11	8	3	2	2
Corn Laws – Retention	11	10	6	0	1	0
Corn Laws – 1846 Vote – Repeal				12	5	8
Corn Laws – 1846 Vote – Formerly Opposed, but in 1846 Voted for Repeal				41	26	23
Corn Laws – 1846 Vote – For Protection				18	9	5
Inquiry into Corn Laws		1	1	0	0	0
Member of the Anti-Corn Law League			2	2	4	3
Navigation Laws Repeal – Support					5	3
Navigation Laws Repeal – Opposed					2	1
Return to Protection – 1850 Vote – Support						5
Return to Protection – 1850 Vote – Opposed						1
Free Trade – Support	28	27	23	26	32	44
Free Trade – Opposed	2	1	0	0	0	0
Free Trade Club, Member	24	13	0	19	0	0
Protection, Agricultural – Support	4	6	2	0	0	2
Protection of Manufactures and Industry – Support	1	1	0	1	1	1
Protection of the Silk Trade	2	1	1	1	1	1
Revision of Excise Laws	1	0	0	0	0	0
Opposed to Protective Duties			1	0	0	0
Anti-Excise Association, Member of					1	1
Direct Taxation in Preference to Excise Duties					1	3
Excise Duties Greatly Modified					1	2
Excise Duties Abolished						2
Timber Duties Reduced			1	1	0	0
Sugar Duties Reduced			1		1	1
Tea Duties Reduced					1	2
Coffee Duties Reduced					1	1
Bank Charter Act Revised						1
Bank of England to Protect Against Note Forgery		1	0	0	0	0
Establishment of Small Bank Notes		1	1	1	1	1
Scotch Banking System – Supporter of						1
Currency Reform					1	1
Currency Based on Gold or Silver	1	1	1	1	1	0
Extension of the Currency	2	1	0	1	0	0
Currency Laws, Repeal of – In Favour				1	0	1
Paper Currency – Opposed to Unrestricted	1	1	1	2	1	1
Currency, Sweeping Changes in – Opposed	1	1	0	0	0	0
Monetary System Revised	2	0	0	0	0	0
Present Monetary System – Opposed	1	2	0	0	0	0
Monopolies Opposed			8	6	2	2
Freedom of Commerce – Support	1	0	0	1	1	0
East India Charter Modified	1	0	0	0	0	0
East India Monopoly Opposed	5	1	1	1	1	1
China Trade Opened	6	0	0	1	0	1
India Trade Opened	2	0	0	0	0	0
Support for Colonial Interest	1	0	0	0	0	0
Perfect Freedom of Labour and Capital	1	0	0	0	0	0
Increase Energy to Trade and Commerce						1
Financial Reform						1
Corn Laws and Trade – total number of appearances	158	114	73	140	102	123

Table 2.4: *Tax and Expenditure Statements in Dod*

Statement	1833	1837	1841	1847	1847NP	1852
Taxes on Advertisements – Opposed	1	0	0	0	0	0
Taxes on Agriculture – Opposed		1	0	0	0	0
Taxes on Bread – Opposed		1	0	0	0	0
Taxes on Industry – Opposed	4	5	0	1	1	1
Taxes on Insurance – Opposed		1	1	1	2	1
Taxes on Knowledge – Opposed	19	15	4	5	3	3
Taxes on Malt – Opposed	6	8	3	2	9	8
Taxes on Necessaries of and Comforts of Life – Opposed	1	2	0	0	0	0
Taxes on Newspapers – Opposed	1	1	0	0	0	0
Taxes on Poor – Opposed					1	1
Taxes on Shops – Opposed	1	0	0	0	0	0
Taxes on Soap – Opposed	1	1	1	1	1	1
Taxes on Tea – Opposed					1	0
Taxes on Tobacco – Opposed	1	0	0	0	0	1
Assessed Taxes – Opposed	12	11	5	4	4	2
House and Window Taxes – Opposed	10	6	4	4	6	1
Income Tax – Opposed					1	2
Property Tax – Support	12	14	8	5	6	5
Property Tax – Opposed	1	0	0	5	0	0
Large Reduction in Taxes – Support	1	1	0	0	0	0
Sweeping Changes in Taxation – Opposed	1	1	0	0	0	0
Removal of Inequalities in Taxation	1	3	1	1	1	3
Cheap Government	1	1	0	0	0	0
Retrenchment	3	3	0	0	0	4
Unnecessary Expenditure – Opposed	1	1	0	1	0	1
Rigid Economy – Supported		1	1	1	1	1
Pension and Sinecure Reform and Abolition – Support	3	10	6	6	6	5
Pension and Sinecure Reform and Abolition – Opposed		1	0	0	0	0
Reduction in Interest on the National Debt	1	1	0	0	0	0
Equitable Adjustment of the National Debt		1	0	0	0	0
Abolition of Naval and Military Sinecures		1	1	2	0	0
Land Should be Liable to Probate and Legacy Duties				1	0	0
Financial System – Revision of						1
Taxes and Expenditure – total number of appearances	82	91	35	40	43	41

Table 2.5: *Irish Statements in Dod*

Statement	1833	1837	1841	1847	1847NP	1852
Repeal of the Union – Strong Support	8	5	4	7	11	13
Repeal of the Union – Mild Support	8	7	1	0	2	1
Repeal of the Union – Opposed	3	2	1	1	4	5
Poor Laws for – Support	1	6	3	2	1	0
Poor Laws for – Opposed	3	0	0	0	0	0
Modified Poor Rate for		1	0	1	0	0
Catholic Establishment for – Support	1	0	0	0	0	0
Catholic Clergy Maintained by Taxes on Irish Land					1	1
Catholic Association, was One of the Founders of		1	1	1	0	1
Church of Ireland Reform – Support	2	0	0	0	1	1
Church Cess Abolition – Support	1	0	0	0	0	0
Appropriation of Church Revenues for Education of Irish Poor		1	0	0	0	0
Tithe Abolition in Ireland	1	1	0	1	1	1
Bishops Reduced in Number and Income	1	0	0	0	0	0
Absentee Landlords, Tax on – Support				1	1	1
Tenant League – Opposed						1
Tenant Right – Support the Idea of				1	6	9
Long Leases, in Favour of					1	1
Removal of Irish Grievances	1	1	1	1	0	0
Ireland Being put on Equal Footing with England	1	0	1	1	0	0
Fair and Impartial Government for	1	0	0	0	0	0
Holding the Imperial Parliament in Dublin Every Third Year	1	1	0	0	0	0
Impeachment of Several Persons Connected with the Government of Ireland		1	0	0	0	0
Supporter of Government Measures in Ireland			1	1	1	1
Liberal Policy Towards				1	1	0
National Education for Ireland						1
Opposed to Stanley's Plans for Education in Ireland		1	0	0	0	0
Repayment of Loan to Ireland Made During the Famine – Opposed to					1	1
Advocate of Reproductive Employment During the Famine					1	1
Jury Bill for	5	0	0	0	0	0
Corporation Reform		1	0	0	0	0
Support Irish Manufactures		1	0	0	0	0
Free Trade Support as Long as it Does Not Interfere with Ireland's Prosperity					1	1
Privileges of the Bank of Ireland – Opposed				1	1	1
Old Ireland Party, Member of					2	2
Ireland – total number of appearances	38	28	15	20	37	43

Table 2.6: *Social Statements in Dod*

Statement	1833	1837	1841	1847	1847NP	1852
Factories Bill – Support	1	0	0	0	0	0
Poor Laws – Support	1	1	0	0	0	2
Poor Laws – Oppose					5	2
Poor Laws Revision	2	1	0	3	2	2
Poor Rates Removed	1	0	0	0	0	0
Establishment of Legal Provision for the Destitute Poor	1	0	0	0	0	0
Make Safe Provision for the Poor	1	0	0	0	0	0
National Education – Support			1	2	3	5
Russell's Education Plan – Support					3	3
Education to All Classes and Creeds			1	1	1	1
National System of Unsectarian Education						1
Diffusion of Education Unconnected with Religious Opinions						1
Increased Comforts for the Humbler Classes					1	1
Health of Towns – In Favour					1	1
Public Walks in Cities – In Favour					1	1
Social Issues – total number of appearances	7	2	2	6	17	20

posters and addresses, MPs who had voted for the Reform Act in 1832 were careful to remind the political public of this. This declined, naturally, as MPs from the 1830 parliament left or died. Further, two of the important reforms of the 1820s, Catholic Emancipation and Repeal of the Test and Corporation Acts, appeared as late as the 1847 parliament. Support for Queen Caroline during her trial in 1820 was important enough for Pryse Pryse, Reformer MP for Cardigan Boroughs 1818–41 and 1842–9, to include throughout his parliamentary career.

Miscellaneous issues that do not fit easily in other categories are listed in Table 2.8. Except for the game laws, flogging in the army in the 1833 volume and the 'No Pledges' statements, these generally displayed the individual interests of an MP. This is perhaps where Liberal Party MPs displayed their 'single issue' politics.

Slavery issues, naturally, played a major role in the 1833 volume of *Dod*, slightly less in the 1837 volume, and disappear thereafter. 'Immediate Abolition' refers to Liberal Party MPs calling for just that, the immediate abolition of slavery without making special provision to slave owners. 'Gradual Abolition' refers to statements that support the abolition of slavery, but with the added modification that some sort of compensation or consideration (often termed 'justice') be taken into account. 'Immediate Abolition Opposed' refers to the appearance of that literal statement, without the modifiers mentioned under 'Gradual Abolition'.

Although the individual statement tables show the distribution of major issues within each year, it is perhaps easier to see how ideas of presentation changed between 1833 and 1852 if we look at the table of the total number of appearances of each category for the selected years. Table 2.10 reveals the clear dominance of parliamentary and elective

Table 2.7: *Voting History Statements in Dod*

Statement	1833	1837	1841	1847	1847NP	1852
Queen Caroline – Voted in Favour of	1	1	1	1	1	0
Repeal of Test and Corporation Acts – Voted For		2	1	1	0	0
Catholic Emancipation – Voted For	1	5	3	2	2	0
Catholic Emancipation – Voted Against	1	1	0	0	0	0
First Reform Bill – Voted Against		1	0	0	0	0
Reform Act – Voted For	19	14	7	4	2	2
Supported Principle of the Reform Bill		1	0	0	0	0
Formerly Thought Reform Bill too Extensive, but Subsequently Changed his Opinion			1	0	1	1
Absent from Reform Bill Divisions	1	0	0	0	0	0
Transfer of Franchise from East Retford to Birmingham – Voted For		1	0	1	1	1
Moved the Address of Confidence in Lord Grey's Government in 1831		1	0	0	0	0
Lord Ebrington's Motion – Voted For	5	3	2	2	1	1
Voted for the Principle, but Differed on Details of Reform Act	2	1	1	0	0	0
£50 Tenant-at-Will Clause – Voted For	1	1	0	0	0	0
Appropriation Clause of Stanley's Irish Church Bill – Voted For					0	0
Appropriation Clause of Stanley's Irish Church Bill – Voted Against			1	0	0	0
Slavery Abolition – Voted For		1	2	1	0	0
Leading Advocate for the Abolition of Slavery		1	0	0	0	0
New Poor Law – Voted For			1	1	1	1
Clause 147 of New Poor Law Act – Voted Against		1	1	1	1	0
Dissenters Admitted to the Universities – Voted For					0	0
Dissenters Admitted to Universities – Voted Against			1	0	0	0
Repeal of Jewish Disabilities – Voted For		1	1	0	0	0
Repeal of the Malt Tax in 1835 – Voted For					2	3
Repeal of the Malt Tax in 1835 – Voted Against					2	1
Bank Restriction Act of 1844 – Opposed						1
Brought in Motion to Prohibit Importation of French Goods		1	0	0	0	0
Impeachment of Lord Melville – Voted For					1	0
Bathurst Pension – Voted Against		1	0	0	0	0
Supported Liberal Measures		1	0	0	0	0
Voting History – total number of appearances	31	39	23	14	15	11

Table 2.8: *Miscellaneous Statements in Dod*

Statement	1833	1837	1841	1847	1847NP	1852
A Whig of the Old School of Charles James Fox, and a Friend of Civil and Religious Liberty			1	0	0	0
Abolition of Death Penalty Except for Murder	2	2	0	0	0	0
Abolition of Useless Places		1	1	0	1	1
An Uncompromising Friend of the People			1	0	1	0
Capital Punishment – Opposed					1	0
Centralisation – Opposed				1	1	2
Chancellor Nominating JPs – Opposed	2	0	0	0	0	0
China War – Supported				1	1	1
Disclaims Finality of Reform Act						1
Emigration to Relieve Property Pressure – Support	1	0	0	0	0	0
Enlarged Scheme of Colonization		1	1	1	1	1
Extreme Measures – Opposed						1
Finality in Legislation – Opposed					1	0
Flogging in Army – Opposed	5	0	0	0	0	0
Friend and Supporter of the Late Charles James Fox	1	0	0	0	0	0
Game Laws – Opposed					6	4
Game Laws – Support					2	3
General Registry Bill – Opposed	1	0	0	0	0	0
Grand Jury System Reform – Support	4	2	1	1	1	0
Impressment of Seamen – Opposed	2	0	0	0	0	0
Jury System Reform – Support	4	3	1	1	0	0
Justice Prompt and Cheap	1	0	0	0	0	0
Liberal in Every Sense of the Word						1
Liberal in the fullest sense of the term					1	1
Liberty of Action, Conscience, and Speech – In Favour of		1	0	0	0	0
Local Courts – In Favour of		1	1	1	0	0
Magistrates Elected – Support	1	2	0	0	0	0
Mitigation of the Criminal Code	2	2	2	2	0	0
No Pledges	1	2	9	6	0	0
No Pledges Except not to Talk Unnecessarily						1
Preservation of Yorkshire Registry – Support	1	1	1	1	0	0
Published an Enquiry into Prison Discipline		1	0	0	0	0
Rate-Paying Clauses of the Reform Act – Opposed					1	0
Reformatory Treatment of Juvenile Offenders					1	0
Remove all Abuses without Injury to the Just Rights of Any			1	0	0	0
Repeal of the Union with Scotland – In Favour				1	0	1
Standing Army – Opposed	1	0	0	0	0	0
Misc. – total number of appearances	30	19	20	16	19	18

Table 2.9: *Slavery Statements in Dod*

Statement	1833	1837	1841	1847	1847NP	1852
Immediate Abolition	107	2	0	0	0	0
Gradual Abolition	4	0	0	0	0	0
Immediate Abolition Opposed	10	0	0	0	0	0
Slavery – total number of appearances	121	2	0	0	0	0

Table 2.10: *Statements in Dod 1833–52*

Statement	1833	1837	1841	1847	1847NP	1852
None	118	142	134	88	98	90
Parliamentary and Elective	200	307	176	145	159	166
Church	88	84	45	44	99	102
Corn Laws and Trade	158	114	73	140	102	123
Taxes and Expenditure	82	91	35	40	43	41
Ireland	38	28	15	20	37	43
Social	8	2	2	6	15	18
Voting History	31	39	23	14	15	11
Misc.	30	19	21	16	21	20
Slavery	121	2	0	0	0	0

statements, followed by corn laws and trade, and then church and religion. This distribution may be seen more clearly in Figure 2.1.

Several preliminary conclusions may be drawn from these tables and the graph, leaving aside, for the moment, the 'None' category.[67] First, it is striking how much greater the appearances of 'Political' (that is, 'Parliamentary and Elective') and 'Trade' (that is, 'Corn Laws and Trade') issues are than church issues, even in the 1830s, when several important church questions were debated in parliament. Brent, Ellens, Parry and Hilton have stressed the centrality of religious and church issues in the 1830s, yet this *Dod* evidence complicates the picture of how MPs balanced their interests and political statements.[68] Equally intriguing is how much church issues rose in appearance in the late 1840s. This may be partly explained by the Maynooth controversy of the mid 1840s, but also, as we shall see when these figures are compared with those of the 1860s (below), religious questions gradually became more important in the minds of Liberal Party MPs. Second, it is quite clear that many Liberal Party MPs wished their attitudes toward political questions (especially the ballot and the possible further extension of the franchise) to be presented

[67] Conservative MPs will not be analysed or, unfortunately, used in comparison. The work required for such a comparison falls outside the scope and time limits of this book.

[68] See R. Brent, *Liberal Anglican Politics: Whiggery, Religion, and Reform, 1830–1841* (Oxford, 1987); J.P. Ellens, *Religious Routes to Gladstonian Liberalism: The Church Rate Conflict in England and Wales, 1832–1868* (University Park, PA, 1994); Parry, *Rise and Fall of Liberal Government*; B. Hilton, *The Age of Atonement: The Influence of Evangelicalism on Social and Economic Thought, 1785–1865* (Oxford, 1988).

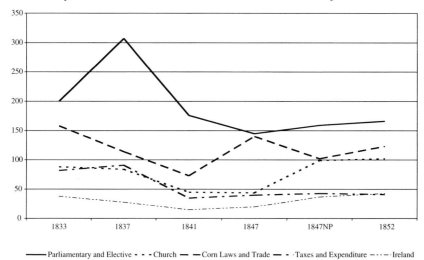

Figure 2.1: *Statements in Dod 1833–52*

above others. If we look at Figure 2.1, we see that these issues dominate *Dod* entries. Clearly, Liberal Party MPs considered these of first importance, and may have used their degree of support for political reform as a way of displaying their overall political ideology. Third, the other categories attracted relatively little comment, which is surprising, given that they contain such issues as the retention and maintenance of the Union, the implementation and modification of the New Poor Law, and Repeal of the Assessed Taxes.

If we now make a comparison with the 1860s, we see a number of other significant things that *Dod*'s political statements can tell us. Using a similar method (which varies slightly in categorisation), Professor Arnstein has shown that, by the mid and late 1860s, MPs on both sides of the House were concerned mainly with questions of religion and the Church, and that the difference in numbers of appearances between political issues and religious issues among Liberal Party MPs was much smaller than in the 1830s and 1840s.[69] His results from examining the 1865 and 1869 volumes of *Dod's Parliamentary Companion* are shown in Table 2.11.

Arnstein did not tabulate the number of MPs who had no parliamentary political statement, but he did note that 'approximately a quarter of the total number of MPs of either party failed, moreover, to name any specific issue whatsoever'. Further, he chose different categories.[70] But, if we modify his tables to match more closely those presented here, we may make a reasonable comparison with the only other study to use *Dod* in this way. If we choose the 1837 *Dod* volume (which was arguably the one in which the editor had regularised his compilation) and the 1852 volume (the final one in the chronological scope of this work), and compare them with his years, 1865 (which, Arnstein argues, saw the last of the 'old' mid Victorian parliaments, before the Reform

[69] W. Arnstein, 'The Religious Issue in Mid-Victorian Politics: A Note on a Neglected Source', *Albion*, vi (1974), 134–43.

[70] Arnstein, 'Religious Issue in Mid-Victorian Politics', 136–7.

Table 2.11: *Statements in Dod 1865 and 1869*

Issue	1865 Liberals	1865 Cons	1869 Liberals	1869 Cons
Political	321	106	284	39
Religious	221	106	280	177
Foreign & Military Policy	52	68	24	19
Economic	42	43	36	38
Education	33	24	79	43
Other Social Issues	30	9	65	21
Colonial	3	0	4	0

Source: Arnstein, 'Religious Issue in Mid-Victorian Politics', 138.

Table 2.12: *Statements in Dod, Comparison 1835–69*

Issue	1837 Liberals	1852 Liberals	1865 Liberals	1869 Liberals
Political	307	166	321	284
Church/Religious	84	102	221	280
Trade/Economic	198	164	42	36
Social/Education	2	18	63	144
Other	47	61	55	28

Act of 1867, and with Palmerston still prime minister) and 1869 (the volume that includes Gladstone's Liberal Party victory and first term in office), we see important differences. Table 2.12 demonstrates this clearly.

Not only do church and religious issues become more prominent in the later 1860s volumes (the dramatic increase is shown in Figure 2.2), but by 1869 social and educational issues also increase in appearance.

We see, therefore, that the liberal politics that MPs chose to present through *Dod's Parliamentary Companion* were largely progressive in terms of church and religious issues. Political issues (mainly the ballot and further parliamentary reform) dominated the 1830s and 1840s, but began to share this dominance with religion later in the century. Miles Taylor is quite correct, therefore, when he states that 'by looking at backbench opinion, as well as the machinations of party leadership . . . it becomes clear that many of the principles by which the party was best known in the 1860s were subscribed to by many MPs by the end of the 1840s'.[71]

While he intends this statement to refer to his 'Reform party', it is clear that it applies to the Liberal Party as a whole, and that the two issues that towered over others – political reform and religious liberty – remained among the most important from the passage of the Reform Act to the first avowedly Liberal government in 1869.

It must not be assumed that the issues presented in *Dod's Parliamentary Companion* display a rigidly uniform liberal ideology, or even that they claim to show the full colours of political opinion among MPs. Local issues are almost completely left out, for

[71] M. Taylor, *The Decline of British Radicalism, 1847–1860* (Oxford, 1995), 345.

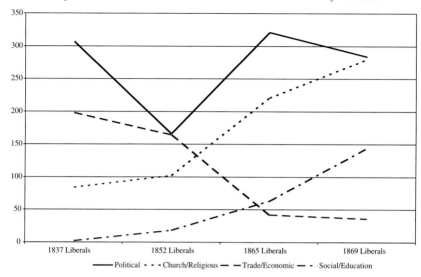

Figure 2.2: *Statements in Dod, Comparison 1837–69*

instance.[72] But they at least show the border points of liberal politics, and allow us some means of comparison. And one final bit of evidence for the recognized existence of a liberal politics is the fact that, beginning in the 1844 volume, *Dod* began to use '&c.' to save space when printing political statements. On its own, this may not seem like much evidence, but it actually reveals an assumption on the part of the editors that readers would have been able to infer the logical progression of political stances of MPs from this printer's device. This was used, for example, in the entries of four different types of Liberal Party MP in 1844. Wynn Ellis, Liberal MP for Leicester 1831–5 and 1839–47 was 'of liberal politics; in favour of [the] ballot and an extension of the suffrage; abolition of the Corn Laws, &c.' Robert Pulsford, Liberal MP for Hereford 1841–7 was 'in favour of the ballot, the repeal of the Corn Laws, &c.' Joshua Scholefield, Radical MP for Birmingham 1832–44, was 'in favour of free trade, the ballot, the repeal of the Corn Laws, &c.' John Vivian, Whig MP for Swansea 1832–55, was 'of Whig principles; in favour of shorter Parliaments, the repeal of the Corn Laws, &c.' Clearly, then, liberal politics was so well understood that *Dod* was able to use this device.

This section has shown that most Liberal Party MPs were very interested in presenting their political thinking in *Dod* summaries. Like their agenda-mongering in electioneering material, liberal politics, as displayed in *Dod*, was relatively strong, as well as consistent with what Parry has defined as his liberal value system. Political reform, steady reform of

---

[72] Rare exceptions included James Brocklehurst, Reformer MP for Macclesfield from 1832 to 1868, who listed 'is in favour of protection of the silk trade' in each of his *Dod* entries from 1832 to 1852, including this from the 1847 volume: 'voted against the corn laws, but is in favour of protection for the silk trade'. Silk trade representatives sometimes targeted certain MPs for help in exempting them from factory legislation. See the pamphlet, *Facts Relative to the Employment of Children in Silk Mills* (Manchester, 1833), in which mill owners argue that silk factories should be treated differently in regard to child labour because silk work did not involve heat, it was light work, the factories were clean and the children had plenty of time to play during the working day. A copy of this pamphlet is in the Norfolk RO, Bulwer Papers, BUL 1/10/31: Henry Lytton Earle.

the Church Establishment, and liberalisation in trade and expenditure remained the most important things during this period. Further, as we have seen in the comparison with the Liberal Party in the 1860s, once some important free trade concerns were largely satisfied, other liberal issues (notably social and education issues) rose in prominence.

Chapter 2 suggests that, between 1832 and 1852, a liberal politics was constructed around a core of important political and social issues, notably further parliamentary reform, church reform and free trade. While most of these, naturally, had antecedents before 1832, this chapter has analysed the new ways in which they were presented to the political public. Through agenda-making in public and private electioneering discourse, and in parliamentary guides, Liberal Party MPs displayed a new emphasis on presenting liberal politics through detailed statements in electioneering material, correspondence with constituents and other MPs, and public statements. Further, we have seen the high degree to which they cohered with private political sentiments. Chapter 3 will show the further importance of both the public and private aspects of liberal politics by examining the ways in which party control was made a part of political life in the 1832–52 period.

Chapter 3. Liberal Party Control

Chapter 2 showed how liberal politics was constructed and presented in the reform period. But, as Alan Sykes has asserted, 'a political mentality is not a political party'.[1] This chapter will show how far the Liberal Party connected liberal politics with party control, and how that control was presented. It will concentrate on the various aspects of party control, especially in and from Westminster, not so much as an attempt to argue whether there were strict and effective party structures for the liberals, but to show the importance of the idea that there were such things, or that, in an ideal liberal political world, there should be.

In a famous sentence that set a paradigm for perceptions of the growth of liberalism and the Liberal Party in Victorian Britain, John Vincent wrote: 'The massive development of party loyalties throughout the country preceded any corresponding full development of party organization by almost a generation'.[2]

The new research in this chapter will show that this is no longer valid. Both inside the house of commons and in the central party electioneering management groups, Liberal Party organisation in the reform years was remarkably extensive, especially given the very different nature of politics at the time. At no time between 1832 and 1852 did MPs owe their seats to party organisations or full party funding. At no time during this period were MPs threatened with losing party support if they refused to follow their leaders into the division lobbies.[3] Yet they were whipped, and more importantly, they expected that they would be whipped; they were given central party funds, and often asked for more; and their successes and failures on the hustings and at the polls were watched carefully by a central group in London. This chapter examines whipping and parliamentary control, party management in terms of electioneering and registration, and the social institutions that made up the central Liberal Party. It shows that, despite the fact that Liberal Party organisation was not as successful as it could have been, and however many difficulties the coalition of liberal groups experienced in working together, the existence of a perception of party organisation, and expectations of behaviour, made the Liberal Party conceptually strong.

Whipping and Parliamentary Control of MPs

Almost nothing is known about whipping and parliamentary control of MPs in the early and mid Victorian period. Most historians suspect that much of the work was done

---

[1] A. Sykes, *The Rise and Fall of British Liberalism 1776–1988* (1997), 21.

[2] J.R. Vincent, *The Formation of the British Liberal Party, 1857–1868* (1966), 82.

[3] For a good, general discussion of the differences between Victorian MPs and late 20th-century MPs, see T.A. Jenkins, *Parliament, Party and Politics in Victorian Britain* (Manchester, 1996), chs 2, 3.

verbally, and consequently, little written evidence survives.[4] Still, some sketchy records are available, and they give the impression that whipping and parliamentary control in this period operated relatively closely to the way they did in later decades. That is, a group of junior ministers, headed by a chief whip, sent out circulars to MPs requesting attendance at debates and divisions. They stressed the urgency of important divisions, acted as tellers on government divisions and arranged pairs for party MPs who had to be absent.[5] Opposition whips in the early Victorian period are even less understood, but it is clear that some sort of organisation on the opposition benches took place.[6] The Liberal Party chief whips between 1832 and 1852 were as follows:

1830–2	Edward Ellice (Whig MP for Coventry)
1832–5	Sir Charles Wood (Whig MP for Halifax)
1835–41	Edward John Stanley (Reformer MP for Cheshire North)
1841	Sir Denis Le Marchant
1841–50	Henry Tufnell (Whig MP for Devonport, 'Liberal' after 1844)
1850–2	W.G. Hayter (Liberal MP for Wells).[7]

Whips became increasingly important after 1832 because of the idea that the reformed parliament had an increased popular responsibility. Edward Ellice wrote to Grey on 5 November 1832 that:

the first point to be decided at every discussion relative to the measures of your Cabinet is not whether you can come to some compromise of opinion amongst

---

[4] The most comprehensive studies of whipping in the 19th-century house of commons are: J. Sainty and G.W. Cox, 'The Identification of Government Whips in the House of Commons 1830–1905', *Parliamentary History*, xvi (1997), 339–58, esp. 339–49; T.A. Jenkins, 'The Whips in the Early-Victorian House of Commons', *Parliamentary History*, xix (2000), 259–86. See also Jenkins, *Parliament, Party and Politics*, ch. 3; P.M. Gurowich, 'Party and Independence in the Early and Mid-Victorian House of Commons: Aspects of Political Theory and Practice 1832–68, Considered with Special Reference to the Period 1852–68', University of Cambridge PhD, 1986, pp. 89–96; Angus Macintyre, *The Liberator: Daniel O'Connell and the Irish Party 1830–1847* (1965), introduction and bibliography. William Whyte's *The Inner Life of the House of Commons* (2 vols, 1897) provides a good description of the nature of whipping from the 1850s to the 1870s. H.J. Hanham also provides a good summary of Liberal Party organisation and the duties of whips after the Second Reform Act in his *Elections and Party Management: Politics in the Time of Disraeli and Gladstone* (1959), 349–56. See A. Ramm, 'The Parliamentary Context of Cabinet Government', *EHR*, xcix (1984), 768–9, for the ways in which Gladstone's whips tried to deal with the problem of parliamentary congestion. See also A.F. Thompson, 'Gladstone's Whips and the General Election of 1868', *EHR*, lxiii (1948), 189–200.

[5] The chief whip was a senior secretary of the treasury, and the junior whips were junior lords of the treasury. See A. Aspinall, 'English Party Organization in the Early Nineteenth Century', *EHR*, xli (1926), 396–7; Jenkins, *Parliament, Party and Politics*, 60–1. They also seem to have handled patronage, but this too is a shadowy area.

[6] See Jenkins, 'Whips in the Early-Victorian House of Commons', *passim*, and his *Parliament, Party and Politics*, 61–4 for an explanation of Conservative whipping in and out of office. On whipping before 1832, see *The History of Parliament: The House of Commons, 1820–32*, ed. D. Fisher (7 vols, 2009), i, 291, 304, 314–15.

[7] This list was compiled from Sainty and Cox, 'Government Whips in the House of Commons', 350–1; Gurowich, 'Party and Independence', appendix i, 369, which corrects the mistakes in C. Cook and B. Keith, *British Historical Facts 1830–1900* (1975), 93. Sir Denis Le Marchant was not an MP until he sat for Worcester City from 1846 to 1847, but he organised the whipping until Tufnell could take over. See J.K. Buckley, *Joseph Parkes of Birmingham and the Part which He Played in Radical Reform Movements from 1825–1845* (1926), 179.

yourselves and act in concert upon it, but whether your decision when made and the proceedings to grow out of it will be satisfactory to a majority of the popular party in the House of Commons.[8]

This advice was not followed very closely, however, and Grey and Althorp (the leader of the Commons) failed to operate the whipping system effectively. Ian Newbould argues that this was because the Whigs did not 'operate from the same principle of party management' as the Conservatives did. Whipping for government divisions was often confused, and many times the ministry had to rely on Conservative support.[9] In 1830, Ellice had been appointed chief whip. In many ways, this was an excellent appointment, even if Grey and Althorp failed to exploit it fully. Ellice was popular among liberal MPs because he had an agreeable personality, and his business interests lent him credence with City MPs and many Radicals. Further, he was a Scot, which helped with Scottish MPs, and his advanced thinking on Irish church issues was welcome with Repealers.[10] In fact, Charles Wood, his successor, said that he was the only government member who could 'keep things together'.[11] Ellice apparently worked very hard at keeping things together, and was successful to a certain extent. The problem was that Althorp, even with his relative lack of interest in party management, sent out whipping circulars in addition to those which Ellice sent.[12] This confused many Liberal Party MPs, particularly since Althorp's whips were vague and did not convey the necessary sense of urgency on specific measures. Since they were coming from the leader of the house of commons, many liberals understandably thought that they superseded Ellice's whips. For example, Althorp's first whip of the 1833 session referred to 'matters of importance' but did not list what they were.

Sir,

Parliament will meet on the 29th instant & immediately proceed to the Election of the Speaker; the other business of the Session will not however commence till the beginning of the following week. I have taken the liberty to give you this information & at the same time beg leave to request your early attendance, as matters of importance must be brought under the consideration of the House at the Commencement of the Session.[13]

Trying to keep Liberal Party MPs in the Commons informed and whipped under these circumstances, which included the heightened mood in the country during the Reform

[8] E. Ellice to Lord Grey, 5 Nov. 1832, quoted in Richard Brent, *Liberal Anglican Politics: Whiggery, Religion, and Reform, 1830–1841* (Oxford, 1987), 72.

[9] I. Newbould, 'Whiggery and the Growth of Party 1830–1841: Organization and the Challenge of Reform', *Parliamentary History*, iv (1985), 137–44; I. Newbould, *Whiggery and Reform, 1830–1841: The Politics of Government* (1990), 10, 24–9.

[10] Newbould, *Whiggery and Reform*, 25.

[11] Grey Papers: Charles Wood to Lord Grey, 3 July 1832, quoted in Newbould, *Whiggery and Reform*, 25.

[12] Newbould, *Whiggery and Reform*, 25–7.

[13] Bodl. Dashwood Papers, MS DD Dashwood, G.2.1: whipping circular from Althorp, 8 Jan. 1833.

Bill years, eventually proved too much for Ellice, and he used his wife's death in July 1832 as an excuse to resign.[14]

Charles Wood, Grey's son-in-law, was then appointed chief whip. He tried to convince Althorp to increase the organisation of his office by appointing assistants but the leader of the House refused.[15] This led to a continuation of the problems that had existed under Ellice. Further, there was some confusion even among cabinet members as to who was in charge of whipping and the government's parliamentary timetable. Thomas Spring-Rice, Whig MP for Cambridge and a secretary to the treasury, helped in an unofficial capacity. For instance, Palmerston wrote to him in May 1833, asking when a certain motion from Hume was coming in and whether he thought Palmerston ought to be there to answer the motion and vote in the division.[16] Wood seems to have soldiered on until 1835, but without much guidance from Althorp or Melbourne.[17] After the 1835 election, E.J. Stanley was chosen to head the whips' office. Apparently this was done because Melbourne became convinced that there needed to be a stronger connection between the liberal electioneering managers Joseph Parkes and James Coppock and liberal parliamentary managers.[18] Parkes knew Stanley and liked him, and there seemed little reason to think that whipping would be as confused and informal as it had been between 1830 and 1835.[19] Under Stanley's tenure, whipping circulars were more specific and instructive, as shown in the following example to Charles D'Eyncourt, dated 10 July 1835:

> The Report of the Corporation Bill will be brought up on Tuesday, when we shall probably have some important divisions on the [illegible], and other clauses. But the most important division of the year will be on going into Committee on the Irish Tithe Bill when Peel has given notice of his intention to move an instruction to the Committee for the purpose of separating the Appropriation from the Commutation. For the vote we ought to have every Member present as the size of the majority will materially affect the future conduct of both the Tories & the Lords & the King.
>
> For that day therefore probably Monday the 20th or Tuesday the 21st we hope to count on your presence for certain; & if you could be here next week we shd be very glad of your company, but it is not such a matter of life and death.[20]

---

[14] N. Gash, *Politics in the Age of Peel: A Study in the Technique of Parliamentary Representation 1830–1850* (1953), 420; Newbould, *Whiggery and Reform*, 26.

[15] Newbould, *Whiggery and Reform*, 26–7.

[16] National Library of Ireland, Monteagle Papers, MS 13,375, folder 8, item 3: Lord Palmerston to Thomas Spring-Rice, 6 May 1833.

[17] The Wood Papers at the Borthwick Institute at the University of York are remarkably silent on whipping and parliamentary management, which is in keeping with the general lack of primary material on the subject. The collection is better on central electoral management, as will be shown below.

[18] Newbould, *Whiggery and Reform*, 27–8.

[19] Parkes (WEST): Parkes to Lord Durham, 3 Apr. 1835.

[20] Lincolnshire Archives Office, D'Eyncourt Papers, TDE/H1/117: E.J. Stanley to Charles Tennyson D'Eyncourt, 10 July 1835.

The reduced Liberal Party majority after 1837 made Stanley's job more difficult, as did the fact that some Whigs thought his connections with Parkes tinged him with Radical tones. During this period, Stanley was particularly careful with whipping and pairing. Again, he wrote to D'Eyncourt on 2 November 1837:

> It will not be safe to be absent on the 15th without a pair, but if you can get one I do not think there will be any occasion for you to be in Town before the 20th on which date however it is most important that every one who can to be present [*sic*] as I think it very probable they [the Conservatives] will try some amendment, & are quite keen to do it if they think us remiss in attendance.[21]

The concerns over the reduced majority, and the lengths to which Stanley had to go to preserve division majorities, may also be seen in the fact that, by 1839, the Conservative electoral manager, F.R. Bonham, did not trust Stanley to pair honestly. In a letter to Thomas Fremantle, the Conservative whip, on 8 February 1839, Bonham wrote:

> The Government are obviously very uneasy as to their position, and I strongly suspect that they are aware of their danger from the *absence* of many of their old supporters . . . I need not say that Stanley is not scrupulous and might use names for pairing *without express authority* tho' once done they might hesitate to annul his act.
>
> I should therefore *most strongly urge* you to decline *all* such negotiation with him *for the next ten days or a fortnight* . . . You will then have . . . ample time for any *legitimate* pairs, and *also* for some inquiry into those he may propose.[22]

By 1839, Stanley was using strong 'Liberal Party' language in whipping circulars, and presenting the party to MPs as if it were already a cohesive unit. A general whip from May 1839 shows this.

> My Dear Sir,
>
> As the Speaker has declared his intention of not resuming the chair after the Whitsun Holidays, I take the liberty of informing you that Mr Shaw Lefevre has announced himself as a candidate for the speakership; and as I trust that all the Liberal Party will unite in supporting that Gentleman's pretensions, I venture to press upon you the very great importance of being present on the 27th Instant, on which date it is probable that the Election will take place.
>
> As I trust that you will feel disposed to give your vote to Mr. Lefevre, I should feel much obliged if you would give me an answer as soon as possible to inform me whether I may rely on your presence and support on this occasion.
>
> Yours ever, EJ Stanley.[23]

---

[21] Lincolnshire Archives Office, D'Eyncourt Papers, TDE/H1/1228: E.J. Stanley to Charles Tennyson D'Eyncourt, 2 Nov. 1837. During this period, MPs often tried to arrange their own pairs first, before turning to the party whips.

[22] F.R. Bonham to Thomas Fremantle, 8 Feb. 1839, quoted in Jenkins, *Parliament, Party and Politics*, 64–5. See also Berkshire RO, Pusey Papers, D/EBp, C2: W. Baring to P. Pusey, 2 Feb. 1837.

[23] Lincolnshire Archives Office, D'Eyncourt Papers, TDE/H1/123: general whipping circular, [no date] May 1839.

Unfortunately, the world of liberal whipping becomes dark again for the 1840s. Henry Tufnell left no manuscript collection, and his letters to Russell in The National Archives do not provide much light. Terry Jenkins surmises that, unlike Conservative MPs, who subscribed to a party fund after 1835 to support opposition whipping, the Liberal Party had no such structure, and attendance at divisions became largely a matter of MPs paying their own individual attention to the parliamentary timetable.[24] And, as we shall see below, the Reform Club attempted to take up the slack and provide a communication system with the house of commons. Liberal Party cohesion in division lobbies during the 1840s, however, suggests that whipping must have remained reasonably effective, as Part 2 will show.

Central Election Management

While it would be an exaggeration to say that early and mid Victorian MPs owed their seats to party machinery and party funds, there was a considerable degree of central Liberal Party electioneering communication and funding. While this may not have been enough to convince Vincent and other historians that there was 'full' party development at Westminster, it was clearly evident, and is all the more significant because of the very individual ways in which candidates were selected in constituencies and the mainly personal ways they used to finance their own elections. But historians have not generally found the 1832–68 period worthy of serious electoral study. Until the appearance of Philip Salmon's crucial work on the mechanics of electoral reform, readers had to rely on Charles Seymour's 1915 study, as well as Norman Gash's more general political texts.[25] Other periods are better served. The late 18th century and early 19th century are discussed fully by Frank O'Gorman and John Phillips, and the work of H.J. Hanham for the period after the 1867 Reform Act has not been seriously challenged.[26]

This chapter will not attempt to carry out the sort of work Salmon, Seymour and Gash have done so well and extensively. Rather, it will show that most central Liberal Party structures (the Reform Association, the Cleveland Square group and the Reform Club) displayed a high level of communication between the centre and the constituen-

---

[24] Jenkins, *Parliament, Party and Politics*, ch. 3.

[25] P. Salmon, *Electoral Reform at Work: Local Politics and National Parties, 1832–1841* (Woodbridge, 2002); C. Seymour, *Electoral Reform in England and Wales: The Development and Operation of the Parliamentary Franchise 1832–1885* (New Haven, CT, 1915); N. Gash, *Reaction and Reconstruction in English Politics, 1832–1852* (Oxford, 1965); Gash, *Politics in the Age of Peel*; J. Prest, *Politics in the Age of Cobden* (1977). See also J. Grego, *A History of Parliamentary Elections and Electioneering in the Old Days* (1886); *The Old and New Representation of the United Kingdom Contrasted* (1833); D.E.D. Beales, 'The Electorate Before and After 1832: The Right to Vote and the Opportunity', *Parliamentary History*, xi (1992), 79–98; K.T. Hoppen, 'The Franchise and Electoral Politics in England and Ireland 1832–1885', *History*, lxx (1985), 202–17.

[26] F. O'Gorman, *Voters, Patrons, and Parties: The Unreformed Electoral System of Hanoverian England 1734–1832* (Oxford, 1989); F. O'Gorman, *The Emergence of the British Two-Party System, 1760–1832* (New York, 1982); F. O'Gorman, 'Electoral Deference in "Unreformed" England: 1760–1832', *Journal of Modern History*, lvi (1984); F. O'Gorman, 'Party Politics in the Early Nineteenth Century', *EHR*, cii (1987), 63–84; J.A. Phillips, 'Popular Politics in Unreformed England', *Journal of Modern History*, lii (1980), 599–625; J.A. Phillips, *Electoral Behaviour in Unreformed England: Plumpers, Splitters and Straights* (Princeton, NJ, 1982); J.A. Phillips, 'The Structure of Electoral Politics in Unreformed England', *Journal of British Studies*, xix (1979), 76–100; Hanham, *Elections and Party Management*. See also E.A. Smith, 'The Election Agent in English Politics, 1734–1832', *EHR*, lxxxiv (1969), 12–35.

cies. This showed an expectation of central interest both at Westminster and among candidates and agents in the constituencies. It is based, among other things, on previously underused sections of the Parkes papers, the papers of Charles Wood, and on evidence from the papers of Sir Denis Le Marchant, which appears here for the first time. The next section discusses central electioneering and registration, and the following section discusses 'Reform' and 'Liberal' 'Associations' in London and the constituencies, as well as the Reform Club in Pall Mall. In terms of competition with the Conservatives, it is a story of failure, but in terms of perception of liberal politics and presentation of party control, it is a story of strength.

Electioneering and Registration in the Centre

While the 1832 Reform Act did little to change the composition of the house of commons, and made only a moderate increase in the size of the franchise, it significantly changed British politics in one very important way – registration. The new requirements for the registration of voters, contained in the Act, fundamentally changed the nature of electoral politics both in the constituencies and in the party centres in Westminster. By the 1835 general election (the first held under the new rules), registration had become a prime concern for parties. Because electoral registration was to take place annually, and because the registration of individual electors could be challenged, highly charged party contests sprang up in the constituencies. This eventually filtered to party leaders in London, and both groups set up central groups to monitor registration and canvassing.[27]

The two years immediately following the passage of the Reform Act saw Whig leaders slow to realize that further attention to their electoral support was needed in order to remain in government. James Atkinson, liberal agent for Kendal and Westmorland, wrote to James Brougham on the last day of the Reform year, 31 December 1832, urging him to exert whatever pressure he could on his brother Henry to convince the Whig ministry to keep the liberal electorate happy by passing church reform, and paying more attention to electoral matters.[28] Whig leaders were very uneasy with notions of increased electoral professionalisation because the Reform Act was partly intended to free the electorate from undue influence and pressure, and replace electoral 'management' with the force of argument. This Foxite notion of politics lingered in the Whig leadership because many of them had been in parliament since the early decades of the century, and were still heavily influenced by the legacy of Fox.[29] Apparently, Melbourne thought Ellice 'a cunning, designing knave', and worried that his easy communication with Parkes meant that he was too willing to listen to ideas about further constitutional reform.[30] For the more conservative Whigs in the cabinet, professional electioneering was perhaps tainted with parliamentary radicalism. But this explanation has been effectively challenged by Salmon and Mandler,

---

[27] Salmon, *Electoral Reform at Work*, 12–38; Seymour, *Electoral Reform in England and Wales*; Gash, *Politics in the Age of Peel*; Gash, *Reaction and Reconstruction*. See also Prest, *Politics in the Age of Cobden*.

[28] University College London Manuscripts Room, Brougham Papers: James Atkinson to James Brougham, 31 Dec. 1832.

[29] For a fuller discussion of this, see Brent, *Liberal Anglican Politics*, ch. 1.

[30] Newbould, *Whiggery and Reform*, 27–32; Salmon, *Electoral Reform at Work*, 40–1.

and by Ellis Wasson, who has shown heavy Whig involvement in managing the press for party purposes before and after 1831.[31] Although some Whig leaders were cautious and may have disdained electioneering work, they were considerably successful in the initial stages. Melbourne received regular communication from Parkes,[32] and Mandler has shown that 'whig aristocrats were instrumental in establishing a Central Reform Association'.[33]

If this unwillingness on behalf of the leadership to get deeply involved with election-eering and registration caused problems for Liberal Party MPs in the house of commons, it also allowed committed Reformers and Radicals to push their own efforts at increased registration unhindered. The most important of these was Parkes, who first came to national prominence as a communications link between the government and the Bir-mingham Political Union during the Reform crisis of 1831.[34] He very rapidly became one of a handful of liberal men in London who were trying to promote reform causes in the press, as well as prepare for liberal electioneering. Parkes thought highly of his own abilities to influence the press, and told E.J. Littleton in early 1833:

> I can command much of the Press for you – the great steam power of the political world. Any [*Morning*] *Chronicle* leader I will do for you in confidence – or in the *Sun*, or in the excellent Sunday paper the *Spectator* which is rather the Sunday paper now of superior ability & high circulation. The *Times* I can directly influence – but certain members of the Government (entre nous) move the helm & also that of the Globe, tho' the Editor of the Globe is a particular & old friend – Mr. W. Coulson. The *Chronicle* I am a frequent & active writer in of leaders, and I have tonight sent up an article – which I penned after seeing in the morning Tory papers of today columns about the speakership.[35]

Thomas Barnes, editor of *The Times*, noted the increased importance of Parkes (still considered new on the political scene) by 1834, when he wrote to Sir Denis Le Marchant that a *Times* reporter had tried to get information on what materials had been used to prepare a speech by Lord Grey, but that he was 'suddenly intercepted by our new ally, the "Birmingham Attorney" – Joseph Parkes: who took them [the details about the speech material] to the Chronicle. The consequence is that Lord Grey's speech is very imperfectly reported [in *The Times*]'.[36]

Parkes neatly summarized the dilemma of non-co-operation of the Whig leaders when he wrote to Lord Durham near the end of 1834: 'Here we are in London, without a penny for Elections or Agitation . . . We are doing better at Ellice's house in Election

[31] E.A. Wasson, 'The Whigs and the Press, 1800–50', *Parliamentary History*, xxv (2006), 70–5.

[32] Salmon, *Electoral Reform at Work*, 54–7.

[33] P. Mandler, *Aristocratic Government in the Age of Reform: Whigs and Liberals, 1830–1852* (Oxford, 1990), 164.

[34] On Parkes, see *ODNB*, xlii (2004), 777–82, and his obituary in *The Times*, 12 Aug. 1865. See also W.E.S. Thomas, *The Philosophical Radicals: Nine Studies in Theory and Practice 1817–1841* (Oxford, 1979), 266; Wasson, 'Whigs and the Press', 82; G.B.A.M. Finlayson, 'Joseph Parkes', *BIHR*, xlvi (1973), 186–201; N. Lopatin-Lummis, ' "With All My Oldest and Native Friends". Joseph Parkes: Warwickshire Solicitor and Electoral Agent in the Age of Reform', *Parliamentary History*, xxvii (2008), 96–108.

[35] Parkes (WEST): Parkes to E.J. Littleton, 2 Jan. 1833.

[36] PA, Le Marchant Papers: Thomas Barnes to Sir Denis Le Marchant, 2 July 1834.

matters; but the Whigs are cold, selfish, factionalizing men, as a Party. I can't make *time & money* for them'.[37]

By the end of 1834, Whig leaders were coming around to the idea that registration was essential for electoral success. Le Marchant was convinced that increased registration was helping the liberal effort in the boroughs, and that 'the counties are the only places where we shall suffer any material losses'.[38] And even Parkes, whose electoral mood swings ranged from despair to elation on nearly a daily basis, thought that registration was becoming more solid by the end of 1834.[39] By the election in January 1835, the central liberal electioneering committee was made up of Duncannon and Mulgrave from the house of lords, Sir John Hobhouse, Whig MP for Nottingham, and Charles Thomson, Whig MP for Manchester, from the house of commons as senior members, and Parkes, Thomas Drummond (formerly Althorp's private secretary) and Le Marchant outside Westminster as junior members. They represented both the liberal groups in the Lords, Commons and outside, as well as different shades of opinion, although all were of the more 'reforming' element of the Liberal Party.[40]

Throughout 1835, the crucial year in the formation of liberal groups within the Liberal Party, Parkes constantly reported to Durham on the various electioneering efforts being undertaken in London – registration, and the establishment of a 'National Club'.[41] He also kept other interested liberal MPs informed of electoral matters, particularly Charles D'Eyncourt, Radical MP for Lambeth.[42] He pushed the idea of liberal unity whenever he got the chance, and worried about the prospect of the continuation of a 'whig family' government. But most often, he stressed that the Liberal Party '*must systematically register*'.[43] For the remainder of the year, he kept in constant contact with the new government whip, E.J. Stanley, discussing election minutiae weekly. An example from October shows this clearly:

We are getting through the registry very well for the reformers, on both sides of the county. In the northern division I expect an addition to our roll of 600 beyond the 2 parties, and in the south we shall I think fully maintain our ground. All our information at Cleveland Row, at the Association highly favourable. . . . but what strikes me most in the country and amounts to a distinct gain, is the organisation and union of the reformers produced by this year's attention to the registration.[44]

Further, he served, informally of course, as a candidate selector for Stanley, especially when an MP took the Chiltern Hundreds and a new candidate was needed for the

[37] Parkes (WEST): Parkes to Lord Durham, 13 Dec. 1834.

[38] UCL MSS Room, Brougham Papers: Le Marchant to Henry Brougham, 23 Dec. 1834. See also Newbould, *Whiggery and Reform*, 31.

[39] Parkes (WEST): Parkes to Lord Durham, 16 Dec. 1834.

[40] D. Close, 'The General Elections of 1835 and 1837 in England and Wales', University of Oxford PhD, 1967, 178–9.

[41] Parkes (WEST): Parkes to Lord Durham, 26 Jan. 1835.

[42] Lincolnshire Archives Office, D'Eyncourt Papers, TDE H31/10: Parkes to Charles Tennyson D'Eyncourt, 31 Jan. 1835.

[43] Parkes (WEST): Parkes to Lord Durham, 3 Apr. 1835.

[44] UCL MSS Room, Parkes Papers: Parkes to E.J. Stanley, 11 Oct. 1835.

by-election.[45] But he had seen too much by the end of 1835 to be confident that the party and, by extension, liberalism, would improve its electoral organisation: 'I see no appearance of any present storm in the political atmosphere. The Registration Returns of the Reform Assocn. *are all good*. We shall gain greatly on average. Still liberalism has many difficult straits to pass in the next 2 or 3 years'.[46]

For the next three years he continued to press the importance of registration, trying to show Liberal Party leaders that it had several positive effects for liberal politics. The registration efforts coming out of the Municipal Reform Act of 1835 'seal[ed] the fate of Toryism', as he wrote to Lord Durham in one of his overenthusiastic moods.[47] He argued strongly to E.J. Stanley that it was vital that a liberal candidate be put up for every seat, in order to show that there was a good degree of party feeling across the country.[48] But he constantly had to beg Stanley for more attention to be paid to registration in the country:

> Some of our Country Registrations are being spiritedly managed this year, but many are wholly neglected in despair – while everywhere the Tories are acting on Peel's advice, R.R.R ['Register, Register, Register']. Nothing will save many English and Scotch country seats we now have, while the system continues as it is.[49]

His concerns about the weakness of Liberal Party central organisation lasted throughout the rest of the 1830s and, by the early 1840s, Le Marchant had largely taken over central electoral administration.

When the Whig government began its final year in 1841, it had more or less run out of electoral steam. As the Reformer backbencher for Shrewsbury, Robert Slaney, wrote in his journal in March 1841, 'the Whig or Reform party [is] still in Office but losing ground in almost every election'.[50] Norman Gash attributed the Conservative victory of 1841 to the 'disciplined opposition organized for electoral purposes'.[51] On the liberal side, the indiscipline may be seen in the work that Le Marchant had to do to pay election bills after the election. There were many complaints from liberal candidates and liberal agents that there was confusion over who was to help with electoral finances, and that the money was not forthcoming. John Guest, agent to the liberal candidate for Southampton, Edward Hutchins, wrote to Le Marchant, outlining the confusing nature of election funding:

> Mr Hutchins the late candidate for Southampton informs me that Mr Coppock wishes me to state to you what was the understanding between the candidate and the Finance Committee which met at the Reform Club upon the subject of the expenses

---

[45] UCL MSS Room, Parkes Papers: Parkes to E.J. Stanley, 29 May 1840. In this case, Sir John Walsh applied for the Chiltern Hundreds, and a new candidate was needed for Radnor.

[46] Lincolnshire Archives, D'Eyncourt Papers, TDE H31/11: Parkes to Charles Tennyson D'Eyncourt, 15 Oct. 1835.

[47] Parkes (WEST): Parkes to Lord Durham, 5 Jan. 1835.

[48] UCL MSS Room, Parkes Papers: Parkes to E.J. Stanley, 9 Oct. 1836.

[49] UCL MSS Room, Parkes Papers: Parkes to E.J. Stanley, 13 Aug. 1837; see also Parkes to Stanley, 24 Sept. 1837.

[50] Shropshire Records and Research Centre, Slaney Papers: journal entry, Robert Slaney, Mar. 1841.

[51] Gash, *Politics in the Age of Peel*, xiii.

of the Southampton contest. By the desire of Mr Hutchins I met Mr Coppock on behalf of the Committee and the arrangement which I reduced to writing was that the candidates Messrs Mangles & Hutchins should each spend £1,000 and the Committee £1,000 and then in case of their being any further sum required Mr Hutchins was to pay if successful £500 and if unsuccessful £250 in addition to the £1,000 and Mr Mangles was also to pay an additional £500 or £250 as the case may be.[52]

Throughout 1841, Le Marchant handled requests for central party money. The correspondence also shows a good deal of party feeling among candidates, as well as the expectation that there was a core group of Liberal Party MPs who were in charge of providing some financial assistance. On 13 May 1841, George Larpent, Liberal MP for Nottingham, wrote that, in an effort to pay his election bills, he would:

engage to apply £900 or £1,000 of it [the money to be sent from London] to satisfy these claims so as to put the party in the most favourable position for the future. I shall then have paid £500 and I cannot but think that you & my friend J.A. Smith [Whig MP for Chichester] who were privy to the terms upon which I was induced to make the attempt [the recent candidacy], will bear me out to the leaders of the party, that I have more than fulfilled what could have been expected of me.[53]

The difficulty in getting enough funding was also shown in a letter from a Stockbridge agent, Mr Etivall, who wrote to Le Marchant in June 1841:

the Southampton men desired me to ask you to send them (to Mr. Sharpe [liberal agent]) the £500 which they understood that they were to have. I am going down on Thursday evening to a meeting of the Reform Association. Pray send me the £30 for Southampton, which I paid there in July last.[54]

Candidates and agents were forced to beg even for these small sums from the central group, and appealed for central help partly in order to ensure that their standing (and that of the Liberal Party) in their community remained good. Thomas Granger, the recently elected Liberal MP for Durham City, pleaded with Le Marchant to make good on the money he had been promised by James Coppock and E.J. Stanley, and that 'I shall be obliged by an early answer to this, for as my opponents have paid their electioneering accounts it is very unpleasant for me to allow mine to remain unsettled besides being injurious to the liberal interest in Durham'.[55]

E.J. Stanley also got his share of these letters. On 31 August 1841, Granger wrote telling Stanley what to do with money he had donated to the central fund. Stanley passed the letter on to Le Marchant:

---

[52] PA, Le Marchant Papers: John Guest to Sir Denis Le Marchant [no date, 1841]. See also *The Politics of 1837 by an Old Reformer, Respectfully Addressed to Viscount Melbourne* (1837).

[53] PA, Le Marchant Papers: George Larpent to Sir Denis Le Marchant, 13 May 1841; see also C. Howard, a Dublin liberal agent, to Le Marchant, 15 Jan. 1841; Mr Travers, a London agent, to Le Marchant, 16 July 1841.

[54] PA, Le Marchant Papers: Etivall to Le Marchant, June 1841 (no exact date given).

[55] PA, Le Marchant Papers: Thomas Granger to E.J. Stanley, 14 Sept. 1841.

I am . . . most anxious about Winnington's election at Bewdley, if you could give him the £200 you promised me you would, I should be very glad . . . I have just seen Mr. Scott MP for Walsall, who says there will certainly be a small balance out of the £1,000 I sent for the E. Worcestershire election, and that he will get the account finished as soon as possible, which balance will after be at your disposal or go to Winnington. Winnington's election cost upwards of £3,000, which makes me so anxious of it.[56]

The defeat in 1841 spurred further organisational activity, as had the losses of 1835. Russell now began to play a more active role in electioneering and in keeping an eye on liberal efforts in the country. Between 1841 and 1852, Russell and Le Marchant, with the fading help of Parkes, began to assert strong control over Liberal Party management. Le Marchant continued to serve as the communication centre, receiving reports from various liberal agents or MPs from most areas, as he had in the past, but also now working more closely with Russell on the question of filling seats that had been vacated (or were about to be vacated) due to an MP's death.[57] On 26 August 1843, Russell wrote to Le Marchant that the dying Sir Matthew Wood should be replaced by the Reformer MP for the City of London, James Pattison.[58] Similarly, he wrote again to Le Marchant, on 10 October 1843, that the government ought to prepare to replace the Whig MP for Middlesex, George Byng, in the event of his death:

I hear Mr. Byng is better but it is necessary to be prepared for an event which his age & severe illness seem to forebode.

I should be much obliged to you if you would try to ascertain what Byng's leading supporters, & the heads of the radical party in Middlesex would do in the case of an election before parliament meets. The seat is now a whig seat. I do not think there is any Cavendish ready to start . . . but Hastings Russell would, if his friends & the party wished it. His opinions are mine, tho' not so much for finality as I am.

But it would not do to start unless all the liberals went with us. I would go up to town for a few days, if there were any question of a contest.[59]

By 1844, Russell had gained a strong sense of the various liberal efforts in the country, and corresponded with Le Marchant more frequently, often discussing several constituencies and candidates in one paragraph, as in this case in the west country.

We must be careful how we touch Portsmouth. There is a strong tory party there headed by the Holdsworths, the former boroughmongers of the place. There is a Judicial attorney, James Smith, a tory . . . sort of chap — if he is still alive — the majority are liberal, but it is very likely that with the fame of [James] Matheson

---

[56] PA, Le Marchant Papers: Lord Foley to E.J. Stanley, 31 Aug. 1841.

[57] David Dundas was Le Marchant's man in Scotland, and Lord Carlisle often fulfilled the role in Dublin. See PA, Le Marchant Papers, *passim*.

[58] PA, Le Marchant Papers: Russell to Le Marchant, 26 Aug. 1843. Sir Matthew Wood was Radical MP for the City of London, 1832–43. James Pattison, a Reformer, defeated Thomas Baring for the seat at the election held after Wood's death in 1843.

[59] PA, Le Marchant Papers: Russell to Le Marchant, 10 Oct. 1843.

[Liberal MP for Ashburton] at Ashburton they will like a generous London merchant to give them employment in shipping, etc. Mr. [George] Moffat [Radical candidate for Dartmouth in 1844, and MP there 1845–52] seems far from being a troublesome [Anti-Corn Law] Leaguer, so that I am disposed to think his election would be the best thing that can happen to us. I need not write to Parkes. I wish you would see him, & say that if Mr. Moffat means to stand the sooner he goes there the better & that he may use my name to any of the Seale family [family of Sir John Seale, Whig MP for Dartmouth, 1832–44].[60]

Further, Russell was clearly in command of party electioneering matters, as the following letter from Lord Brougham to Le Marchant shows. On 17 December 1845, Brougham wrote to Le Marchant, mentioning, among other things, 'the general fund'. Le Marchant had stood for Harwich in the election of 1841, but, according to Brougham, had been remiss in settling his election bills and repaying election loans. He asked Le Marchant to settle the debt, and 'If you take any other view of the matter, I shall very cheerfully submit it to the decision of Lord Bessborough, Lord John Russell, or Sir J.C. Hobhouse'.[61]

Threatening to take this election financing matter to a 'higher court' consisting of Bessborough, the leader of the Liberal Party in the house of lords, Russell, the general party leader, and Hobhouse, who had been president of the board of control under Melbourne and would be again under Russell after 1846, shows that, although Whig leaders may not have been attentive to party matters between 1833 and 1841, they certainly became so after losing to Peel. This was echoed by the sentiments of the second Lord Grey, who wrote to Russell in late 1846 that the new liberal administration must not only pay more attention to the perceived popular nature of electioneering and ministry formation, but must transfer that to governing.[62]

The lesson seemed to have been learned, at least as far as electioneering was concerned. Le Marchant continued to send out money to candidates. For instance, on 23 November 1846, he wrote to Charles Wood about advancing £1,200 for contests in Southampton and Weymouth.[63] He continued to manage seats and candidates, which seemed to increase in importance. E.J. Stanley wrote to Edward Lytton that there were many seats available for him to try (since he was not interested in contesting his old seat at Lincoln, where he had been MP from 1832 to 1841), including St Albans and Hull, and that he had spoken to Tufnell and Le Marchant, in the interest of aiding Lytton's search.[64]

Whipping and central election management, although often confused and inefficient, were central to Liberal Party organisation. But the efficiency and order of these structures and ideas were not as important as the sense of perception and expectation in the whipping and correspondence about parliamentary seats. MPs were increasingly whipped as members of the Liberal Party (or 'all Liberal Members'), and they expected to be

[60] PA, Le Marchant Papers: Russell to Le Marchant, 4 Dec. 1844; see also Russell to Le Marchant, 16 Oct. 1845.

[61] PA, Le Marchant Papers: Brougham to Le Marchant, 17 Dec. 1845.

[62] Univ. of York, Borthwick Institute of Historical Research, HalifaxPapers: Lord Grey to Russell, 17 Dec. 1846. This letter is reproduced in typescript in A8, i, 17–20.

[63] Univ. of York, Borthwick Institute, Halifax Papers: Le Marchant to Charles Wood, 23 Nov. 1846.

[64] Hertfordshire RO, Lytton Papers, D/EK/023, item 6: E.J. Stanley to Edward Bulwer Lytton, 5 June 1847.

whipped as such. Further, there was a greatly increased perception that there was a group in London that monitored electoral successes and tried to keep the central party funding afloat. The same sorts of perceptions and expectations may be seen in the next section on electoral and registration organisations.

Associations and Societies: Liberal Registration and Electioneering in the Centre and the Constituencies

The previous section focused on individuals in London, and on how they gradually increased their attention to liberal electioneering throughout the Reform period. It also showed the degree of liberal language used and the increasing expectations of party from 1832 to 1852. This section will examine liberal attempts to organise more fully in London and in the constituencies and, more importantly, to organise more impersonally, in order to give a sense of continuity to liberal election efforts, and provide structures for elections beyond the immediately forthcoming one. There was, of course, a good deal of disagreement among liberal groups about the direction that registration and election-eering should take, and there was some degree of factionalising. But overall, this section shows how much organising liberals wanted to create an ongoing liberal presence at elections and the registration courts, that they realized the necessity of doing so, and that the political language they employed showed a high degree of party consciousness and feeling.

Historians now generally agree that one of the most significant results of the Reform Act of 1832 was that its registration clauses increased party activity in the constituencies. Electors were pushed to the registration courts by party agents, their electoral status was questioned by opposing party agents, and contests were often won or lost in the annual registration battles.[65] 1832–52 became, as Gash has written, 'the age of registration societies, [and] constituency associations'.[66] And, as John Phillips has argued, the party contests each year in the registration courts helped lead to a general understanding of the

---

[65] Salmon, *Electoral Reform at Work, passim*; O'Gorman, 'Party Politics', 84. See Prest, *Politics in the Age of Cobden*, 15, for a discussion of the registration clauses of the Reform Act causing a 'little election' in each constituency every year. For works regarding election law and the consequences of the 1832 Reform Act, see J.D. Chambers, *A Complete Dictionary of the Law and Practice of Elections of Members of Parliament, and of Election Petitions and Committees for England, Scotland, and Ireland* (1837); J. Clerk, *The Law and Practice of Election Committees* (1852); A.E. Cockburn, *Questions on Election Law Arising from the Reform Act* (1834); W.H. Cooke, *Plain Instructions for Overseers and Electors in the Registration of Voters for Counties and Boroughs in England and Wales* (1835); E.W. Cox, *Instructions to Committees and Agents of Candidates and to Returning Officers for the Management of an Election* (1847); E.W. Cox, *The Law and Practice of Registration and Elections* (1847); R.R. Detrosier, *Lecture on the Utility of Political Unions* (1832); G.P. Elliot, *A Practical Treatise on the Qualifications and Registration of Parliamentary Electors in England and Wales* (1839); Liberal Registration Society, *Rules* (1860); *The Origins, Objects, and Advantages of Political Unions* (1832); J. Paget, *The Registration of Voters Act* (1843); *Parliamentary Agents Rules*, Parliamentary Archives, Historical Collection 68 (1836); Parliamentary Candidate Society, *Proceedings* (1831); G. Price, *Complete Election Guide: The Reform Act* (1832); R.C. Sewell, *A Manual of the Law and Practice of Registration of Voters in England and Wales* (1849); C. Wordsworth, *The Registration of Voters Act* (1843).

[66] Gash, *Politics in the Age of Peel*, xiii. See also M.M. Ostrogorski and F. Clarke, *Democracy and the Organization of Political Parties* (New York, 1902), 142–3; J.A. Phillips, *The Great Reform Bill in the Boroughs: English Electoral Behaviour, 1818–1841* (Oxford, 1987), 230–1; F.M.L. Thompson, 'Whigs and Liberals in the West Riding, 1830–1860', *EHR*, lxxiv (1959), 214–39.

'stances of the parties'.[67] Even before the Reform Act had passed, certain groups were preparing to push their political agendas through new types of organisation. As early as March 1831, liberal (especially Radical) MPs were attempting to organise for the purposes of getting like-minded MPs into the House. 'Liberal' and 'Reform' associations for candidate selection, for organising electoral registration and for orchestrating this on a national level were founded throughout the period. Usually, they appealed for members and subscribers, had a brief period of activity and then folded. This process continued right up to 1860, when the Liberal Registration Association was founded, which lasted well into the 1870s and was eventually replaced as the central Liberal Party organisation by the National Liberal Federation in 1877. Very few of the groups managed to retain interest among their members and subscribers past a general election. The Parliamentary Candidate Society, a radical group in London with Hume at its head, proposed in March 1831:

> that in the event of the measure of parliamentary reform, brought forward by his majesty's ministers, being defeated, or rendered less efficient, by a corrupt faction of borough-mongers, and of parliament being dissolved, this society will use every constitutional exertion to aid the return of the friends of reform, and to exclude the enemies of that measure.[68]

They never had to exercise this purpose, however, because the Act passed, and other societies and associations rose to take up the task of promoting ideologically sound candidates for each of the parties.[69]

As will be seen in Chapter 4, 1834 and 1835 saw much agitation for a 'Union of Reformers'. In December 1834, Charles D'Eyncourt, Radical MP for Lambeth, wrote to Edward Heneage, Whig candidate for Great Grimsby, saying that he would support Heneage's candidature and that:

> I have it also at Heart to aid in rescuing the country from the Hands of those who would now either arrest the progress of Reform, or otherwise degrade the character of Public men, by surrendering points, on the consistent maintenance of which credit for political Honesty exclusively rests. For this object I have, at the present juncture, as well as when Lord Melbourne's government was formed, earnestly promoted union between the Whig and Liberal Reformers; and I had a full persuasion that the Melbourne cabinet would have justified that union.[70]

Similarly, Durham argued for the co-ordination of Liberal registration, to pay more attention to the mechanics of elections and electioneering, and for the creation of a National Reform Association.[71] Richard Potter, Radical MP for Wigan, wrote to Joseph Hume, suggesting much the same thing: 'it has often occurred to me lately that the

---

[67] Phillips, *Great Reform Bill*, 52–3.

[68] *Proceedings of the Parliamentary Candidate Society* (1831), 6.

[69] Close, 'General Elections of 1835 and 1837', 194–5; Salmon, *Electoral Reform at Work*, ch. 2.

[70] Lincolnshire Archives Office, D'Eyncourt Papers, TDE H4/9: D'Eyncourt to Edward Heneage, 8 Dec. 1834.

[71] Salmon, *Electoral Reform at Work*, 45.

liberal members ought to form a bond of union so that they may act together for the public good. The Tories have their clubs, Conservatives Associations & success in many instances has followed their efforts'.[72]

In late 1834 and early 1835, therefore, the phrase 'Union of Reformers' came to stand for an idea of a national liberal organisation, without there being much practical application of electioneering methods. There was a variance of support for the union in the localities. In Dudley and Bedford, Whigs and Radicals were not on good terms, for instance, and the union was hardly mentioned in electioneering material. And the general feeling of discomfort felt between liberal groups meant that the only feasible aim of such a union was to keep the Tories out of office.[73] This was, of course, successful enough in keeping out the Tories in the 1835 election, but the general lack of enthusiasm for a stronger bond may have been one of the reasons the Liberal Party lost MPs at that election. Parkes certainly thought so, and urged the Liberal whip, E.J. Stanley, to retain the union: 'The great point now is to preserve that national union of Reformers which the tories so dread and which has so safely ridden out the storm of this session'.[74]

Parkes set out much of the reasoning for the need for, as well as the eventual structure of, a central liberal association, when he wrote to Lord Durham in early 1835, complaining that the Warwickshire North Division seat had been lost due to inadequate liberal organisation:

> We must organize an Association in London to *work* the Reform Bills – to point out to the Country the facility & effect of orginization [sic], pre-arrangement, & funds by small annual subscription for registration especially. Since 1832 the great addition of 1037 persons has been made to our ND. [Northern Division] Warwickshire Register, 3/4ths of the addition I should think Tory, while our party with hundreds in the towns non-registered have never taken a step either to register Reformers or to oppose foul registered Tories. Now what can we expect from the neglect, but the loss of much of the benefit of the Reform Bills? We are here immediately forming Associations local for the purpose of remedying our defects & neglects.[75]

Parkes helped to found the Reform Association on 21 May 1835, with T.W. Coke as chairman.[76] Initially, they met in the upper floor of Parkes' house, but soon moved to Cleveland Square, where they were often referred to as 'the Cleveland Square group'.[77] The day-to-day running of the Association was mainly handled by James Coppock, a

---

[72] British Library of Political and Economic Science, London, Potter Papers, Coll. Misc. 146: Potter to Hume, 25 Jan. 1835.

[73] Close, 'General Elections of 1835 and 1837', 82–4.

[74] UCL MSS Room, Parkes Papers: Parkes to E.J. Stanley, 6 Sept. 1835.

[75] Parkes (WEST): Parkes to Durham, 18 Jan. 1835.

[76] *The Times*, 22 May 1835; Salmon, *Electoral Reform at Work*, 46; *The Spectator*, viii, no. 360, 23 May 1835, 483. Close, 'General Elections of 1835 and 1837', 437; J.P. Parry, *The Rise and Fall of Liberal Government in Victorian Britain* (New Haven, CT, 1993), 130–1; Newbould, *Whiggery and Reform*, 31–3. Gash credits Durham with the founding of the Reform Association in 1834, based on S.J. Reid, *Life and Letters of the First Earl of Durham, 1792–1840* (2 vols, 1906), ii, 3–4. But this seems to have been the sketching of a general idea, with the real work left to Parkes and Ellice. See Gash, *Politics in the Age of Peel*, 403–4.

[77] Parkes (WEST): Parkes to Durham, 1 June 1835.

parliamentary agent and expert in the new electoral law.[78] One of the main purposes of the Association was to raise money for distribution to local liberal registration societies.[79] The Reform Association appealed directly to liberal candidates and MPs to support its central efforts. In a poster addressed to 'the People of Great Britain', it said:

> The extensive formation of 'Tory Associations', or 'Conservative Clubs', throughout Great Britain, calls upon Reformers to unite for the protection of the constitutional power of the people . . . The counteraction of these [the Tories'] formidable efforts requires the closest union and the utmost vigilance of all classes of Reformers, and is the sole purpose of this Association . . . Subscriptions, will be received from all friends of the liberal cause who may be disposed to aid more the general views of the Association but it is not desirable that contributions which may be more usefully employed by Local Societies, should be diverted from local objects to the general fund; it being of the utmost importance that all, in their several districts, should organize and prepare their separated means for the approaching REGISTRATION.[80]

By the end of the year, Parkes was generally pleased both with the efforts of the Association in London, and also its work in helping local liberals form their own associations. He wrote to E.J. Stanley in October 1835:

> All our information in Cleveland Row, at the Association, is highly favourable . . . When the Regn. is completed & the Lists out I have directed Coppock to send round a private Circular letter to all our confidential Emissaries & 'Branches' to obtain accurate Returns. . . . But what strikes me most in the country, & amounts to a distinct gain, is the orginision [*sic*] & Union of the Reformers produced by this year's attention to the Registrn.[81]

Local organisations, of the type mentioned by Parkes, were being formed in many parts of the country between 1835 and 1837. Many of these had relied on the central Reform Association for help and advice.[82] The Middlesex Reform Club, a liberal registration association, was formed in May and June of 1835.[83] The Finsbury Reform Club, one of the earliest groups, was praised by James Coppock for its spirit of 'reform, and the promotion of the purity of elections'.[84] Liberals in Staffordshire struggled to establish clubs, especially after the founding of the Walsall Conservative Club and others.[85] By the

---

[78] Gash, *Politics in the Age of Peel*, 424.

[79] See Salmon, *Electoral Reform at Work*, 46–7, for a description of how this process helped fund local liberal efforts to work the annual registration revisions. See also TNA, Russell Papers, 30/22/2c, f. 221: Parkes to Russell, 6 Oct. 1836; Parkes (WEST): Parkes to Durham, 6 Sept. 1835.

[80] Durham County RO, Bowes Papers, D/St/C1/16, 263: Reform Association poster, 20 May 1835.

[81] Parkes (WEST): Parkes to E.J. Stanley, 11 Oct. 1835.

[82] Close, 'General Elections of 1835 and 1837', 198; Salmon, *Electoral Reform at Work*, 58–9.

[83] Norfolk RO, Bulwer Papers, BUL 1/6/7: James Davies, secretary to the Middlesex Reform Club to Henry Lytton Bulwer, 1 June 1835.

[84] J. Coppock, *The Elector's Manual: Or Plain Directions by which Every Man may Know His Own Rights, and Preserve Them* (1835), dedication page.

[85] Staffordshire RO, Littleton Papers, D260/M/F/5/27/11/8: C.F. Cotterill to E.J. Littleton, 9 Apr. 1835; see also D260/M/F/5/27/11/9: W. Cotterill to Littleton, 9 Apr. 1835.

summer, the central Association in Cleveland Square was appealing for more local Reform Associations, and for subscriptions 'from all friends of the liberal cause who may be disposed to aid the general views of the Association'.[86] By the end of August 1835, the Staffordshire Reform Association was being formed.[87] The Denbyshire Reform Association overtly set itself up as a 'branch of the "British Reform Association in London" '.[88] There were quite a few local reform associations that never succeeded to any significant degree. Canterbury Radicals split from the local Reform Association over opposition to the poor law and formed their own Radical association. The Newcastle Reform Association repeatedly failed to organise, and the Durham Association split into liberal and whig factions.[89] Parkes wrote to Durham in June 1835:

> We are by Circular, to the Country members of the R.A., collecting & filing sets of all the Rules & Constitutions of the Tory & Liberal Associations . . . I am happy to say that the country accounts display great activity & moving zeal among the Liberals. Put them in the right path & they will crop their enemies.[90]

Parkes was over-optimistic about the potential success of these liberal associations, but the fact that the central party managers were collecting and organising the rules and constitutions of local associations shows how prevalent they were becoming and, more importantly, that it was being accepted that they were to be the new model for local political activity.

The Reform Association was not to last. Beset by organisational problems and over-centralisation, by 1837 it found itself having difficulty keeping local organisations going. The emphasis on central management proved, in the end, to weaken liberal and reforming associations in the constituencies by keeping them at one remove from daily politics in the localities. The structure also put too great a burden on Coppock and Parkes, who had other parliamentary business to attend to. Parkes tried to keep the Association going, but it gradually faded out, and its organisational and financing duties had transferred to the Reform Club by 1841.[91] Local liberal organisations were forced by necessity to keep going, although many of them did not survive the 1830s and new ones were constantly being founded.[92]

By the 1840s, registration was not simply an electoral concern. Some agents wrote to their MPs that the weakness of the Melbourne administration was hampering liberal registration efforts, and that the government ought to pay more attention to how its progress in Westminster was being viewed in the constituencies.[93] And, during Peel's administration, local liberal groups worried that the registration efforts of the 1830s were

---

[86] *Morning Chronicle*, 10 July 1835, quoted in Salmon, *Electoral Reform at Work*, 42, 58–9.

[87] Staffordshire RO, Sutherland MSS: Thomas Cotton Sheppard to the Duke of Sutherland, 31 Aug. 1835; see also Sheppard to Sutherland, 2 Nov. 1837.

[88] Founding address of the Denbyshire Reform Association, 1836, quoted in Salmon, *Electoral Reform at Work*, 60.

[89] Salmon, *Electoral Reform at Work*, 62–3.

[90] Parkes (WEST): Parkes to Durham, 1 June 1835.

[91] Salmon, *Electoral Reform at Work*, 55–7.

[92] Salmon, *Electoral Reform at Work*, 62–3.

[93] See Univ. of York, Borthwick Institute, A/14, Halifax Papers: William Tottie to Sir Francis Wood, 31 Aug. 1840; see also Tottie to Wood, 26 June 1838, 6 May 1839.

slowing down. As F.H. Hawkes, the chair of the West Riding Registration Association, wrote to Charles Wood on 1 August 1844, 'The once strong Party which prior to the last Reformation of Parliament, called itself Liberal, ... is ... now such a Hash as it appears at least to me of conflicting opinions, [that] nothing but the most critical danger to the Country can reunite [it] in one common Sentiment'.[94]

Although this sentiment was not rare, it tended to exist only among existing registration associations. Newly formed ones continued to present their own liberal-ness. The South Durham Reform and Registration Association was formed in 1841 to work the registration, 'with a view to preserve as far as possible the ascendancy of Liberal Principles'.[95] The North-Riding Liberal Registration Association similarly used liberal language, mixing 'liberal' and 'Reformer' as synonyms, and calling for a 'general meeting of the Liberal Party' to be held in Northallerton.[96] At nearly the other end of the country, the new South Essex Reform Association's objects were 'the advancement of liberal principle by attending carefully to the registration, and promotion of general organization of the constituency for the purpose of securing the return of liberal members of parliament'.[97]

Further, Liberal Party MPs continued to keep in close contact with their local associations. William Tancred, Whig MP for Banbury, attended every Banbury Reform Association dinner from 1837 until 1859, and usually brought along with him another MP respected by the Association.[98] William Pinney, Liberal MP for East Somerset, continued his membership of the East Somerset Liberal Association until 1865.[99] And, most diligently of all, Thomas Thompson sent the secretary of the Bradford Reform Association weekly summaries of the doings in parliament, published in the *Bradford Sun*.[100]

These associations continued to work well in some constituencies, but floundered in others. New ones were founded in some constituencies, and in other places they disappeared. Although not all liberal associations were well run and effective in the 1830s and 1840s, their sheer existence, and the fact that many of them tried to improve their organisations rather than starting again, demonstrates well the expectation of permanence of local liberal groups.[101]

---

[94] Univ. of York, Borthwick Institute, A/14, Halifax Papers: F.H. Hawkes to Sir Charles Wood, 1 Aug. 1844.

[95] Durham County RO, Bowes Papers, D/St/C1/16/317: draft rules and regulations of the South Durham Reform and Registration Association, 1841.

[96] Sheffield City Archives, Wentworth-Fitzwilliam Papers: Rules of the North-Riding Liberal Registration Association, 15 Sept. 1837.

[97] Essex RO, Barrett-Leonard Papers, D/DL/O44/1: printed flyer from the South Essex Reform Association, 13 Dec. 1841.

[98] B.S. Trinder, *A Victorian MP and His Constituents* (Banbury, 1969), xix–xxi. See also Staffordshire RO, Littleton Papers, D260/M/F/5/27/14/38: Thomas Bolton to Lord Hatherton, 22 Aug. 1841, for the importance of attending dinners.

[99] Bristol UL Special Collections Department, Pinney Papers: Thomas North to William Pinney, 11 Dec. 1849.

[100] A collection of these is in Univ. of Hull, Brynmor Jones Library, Thompson Papers, DTH.

[101] See Univ. of York, Borthwick Institute, A/14, Halifax Papers: Thomas William Tottie to Sir Francis Wood, 30 Dec. 1840, in which he discusses mainly questions of attendance and tinkering with the division of labour between the central committee and local committees. See also J.A. Thomas, 'The System of Registration and the Development of Party Organization, 1832–1870', *History*, xxxv (1950), 87; J.D. Chambers, *The New Bills for the Registration of Electors Critically Examined* (1836).

Political club life in London started slowly after the passage of the Reform Act. While Brooks's and White's had sometimes served as meeting places for Whigs and Tories, this was often simply a matter of convenience. Real political social life still revolved around the great houses, such as the Whigs' Holland House. But between 1832 and 1836, Conservatives and Liberals began to realize that central political clubs would not only be able to absorb those who would have seemed out of place in aristocratic houses, but also as a place for provincial party men to use as a base when visiting London and, most importantly, as continuing institutions which did not rely on the personalities and interests of political hosts.

The Reform Club was to become the liberal centre well into the 20th century. Its precursor was the Westminster Reform Club, founded on 7 March 1834, in St George Street. Parkes caused a controversy by trying to gain membership for Coppock (who, presumably, did not meet the social standards required). This may have been a major impetus for Parkes to start working on the formation of a new club for reformers and liberals.[102] The Club was founded on 6 February 1836 at a meeting held at Tendall's Hotel. Joseph Hume was in the chair, and the resolution read:

> 1st That a Club consisting of Reformers only be forthwith established in the metropolis, to be called The Reform Club; for the purpose of bringing together the reformers of the United Kingdom. 2nd That the following 35 gentlemen be appointed to the provisional committee, to organize and establish the Reform Club viz: Henry A. Aglionby Esq. MP, Alexr Bannerman Esq. MP, John Blackburne Esq. MP, Montague S. Chapman Esq. MP, William Clay Esq. MP, J.W. Cook Esq. MP, O'Connor Don MP, Edward Divett Esq. MP, Lord Ebrington MP, William Ewart Esq. MP, General Sir Ronald Ferguson MP, George Grote Esq. MP, Joseph Hume Esq. MP, Lord King, Charles Lefevre Esq. MP, William Marshall Esq. MP, Honble Fox Maule MP, Sir William Molesworth Bart MP, James Morrison Esq. MP, Lord Morpeth MP, John A. Murray Esq. MP, Daniel O'Connell Esq. MP, Richard Moore O'Ferrall Esq. MP, William H. Ord Esq. MP, James Oswald Esq. MP, Joseph Parkes Esq., Honble Charles A. Pelham MP, Edward Wynn Pendarves Esq. MP, Lord Radnor, Richard Lalor Sheil Esq. MP, Edward J. Stanley Esq. MP, Edward Strutt Esq. MP, Henry Warburton Esq. MP, Henry George Ward Esq. MP . . .[103]

Edward Ellice was to host a meeting of the provisional committee at his house in Carlton House Terrace to attend to the details of forming the Club. There had been a

---

[102] L. Fagan, *The Reform Club: Its Founders and Architect* (1887), 19. Fagan claims that Disraeli was a member from 2 July 1834 to 8 February 1835, and cancelled his membership when he could not pay his bill. See also Reform Club Archives, Pall Mall, London: Sir Robert Sidney to the Reform Club Library Committee, [no date] 1873, donating the minute book of the Westminster Club, in which he says that Disraeli tried to join and was rejected. See also Michael Sharpe, *The Political Committee of the Reform Club* (1996), 7–18; W.F. Rae, 'Political Clubs and Party Organization', *Nineteenth-Century*, iii (1878), 919–20. The issue of political dinners is somewhat related to club life during this period. See Marc Baer, 'Political Dinners in Whig, Radical, and Tory Westminster, 1780–1880', in *Ideas and Institutions of Victorian Britain, Essays in Honour of George Kitson Clark*, ed. R. Robson (1967), 1–19; P. Brett, 'Political Dinners in Early Nineteenth-Century Britain', *History*, lxxxi (1996), 527–52.

[103] Reform Club Archives: memorandum on the founding of the Reform Club, 6 Feb. 1836. See also Parkes (WEST): Parkes to Durham, 7 Feb. 1836.

squabble between Ellice and Parkes over the necessity of the Club, and the form it would take, but this seems to have resolved itself one way or another for, as Parkes wrote to Durham on 1 March 1836, the Club grew quickly in its first few months. 'We have now all cordiality – the Whigs *forced* in . . . We have nearly 250 MPs and 1,000 Members'.[104]

The Reform Club was perhaps the liberals' greatest organisational success, although very little is known about its workings.[105] By May 1836, a messenger had been appointed to run back and forth to the house of commons, to report proceedings and to help the whips increase attendance.[106] By the beginning of the parliamentary session of 1837, there was a weekly parliamentary dinner for liberal MPs.[107] The 1840s saw the Club take a more direct role in political and electoral affairs. There was a central election fund at the Club, which was distributed to constituencies where it was needed.[108] And in February 1845, a political committee was formed to 'strengthen the union of the Liberal party'.

At a meeting of the Liberal Members, held at the Reform Club, on Wednesday the 12th of February 1845 (Mr. Tancred in the chair) it was resolved that a committee be appointed, to devise means by which the union of the Liberal party may be strengthened, and the efforts of Independent liberal Members in the House be supported. That the committee consist of Mr. Chas. Villiers, Mr. Ward, Mr. Duncombe, Mr. Hawes, Mr. Tancred, Mr. Hayter, Mr. Ross, with power to add to their number. That Mr. Blunt be appointed secretary to the above committee.

The committee met and recommended 'that a permanent Committee be appointed, whose business it shall be to meet at 3 o'clock on every Monday during the sitting of Parliament for the purpose of considering the Notices which have been given, of receiving communications from members, on the subject of notices, of taking necessary measures for securing the necessary attendance of members at debates, and, divisions, and of consulting generally as to the best means of promoting the objects and principles of the Liberal party. Signed Charles P. Villiers (Wolverhampton), Thomas S. Duncombe (Finsbury), B. Hawes (Lambeth), H.W. Tancred (Banbury), W.G. Hayter (Wells), H.G. Ward (Sheffield), D.R. Ross (Belfast) . . .'[109]

[104] Parkes (WEST): Parkes to Durham, 1 Mar. 1836; Reform Club Archives: Reform Club Resolution, 8 Feb. 1836, and List of Members; Sharpe, *Political Committee of the Reform Club*, 7–18. See also Gash, *Politics in the Age of Peel*, 424. The Club used Gwydyr House in Whitehall before moving to its present site in Pall Mall. See Salmon, *Electoral Reform at Work*, 53; G. Woodbridge, *The Reform Club, 1836–1978* (New York, 1978), introduction and ch. 1; T.H.S. Escott, *Club Makers and Club Members* (1914), 225; Mandler, *Aristocratic Government*, 164–5; J.C. Clarke, 'The Fortunes of the Ellice Family: From Business to Politics 1760–1860', University of Oxford PhD, 1973, 371–2.

[105] The Reform Club Archives hold little information, which may not be surprising since it may be reasonably assumed that the majority of Club business was conducted verbally.

[106] Reform Club Archives: Minutes of the General Committee of the Reform Club, 31 May 1836. The forthcoming Warwick University PhD thesis of Seth Thévoz will substantially enhance our understanding of the role played by London clubs in the whipping process.

[107] Univ. of Manchester, John Rylands Library, Fielden Papers, FDN/1/2/1 item 20: Lord Marcus Hill to John Fielden, 22 Feb. 1837.

[108] Staffordshire Record Office, Littleton Papers, D260M/F/5/26/22: diary entry, Lord Hatherton, 6 July 1841; Salmon, *Electoral Reform at Work*, 57; Gash, *Politics in the Age of Peel*, 405–6.

[109] Reform Club Archives: memorandum of the political committee of the Reform Club, 12 Feb. 1845.

Unfortunately, little is known about this committee in the 1840s.[110] There are no records of the meetings until 1869, and even those simply list the new appointees. Like whipping and parliamentary control, political club life almost disappears from the historical record for years at a time. There is very little surviving material about the Reform Club during the 1840s (except what has been noted above), and it seems that, like whipping, it settled down into the rather mundane daily operation of party politics in Westminster. But the fact that the Reform Club was maintained as the centre of liberal political life until the establishment of other liberal clubs in the 1870s implies that it must have succeeded well enough in its stated aims.[111] Further, the mere continued existence of a central club, with its political mirror at the Carlton, shows that ideas of the Liberal Party were strong enough to extend to the social sphere. By the mid 1830s, therefore, the Liberal Party was becoming a more complete entity in perception and practice.

This chapter has traced the importance of the growth of liberal organisations and institutions for ideas of a Liberal Party. Historians have been interested in the functioning of these organisations and whether they were successful. But they have not generally examined the degree of expectation displayed by those founding and running these groups. In contrast to the pre-Reform period, political organisation became deperson-alised and, to a degree, institutionalised. Those forming and organising the Reform Association, the Reform Club and local liberal and reform associations and societies sought to institutionalise their ideological differences from the Conservatives, and to present them both to MPs at Westminster and the political public, with an expectation (however unrealistic) of permanence. The whiggish notion that a reformed electorate and parliament would find its own, natural and liberal course was quickly abandoned after 1835. The realization that electoral and parliamentary politics would have to be profes-sionally run may not have resulted in strong and rigid party structures comparable to 20th- and 21st-century ones, but it did result in a marked degree of party thinking and conceptualisation. It is clear, therefore, that there were significant developments that affected the Liberal Party in terms of party labelling, the outlines of liberal politics, as well as party management. The next chapter will take this analysis one step further by showing the ideas of co-operation inside the house of commons among Liberal Party MPs in the mid 1830s.

---

[110] For subsequent decades, see Sharpe, *Political Committee.*
[111] Hanham, *Elections and Party Management,* 100–3.

Chapter 4. The Liberal Brigade, the Speakership and Lichfield House: Ideas of Co-operation among Liberal Groups in 1835

The previous chapter showed the degree of party control in London, and the extent of party communication between London and the constituencies. This chapter refocuses attention on MPs inside the house of commons. It will examine the well-known events of 1835, particularly the party struggle over the choice of Speaker in 1835, the attempts at forming a 'Liberal Brigade', and the Lichfield House meetings. Emphasis has been placed on 1835 because, as will become apparent, it was the formative year of the party. The reaction in the parliamentary party and among liberal electors to the Whig government's dismissal in 1834, and what was loosely and generally agreed to in the 1835 Lichfield meetings, taken together with the formation of central Liberal Party electoral and registration organisations and the founding of the Reform Club in 1835–6 discussed in Chapter 3, provide a good chronological dating for the beginning of the party.

The dismissal of the Whig government in November 1834 brought the liberal groups in the house of commons closer to each other, if only in a surprised reaction to such a strong move by the king.[1] The *Eclectic Review* overstated the case when it wrote in 1837 that 'the division of reformers instantly ceased. The whigs and radicals and the Irish . . . became instantly one'.[2] But the months between November 1834 and May 1835 saw liberal groups in the house of commons agree to act together on certain issues, as well as coming to a realization that common action was becoming more and more important since it appeared that the electors were not going to reward them forever for passing the Reform Act.[3] No matter how much Whig leaders were concerned that an agreement with the Radicals was politically dangerous, they were willing to agree to a sort of party unity on the issue of the dismissal, Irish church appropriation and opposition to the Speaker. For their part, the Radicals tried to form their own sub-party initially, but soon came to the conclusion that their agreement with the Whigs over these issues was enough to allow a broader alliance for the time being. O'Connell and the Repealers were in a similar position. Too small a party to get the Union repealed, they realized they had to join the Whigs if they were going to see any other Irish reforms. A.H. Graham summarized it neatly when he wrote that the liberal groups were 'driven towards each

---

[1] 'The unexpected turn out of the Ministers has so astounded the Public that neither Tories, Whigs or Radicals, have as yet recovered from the blow'. Lambeth Archives Department, Minet Library, D'Eyncourt Papers, IV/3/8: Samuel Palmer (Lambeth electioneering agent) to Charles Tennyson D'Eyncourt, 18 Nov. 1834.

[2] *Eclectic Review* (new ser., ii, 1837), 209; *The Times*, 19 Nov.–4 Dec. 1834.

[3] *The Times*, 21 Nov. 1834; D. Close, 'The General Elections of 1835 and 1837 in England and Wales', University of Oxford PhD, 1967, 43–4, 48. See also Southampton UL, Broadlands Archives Trust, Parnell Papers, bundle 15, item 24: Alexander Kay to Henry Brooke Parnell, MP for Dundee, 15 Dec. 1834.

other by their individual policy aims and the existence of a delicate balance of power in the House of Commons'.[4] And by May 1835, there was a general assumption that a Liberal Party existed in the house of commons, and that each of the groups in it owed some allegiance to the others, and to the new liberal politics.

The Liberal Brigade

As mentioned above, the original idea to have a meeting of liberal opposition groups came from the Radical camp. This is often referred to as the 'Radical Brigade', but, as will be seen in the quotations below, it should be more accurately be called the 'Liberal Brigade', since 'Radical' never appears in the existing correspondence relating to it or, more significantly, in the resolution drawn up (and reproduced in full here for the first time).[5] 'Liberal', on the other hand, appears quite often. John Hobhouse, Reformer MP for Nottingham, in conjunction with Charles Thomson, Reformer MP for Manchester, seems to have been the first to suggest a meeting of opposition MPs early in 1835. He wrote to Melbourne on 19 January 1835, saying:

> Thompson [*sic*] & myself agreed yesterday that we ought to get together all the members returned by reformed constituencies a few days previous to the session – & that the best mode of doing this would be by having a dinner – say on the 19th of Feby, the day on which the writs are returnable.

> Our plan is to write to every M.P. who can be called a Reformer telling him that such a scheme is in agitation & that if he wishes to attend he will signify his intention to Mr. Drummond at Cleveland Square.[6]

At Joseph Parkes' house on 23 January 1835, leading Radicals discussed the idea of a brigade. As Parkes reported to Durham on 26 January 1835,

> We are losing no time, for scheming measures to prevent the Opposition being a rope of sand – to head the three Sections of MPs, viz. the Whigs, the Reformers & Irish Brigade . . .

> On Tuesday we had a preliminary meeting at my house – & again on Friday. Warburton, Clay, Grote, Hawkins, Ward, Ewart, Bulwer, Ewart [*sic*] & others are scheming to form a party of 70 or 80 Reformers with their own head – the Whigs to have a head – & O'Connell to head the Irish wild men. The three heads on all important questions to arrange a combined opposition &c. &c. I think this the only practicable scheme. I have many objections. But what Whig has the power, or public confidence to be the General Leader? However we meet again on Wednesday at 12, & Joey Hume & others meet, when it will be again discussed . . .

---

[4] A.H. Graham, 'The Lichfield House Compact, 1835', *Irish Historical Studies*, xii (1961), 209–13. See also Close, 'General Elections of 1835 and 1837', 84–9; Angus Macintyre, *The Liberator: Daniel O'Connell and the Irish Party 1830–1847* (1965), 128–9.

[5] See I. Newbould, *Whiggery and Reform 1830–1841: The Politics of Government* (1990), 166, for the use of 'Radical Brigade'.

[6] J.C. Hobhouse to Melbourne, 19 Jan. 1835, quoted in A.D. Kriegel, 'The Politics of the Whigs in Opposition, 1834–1835', *Journal of British Studies*, vii (1968), 82–3.

It will be mortifying to the death if with such overwhelming numbers & talents in Opposition we cannot work out the fall of the Tories & the construction of a really liberal Ministry.[7]

Henry Warburton then reported the meeting to Henry Lytton, enclosing a copy of the resolution, which read:

It is proposed to make arrangements for holding frequent and regular meetings to be attended by Members of parliament of Liberal Politics. The great advantage of such meetings during the ensuing Session of Parliament will present themselves in a moment's reflection.

The recent elections have introduced into parliament a large body of Tories, strenuous and well-disciplined supporters of the present Ministry. It therefore behoves the Liberal Members to study, as much as possible, the means of concert and cooperation among themselves. On the extent to which such union may be found practicable, the success of the Liberal cause during the ensuing Session will greatly depend.

Considering the great diversity of opinion which prevails among various sections of Liberal Members, no successful attempt will be made to unite them all into one coherent body; nor to single out one leading person, in whom all would have the requisite degree of confidence. It is presumed that those Members who have been accustomed heretofore to consider themselves acting systematically with the Whig Party, will still retain the same intimate conjunction, both among themselves, and with the Members of the late Ministry. It is presumed, also, that a considerable body of the Irish Liberals will be, in like manner, disposed to act in union under a presiding head of their own choice. There remains, however, a large number of Liberal Members, who fall under neither of those classes; and for them, especially, the proposed meetings are intended, as means of facilitating the requisite cooperation for common public objects.

If this plan should be put in execution, the Members would, of course, choose, out of their own number, some one person to serve as an organ of communication with the other sections of the liberal body. Frequent meetings would be held for the purpose of deliberation on the course to be pursued in Parliament respecting political questions of importance. If the Members should differ in opinion, no individual could, of course, be held bound to comply with the views of the Majority when he thought it his duty to act otherwise. But though no such unconditional compliance could ever be expected, it is certain that much disagreement on minor points, and many obvious inconveniences might be avoided, by their preliminary discussion: and the whole result would be, to facilitate greatly effective and harmonious cooperation among the aggregate both of the Liberals, towards such public objects as they might jointly approve.[8]

This proposal contained the dilemma of liberal politics during the reform period. On the one hand, much is made of the need for all 'Liberal Members' to co-operate to oppose

---

[7] Parkes (WEST): Parkes to Lord Durham, 26 Jan. 1835.

[8] Norfolk RO, Bulwer Papers, BUL 1/3/52: Henry Warburton to Henry Lytton Bulwer, 24 Jan. 1835. This is the only full extant copy of this proposal that I know of, and is presented here for the first time.

the Tories, which is a distinct sign of party feeling. Some of the language of party co-operation is used: the 'union' of liberal members will be necessary for liberal success in the coming parliamentary session; meetings between the recognized liberal groups were to be held 'as means of facilitating the requisite cooperation for common public objects' and 'for the purpose of deliberation on the course to be pursued in Parliament respecting political questions of importance'; and that minor disagreements should not get in the way of co-operation on major questions. On the other hand, there is the recognition that there was a 'great diversity of opinion' among liberal MPs, and that no 'attempt will be made to unite them all into one coherent body; nor to single out one leading person, in whom all would have the requisite degree of confidence'. But the frequent use of liberal language displayed in 'Liberal Members', 'Liberal cause' and 'the liberal body' implies that, even though the Radicals made a point of emphasizing that they thought a party as unified as the Conservatives was not likely, and therefore not worth proposing, there was a strong idea of a liberal group of MPs who must act together to promote liberal measures ('the liberal cause'). Parkes wrote to Charles D'Eyncourt on 31 January 1835, stressing the proposed co-operation between the three liberal groups, referring to 'the general body':

> The whigs will be led by Lord John Russell, the ultra whigs by their hereafter to be appointed leader, the Irish brigade by King Dan. The three, as representing their different sections, to be in communication to concert opposition & prevent collisions and follies in the general body. All those already communicated with approve this 'scheme of governmt'.[9]

Further, Warburton wrote again to Bulwer on 4 February 1835 that he had signed up an additional 35 MPs who were willing to join the proposed 'Liberal Brigade':

> My Dear Sir,
>
> I send you the list of 35 Members, who have sent in their adhesion to the proposed plan of a Liberal Brigade.
>
> The names, as you will see, are highly respectable. I propose calling on you tomorrow, to ask you to look over the list of the most likely to join us; and to beg you, if you know any of them to apply to them on the subject.[10]

Progress toward a 'Liberal Brigade' was pre-empted by Russell, who decided to attend the already arranged meeting at Lord Lichfield's house and took charge of it.[11]

The Speakership and Lichfield House

On 29 January 1833, Richard Potter, Radical MP for Wigan, wrote in his diary that he voted in the Speakership contest for E.J. Littleton, Whig MP for South Staffordshire, over

---

[9] Lincolnshire Archives Office, D'Eyncourt Papers, TDE H31/10: Parkes to Charles Tennyson D'Eyncourt, 31 Jan. 1835.

[10] Norfolk RO, Bulwer Papers, BUL 1/3/53: Warburton to Bulwer, 4 Feb. 1835. Unfortunately, the enclosed list is not extant.

[11] See Newbould, *Whiggery and Reform*, 166–7.

Charles Manners-Sutton, Conservative MP for Cambridge University and the current Speaker of the house of commons, 'on several grounds, first that we ought rather to have a man of liberal opinions than a rank Tory'.[12] And even though the Whig MP Richard Slaney expressed the views of many moderate Whigs and Reformers when he wrote to Spring-Rice by the end of that year that 'The greatest *party* questions are now settled',[13] Whig leaders, and many Radicals, used party mechanisms and party language two years later to organise a successful opposition to Manners-Sutton, in an expression of their anger and feelings of impropriety over the 1834 dismissal.[14] Further, Manners-Sutton was seen as hardly a neutral speaker when it came to the formation of ministries. He had approached Wellington in May 1832, volunteering to help form a Tory administration. Although 'Grey forgave him for this', Manners-Sutton then attended privy council meetings in November 1834 which led to the Whig government's dismissal. This was going too far, and if Grey was reluctant to claim that this was a question of principle, Russell and Melbourne were not.[15] The Speakership contest was, therefore, an immediate rebuke to the king for what were seen as his unconstitutional actions.

The combined effort to oust Manners-Sutton was the first in a series of individual agreements that eventually led to a sort of coalition of liberals in 1835. On the surface, the argument against Manners-Sutton was that he was partial in his selection of speakers during house of commons debates. Parkes was perhaps the most critical of the way Manners-Sutton exercised his duties during sittings. He wrote to Charles D'Eyncourt, Radical MP for Lambeth:

> He is not impartial in the chair; he is not courteous . . . Have you never seen him call up just that wild Irishman [O'Connell] . . . who he knew would spoil a Liberal Debate, & see a tory where he could not discern a Liberal? Have you never seen or heard of his treating men who he did not approve like dogs? Why do the Tories saddle and bridle such an old plate horse again? Because he will suit their present party purpose by stopping out a Liberal Speaker.[16]

Other liberals were less stringent, but still displeased, arguing that Manners-Sutton generally chose the best Conservative orator, and the worst liberal, whenever he could.[17] In a leader on 30 January 1835, the *Morning Chronicle* wrote:

[12] British Library of Political and Economic Science, London, Potter Papers, Coll. Misc. 146: diary entry, 29 Jan. 1833.

[13] National Library of Ireland, Monteagle Papers, MS 13,372, folder 15, item 6: Richard Slaney to Thomas Spring-Rice, 9 Dec. 1833.

[14] See Southampton UL, Parnell Papers, bundle 15, item 24: Alexander Kay to Henry Brooke Parnell, MP for Dundee, 15 Dec. 1834.

[15] J. Prest, *Lord John Russell* (1972), 86–7.

[16] Lincolnshire Archives Office, D'Eyncourt Papers, TDE H31/10: Parkes to Charles Tennyson D'Eyncourt, 31 Jan. 1835.

[17] For example, see James Grant's description of Manners-Sutton in his *Random Recollections of the House of Commons from the Year 1830 to the Close of 1835, including Personal Sketches of the Leading Members of All Parties, by One of No Party* (1836), 15. Although Grant calls himself 'One of No Party' in the full title of this book, he was clearly a Whig journalist, writing for the *Morning Chronicle*. See also *The Literary Companion to Parliament*, ed. Christopher Silvester (1996), 83, 209–11, 313–14, 356–9, 503–6 for handy extracts of Grant's reporting.

whoever votes for Sir Charles Sutton is no Reformer. He may not call himself a Tory; but it would be far better that he were; as the man who has not sense to discover the folly of wavering on the question of this nature, only injures the cause he professes to support. It ought to be a sufficient reason with all good Reformers, to vote against Sir Charles Sutton, that the Tory Ministry have this object greatly at heart. That must be strange policy which benefits the Tories benefits the Reformers at the same time.[18]

The chronology of the Speakership contest is well known, but presented here for the first time are some of the challenges faced by liberal backbenchers when discussing the liberal plans with leaders and with their constituents, and the importance of this new material for the history of the formation of the Liberal Party.[19] Radical MPs had been eager since 1833 to replace Manners-Sutton, but Whig leaders had been less willing to take such a bold step, which had never been done before on a party basis.[20] Thomas Spring-Rice, Whig MP for Cambridge, had been interested in the post since 1833, but had consistently been talked out of it. In late 1834 and early 1835, he let it be known among his Whig friends that he would like the position. Spencer wrote to him on 18 January 1835, trying to dissuade him: 'I am surprised I own that you should choose to lower yourself to so faceless an office as that of Speaker, standing as high as you do at the present time'.[21] There were many reasons for Whig leaders to dissuade Spring-Rice from standing. He was considered one of the most able, and most constitutional, Whigs in the house of commons.[22] Further, the Radicals would never have voted for him. The realization by the Whigs that the Radicals must be courted was a very significant step in the formation of the Liberal Party coalition, and Russell especially began to court liberal backbenchers. The preferred candidate of the Radicals and Reformers, James Abercromby, Whig MP for Edinburgh, was chosen, and a campaign to get him elected was begun. It was clear that Stanley and his followers would not vote against Sutton. This was not a surprise to Russell, but Grey had hoped that the Stanleyites might return one day.[23]

Melbourne and Russell had discussed the difficulties of courting Irish and Radical support, with Melbourne initially refusing to have anything to do with Brougham, Durham or O'Connell. Eventually, Melbourne agreed that the whips should send out letters for a meeting to oppose Manners-Sutton.[24] In a circular letter to liberal MPs, dated 31 January 1835, Russell wrote:

---

[18] *Morning Chronicle*, 30 Jan. 1835.

[19] For the Speakership, see Prest, *Lord John Russell*, 87–90; Newbould, *Whiggery and Reform*, 164–81; P. Mandler, *Aristocratic Government in the Age of Reform: Whigs and Liberals, 1830–1852* (Oxford, 1990), 159–60; T.A. Jenkins, *The Liberal Ascendancy, 1830–1886* (1994), 23–4; W.E.S. Thomas, *The Philosophical Radicals: Nine Studies in Theory and Practice, 1817–1841* (Oxford, 1979), 274–6.

[20] Newbould, *Whiggery and Reform*, 161.

[21] National Library of Ireland, Monteagle Papers, MS 13,379: Spencer to Spring-Rice, 18 Jan. 1835. Spring-Rice had been at the treasury under Althorp, was a central figure in the Whig administration and would become chancellor of the exchequer in April 1835 under Melbourne.

[22] National Library of Ireland, Monteagle Papers, MS 13,379: Viscount Howick to Thomas Spring-Rice, 24 Jan. 1835. In this letter, Howick told Spring-Rice that he was one 'of those few remaining persons who can lead the constitutional Whigs'.

[23] Prest, *Lord John Russell*, 86.

[24] Prest, *Lord John Russell*, 87–8.

My Dear Sir,

We have determined, as you will see, on trying the question of the speakership, & I found the wishes of our friends so strongly in favour of Abercromby, to whom I had spoken on the subject a few days after the dissolution of the late ministry, that I would not hesitate to press him again upon that to acquiesce.

It was quite impossible to re-elect Sutton without a Division. His failure of duty has been glaring. I hope you will attend.[25]

Sir Matthew Ridley, Whig MP for Newcastle-upon-Tyne, replied that he could not vote against Manners-Sutton, which prompted Grey's son, Lord Howick, to write to him to urge voting for Abercromby. This is a very significant letter, because it shows that Howick was uneasy with the idea of combining with the Radicals and Repealers, but that he was going to vote for Abercromby on party grounds (however much he disliked it), and that Ridley should do the same. The postscript gives the strongest sense of this:

I am not quite sure that I think the policy of bringing him [Abercromby] forward was very good, but of this it is now too late to think, the step having been taken, it wd I fear do very great mischief if the liberal party were to be shewn so weak as not to be able to carry their candidate. You must not presume because I say this that I am one of those who are prepared to go into headlong & factious opposition, & to make common cause with Hume, O'Connell & Co. I will do no such thing; . . . This is the view by which my conduct shall be governed though at the same time I shall avoid most carefully anything which I consider factious, & shall take the earliest opportunity of expressing my undiminished dislike to O'Connell . . . It seems to me that if the really conscientious & constitutional Whigs were to shrink from opposing the present Govt, the necessary consequence wd be that we shd drive into the ranks of the radicals all those people (& they are very numerous) who unite moderate views as to measures with a rooted distrust of, & eager hostility to the men now in power. Pray excuse this long & rambling letter & allow me to hope that we shall meet & vote on the same side on the 19th. I am going to town tomorrow. [PS] Pray burn this. It is only meant for your eye or I shd not have said so plainly what I think of persons with whom we are acting. I forgot to say that if you feel an objection to voting for Abercromby I hope you will not think it necessary to come up in opposition to all those with whom you have so long acted.[26]

O'Connell's reply to Russell's invitation was enthusiastic. He wrote:

the Irish members of the popular party will avoid all topics on which they differ from you and your friends *until the tories are routed*, and that you will find us perfectly ready to co-operate in any place which your friends deem most advisable to effect that purpose. In short, we *will be steady allies* without any mutiny in your camp.[27]

---

[25] Northumberland RO, Ridley Papers, ZRI 25/75: Speakership whip from Russell to Matthew White Ridley, 31 Jan. 1835.

[26] Northumberland RO, Ridley Papers, ZRI 25/75: Lord Howick to Sir Matthew White Ridley, 12 Feb. 1835.

[27] Graham, 'Lichfield House Compact', 218.

The excitement in political circles built up greatly in mid February, and was even felt in Paris, where Thomas Raikes wrote in his journal: 'Party spirit rages with great violence throughout society in London. The disappointed Whigs are ready for any measures which may perplex the Duke's government, and are publicly coalescing with the Radicals to turn them out'.[28]

At the first Lichfield House meeting on 18 February 1835, Whig leaders had clearly not intended for there to be an overt discussion of future co-operation. Russell turned the agenda away from a potential discussion of a union of liberal groups, and towards the specific issues of the Speakership, the dissolution, the church of Ireland, English dissenters and English corporations.[29] He took charge of the meeting, and asked MPs to vote for Abercromby, but not to cheer if he was successful. The meeting was a success, and Manners-Sutton was defeated the next day in the house of commons by 318 to 308.[30]

According to Dr John Allen,

> Abercromby has been elected Speaker by a majority of 316 to 306. Stanley and his friends voted against him. Several persons calling themselves Reformers voted the same way. How many I cannot say. Of the members who were absent and did not vote, the Morning Chronicle reckons 25 Reformers and 7 Tories, which with the two Tellers and one pair during the debates makes up the whole of the House. Burdett had determined till this morning to attend and vote for Sutton, but was persuaded by Otway Cave to stay away. Of the Scotch reformers Sinclair and Agnew voted for Sutton, McTaggart staid [sic] away.[31]

Joseph Brotherton, Radical MP for Salford, reported the success of all this to J.B. Smith, crowing: 'You see what *union* will do!'[32] As Table 4.1 shows, the Liberal Party votes in favour of Abercromby were overwhelming: 87.6% voted for him, and 12.4% for Manners-Sutton. The most significant numbers of Manners-Sutton supporters, on the opposition benches, came from the reformers, where a good many conservative-leaning MPs called themselves 'moderate Reformers'.

There were two more Lichfield House meetings to come after the one in which the Speakership opposition was decided, which have generally been overlooked. These subsequent meetings were lesser in stature and immediate political importance than the first, but

[28] T. Raikes, *A Portion of the Journal Kept by Thomas Raikes, Esq, from 1831 to 1847* (1856), 71–2, journal entry, 16 Feb. 1835.

[29] Newbould, *Whiggery and Reform*, 166; Prest, *Lord John Russell*, 188–90.

[30] As with all divisions in this book, this includes tellers and pairs. The numbers of this division are generally reported as 316 to 306, Hansard, *Parl. Debs*, xxvi, cols 56–61 (19 Feb. 1835). See also Graham, 'Lichfield House Compact', 216–19; Diary of Dr John Allen, 18 [Feb. 1835], in *The Holland House Diaries 1831–1840*, ed. A.D. Kriegel (1977), 278; Prest, *Lord John Russell*, 87.

[31] 19 [Feb. 1835], *Holland House Diaries*, ed. Kriegel, 279. According to the *Morning Chronicle*, the 'Reformers Absent' on the Speakership contest were: Belfast, earl of; Bennett, John; Burdett, Sir F.; Campbell, W.F.; Clements, Lord; Cobbett, W.; Colbourne, N.W.R.; Dillwyn, L.W.; Ellice, Edward; Ferguson, Robt; Fielden, John; Glynnes, Sir; Howard, Ralph; Johnstone, Sir J.W.B.; Lennox, Lord Arthur; M'Taggart, John; Milton, Lord; Ponsonby, J.G.B.; Pryse, Pryse; Sanford, E.A.; Scott, Sir E.D.; Smith, R.J.; Smith, J.A.; Stuart, Lord James; Talbot, Chr. R.M. The 'Anti-Reformers Absent' were: Calcraft, J.H.; Cartwright, W.R.; Knightley, Sir Chas; Pechell, G.R.; Pollen, Sir John; Pollington, Lord; Walpole, Lord. Paired off for – Langton, W. Gore. Paired off against – Wynn, Sir W.W. *Morning Chronicle*, 20 Feb. 1835.

[32] Manchester Central Library, John Benjamin Smith Papers, MS 923.2 S.334, item 85: Joseph Brotherton to J.B. Smith, 27 Feb. 1835. See also *Reflections on the O'Connell 'Alliance' or Lichfield House Conspiracy* (1836).

Table 4.1: *Division on the Speakership, 19 February 1835*

Liberal Party groups	Abercromby	Sutton
Administration	3	1
Liberals	1	0
Radicals	38	1
Reformers	123	34
Repealers	24	0
Whigs	107	9
None listed	22	0
All Liberal Party	318	45
Conservative Party	0	263
Totals	318	308

Source: Hansard, *Parl. Debs*, xxvi, cols 56–61 (19 Feb. 1835); *The Times*, 20 Feb. 1835.
Note: The Liberal Party groups are taken from the relevant *Dod's Parliamentary Companion* volumes, a convention adopted for all division tables in this book.

their significance lies in the fact that there was more than one meeting simply to oust the Speaker, and that, with each meeting that agreed on opposition strategies to Peel's government, there was a drift towards an increased assumption of common action among liberal groups. The purpose of the second meeting on 12 March 1835 was to decide what to do about Hume's motion on naval supplies. After a lengthy discussion, Hume was convinced to withdraw his motion, and the group agreed that, if Russell's forthcoming appropriation motion succeeded (see Chapter 5), the Liberal Party would press a motion of no confidence. Clearly, Hume was eventually willing to withdraw his motion for party ends, and a party strategy was agreed upon. At the third and final meeting on 23 March 1835, they agreed that liberal MPs would support Russell's appropriation motion.[33]

Perhaps the most symbolic evidence of the party effects of the Lichfield House meetings was the fact that O'Connell and his party moved to sit behind the reinstated Whig ministry on 18 April 1835. Since the opening of the 1833 session, some Radicals and most Repealers had continually sat on the opposition benches. O'Connell, in fact, moved the opposition to the reply to the king's speech in 1833. Sir George Hayter's famous painting of the 1833 house of commons shows this clearly.[34] James Grant, also, noted that 'a few members of the extreme Radical Party . . . never change their seats . . . because no men sufficiently liberal for them have ever been in office'.[35] But after O'Connell's agreements made at the Lichfield House meetings, and after the success in ousting Peel, he accepted that alliance with Russell and the Whigs, and the general acceptance of a liberal coalition.[36] The Repealers, and most Radicals, then moved across the floor of the house of commons and sat behind the Whig ministry.[37]

[33] See Graham, 'Lichfield House Compact', *passim*, esp. 221–2.
[34] Sir George Hayter, *The House of Commons, 1833* (1833–43), National Portrait Gallery, Reg. No. 54.
[35] Grant, *Random Recollections*, 4.
[36] Macintyre, *The Liberator*, 128–9; Graham, 'Lichfield House Compact', 223.
[37] Graham, 'Lichfield House Compact', 223; Grant, *Random Recollections*, 5.

Angus Macintyre wrote that 'The making of the Lichfield House Compact was one of the most decisive events in British political history between 1832 and 1847', and the emphasis should be placed on the 'making' rather than the 'Compact' itself. 'Compact' was applied by the Tories to damage the Whig government by trying to tar them with associating with Radicals and O'Connell. There was no official agreement in the sense of a written compact at the Lichfield meetings. But the 'making', in terms of the initial scramble by Russell and the Whigs to take control of what they saw as a growing group of liberal MPs willing to join the Liberal Brigade, and the step-by-step strategies to overthrow Peel based on political opportunities, was unprecedented in liberal politics since 1830.[38] The Lichfield House meetings were never intended to have the ultimate significance that they eventually gained. They became important because the grouping together for specific parliamentary ends was the beginning of a drift towards greater co-operation.

The other major effect of the events of January and February 1835 was that they indicated to liberal constituents and MPs that a strategy of inclusion for liberal groups would dictate the party's action in government and, potentially, in opposition. Some constituents found this unacceptable and, in one case, even unnatural. Robert Hankinson wrote to his MP Sir William Ffolkes, Whig MP for West Norfolk, deploring the partisan nature of the Speakership contest: 'this opposition to the late Speaker (qualified in respect for the office) is founded on faction, – on an unnatural alliance between the Whigs and Radicals, formed for no other purpose but to oust the present ministers'.[39] The Reverend W. Leigh wrote to E.J. Littleton that he thought an alliance with O'Connell 'would prove fatal to the [Whig] Administration'.[40] Priscilla Johnston, wife of Alexander Johnston, Whig MP for St Andrew's District, and daughter of Sir Thomas Buxton, Whig MP for Weymouth and Melcombe Regis, wrote to her younger brothers, saying that things would be much easier for Russell and the Whigs 'if a few of their friends would but die', and listed Hume, Warburton and O'Connell as among those whose demise 'would wonderfully help'.[41] And for W.H. Hyett, Whig MP for Stroud, an alliance with Radicals and Repealers was enough for him to leave the party and concentrate on local politics. He wrote to a friend: 'no one likes to feel himself forced to cut the last link that bound him to a party . . . [but] I cannot overcome the conviction that Lord John Russell as the leader of his Party has adopted a mode of opposition in every way wrong'.[42] Hyett became an important local politician in Gloucestershire, and eventually drifted to the Tories.

The period 1833–7 also saw the drift of other Whigs and moderate Reformers to the Conservative party. This was owing to several factors: unhappiness with the extent of the

---

[38] Macintyre, *The Liberator*, 144–5; N. Gash, *Reaction and Reconstruction in English Politics, 1832–1852* (Oxford, 1965), 168–70.

[39] Norfolk RO, Ffolkes Papers, NRS 8740/21/D/4: Robert Hankinson to Sir William Browne Ffolkes, 18 Feb. 1835.

[40] Staffordshire RO, Littleton Papers, D260/M/F/5/27/11/17: Rev. W. Leigh to E.J. Littleton, 12 Apr. 1835; see also D260/M/F/27/11/19: John Howells to E.J. Littleton, 14 Apr. 1835, where he warns Littleton that alliance with O'Connell would damage his election chances.

[41] Bodl., Buxton Papers, MS Britain Emp. s444, xvi, 445: Priscilla Johnston to her brothers, 11 Apr. 1835.

[42] Gloucestershire RO, Hyett Papers, D6/F32/f. 89: draft of letter from W.H. Hyett, 13 May 1835 [recipient not evident].

1832 Reform Act, the seeming unwillingness of the Whig cabinet to resist pressures for further reforms,[43] and proposals to appropriate Irish church revenues.[44] And, as we have seen, alliance with O'Connell, however temporary, proved too much for some MPs. Robert Stewart has estimated that at least 41 MPs had left the liberal coalition and joined the Conservatives by 1837.[45] Ridding itself of those unwilling to brook co-operation with the Radicals and the Irish at any price, the emerging Liberal Party found it even easier to assume co-operation as the 1830s and 1840s progressed. Combined with the loss of the Derby Dilly, this would ensure fewer difficulties from the more conservative elements on the liberal side of the House.

While the ideas of co-operation among liberal groups in 1835 did not result in a tight and disciplined Liberal Party in the modern sense of the word, they clearly provided the impetus for the beginnings of the parliamentary party. Further, the emphasis placed on co-operation among liberals was highly significant. Some Whig, Reformer, Radical and Repealer MPs looked to 'liberal' as an umbrella term for an idea of party, which they could huddle under when necessary. Others clearly thought that greater direct co-operation was both needed and desirable. Either way, the strength of this *idea* of liberal co-operation lends a good deal of weight to the overall argument that ideas of the Liberal Party were central to liberal politics in this period.

---

[43] M. Brock, *The Great Reform Act* (1973), 315.

[44] See Chapter 5.

[45] R. Stewart, *The Foundation of the Conservative Party 1830–1867* (1978), 108–9, 110–18. See also his appendix 2 (374–5) for Conservative gains in the house of commons 1833–7, and appendix 3 (376–7) for Stanley's own list of members of the Derby Dilly. Of the 'Reformers who became Conservatives, 1833–1837' Stewart lists on p. 374, several seem to have stayed in the Liberal Party, according to *Dod's Parliamentary Companion*, and others are questionable. These include: Lord A. Chichester (Belfast) who was a Whig from 1833 to 1835; R. Godson (Kidderminster) who remained a Reformer until 1842; G. Granville Harcourt (Oxfordshire) who was a moderate Reformer until 1842; W. Hughes Hughes (Oxford) who was a moderate Reformer from 1832 to 1837, when he left the House; J. Pemberton Plumptre (Kent East) who remained a moderate Reformer from 1833 to 1837; and S. Spry (Bodmin) who was a moderate Reformer from 1833 to 1835, a Reformer from 1836 to 1838, and Administration from 1839 to 1840.

Part 2: Liberal Agendas in Conflict and Consensus: Ideas, Issues, Language and Behaviour among Liberal Party MPs 1832–52

Chapter 5. Appropriation and the Formation of the Parliamentary Liberal Party

If Part 1 was about the 'structures' of party, and the ways in which those structures were constructed and presented, Part 2 is about 'issues'. It analyses the ways in which Liberal Party MPs behaved both in terms of applying liberal politics to specific questions, and how they moved through the division lobbies, that is, acting as a party in the most fundamental manner – voting together. There are many issues that could have been included here, including the secret ballot, various centralisation concerns, and education, but Part 2 will concentrate on Ireland, reform of the church of England, and free trade, because of the clear expressions of (and disagreements over) liberal politics on these matters. This chapter will examine the party dynamics of political language and voting in divisions during the debates over the appropriation of the excess revenues of the church of Ireland. Parry has suggested that MPs' behaviour on appropriation 'was probably the most important single step in the formation of the Liberal party'.[1] Throughout the 'appropriation parliaments',[2] Liberal Party backbenchers played a crucial role in keeping the issue alive in debate. Their support was also carefully weighed in the calculations and party management strategies Whig leaders had to employ to retain parliamentary support. In 1833, Charles Wood, who succeeded Ellice as party whip, counted heads to inform Stanley that between 200 and 250 liberal MPs supported appropriation, depending on the extent of any government proposal.[3] Further, the direct action of backbenchers themselves was crucial. They tabled appropriation motions at various times between 1833 and 1838, usually trying to force a more resolute application of church funds to general purposes than the government was willing to accept. They also kept the issue alive by presenting petitions.

Reform of the church of Ireland (in the 1830s and late 1860s) has been discussed and interpreted in terms of cabinet politics, nascent Liberal Party ideology, religion and Irish affairs. 'Appropriation', shorthand for the application of the surplus revenues of the church of Ireland to other purposes, such as education, has not been ignored in the works that deal with the 1830s. Various high political aspects of the controversies, such as the reaction of the Irish party, cabinet divisions and resignations in 1834, and the potential Lords–Commons clash over the larger issue of church disestablishment, have all been well discussed.[4] But, although their contributions and actions have been recognized,

---

[1] J.P. Parry, *The Rise and Fall of Liberal Government in Victorian Britain* (New Haven, CT, 1993), 108.

[2] John Prest, *Lord John Russell* (1972), 115.

[3] Wood to Stanley, 5 Jan. 1833, cited in R. Brent, *Liberal Anglican Politics: Whiggery, Religion, and Reform, 1830–1841* (Oxford, 1987), 73.

[4] For cabinet politics, see especially I. Newbould, *Whiggery and Reform, 1830–1841: The Politics of Government* (1990), 86–9; Prest, *Lord John Russell*, 112–17. See also M. Condon, 'The Irish Church and the Reform Ministries', *Journal of British Studies*, iii (1964), 120–42; Angus Macintyre, *The Liberator: Daniel O'Connell and the*

the role Liberal Party backbenchers played in the parliamentary struggle over these issues, and the question of whether they displayed party feeling or loyalty, has not received adequate attention.[5] The purpose of this chapter is to fill this gap in an otherwise much-discussed field. It will show how MPs who sat on the liberal side of the Commons reacted to Irish church reform proposals as members of a forming Liberal Party. It will focus on the increase in Liberal Party voting cohesion over appropriation, the use of appropriation as a defining issue for liberal MPs, and the employment of 'liberal' language. There were several areas where liberals disagreed on Irish church reform, as will be shown. This chapter, however, is concerned with the points of agreement, and whether these came from a similar sense of liberal politics, which, combined with common action in divisions, is enough to consider the liberals a viable party in the contemporary 1830s meaning of the term. The question addressed will be whether appropriation was a staging post in the formation of the pre-Gladstonian Liberal Party, as Lord John Russell thought, and as Parry has argued.[6]

The Nature and Make-Up of the Church of Ireland

An understanding of the nature and make-up of the church of Ireland is necessary for what will be discussed here. The church of Ireland was the established anglican church in Ireland, joined to the church of England under the Act of Union, which took effect in 1801. The doctrine and personnel of the church of Ireland were the same as that of the church of England, and Irish church prelates sat in the house of lords alongside English prelates.[7] According to a census taken for the Commission on Public Instruction in Ireland, there were 852,064 members of the church of Ireland in 1835.[8] The religious census of Ireland, however, shows how small a proportion the church of Ireland made in the overall population. The same census in 1835 gave the figures shown in Table 5.1. The church of Ireland represented just over 10% of the population, whereas the catholic church represented 81% (and the total non-anglican percentage was 89%).[9] The church

---

[4] *(continued)* *Irish Party 1830–1847* (1965); J.P. Parry, *Democracy and Religion: Gladstone and the Liberal Party, 1867–1875* (Cambridge, 1986), 261–88. For an interesting analysis of the church of Ireland and the Oxford Movement, see P. Nockles, 'Church or Protestant Sect? The Church of Ireland, High Churchmanship, and the Oxford Movement, 1822–1869', *HJ*, xli (1998), 457–93.

[5] A brief acknowledgment of the importance of backbenchers is given in Brent, *Liberal Anglican Politics*, 77.

[6] Parry, *Rise and Fall of Liberal Government*, 108.

[7] D.H. Akenson, *The Church of Ireland: Ecclesiastical Reform and Revolution, 1800–1885* (New Haven, CT, 1971), introduction; Condon, 'Irish Church', 121. There were four seats for Irish prelates (one archbishop and three bishops) and 26 seats for English prelates (two archbishops and 24 bishops).

[8] T.H. Lister, 'State of the Irish Church', *Edinburgh Review*, lxi (1835), 494. This figure, which Lister took from the Report of the Commission of Public Instruction (Ireland), 1835, includes wesleyan methodists, who would not have been included in an English census. The Lister article is excellent for a description of the church of Ireland and statistics relating to it. See also Condon, 'Irish Church', 120. Caution must be used when reading pre-Famine Irish demographic statistics, since their accuracy has been questioned. In this instance, the individual categories may vary slightly in accuracy, but the significance is to be found in the percentage of church of Ireland adherents compared with other Irish religions.

[9] Lister, 'State of the Irish Church', 495–6. The census goes on to state that the proportion of church of Ireland members to those of other religions was 1 to 4¼. The proportion of all protestants to catholics was also 1 to 4¼.

Table 5.1: *Religious Affiliation in Ireland, 1835*

Overall population of Ireland	7,943,940
Religious affiliations:	
Church of Ireland	852,064
Roman catholic	6,427,712
Presbyterian	642,356
Other protestant dissenters	21,808

Source: Lister, 'State of the Irish Church', 494.

of Ireland's revenue in 1835 was considered to be around £800,000 p.a., which came mainly from tithes, revenue from land confiscated in the 16th and 17th centuries and an Irish church rate (called a 'cess').[10]

The major grievances against the state of the church of Ireland were that its revenue came from the entire population (overwhelmingly non-anglican), and that there were many parishes in which no religious duties were performed, even though money was collected in them. In Britain as well as Ireland, this seemed like a glaring injustice. William Ord, Reformer MP for Newcastle-upon-Tyne, told his constituents in 1834: 'I look upon a great, rich, ecclesiastical establishment, in the midst of a people having another faith, to be a political absurdity'.[11] Various ideas for correcting it had been discussed since 1829.[12] In the 1830s, Whig leaders proposed appropriating revenue beyond the amount the Church needed to fulfil its ecclesiastical duties, and put it towards more general purposes, including funding the Irish National Board of Education, set up in 1831. The idea behind this was that church property was held in trust to perform certain duties. Whenever there was money not directed towards this end, parliament had a responsibility to see that it was used in the terms of a national institution, providing guidance and education for the population.[13]

While proponents of this reform thought it necessary for some measure of justice, and to preserve the anglican church establishment in Ireland by removing a grievance held against it, opponents of such reforms thought that the end result would be to destroy the church of Ireland, and eventually the church of England. They stressed that, since Ireland was in union with Britain, the overall majority of the United Kingdom was protestant, and the establishment should reflect that. Before the church of Ireland could be treated differently from the church of England, the union would have to be dissolved.[14] Spring-Rice thought that linking the defence of the church of England to the church of Ireland was illogical and impractical. 'To defend York and Canterbury', he wrote to Sir Richard Musgrave, Reformer MP for Waterford County, 'a battle ought to be fought in

[10] Condon, 'Irish Church', 121–2.

[11] Northumberland RO, Ord Papers, NRO 324/A, 69: electoral address, 22 Dec. 1834.

[12] R.W. Davis, 'The Whigs and Religious Issues, 1830–1835', in *Religion and Irreligion in Victorian Society: Essays in Honor of R.K. Webb*, ed. R.W. Davis and R.J. Helmstadter (1992), 32–3.

[13] Brent, *Liberal Anglican Politics*, 65–6.

[14] See Sir James Graham's speech in the house of commons, Hansard, *Parl. Debs*, xxvii, cols 426–8 (30 Mar. 1835).

a better position than in Connemara'.[15] Other political opponents of Irish church reform thought it was simply party political manoeuvring for the whigs to retain their parliamentary strength by courting Radical and Irish members.[16] Connected to the appropriation issue was the question of tithes and tithe commutation in Ireland. But while tithe reform, and the various efforts to end the 'tithe war' in Ireland through coercion, were important issues in the 1830s, the question of appropriation is more suitable to an analysis of the formation of the Liberal Party because it was the idea of a redistribution of church of Ireland wealth that made it a defining issue for Liberal Party politics. Tithes could never be as important for the Liberal Party because they were a topic only addressed as a reform for Ireland. Appropriation, on the other hand, addressed many aspects of liberal politics, including the nature of the constitution, church establishment and national institutions, as well as Irish reform.

Parliamentary Action on Irish Church Reform

After the struggle for parliamentary reform in 1832, and before the rise and threat of larger social movements in the 1840s, Irish church reform was at the forefront of parliamentary debate. Whig cabinets split over the issue in 1833, it contributed greatly to the dismissal of the Whig government in 1834, Peel's first ministry fell over it in 1835 and the reappointed Whig government struggled with it until 1838.[17] Although there had been proposals to reform Irish church revenues before the Reform Act, it was not until late 1832 that the Whig cabinet took up the issue in earnest.[18] Stanley proposed mild reforms that would reduce the number of 'empty' parishes, place Irish church revenues into the hands of a commission and make minor reforms in the way the Church handled its finances.[19] The cabinet split in its reaction to Stanley's proposal between those who thought the plans did not go far enough (Althorp, Durham, Russell, Anglesey), and those who thought that these mild reforms were all they could expect to pass both houses of parliament (Grey, Stanley, Richmond, Graham). But the election in 1832 brought in MPs interested in pushing Irish church reform further than Stanley wanted it to go. Althorp told Grey that, unless the government took a strong lead on Ireland, the backbenches would rebel.[20] In the new session of parliament in 1833, therefore, Althorp introduced the Whig government's Irish Church Temporalities Bill (which was mainly the work of Stanley), and he stressed its structural reforms.[21] The Bill

---

[15] National Library of Ireland, Monteagle Papers, MS 13,375, folder 13, item 5: Spring-Rice to Musgrave, 30 Jan. 1833.

[16] Brent, *Liberal Anglican Politics*, 66–7; A.D. Kriegel, 'The Politics of the Whigs in Opposition, 1834–1835', *Journal of British Studies*, vii (1968), 85–6.

[17] Macintyre, *The Liberator*, xv.

[18] Davis, 'Whigs and Religious Issues', 32.

[19] Condon, 'Irish Church', 125–7.

[20] Prest, *Lord John Russell*, 59.

[21] G.I.T. Machin, *Politics and the Churches in Great Britain, 1832–1868* (Oxford, 1977), 32–3. The changes proposed were: the abolition of ten sees out of 22, reducing two archbishoprics to bishoprics, to cease appointments to parishes where three years had passed without a service, to remove the Irish church rate, to tax clerical incomes over £200, to reduce the wealth of Armagh and Derry (the richest sees), and other minor changes.

included a mild sort of appropriation, but Althorp specifically did not rule out the possibility of further appropriation in future.[22] The House reacted calmly at first, but as Althorp outlined the details of the Bill, especially the abolition of the cess (the Irish church rate) and the dissolution of ten bishoprics, hearty cheers and applause flowed from liberal groups.[23] Ultra-conservative churchmen expressed great fear that this was simply the first step in destroying the Church establishment as a whole.[24] 'The tories are in a great rage against what they call indecent precipitancy', Joseph Brotherton, Radical MP for Salford, wrote to J.B. Smith after the first reading.[25]

It was not long, however, before the question of the degree of appropriation was brought up in the House. On 1 April 1833, William Gillon, Radical MP for Falkirk, announced that he would move an amendment in committee to the effect that surplus Irish church revenue should be appropriated for the purposes of 'general utility'.[26] Although his motion failed during the committee stage, the tenor of debate around it heightened concerns about the government's appropriation proposals.[27] In this atmosphere, and with cabinet concerns that the Bill's appropriation clause[28] would drag the rest of the Bill down with it (if not in the house of commons then certainly in the house of lords), Stanley moved to drop appropriation from the Bill. Arguing that there was much-needed reform contained elsewhere in the measure, he stressed that it was more important that the rest of the Bill should not be lost on this point.[29] Clause 147 was the most controversial aspect of Stanley's Irish Church Temporalities Bill. Although Stanley was opposed to parliamentary interference with existing church property, he accepted the mild form of appropriation contained in Clause 147.[30] The problem for the cabinet was that 147 seemed to contain the principle of appropriation, or at least that was the interpretation that appropriation-minded MPs placed on it during the Bill's debate. When faced with potential opposition from the Lords and the king, the cabinet decided to amend the clause and reduce its immediate effect, but Stanley was able to engineer its withdrawal.[31] On 21 June 1833, therefore, Stanley announced to the House that the government would omit Clause 147. His arguments in support of this were that the amount of money that would have been redistributed under its provision was not that great, and that, even without it, the Bill was a great relief to the Irish people (particularly

---

[22] Hansard, *Parl. Debs*, xv, col. 576 (12 Feb. 1833).

[23] E.A. Wasson, *Whig Renaissance: Lord Althorp and the Whig Party 1782–1845* (New York, 1987), 279–80; Condon, 'Irish Church', 128–9.

[24] Machin, *Politics and the Churches*, 33.

[25] Manchester Central Library, John Benjamin Smith Papers, MS 923.2 S.333, ii, item 177: J. Brotherton to J.B. Smith, 11 Mar. 1833.

[26] Hansard, *Parl. Debs*, xvii, col. 138 (21 Apr. 1833). In his words, 'the revenues of the Church of Ireland should be thrown into the general mass of public property'.

[27] Hansard, *Parl. Debs*, xvii, col. 1386 (20 May 1833). Gillon's motion failed: Ayes 16, Noes 126, majority 110.

[28] Clause 147, which stated that excess revenue earned from church lands gained *after* the Bill had passed would be appropriated towards education.

[29] Hansard, *Parl. Debs*, xvii, cols 1073–4 (21 June 1833).

[30] Clause 147 set up a fund from the sale of bishops' land. Since this fund was a new creation of parliament and would not affect existing church property, Stanley agreed to it. See Newbould, *Whiggery and Reform*, 141–2.

[31] Machin, *Politics and the Churches*, 35–7; Newbould, *Whiggery and Reform*, 92. The backstairs chronology of this decision, and Stanley's decision to drop the clause, are presented most clearly by Newbould.

since it abolished the Irish church rate).[32] O'Connell reacted immediately and angrily to this announcement. He argued vigorously that the government had based the passage of the Coercion Bill on the promise that there would follow a great reform of the Irish church. Without Clause 147, there was no great reform of the Irish church.[33] Further, he argued, 'Ministers had sacrificed their principles in order to keep their places; but when their principles were gone, what was the value of their places?'[34]

O'Connell and his Irish followers saw Stanley's action as a betrayal of a promised redress for Ireland, but other MPs saw it as a betrayal of the forming Liberal Party, and the party language they used was strong. Joseph Hume, Radical MP for Middlesex, reiterated that the 1833 Coercion Bill had been passed based on the promise of reform in the Irish church, and that 'the tories themselves' would never have done this.[35] Similarly, Daniel Harvey, Radical MP for Colchester, complained that 'In the worst days of toryism, when the tories sat on that hotbed of corruption, the ministerial bench, nothing so paltry as this Church Reform Bill ever sprang from it'.[36] 'If [we] are to have tory measures', echoed Colonel Davies, Reformer MP for Worcester, 'let them be carried under tory banners'.[37] Richard Sheil's biographer referred to the 'bitter reproaches' directed at ministers by English and Irish MPs who supported appropriation.[38] Some Whigs came to the defence of the government by arguing that appropriation was not the overriding principle of the Bill, and that the cautious reforms the Bill did contain were not worth losing by having a pitched battle with the Lords.[39] Russell himself argued that dropping the clause was the pragmatic thing to do, since the country could not stand a Lords–Commons clash every year.[40]

The House divided on the retention of Clause 147, as shown in Table 5.2. The Conservatives, of course, were in nearly complete agreement over removing the clause.[41] The Liberal Party, however, was almost evenly split, with a slender majority voting with Stanley. As seen in Table 5.2, in an analysis of the different sections within the party, it was the Whigs who tipped the scale in Stanley's direction. The even split in the Reformer vote should also be noted. Radicals and Repealers were consistently cohesive. At this stage, Liberal Party MPs were divided over whether to stick strictly to their ideas of liberal politics, or to accept the reality that appropriation would have wrecked the rest of the Bill, and therefore they should vote against it. Paradoxically, it seems that both types of behaviour had Liberal Party interests at heart. Those who voted to retain the clause thought the appropriation principle was so central to liberal

---

[32] Hansard, *Parl. Debs*, xviii, cols 1073–4 (21 June 1833).

[33] The Irish Coercion Act (Suppression of Disturbances Act, 1833, 3 Will. IV, c. 4) was the culmination of a series of measures that allowed the lord lieutenant of Ireland to declare an area 'disturbed', and enforce curfews, other restrictions on movement, and detention without trial for up to three months.

[34] Hansard, *Parl. Debs*, xviii, cols 1075–9 (21 June 1833).

[35] Hansard, *Parl. Debs*, xviii, cols 1881–2 (21 June 1833).

[36] Hansard, *Parl. Debs*, xviii, col. 1084 (21 June 1833).

[37] Hansard, *Parl. Debs*, xviii, col. 1092 (21 June 1833).

[38] W. Torrens McCullagh, *Memoirs of the Right Honourable Richard Lalor Sheil* (2 vols, 1855), ii, 144.

[39] T.B. Macaulay, Hansard, *Parl. Debs*, xviii, cols 1083–4 (21 June 1833).

[40] Hansard, *Parl. Debs*, xviii, col. 1095 (21 June 1833).

[41] The one conservative, W.S. Bernard, an Orange Tory, who was listed as voting Aye was a mistake in the division list (which is not rare), but there is no way of proving it.

Table 5.2: *Division on Clause 147 of the Irish Church Temporalities Bill*

Liberal Party groups	Ayes	Noes
Administration	0	8
Liberals	0	0
Radicals	23	4
Reformers	59	58
Repealers	24	0
Whigs	43	102
None listed	18	10
All Liberal Party	167	182
Conservative Party	1	96
Totals	168	278

Sources: Hansard, *Parl. Debs*, xviii, cols 1098–102 (21 June 1833); *The Times*, 24 June 1833.
Note: Official division lists were not compiled until 1836. As with most divisions, this one took place 'backwards'. Stanley wanted the clause dropped, but the actual motion was that it be retained. So, supporters of the clause's removal voted 'no'.

politics that it should be defended completely. Those who voted for dropping the clause did so from a pragmatic liberal stance that mild reform in Ireland was better than no reform at all. Right up until the end of the committee stage, the government faced pressure from its own backbenchers to reintroduce appropriation.[42] Disagreement was also found on the ministry bench. On 21 June 1833, Russell declared that church property was national property, and as such, could be appropriated for larger benefits.[43]

In 1834, the government introduced another tithe reform bill, in an attempt to quell land disturbances in Ireland with reform as well as coercion. During the debate on its second reading, Russell thought Stanley had said that the government was against appropriation. He stood up on 6 May 1834 and made a statement in favour of appropriation similar to the one he had made the previous year,[44] 'but it was said to a much more militant House of Commons which had known that this was an issue upon which ministers were at odds'.[45] Further, the more liberal section of the government had been bolstered by the promotion of Edward Ellice and James Abercromby to the cabinet. Stanley apparently decided that this continued support of appropriation meant that either he or Lord John must resign.[46] And after the Radical backbencher H.G. Ward moved a strong appropriation motion on 27 May 1834, Stanley did resign (along with Graham, Ripon and Richmond).[47]

H.G. Ward's motion during the debate on the Whig government's 1834 tithe bill encapsulated the general liberal backbench position on appropriation. The wording was:

[42] Including Richard Sheil's motion of 8 July 1833, Hansard, *Parl. Debs*, xix, col. 260.

[43] Hansard, *Parl. Debs*, xviii, col. 1095 (21 June 1833).

[44] Hansard, *Parl. Debs*, xxiii, cols 664–6 (6 May 1834).

[45] Prest, *Lord John Russell*, 65.

[46] Macintyre, *The Liberator*, 131–2.

[47] Hansard, *Parl. Debs*, xxiii, cols 1368–96 (27 May 1834); Condon, 'Irish Church', 132–3.

Table 5.3: *Division on H.G. Ward's 1834 Appropriation Motion*

Liberal Party groups	Ayes	% of total (125 Liberal Party MPs voting)
Administration	0	0
Liberals	1	0.8
Radicals	24	19.2
Reformers	42	33.6
Repealers	17	13.6
Whigs	14	11.2
None listed	8	6.4
All Liberal Party	125	100

Sources: Hansard, *Parl. Debs*, xxiv, cols 86–7 (2 June 1834); *The Times*, 4 June 1834.

> That the Protestant Episcopal Establishment in Ireland exceeds the spiritual wants of the Protestant population; and that, it being the right of the state to regulate the distribution of church property, in such a manner as parliament may determine, it is the opinion of this house, that the temporal possessions of the Church of Ireland, as now established by law, ought to be reduced.[48]

A lengthy debate (with few new arguments) ensued, and the motion failed on 2 June 1834, by 120 to 396. Owing to non-extant sources, a complete analysis of the division on Ward's motion is not yet possible.[49] Including pairs and tellers, there were 125 MPs in favour of Ward's motion, all from the Liberal Party. Table 5.3 provides an analysis of each group of liberals' contribution to the overall Liberal Party vote.

Later, in July 1834, a debate over promises made to O'Connell about the renewal of the 1833 Coercion Act forced Althorp and Grey to resign rather than face the charge of, at best, government inconsistency (at worst, dishonesty). Melbourne formed a new administration and passed coercion, along with stringent tithe reform (coercion passed the house of lords, but tithe reform was rejected).[50] The stronger approach Melbourne took to tithe reform caused some liberal optimists to claim that 'with these proceedings may be said to close the parliamentary struggle between the Irish popular party and the whigs'.[51] But it was Russell's lead on appropriation that led backbenchers to regard him as the strongest supporter of appropriation in the cabinet and, in many ways, led to stronger party cohesion. We have seen earlier that Lord John took an early view that the church of Ireland needed reform, that its income far exceeded its requirements and that the surplus ought to be put towards general education for the Irish people.[52] As he wrote to Spring-Rice in January 1835,

---

[48] See Ward's speech, Hansard, *Parl. Debs*, xxiii, cols 1368–96 (27 May 1834).

[49] It has proved impossible to locate the full division list for Ward's motion. Official division lists were not compiled before 1836. Hansard followed press reports in providing a list of the Ayes, which is of limited value, but reproduced here nonetheless. No conservative MPs voted Aye.

[50] McCullagh, *Sheil Memoirs*, ii, 195–7; Condon, 'Irish Church', 135.

[51] McCullagh, *Sheil Memoirs*, ii, 197–8.

[52] Hansard, *Parl. Debs*, xli, col. 377 (13 July 1832); Prest, *Lord John Russell*, 57–8; see also 'Memorandum by Lord John Russell on Irish Policy, 18 October 1833', in R. Russell, *Early Correspondence of Lord John Russell, 1805–1840* (1913), 42–4.

My belief is . . . that when the spiritual satisfaction of protestants had been fully provided for in any district it was right & expedient to apply any surplus which might remain, to the education of all classes of the people according to the system now [used] by the National Board of Education in Ireland.[53]

It was his 1834 statement in the house of commons on excess church revenues, however, which brought him prominent attention from backbenchers. As stated above, during the debate on the second reading of the 1834 Irish Tithe Bill, Russell rose and said that church of Ireland revenues were too great for the Church's purpose and ought to be appropriated. Sheil's biographer overstated the case when he said that 'these sentiments were hailed by a numerous section of the Liberal Party as inaugurating a new policy',[54] but the statement at least helped to force a new ministerial arrangement, allowing Russell more prominence after the resignations of Stanley, Graham, Richmond and Ripon. Before he 'upset the coach' in this way, Russell had been circumscribed in his public pronouncements on appropriation, but after the resignations he could speak freely.[55]

It was while out of office during Peel's short ministry in 1835 that Russell made his most significant contribution to the appropriation debate. Having already told Melbourne that he would not take part in a future government that was not committed to appropriation, Russell reflected this private commitment with a public statement in the house of commons.[56] During Peel's minority government, Hardinge (chief secretary for Ireland) brought in another tithe reform bill, without an appropriation clause. In a mid length speech during the tithe bill's committee stage on 30 March 1835, Russell moved that the House go into committee on the question of the 'Temporalities of the Church of Ireland'. He then announced that during that committee he would move for appropriation of surplus church of Ireland funds, and place them towards general education in Ireland.[57] Debate on the motion took four days, and was quite heated at times.[58] Yet, precious few new arguments were advanced on either side. MPs discussed the questions of who was responsible for the administration of church funds, redress (or 'justice') for Ireland, and the gross inconsistency between the population of the Irish church and the contributing Irish population as a whole.[59] Supporters argued, as they had in 1833 and 1834, that appropriation was necessary to placate Ireland, to overcome a religious injustice and to strengthen the church of Ireland by removing what was seen

---

[53] National Library of Ireland, Monteagle Papers, MS 11,140, folder 2: Russell to Spring-Rice, 23 Jan. 1835.

[54] McCullagh, *Sheil Memoirs*, ii, 193.

[55] Prest, *Lord John Russell*, 56. 'Johnny has upset the coach' was the phrase Stanley used in a note to Ellice during Russell's speech. Prest contends that it was written in good humour (see p. 65).

[56] For the Russell–Melbourne letter see Macintyre, *The Liberator*, 143.

[57] Hansard, *Parl. Debs.*, xxvii, cols 361–84 (30 Mar. 1835).

[58] Akenson, *Church of Ireland*, 185.

[59] Hansard, *Parl. Debs.*, xxvii, cols 361–455, 466–539, 547–640, 654–777, 790–828, 837–64, 878–974 (30 March–7 April 1835). See also, Bodl., Buxton Papers, MSS Britain Emp. s444, xvi, f. 429: Richenda Buxton to Charles Buxton, 3 Apr. 1835. The young William Forster, who, as a liberal MP for Bradford from 1860 to 1884, would have much to do with Ireland (as well as with education), sat and watched the entire debate from the gallery, writing reports to his aunt Sarah Buxton. See Bodl., Buxton Papers, MSS Britain Emp s444, xvi, ff. 423–36: W.E. Forster to Sarah Buxton, 3 Apr. 1835.

Table 5.4: *Division on Russell's 1835 Appropriation Motion*

Liberal Party groups	Ayes	Noes
Administration	0	0
Liberals	0	0
Radicals	29	0
Reformers	121	17
Repealers	25	0
Whigs	109	14
None listed	21	0
All Liberal Party	305	31
Conservative Party	3	225
Totals	308	256

Sources: Hansard, *Parl. Debs*, xxvii, cols 969–99 (7 Apr. 1835); *The Times*, 8 Apr. 1835.

as an abuse. Opponents feared the destruction of protestantism in Ireland, and the application of such an anti-establishment principle in England.[60]

Given that Peel was commanding a minority government, it was not surprising that many conservatives accused Russell and the opposition of putting appropriation forward only as a question of confidence. Thomas Buxton, Whig MP for Weymouth and Melcombe Regis, replied sharply that 'the maintenance of the Church, and the spread of education in Ireland are subjects of such deep and vital importance, that all consideration of party politics are but feathers in the scale'.[61] Although Liberal Party MPs generally decried the accusation of mere party politicking, not all were convinced of the purity of Russell's motives or the propriety of handling opposition in this way. For W.H. Hyett, Whig MP for Stroud, this was the last straw in his disillusionment with the new Whig leadership.

> Although I could make every allowance for individuals, who belonging to the party, found themselves in such difficult circumstances that they were forced to vote with him, still when as an Elector, I am called upon to express my approbation of the very person who brought them with such difficulties, I felt that I had no other alternative but to say at once, that I can not give it.[62]

The division on Russell's motion shows the strong support that the Liberal Party gave to appropriation by 1835 (Table 5.4). Within the Liberal Party, we see the dramatic shift in Whig opinion from 1833, as well as the almost complete agreement among other MPs

[60] The length of the debate on the motion threatened to impinge on Russell's private life. On 2 April 1835, Priscilla Johnston (daughter of Thomas Buxton and wife of liberal MP Andrew Johnston) wrote to Sarah Buxton: 'Well this weighty Irish question is still as it were stopping our breath but it is to be ended tonight, that Lord John may be married tomorrow morning'. Bodl., Buxton Papers, MSS Britain Emp. s444, xvi, f. 423.

[61] *Speech of Thomas Fowell Buxton, Esq. MP, in the House of Commons on Thursday, April 2, 1835* [on Russell's appropriation motion], Mirror of Parliament Pamphlet, London, 1835, p. 3, in Bodl., Buxton Papers, ix, item 6.

[62] Gloucestershire Record Office, Hyett Papers, D6/F32/f. 89: draft of a letter (recipient not given), 13 May 1835. Hyett did not stand in the 1835 election, withdrew from the national scene and concentrated on local politics, where he gradually became more and more conservative.

in the party. On 7 April, Russell's motion passed with a small majority of 27, and Peel resigned over what he had taken as a confidence motion.[63]

The ministry that replaced Peel introduced another Irish church reform bill in 1835, guided by Lord Morpeth. Proposing to replace tithes with a more equitable and consistent land rent and to allocate surplus Irish church revenues to general education, the bill passed its first and second readings, and successful whipping surmounted an attempt by Peel to split it in two (to deal with tithe reform and appropriation as separate issues).[64] But it stalled in the house of lords, and the cabinet decided to drop it rather than risk their survival on it.[65] In 1836, Russell introduced an Irish church reform bill, similar to the one in 1835, but with stronger (and more detailed) appropriation provisions. The bill again passed the Commons, but had its appropriation proposals stunted by the Lords. Russell chose to drop the entire bill, rather than abandon a principle he had professed since 1832.[66] And the king's death in 1837 afforded the Whig ministry a chance to dissolve parliament and drop measures they had been unable to pass. Appropriation faded as an important issue by 1838, and serious Irish church reform in parliament had to await Gladstone's disestablishment bill of 1869.[67]

Appropriation as a Defining Issue for Liberal Politics

Charles Grant, Whig MP for Inverness-shire, wrote that appropriation was so closely tied to liberal politics that 'no Reformer could shrink from asserting that principle. There was no room for the imputations of factious motives on the part of the Liberal Party'.[68] Brent and Parry have agreed. For Brent, 'The government's policy on the Irish Church encapsulated the liberal position on religion. It recognized the importance of religion for the welfare of the state and of individual citizens, while maintaining that sectarian differences were both negligible and incapable of authoritarian resolution'.[69] Parry sees appropriation as being nearly all things to all liberals. It appealed to the various sections of the emerging Liberal Party because it held that 'established churches should be upheld as genuinely national institutions' and 'that their present exclusiveness was intolerable'. Appropriation 'attracted Radicals and dissenters who looked forward to measures to "unaristocratize" the established Church of England'. It was rational and utilitarian to distribute the excess funds to the larger population. 'It was a symbol of the responsiveness of the reformed parliament to Irish needs.' It would correct past tory misrule of Ireland

---

[63] Hansard, *Parl. Debs*, xxvii, cols 969–74 (7 Apr. 1835), Ayes 285 to 258; cols 980–5 (8 Apr. 1835) (Peel's resignation); see also Macintyre, *The Liberator*, 144.

[64] See Lincolnshire Archives Office, D'Eyncourt Papers, TDE/H1/117: E.J. Stanley to Charles Tennyson D'Eyncourt, 10 July 1835.

[65] The bill's introduction: Hansard, *Parl. Debs*, xxviii, cols 1319–60 (26 June 1835); first reading: Hansard, *Parl. Debs*, xxix, col. 287 (7 July 1835); second reading: Hansard, *Parl. Debs*, xxix, col. 458 (13 July 1835); Peel's challenge: Hansard, *Parl. Debs*, xxix, cols 790–822 (21 July 1835). See also Akenson, *Church of Ireland*, 186–8.

[66] Prest, *Lord John Russell*, 106–7. See also Univ. of Manchester, John Rylands Library, Fielden Papers, FDN/1/2/1, item 11: George Bull to John Fielden, 7 June 1836.

[67] Akenson, *Church of Ireland*, 188–9; Prest, *Lord John Russell*, 106–7, 115–16; Condon, 'Irish Church', 142.

[68] J. Grant, *Random Recollections of the House of Commons from the Year 1830 to the Close of 1835, including Personal Sketches of the Leading Members of All Parties, by One of No Party* (1836), 435.

[69] Brent, *Liberal Anglican Politics*, 66.

that had 'degraded Irish morals'. 'It would show that Whig principles promised order, yet also liberty and brotherhood.' Finally, it was a reform that could go towards placating Catholics in Ireland.[70] This section will discuss appropriation as a Liberal Party defining issue, taking its cue from Parry and Brent, yet examining the depth of feeling on the backbenches. It will examine appropriation as a debate on: the nature of church establishment, parliament as guardian and controller of church establishment and church funds, strengthening protestantism in Ireland, as support for education and as a reform for the Irish people.

The idea of church establishment as a national institution, with duties to the population at large (and not only the population of the Established Church), was nowhere better described and argued than by the Irish Repealer MP for Tipperary, Richard Sheil: 'the property in the possession of the established church in Ireland is public property . . . and the surplus of said property is applicable . . . to the community at large'.[71] Cuthbert Rippon, Radical MP for Gateshead, also succinctly summarized the idea when he said during the debate on the Irish Church Temporalities Bill:

> The welfare of the many was the end of all government; a national establishment should promote the interests and be in harmony with the feelings of the majority of the nation; but who was audacious enough to assert that the Church of Ireland promoted the interest, or was in harmony with the feelings, of the people at large?[72]

Other Liberal MPs took the argument further. Henry Barron, Repealer MP for Waterford City, said that 'the property of the church was . . . that of the state, and the state had a right to make what arrangements it pleased with respect to that property'.[73] Sheil reminded the House in the same debate that the English state, and many European states, had always interfered with, and controlled, church property. So it made perfect sense that church property be controlled by parliament.[74] The trust in which parliament held church property was also a principle held by anglicans, but they objected to it being exercised in this way. The low-church *Watchman* wrote on 4 April 1835, after Russell's motion had passed, that 'higher principles are obviously sacrificed to expediency in the intended appropriation of the surplus in question to purposes not strictly ecclesiastical. Our liberal legislators thus venture to abuse the trust confided to their guardianship'.[75]

Dissenters also used the debate on church establishment that occurred during appropriation debates to raise the subject of anglican establishment in England. Cuthbert Rippon, Radical MP for Gateshead, tried to turn the 1833 Irish Church Temporalities Bill debate into one on church establishment.

---

[70] Parry, *Rise and Fall of Liberal Government*, 108–10.

[71] Hansard, *Parl. Debs*, xix, col. 260 (8 July 1833). Arguments from Irish MPs did not always fall on receptive ears, even when Liberal Party MPs may have agreed with the sentiments expressed. Some Whigs' attitudes to Irish members may be gleaned from a letter from M.F.F. Berkeley, Whig MP for Gloucester, who wrote to W.H. Hyett on 25 June 1831: 'Sheil's voice is horrible, his Irish brogue detestable, and though his ideas and words pour on in a rapid stream he is not pleasant to listen to'. Gloucestershire RO, Hyett Papers, D6/F32/f. 13.

[72] Hansard, *Parl. Debs*, xvii, cols 1382–3 (20 May 1833).

[73] Hansard, *Parl. Debs*, xv, col. 591 (12 Feb. 1833).

[74] Hansard, *Parl. Debs*, xvi, col. 1377 (1 Apr. 1833).

[75] Bodl., Buxton Papers, MSS Britain Emp s444, ix, item 47, *The Watchman*, 4 Apr. 1835.

The present pretended measure of Reform was a mere wily attempt to perpetuate the monstrous grievance, the iniquitous principle, of compelling the majority of a nation to support the Church Establishment of a small minority. The Dissenters and Catholics constituted the majority of the people of the United Empire . . . A double tax for the support of their own Church and another Church was now paid by the middle and lower classes of the people of Ireland, while the church of the aristocracy was paid for, not by the aristocracy itself, but by the whole body of the people for their benefit.[76]

Appropriation was also seen as a way to strengthen and expand protestantism in Ireland through the goodwill of removing an abuse and educating the populace. But Liberal Party MPs who spoke on these lines were careful not to anger O'Connell and his Irish party through strong language. Instead they emphasized increased general education, which would lead to protestantism through enlightenment. The implication, of course, was that catholicism had such a strong hold on the Irish because they did not have the benefit of the clear thinking and individual decision-making that education could provide.[77] Sir Thomas Wilde, Reformer MP for Newark, argued that the educational end product of appropriation would 'lay a strong hold upon the intelligence of Ireland, and would eventually increase the number of the Protestant population . . . The only means of placing Irishmen in a situation truly to estimate the principles of the Protestant Church, was the education of the people'.[78]

There were many such sentiments expressed in the house of commons during the appropriation debates, and most liberal MPs agreed, although some worried that appropriating church property might damage the cause of protestantism in Ireland.[79] The *Edinburgh Review* argued that, since protestantism was on the rise in Europe, Liberal Party MPs should not feel unduly concerned about its future in Ireland.[80] Further, appropriation had a more general educational benefit. The Irish National Board of Education, set up in 1831, was to be the recipient of appropriated revenues.[81] Some Liberal Party MPs argued that education was a debt owed to the Irish people due to English misgovernance. If the history of Ireland was 'a system of war, and bloodshed, and riot', asked Thomas Buxton, 'was there any cure for this but education?'[82]

This was all part of a larger aspect of appropriation – as judicious redress for the Irish people. Parry has defined part of his liberal value system as 'the belief that Irish grievances were the result of previous tory mis-rule'. And it is here, along with the belief in the responsibility of national institutions to the general populace, that we find the greatest degree of agreement among Liberal Party MPs. Parliament, especially the Liberal Party, had the duty to see that the effects of this misrule were addressed. As Sheil pleaded to the House,

---

[76] Hansard, *Parl. Debs*, xvii, col. 1382 (20 May 1833).

[77] Newbould, *Whiggery and Reform*, 136–7; Brent, *Liberal Anglican Politics*, 51.

[78] Hansard, *Parl. Debs*, xxvii, col. 1359 (2 Apr. 1835).

[79] See Paul Beilby, Whig MP for Yorkshire East, Hansard, *Parl. Debs*, xxvii, cols 568–9 (1 Apr. 1835). See also Newbould, *Whiggery and Reform*, 138.

[80] *Edinburgh Review* (1835), lx, 518.

[81] Brent, *Liberal Anglican Politics*, 65–6; Newbould, *Whiggery and Reform*, 179.

[82] Hansard, *Parl. Debs*, xxvii, col. 708 (2 Apr. 1835).

the heart grows sick at the thought of what she [Ireland] might be and what she is – of what she was made by nature, and what she has been made by you; for she is yours; she belongs to you; her faults are yours, her follies are yours: you are answerable for her errors; for her transgressions you are responsible: her crimes, her atrocities, her blood-shed, her horrors, her madness – all, all are yours; and if I tell you this, it is not for the purposes of unavailing crimination – no, it is in order that I may awaken in your minds, and in your hearts, a sense of the strong coincidence between your palpable interest and your obvious duty, and persuade you to adopt a policy by which the source of all this calamity and all this crime shall be closed; for which it is not superstitious to say, that those who, from factious motives, shall be instrumental in its continuance, will have to pass, before a higher than any human tribunal, a terrible account.[83]

Much of the Irish Church Temporalities Bill was initially characterised as a 'measure of a healing and wholesome nature', by Richard Keane, Whig MP for Waterford County.[84] O'Connell thought it 'contained within itself the seeds of future amelioration'.[85] In his private journal, John Abel Smith, Whig MP for Chichester, bemoaned the loss of parliamentary momentum on appropriation, and wrote that its absence would always be 'a stumbling block in the way of Liberal Government in Ireland'.[86]

The other striking thing under this category was the mythical (almost mystical) belief that the 'Irish people' would show their gratitude for reforms by ceasing agricultural violence and would almost instantly become more loyal subjects. Russell ended his appropriation motion speech in 1835 with the following:

no traveller ever goes into Ireland who does not declare that he has been received everywhere, by the poorest peasant, not only in the most hospitable manner, but with the utmost friendly and open-hearted kindness . . . Such being the feeling, and such the conduct of that nation to individuals, the House has now an opportunity of earning the gratitude and making that affection its own, by asserting the principle for which I contend, and by thus doing justice to the people of Ireland.[87]

William Roche, Repealer MP for Limerick, said that if appropriation became policy, the Irish would become the kingdom's most loyal subjects. His hyperbole is telling:

so susceptible is the Irish character of grateful emotions, so disposed towards an oblivion of the past, in anticipation of the future, [that if appropriation became law, the news of it would mean that] 10,000, nay 100,000 Irish swords will leap from their scabbards to avenge a wrong or an insult to their King and Country, and peace, contentment and prosperity will at length prevail in that hitherto abused, and therefore distracted, land.[88]

---

[83] Hansard, *Parl. Debs*, xvii, col. 47 (31 Mar. 1835).

[84] Hansard, *Parl. Debs*, xv, col. 615 (12 Feb. 1833).

[85] Hansard, *Parl. Debs*, xv, col. 577 (12 Feb. 1833). See also Davis, 'Whigs and Religious Issues', 132, for the broad consensus among whigs for what purposes appropriation could be applied.

[86] West Sussex RO, John Abel Smith Papers, Add. MS 22, 34: journal entry, 10 May 1838.

[87] Hansard, *Parl. Debs*, xxvii, cols 383–4 (30 March 1835).

[88] Hansard, *Parl. Debs*, xvii, cols 1366, 1368 (1 Apr. 1833).

'Party' Politics and Appropriation

Charles Wood, government whip in 1833, drew up a list of MPs and categorised them as 'tories', 'waverers', 'steady supporters', 'supporters', 'English and Scotch Radicals' and 'Irish Repealers'. And it was this sort of party head counting of backbenchers that found its way into cabinet discussions of the course of action on the Irish Church Temporalities Bill. Stanley argued that coercive and less reforming measures had greater support in the House as a whole (which meant garnering tory support). Russell argued that relying on tory support would drive many liberal backbenchers to be more radical.[89] The backbenchers over whom cabinet members worried also expressed a great deal of party concern over Irish church reforms. Their use of 'party' language, especially in 1835, is significant. In a letter to Russell, H.G. Ward wrote that 'I shall do more towards satisfying its [Irish church reform] settlement by leaving it in your lordship's hands, and thus identifying interests of the great party, and with the existence of a liberal cabinet [than I could on my own]'.[90]

Henry Grattan, Repealer MP for Meath and son of the great Irish parliamentarian, thought that party was at least as important as proposals during the Irish church debates. He said to Peel during the debate on the Conservative tithe bill of 1835:

> The difference . . . between these two measures [Peel's tithe bill and Russell's appropriating alternative] is the difference between the two parties. The people would object to that measure in your hands, which they might agree to if proposed by the noble Lord [Russell] because in you they place no confidence: they look to men no less than measures, and they judge of you from the men you have promoted, as well as from the principles you have acted on.[91]

Conclusion

In terms of party action, it is quite clear that appropriation as an issue gained support among Liberal Party MPs during the 1830s. Even when taking into account the differences in circumstances between the 1833 division on Clause 147 and the 1835 division on Russell's motion,[92] the increase in Liberal Party support for appropriation was dramatic. In 1833 47.9% of Liberal Party MPs voted for appropriation; 90.7% did so in 1835. This is of further significance because there was a fundamental ideological difference between the type of appropriation offered in Clause 147 and that in Russell's proposal. In 1833, Stanley proposed to set up a fund from the sale of bishops' land. Since this fund was a new creation of parliament and would not affect existing church property, it was considered a very mild form of appropriation, one aimed at placating the

---

[89] Newbould, *Whiggery and Reform*, 83–6.

[90] TNA, Russell Papers, 30/22, 1E, ff. 33–4: H.G. Ward to Russell, 16 July 1835.

[91] Hansard, *Parl. Debs*, xxvii, col. 891 (7 Apr. 1835).

[92] Care must be taken when comparing 1833 and 1835 (especially for the whigs and frontbenchers), because in order to vote 'for' appropriation in 1833, liberal MPs would have had to vote against the government (which many were reluctant to do). Further, if Stanley's Irish Church Temporalities Bill had gone to the Lords with Clause 147 intact, there almost certainly would have been a Lords–Commons clash, which most MPs feared, especially coming so soon after the reform clash.

Table 5.5: *Support for Appropriation among Liberal Party MPs, 1833 and 1835*

Liberal Party group	1833 (Clause 147) % of support	1835 (Russell's motion) % of support	% increase
Radicals	85.2	100	14.9
Reformers	50.4	87.6	35.7
Repealers	100	100	0
Whigs	29.6	88.61	19.3
All Liberal Party	47.9	90.7	42.8

Note: No 'Liberal' MPs voted on either motion. Eight 'Administration' MPs voted against retaining Clause 147 but, of course, there were no 'Administration' MPs during the division on Russell's motion, so that category has been left out. So too have the 'None listed' MPs, since the comparison would not be useful.

anglican hierarchy and the house of lords. Russell proposed, however, to take all church of Ireland finances into account when calculating the amount to be appropriated, and using those funds for general education. This would have touched existing church money and land, and was, therefore, a much more far-reaching proposal. If anything, it should have attracted hostility from establishment Whigs and mild Reformers (both for ideological reasons and for fear of the reaction of the Lords and the Church). Yet it gained deep support overall. The increase in Whig and Reformer support for appropriation by 1835 is shown in Table 5.5.

This may, of course, be explained not so much as an effect of liberals changing their minds in 1835 as their banding together to bring down Peel. But, as will be argued at the end of this chapter, either explanation provides support for the conclusion that it was the combination of ideology and party action that aided the birth of the parliamentary Liberal Party.

From an ideological standpoint, appropriation has been shown to be central to liberal ideas on the nature of church establishment, parliament as guardian and controller of church funds, and as a needed Irish reform. But what made appropriation as a liberal issue a 'progression' from earlier Whig ideas of simple liberality lay in the fact and nature of the redistribution of national wealth. There was, of course, a strong utilitarian streak in the argument that the church of Ireland's income exceeded its needs and ought to be reduced. Rather than arguing that the income itself ought to be reduced (lightening the 'tax' burden through lower tithes and rent charges), and leaving the individual as a free agent to decide what to do with the money he no longer paid to the establishment, the liberal proposals (even that of the Radical businessman H.G. Ward) retained the income, and redistributed its excess. Further, they redistributed it in a highly national and liberal way, through either the Irish National Board of Education (as the government had proposed in 1832–3, and Russell had in 1835) or for 'the purposes of general utility' (as Gillon and Ward had argued). This broad use of ecclesiastical funds provides the strongest support for the argument that there was a new liberal emphasis on the responsibilities of national institutions. And the fact that nearly all Liberal Party MPs came round to this conclusion indicates relatively strong ideological cohesion.

We may, therefore, draw the preliminary conclusion that the liberal groups satisfy generally accepted criteria for the formation of a modern political party. But how does this fit in with the historiography of appropriation? Newbould clearly overstates the case in his emphasis on the mechanistic side of Liberal Party behaviour. He sees Irish church reform as a question of the level of support for the Whig governments inside the House, and among the electorate. Although there were severe concerns in the cabinet in 1832–3 over Commons and electoral matters, and over how Clause 147 would affect them, by 1835 Liberal Party solidarity on appropriation was strong enough that Whig leaders did not feel the need to address the possibility of losing Russell's division. While there was, no doubt, some interest in using appropriation to help topple Peel, it is highly unlikely that so many Whigs would have changed their minds (and supported a stronger appropriation measure) from 1833 to 1835 simply on party political grounds. This is further bolstered by the fact that the Liberal Party could have forced a confidence vote on almost anything, but did it over appropriation. A far more likely scenario is that the difference may also be attributed to a shift in attitude. Newbould's contention that ideological clashes were only to be found on the backbenches is also clearly too strong.[93] By 1835, backbench cohesion was nearly complete.

One way of summarizing Brent's arguments might be: the liberalisation of the Whigs through the influence of the liberal anglicans led to the party leadership taking a progressive direction. The liberal anglicans were able to capture the leadership of an increasingly 'liberal' party by being ideologically progressive themselves. There is a good deal of support for this conclusion in the appropriation parliaments. Both the Whig leadership and the Whig backbenches developed a liberal attitude towards appropriation, redistribution and the role of national institutions that was essentially fresh at Westminster. Whether this change was the result of the new anglicanism in liberal anglicanism (that is, whether the theological ideas behind political inclusion were paramount), is beyond the scope of this chapter, but a change was clearly evident. Further, Brent's assertion that there was a fundamental change in the conception of the constitution and state among liberals bears some discussion. The change from Foxite ideas of the constitution, with their emphasis on mechanistic reform, to a form of constitutional moralism (whereby an important duty of national institutions was to help define and guide the nation through education, inclusion and example), may be reflected in the strength of feeling towards the redistribution of Irish church funds.[94]

While Parry's 'liberal value-system' paradigm holds up well when discussed in terms of appropriation, his contention that appropriation was, essentially, all things to all liberals is a bit too broad. Had the Whigs been in government when Russell brought in his strong appropriation motion, it is not at all clear that Liberal Party MPs would have risked the party political damage of defending it against the Lords in order to confirm their cohesive ideology. It was the *timely* application of coherent voting that Parry missed when he intellectualised appropriation support. And this political use of ideology must give strong support for the idea of a Liberal Party in the 1830s.

---

[93] Newbould, *Whiggery and Reform, passim.*

[94] Brent, *Liberal Anglican Politics, passim.*

The evidence presented in this chapter shows a large degree of party unity in ideology and action on appropriation, despite the difficulties and vagueness of party politics at the time. There were enough points of agreement and common action to consider the Liberals a viable party. The change in attitude and action among MPs suggests that appropriation was an important staging post in the formation of the Liberal Party. What has been newly presented here is the importance of backbenchers in driving party unity and direction. They continued to force appropriation on to the agenda. They constantly reinforced the idea that appropriation was necessary for contemporary justice of a liberal kind, and voted as a block by 1835. Further, rather than an idea of party being overly mechanistic or overly ideological, this chapter has shown the importance of the convergence of these two necessary political attributes. By 1835, Liberal Party MPs applied their ideology in a timely political fashion, and in doing so displayed, if not to themselves then perhaps to us, the hallmarks of a modern political party.

Although appropriation never became law, and the liberals were ultimately forced to abandon it, we shall see in the discussion in Chapter 6 how there was a similar transformation in attitude, and a similar solidification of the ideas of national institutions and central government, over the topic of church rates. Not surprisingly, there was also similar unwillingness to champion an ultimately fruitless issue, and a similar reliance on local solutions and half-measures to palliate public opinion. An enduring impression of the appropriation years is the realization that, for Liberal Party MPs, the importance of raising an issue, and being seen to raise and debate it, satisfied notions of the responsiveness of government and parliamentary responsibility, regardless of their ultimate and complete success.

Chapter 6. Symbolism and Responsibility: Church Rates and Expectations of the Liberal Party

In the previous chapter we saw how Liberal Party MPs reacted to the movement for a type of religious toleration in Ireland, based partly on the idea that non-anglicans should not be forced to pay for the establishment and maintenance of a state religion that was exclusive in character and practice. There were many reasons why this appealed to them, but one of the most frequently cited was that Ireland should be treated as a special case, and consequently that there need be no fear of a similar movement against the anglican church in England. This chapter will show how much the same group of MPs supported the idea of an anglican church establishment in England, and how their arguments for it related to the issue of church rates. For the majority of Liberal Party MPs, the church of England, unlike the church of Ireland, was an institution to be supported and improved so that it would continue to provide moral guidance for the nation. The varying degrees of support that the church of England could rely on from Liberal Party MPs was shown quite clearly during the 1830s and 1840s. A number of proposed reforms (mostly aimed either at relieving dissenters from obligations to the church of England, or at opening exclusively anglican institutions such as the universities) moved through the house of commons and, among other things, threw into relief the differing strains of opinion among Liberal Party MPs, and displayed the difficulties facing such a coalition.

One of the attempted church reforms was the modification, or abolition, of the church rate. The church rate, essentially a parish property tax to support the local anglican church, was applied to occupiers of property, not just to owners. In this way it burdened nearly everyone, and has accurately been called 'a form of national taxation in the interests of the Anglican church', said to raise £560,000 p.a.[1] The significance of the church rate for the purposes of this book, however, lay in its symbolic importance. The church rate was seen as a national anglican tax, supported by many churchmen as a recognition of the supremacy of the Established Church in a pluralist christian country, and opposed by many dissenters as an unfair burden on non-anglicans and a drag on the free exercise of religious conscience. In a simple and easily understood form, the church rate displayed and symbolised that non-anglican religions had inferior status. Owen Chadwick neatly summarized both the frustrating nature of the church rate for dissenters, and the important role that parliament played in the controversy, when he wrote that the rate was the 'giant sore' in dissenters' grievances, and that it 'kept the flames of

---

[1] R. Brent, 'The Whigs and Protestant Dissent in the Decade of Reform: The Case of Church Rates, 1833–1841', *EHR*, cii (1987), 889–90; O. Chadwick, *The Victorian Church* (vol. 1, 1966), 81–3; G.I.T. Machin, *Politics and the Churches in Great Britain, 1832–1868* (Oxford, 1977), 45–7; G.F.A. Best, 'The Whigs and the Church Establishment in the Age of Grey and Holland', *History*, xliv (1960), 103–18. For a more lengthy explanation of the nature and application of church rates, see J.P. Ellens, *Religious Routes to Gladstonian Liberalism: The Church Rate Conflict in England and Wales, 1832–1868* (University Park, PA, 1994), introduction and ch. 1. In different parts of the country, the church rate was known as a levy, cess, lay or ley.

bitterness flaring'. This was because the church rate was the one thing that dissenters could contest within the parish, which kept it alive and close as an issue. Sometimes they were prosecuted, sometimes they were not.[2] All other grievances could only be solved by parliamentary action. Further, according to Chadwick, the church rate controversy showed that 'religion and politics were inextricable'. In the parish, to vote for assessing rates was a statement of defence of the Established Church and its main champion, the Conservative Party. To vote similarly in parliament was an extension of those same religious and political sentiments. To fight against the church rate was to show toleration to dissenters, as well as a belief in institutional reform, both at the parish and the parliamentary level. These were hallmarks of liberalism.[3]

The church rate controversy has a further, deeper, significance for Victorian history, however. The political attempts to abolish or modify it highlight the symbolism of a growing element in Victorian politics. This was the question of the accommodation of the rights of different groups within the polity to a public recognition and redress of their grievances, combined with a more practical elimination of a financial burden. For, although church rate difficulties were often being solved at the local level throughout the period concerned in this chapter, pressure on the house of commons to act publicly and nationally remained strong until the church rate movement was overtaken by chartism. Not only were bills brought in to abolish or modify church rates, but motions regarding the imprisonment of dissenting individuals for the non-payment of their rate were introduced by Liberal Party backbenchers. In terms of the practical effect on dissenters throughout the country, the church rate debates and bills in parliament were of little value, but their symbolic value was great. And the increasing desire to use parliament as the centre for the redress of grievances, and the willingness and eagerness of Liberal Party MPs to stomach, as well as speak in, long debates on an issue that was often being resolved piecemeal (and locally),[4] tells us a great deal about liberal ideas on the nature of national institutions, as well as the liberal idea, held by most Liberal Party MPs, that it was important (and sufficient) to discuss and debate issues in parliament as a national forum, whether or not any legislation might result. This chapter, therefore, addresses the following questions. Did the church rate issue follow appropriation in the sense that the Whig government proposed a mild, establishment-supporting reform early in its ministry (which drew fire from Radicals and Repealers), and as the 1830s progressed, stricter church rate reform (and abolition) gathered general Liberal Party support? Was there, in other words, a parallel between church of England and church of Ireland reform during the 1830s and 1840s? Further, what might church rates, seen as an accommodation issue,

---

[2] Chadwick, *Victorian Church*, 81.

[3] Chadwick, *Victorian Church*, 82.

[4] In many places, the difficulties of raising funds for church maintenance were overcome relatively amicably at parish meetings. David Eastwood, for instance, has shown that, in some Oxfordshire parishes, 'Where dissent was strong Anglicans were usually compelled to moderate their demands upon ratepayers. In some parishes, whilst the cost of essential maintenance continued to be covered from the rates, other expenses were met by subscriptions and collections'. In some parishes, parishioners avoided church rates by electing churchwardens who would hold down spending. Some dissenters in Witney refused to pay church rates. In other areas, relatively complex arrangements and agreements on a balance between rates, self-funding and subscriptions had to be reached. See D. Eastwood, 'Governing Rural England: Authority and Social Order in Oxfordshire, 1780–1840', University of Oxford PhD, 1985, pp. 288–90. See also Chadwick, *Victorian Church*, 152.

say about the development of the Liberal Party in parliament, and lead us to conclude about liberal reactions to other civil rights issues in the following decades? Finally, how central to liberal politics was the symbolic role that parliament played in the church rate issue, and what hold did the expectations of dissenting constituents have on MPs beyond that symbolism? The reaction of MPs from the various strains of the Liberal Party towards church rate reform may shed further light on their reaction to other popular movements such as chartism and more parliamentary reform.

Although it was a confused, and ultimately failed, attempt at accommodation and inclusion, the church rate abolition movement holds large significance for many other issues. Historians have not failed to notice this. Jacob Ellens, in his *Religious Routes to Gladstonian Liberalism*, makes perhaps the boldest claim concerning the significance of the church rate abolition movement. His overarching idea is that the church rate abolition movement (from 1832 to 1868) helped lead to the formation of the liberal state, that local agitation and central action brought about the reassessment of relations between religion and politics, and that Victorian liberalism, as expressed in the inclusive ideas espoused by Gladstone through the 1870s and 1880s, had its roots in the church rate controversies of the previous generation.[5] Richard Brent, in his article 'The Whigs and Protestant Dissent in the Decade of Reform: The Case of Church Rates, 1833–1841', follows the main argument employed in his *Liberal Anglican Politics*, that is, that liberal anglican Whig governments of the 1830s responded positively to the idea of reform of church finances because their version of anglicanism was increasingly liberal, and pro-gressively inclusive and latitudinarian.[6] G.I.T. Machin, in his *Politics and the Churches*, provides perhaps the broadest application of the church rate experience to the question of relations between religion and politics in early mid Victorian England and Wales. He argues that early Victorian governments employed a dual strategy of gradual liberalisation while retaining the core Church establishment. But, unlike Jews and catholics, noncon-formists were able, eventually, to see most of their grievances addressed, due to their more sophisticated political awareness and pressure.[7] This chapter will argue that a close examination of the attitudes and actions of Liberal Party MPs not only shows the symbolic nature of the political response to church rate agitation, but also that, like many of the other issues in this book, the church rate issue and the Liberal Party were mutually defining in the 1830s and 1840s. It may seem obvious that the political aspects of an issue such as church rates partly defined the developing Liberal Party, particularly since the party relied on the support of dissenters, but how the early Liberal Party could have partly defined the church rate controversy is less clear. The chapter will take the following form: a brief introduction to the general background of the church rate controversy, followed by a summary of the parliamentary action on church rate reform and abolition, an analysis of the debates and divisions on crucial church rate motions, a short discussion of the outside pressure placed on Liberal Party MPs by constituents, and the importance of symbolism for the entire debate and its meaning for the Liberal Party in parliament.

---

[5] Ellens, *Religious Routes*, vii and *passim*. Ellens' book is the most complete study of the church rate conflict between the 1832 Reform Act and Gladstone's abolition of compulsory church rates in 1868.

[6] Brent, 'Whigs and Protestant Dissent', 888–9.

[7] Machin, *Politics and the Churches*, 380.

General Background of the Church Rate Controversy

Although there had been local disturbances over refusals to pay church rates early in the 19th century,[8] the passage of the Reform Act of 1832 may be seen as the acceptable starting point of the major church rate refusal and abolition movements. While the Reform Act obviously did not grant additional political rights to dissenters per se, the redistribution of parliamentary seats to include some towns with large dissenting populations effectively meant that some increase in attention had to be paid to the grievances of nonconformists. After 1832, the church rate became a sort of 'political' tax as well. As Salmon shows, it was often collected as part of the assessed rates required for the new £10 franchise. A ratepayer could lose his parliamentary vote if he refused to pay the church rate as part of his total assessment.[9] Further, the perception that the reformed parliament was a new parliament in terms of purpose, representation and responsibility, gave existing religious tensions new political meanings. William Ord, Reformer MP for Newcastle-upon-Tyne, echoed this idea in 1834, when he told his constituents that church rates were not worth retaining owing to the ill-feeling they caused among dissenters:

> If the church-rate was ten times in value . . . than it is, it would be purchased too dear by the price we are paying for it (cheers). I believe there is no point of political wisdom greater than 'well to know the time and the means of yielding that which is impossible to keep'.[10]

The Reverend Charles Girdleston, vicar of Sedgley in Staffordshire, published his sermon, 'Church Rates Lawful but not Expedient', as a pamphlet in 1833, arguing similarly. Although church rates were not illegal or unconstitutional, he said, they prevented 'the reconciliation of the Church with the Dissenters, and the Reform of the Church itself', and should be abolished on those grounds alone.[11]

While many dissenters and anglicans welcomed local abolition of church rates, strict supporters of the establishment feared that the removal of church rates would lead eventually to disestablishment, and to an irreligious society.[12] It would be a mistake, however, to assume that the church rate question in the 19th century divided anglicans completely from dissenters. Although the majority of opponents of church rate reform were high church anglicans, many dissenters (notably wesleyans) supported the retention of church rates as a necessary aspect of having a state religion.[13] Strict opponents of church rate abolition found strength in the fact that church rates could only be levied

---

[8] Particularly after 1818 and 1819, when parliament allowed church rates to be levied for new church building, not just to maintain existing church fabric. See Ellens, *Religious Routes*, 14–15.

[9] P.J. Salmon, 'Electoral Reform at Work: Local Politics and National Parties, 1832–1841', University of Oxford PhD, 1997, pp. 206–7.

[10] Northumberland RO, Ord Papers, NRO 324/A.69: William Ord, address to electors [n.d.] 1834.

[11] Rev. C. Girdlestone, *Church Rates Lawful, but Not Always Expedient: A Sermon* (1833), 3.

[12] See *Church Rates: A Letter to William Stratford Dugdale, Esq. Member of Parliament for the Northern Division of the County of Warwick, by a Birmingham Manufacturer, One of His Constituents* (Birmingham, 1837); *A Letter to Sir John Campbell on the Law of Church Rates* (1837); *The Real Character of the Provisions of the Bill for Abolishing Church Rates, Viewed Chiefly with Reference to the Coronation Oath* (Durham, 1837).

[13] For a complete discussion of the varying opinions on church rates, see Ellens, *Religious Routes*, ch. 1.

by the consent of the majority of ratepayers in a parish, and so, when church rate opponents had a majority in a local parish, they were not levied. This led, in places, to a desire to see the church rate question settled on a national scale, for the political muscle shown by dissenters and others at the local level to be flexed nationally, and hence lead to the redress of other grievances. This was one of the reasons why dissenters and church rate opponents were able to maintain pressure on parliament for such a long period.[14] Their main stumbling block, however, turned out to be internal dissension over whether to push the church rate abolition movement in a voluntaryist direction, and to demand secularisation of church–state relations, or to concentrate on the abolition of the church rate alone, and avoid the establishment question.[15] Dissent became increasingly voluntaryist throughout the 19th century, and the reaction to it from non-voluntaryist dissenters caused a rift in the church rate abolition movement.[16]

Similar divisions were to be found among Liberal Party MPs in the house of commons. Before we turn to an analysis of parliamentary action on the church rate issue and how it related to the Liberal Party, a short introduction to the differing initial attitudes towards church rates is necessary, so that their subsequent behaviour may be better understood. To begin with, it is important to remember that the differences in attitudes towards church rates among Liberal Party MPs were disagreements among religious men. Radicals and some Reformers argued for church rate abolition on the grounds of equality among sects, and the removal of state preference for anglicanism. Other Reformers, and most Whigs, sought to abolish church rates, while retaining church establishment, including financial support from the government. No Liberal Party MP argued that church rates should be abolished on secular grounds. Ellens asserts that this was explained by many political differences between English liberalism and continental liberalism. English liberalism was not anti-christian and anti-clerical like continental liberalism. It was a hybrid species that was given birth through the midwifery of religion (including the participation of high church and broad church anglicans) and dissenting voluntaryism.[17] The Liberal Party, therefore, represented a broad range of liberal opinion, which sometimes displayed divisiveness during the debates and divisions on the various church rate reform proposals. The majority of the Whigs believed in church establishment, and that only minor reforms were needed to remove dissenters' grievances. Further, these reforms would strengthen the Established Church, and provide a stronger base from which it could continue to act as a guardian of national morality.[18] Brent argues, however, that there was a significant difference between younger liberal anglican Whigs and older, traditional ones. Liberal anglicans, such as Russell and Morpeth, 'defended the Anglican establishment as a liberal institution open to all members of a Christian nation. Its utility was dependent on its popularity'. More conservative Whigs, such as Grey and Stanley, wary of Radical demands, and fearing a return to the reform agitation of 1830–2, sought to conserve the existing state of the

---

[14] Ellens, *Religious Routes*, 3–5.

[15] Machin, *Politics and the Churches*, 45–7; Chadwick, *Victorian Church*, 81–9, 146–58.

[16] Ellens, *Religious Routes*, 19–20.

[17] Ellens, *Religious Routes*, 2.

[18] Machin, *Politics and the Churches*, 19.

church of England.[19] Both Whig groups believed, however, that if church rates were to be abolished, another source of church revenue must be found, even if that meant state money from another source.[20]

Radicals, as we shall see, were almost universally in favour of church rate abolition, and most favoured a greater degree of distance between church and state. When they were at odds, it was over the degree of secularism and voluntaryism they supported.[21] Reformers, arguably the most interesting group, were more or less equally divided between whiggish support of church defence and the more moderate radicalism, stopping short of voluntaryism and disestablishment. As we shall see, they voted equally on either side of church rate divisions and, more importantly, their political ideology, as expressed in debate, was divided as well. Further, their behaviour as a subgroup was more or less identical with the behaviour of the party as a whole, even though they were not the largest constituent group. Although generally silent during the church rate debates, Repealers were universal in voting together (for church rate abolition), and in significant numbers, possibly to show ideological consistency with the appropriation debates, and possibly to help English Radicals and Reformers who had supported reform of the Irish church. As in the previous chapter, we shall see that the reaction among Liberal Party MPs shows the difficulties that a loose coalition such as the Liberal Party faced over religious issues. But, unlike appropriation, the church rate debates do not show a party increasing its ideological and political cohesion. They reveal a much more chaotic situation, where Liberal Party government ministers supported only government church rate reform bills, while Liberal Party backbenchers almost universally supported dramatic church finance reform, and even church rate abolition. It was as if, unlike Irish appropriation, the problem for the Liberal Party was that the church rate controversy was too close to home either for a solution to be found or for there to be a reasonable level of party cohesion.

Parliamentary Action on Church Rates 1832–52

On 31 December 1832, James Atkinson, Whig electioneering agent for Kendal and Westmoreland, wrote to James Brougham that, in order to satisfy a still reform-minded country, the Whig ministry must follow parliamentary reform with church reform. But, he added in a highly prescient note, 'It is quite a difficult subject, [and] must be touched by a masterhand, to produce anything like satisfaction in the country'.[22] Soon after, a deputation from the United Committee of Dissenting Deputies, a nonconformist pressure group, sent an address to Grey on 2 May 1833, asking for church rate relief, as well as other dissenting reforms.[23] Dissenting interests kept up the pressure on the government in 1834. Grey received a deputation from the United Committee on 15 January

---

[19] Brent, 'Whigs and Protestant Dissent', 888–90. See also B. Hilton, 'Whiggery, Religion and Social Reform: The Case of Lord Morpeth', *HJ*, xxxvii (1994), 829–59.

[20] Brent, 'Whigs and Protestant Dissent', 909.

[21] Ellens, *Religious Routes*, 25.

[22] UCL Manuscripts Room, Brougham Papers: James Atkinson to James Brougham, 31 Dec. 1832.

[23] Ellens, *Religious Routes*, 34–5.

of that year. They asked for a broad range of church reforms and for relief of standard dissenting grievances. Grey replied that he was sympathetic to their practical grievances, but that he would never support disestablishment. Further, he argued, calls for disestablishment would simply alienate the Whigs in the house of commons, which would make them less likely to listen to calls for general church reforms, including the abolition of church rates.[24] Five days later, the committee went to Russell, who listened more sympathetically, but told them that the abolition of church rates would bring up the larger question of the connection between church and state, which he would oppose severing.[25] Not satisfied with their reception, the United Committee withdrew to consider other modes of attack or persuasion.

When the parliamentary session started, however, the movement for church rate abolition had taken hold with some backbenchers. On 18 March 1834, Edward Divett, Whig MP for Exeter, moved to abolish the compulsory payment of church rates in England and Wales. He had given notice of the motion at the end of the previous session, and had hoped that the ministry would have been able to bring in an acceptable church rate measure. Seeing that the United Committee had had little success with Grey and Russell, he decided to introduce his motion early in the session.[26] In a relatively short speech, Divett brought up a larger question of church reform, even though his motion dealt only with church rates.[27] 'His opinion was that no man could be justly charged for the support of a religion to which he dissented.' He argued further that there was no reason why the Church could not survive on voluntary contributions, as dissenting chapels were forced to do.

> The principle upon which money should be raised for the necessary expenses of the Church was exclusively that of voluntary contribution. But it would be said, that it was impossible to maintain a Church by such means. To disprove that assumption, he would refer to the case of the Dissenters, who had 8,000 places of worship, and for their maintenance they did not raise in any one year less than a million. Surely, if the dissenters could effect this, the members of the Church of England might be called upon to do something also for the support of their religion.[28]

Further, he argued near the end of his speech, church rate abolition was an almost certain way to improve dissenting attitudes and to lessen acrimony towards the church of England. In what was perhaps an incautious statement, Divett said that dissenters were bitter towards the church of England, but that certain conciliatory measures, such as the abolition of church rates, would go a long way towards dampening that hostility.

> He wished . . . to impress upon the minds of members of the Church of England, that, by showing a conciliatory spirit to their dissenting fellow subjects, they would

---

[24] Machin, *Politics and the Churches*, 40; Raymond Cowherd, *The Politics of English Dissent: The Religious Aspects of Liberal and Humanitarian Reform Movements from 1815–1848* (1959), 84–5; Ellens, *Religious Routes*, 37.

[25] Ellens, *Religious Routes*, 37.

[26] Hansard, *Parl. Debs*, xxii, col. 381 (18 Mar. 1834); J.P. Ellens, 'Lord John Russell and the Church Rate Conflict: The Struggle for a Broad Church, 1834–1868', *Journal of British Studies*, xxvi (1987), 234.

[27] Hansard, *Parl. Debs*, xxii, cols 381–2 (18 Mar. 1834).

[28] Hansard, *Parl. Debs*, xxii, cols 383–4 (18 Mar. 1834).

best promote the interests of that church to which they were attached, and contribute to its stability hereafter. In almost all parishes, particularly in large towns, there was at present a bitter feeling of hostility entertained by the Dissenters towards the Church of England. He believed it was yet possible to do away with the acrimony which existed.[29]

Divett was followed in the debate by several Liberal Party backbenchers, most of them echoing his call for the abolition of church rates and the removal of other dissenters' grievances. Edward Baines, in a speech typical of these, brought up the subjects of admission to the universities, civil registration of births, deaths and marriages, burial rites and other dissenting grievances. Baines placed church rates in a privileged position among dissenting grievances.[30] Right from the very beginning of backbench efforts at church rate reform, the symbolic nature of the question was emphasized. Althorp rose for the government and responded in the same vein, addressing church rates as a symbol of dissenting grievances. He went through Divett's and Baines' list of grievances and spoke to each one. This response showed that, once the subject of church rates was opened, even the government was prepared to discuss the range of dissenting grievances.[31] Russell followed, saying that ministers would act liberally towards dissenters, now that they were in power, and the great question of parliamentary reform had been settled.

> Present ministers were the friends of the just claims of the dissenters, because they were the friends of civil and religious liberty . . . they were men bound together as a party for the support of those principles; out of power they had endeavoured to forward them – out of power they had succeeded in getting a great portion of the just claims of dissenters conceded; and now that they were in power, there surely should be no doubt and no want of confidence in them as to their bringing forward, in due time, and season, the question by which the dissenters would find, that all their claims would be satisfactorily arranged.[32]

Given these indirect assurances from Althorp and Russell that the government would bring in a church rate bill, Divett agreed to withdraw his motion and wait upon government action.[33]

On 21 April 1834, Althorp introduced the government's plan for church rate reform, outlining a measure abolishing church rates and replacing them with a fixed sum of £250,000 to be granted out of the proceeds of the land tax, 'to be applied to the fabrics of the parish churches and chapels in such a manner as parliament may direct'.[34] The reaction to Althorp's plan was strong opposition from dissenters and Radicals, and mild support from Conservatives. Joseph Hume, Radical MP for Middlesex, summarized the utilitarian opposition to the government's scheme when he rose and said that Althorp 'had merely changed the manner in which the payment was to be made. It was merely

---

[29] Hansard, *Parl. Debs*, xxii, cols 385–6 (18 Mar. 1834).

[30] Hansard, *Parl. Debs*, xxii, cols 395–7 (18 Mar. 1834).

[31] Hansard, *Parl. Debs*, xxii, cols 388–92 (18 Mar. 1834).

[32] Hansard, *Parl. Debs*, xxii, cols 398–9 (18 Mar. 1834).

[33] Hansard, *Parl. Debs*, xxii, col. 401 (18 Mar. 1834).

[34] Hansard, *Parl. Debs*, xxii, cols 1013–19 (21 Apr. 1834).

paying the money out of one pocket instead of the other'.[35] That evening, Joseph Brotherton, Radical MP for Salford, reported to John Benjamin Smith in Manchester on the reception of Althorp's bill, and the Radical reaction to it. He wrote that Radical opinion and potential action could be gleaned from the simple sentence, 'Mr Hume is opposing the plan'.[36] Edward Divett, who had given up his motion of 18 March based on Althorp's and Russell's hints that the government would bring in an acceptable measure for church rate reform, was disappointed. Like other Liberal Party MPs who thought themselves representatives of nonconformists, he could not abide replacing the church rate with a payment from the land tax: 'He knew that he was speaking the sentiments of his constituents [when he said] that he could not agree to that part of the noble Lord's plan which went to providing the substitute'.[37] Further, argued Daniel Harvey, Radical MP for Colchester, dissenters found themselves disappointed with the Whig government very soon after they expected the Whigs to follow the Reform Act with church reform.

> We are cautioned, night after night, not to work willing men to death . . . if we will be patient, they will try and do something for us. But surely it would have been better for them to have come forward at once and said, 'we are of the opinion that the same principles which we have applied to the Church of Ireland ought to be applied to the Church of England; at the same time we are firm and decided friends of establishment, and are averse to the experiment of dissolving its connection with the state'. These feelings, honestly expressed, would have been understood and respected by dissenters, who would have been prepared to make great concessions, and the adoption of sound principle of making the church in England, as in Ireland, support its own fabric, would have accumulated upon them the affections and attachment of the dissenting body.[38]

Thomas Barrett-Leonard, Reformer MP for Maldon, opposed the plan, but for entirely different reasons. He recorded in his political notebook, that:

> Lord Althorp's plan deprives the Parishioners of the controul [*sic*] they can now exercise over the rate: takes away the prerogative of taxing themselves for the support of the Church, & places a dangerous & discretionary power in the hands of High Church commissioners; whose office is already sufficiently unpopular.[39]

These objections, however, were not enough to stop Althorp's motion from passing by 258 to 142, with a majority of 116.[40] But the Whig government had had to rely on

[35] Hansard, *Parl. Debs*, xxii, cols 1019–22 (21 Apr. 1834). See also Ellens, *Religious Routes*, 4; Cowherd, *Politics of English Dissent*, 89–90; Machin, *Politics and the Churches*, 44.

[36] Manchester Central Library, John Benjamin Smith Papers, MS 923.2 S.333, ii, item 179: Brotherton to J.B. Smith, 21 Apr. 1834.

[37] Hansard, *Parl. Debs*, xxii, col. 1029 (21 Apr. 1834).

[38] Hansard, *Parl. Debs*, xxii, col. 1047 (21 Apr. 1834).

[39] Essex RO, Barrett-Leonard Papers, D/DL, O48/1: Thomas Barrett-Leonard, entry in political notebook, 24 Apr. 1834.

[40] Hansard, *Parl. Debs*, xxii, cols 1059–63 (21 Apr. 1834).

Table 6.1: *Division on Althorp's 1834 Church Rate Motion*

Liberal Party groups	Ayes	Noes
Administration	7	0
Liberals	0	1
Radicals	6	14
Reformers	60	53
Repealers	4	23
Whigs	77	39
None listed	16	12
All Liberal Party	170	142
Conservative Party	88	0
Totals	258	142

Sources: Hansard, *Parl. Debs*, xx, cols 1059–63 (21 Apr. 1834); *The Times*, 22 Apr. 1834.

Conservative support. As the division analysis in Table 6.1 shows, there was an almost complete divide among Liberal Party MPs between the Whigs and everyone else.

As with all the divisions on church rates, there was no surprise in Conservative Party behaviour. It was also no surprise that the Liberal Party was close to being evenly split. The debates had indicated this, with roughly half the MPs speaking opposing Althorp's plan along the same lines that Hume had used to object to it – that the new church funding would be rating in another form. The depth of Liberal Party disagreement shows how divided the party was over the question of any payment by dissenters, whether it came from church rates or from the land tax. The split among Reformers indicates that they were the Liberal Party writ small. As we shall see below, this was the beginning of the indications that the fundamental divide in the Liberal Party during the 1830s was with the Reformers, ideologically the 'middle group' between the Whigs and the Radicals. One important reason why the church rate problem was never solved by Liberal Party legislation was not because of the tension from Radicals or from establishment-minded Whigs, but that this core of the party could not agree. Further, there was a large section of moderate Whigs who voted 'No', showing that a significant number of Whigs were willing to vote for complete abolition. It became clear, then, that Althorp's motion would attract too much hostility from dissenters for the government to push it through to law, and the measure was quietly dropped.[41]

After being disappointed in this way, many dissenters became wary of the Whigs. Some of them called upon their fellow nonconformists to support only those candidates who would champion some form of voluntaryism; others clung to the Whigs as the only acceptable alternative to a Conservative government under Peel, which, they thought, would be too defensive on church matters.[42] According to Brent, the reaction to the 1834 church rate motions showed an increasing distance between liberal and conservative Whigs, as symbolised by the distance between Grey and Russell. Grey's attitude towards church rate abolition was this: he was reluctant to offend high church Whigs

[41] I. Newbould, *Whiggery and Reform, 1830–1841: The Politics of Government* (1990), 150; Ellens, 'Lord John Russell', 234–5.

[42] Ellens, *Religious Routes*, 40–9.

such as Graham, so he stalled and refused to take action on church rate abolition, antagonising dissenters in the country. Russell realized that church rates would have to be modified or abolished in order to mollify dissenters, but he was unable to move against Grey.[43] Russell, therefore, tried to straddle both camps, while pushing the cabinet in a 'liberal anglican' direction. In late 1834, Melbourne asked him to try to solve the church rate problem without allowing the issue of establishment to arise. Russell realized that the government could not abolish church rates because it would have to make up the lost revenue from the Consolidated Fund, and that church upkeep would have to become a permanent charge on the Fund. The house of commons, he thought, would never agree to this. His solution to this dilemma would be to keep the rate until the Church's finances could be restructured and a surplus created that would equal the revenue the rate took in.[44] This was his way of showing the dissenters that the Whigs were still the reforming party, even though he thought the basic idea of rating in order to support the church of England as a national institution was sound.[45]

The year 1835 saw little action on church rate questions in the house of commons, even though Peel conceded at Tamworth that dissenters had a basic right to appeal for their list of grievances to be acted upon, and he thought deeply about replacing rating with some other form of finance. But he was not in office long enough to do anything more than convince the Church hierarchy that a commission should be appointed to inquire into church finances.[46] Back in office in April, the Whig cabinet began to plan a church rate bill under the leadership of Russell. He argued that a plan that abolished church rates could be acceptable to anglicans if church finances were restructured (especially redistributed to equalise the income disparity among the clergy). This would maintain the Church as a national institution, yet reform it to satisfy the reasonable elements among both churchmen and dissenters. But the cabinet cautioned delay, in order to hear the report of the commissioners on church revenue. They hoped to avoid, or blunt, a tory 'Church in danger' cry. Further, they wanted to wait until the Registration of Births, Deaths and Marriages Bill had passed.[47] When the report of the ecclesiastical commission on church finances was published, it only strengthened the call for delay. It found that church revenue was inadequate to provide enough clergy and churches for the expanding population. The cabinet then realized that it must restructure church finances before touching the subject of church rate abolition.[48]

Dissenters reacted strongly to this delay. The United Committee asked Melbourne and Russell simply to let the church rate question be settled in each vestry. *The Patriot*, a leading dissenting journal, encouraged its readers to refuse to pay their rates. It also said that the Whigs were no longer to be trusted and that the nation's dissenters should take church rate matters into their own hands. Whig successes with the marriage ceremony and registration bills did not receive due credit because church rates had not

---

[43] Brent, 'Whigs and Protestant Dissent', 892.

[44] Newbould, *Whiggery and Reform*, 157; Ellens, *Religious Routes*, 48–9.

[45] Ellens, 'Lord John Russell', 233.

[46] Cowherd, *Politics of English Dissent*, 90; Ellens, *Religious Routes*, 49–50.

[47] Brent, 'Whigs and Protestant Dissent', 901–2; Ellens, 'Lord John Russell', 236–7; Ellens, *Religious Routes*, 53–4.

[48] Ellens, *Religious Routes*, 63–4.

been addressed. This failure to gain dissenting support cast a pall over the 1836 session.[49] That session ended with the founding of the Church Rate Abolition Society, whose purpose was to consolidate dissenting opinion and unite behind the demand that church rates be abolished totally.[50] And, although Russell told the United Committee on 24 January 1837 that the government planned to bring in an acceptable church rate measure in 1837, the Church Rate Abolition Society held a meeting in London on 3 February 1837, which coincided with the opening of parliament. It passed resolutions focusing on abolition, refusing to consider any question of commutation, but it stopped short of calling for disestablishment.[51]

The Church Rate Abolition Society was pleased, therefore, when the government, under the chancellor of the exchequer, Thomas Spring-Rice, introduced its church rate abolition bill on 3 March 1837. Amid a mass of petitions introduced, Spring-Rice proposed that church rates be abolished, and that the upkeep of the Church was to come from surplus revenues generated by better management of church lands.[52] Further, he said, the control of church property was to pass to a government commission:

the plan of his Majesty's government . . . proposed to abolish Church rates altogether; not for the purpose of leaving the fabric of the Church unprovided for, but with a view to providing for its repair, and maintaining it in a manner equally permanent, equally fixed, as before, but by a mode differing from the present in this main and essential distinction, that while the present system seeks for its support through contests painful in prosecution, and doubtful in result – while in levying rates it creates religious animosity – we propose to maintain the fabric of the Church without injury to the Church itself, or to any class of persons, and under a system by which these heats and animosities will be extinguished.[53]

As expected, dissenters were largely satisfied and Conservative churchmen were strongly opposed. The church commissioners who had reported that the Church's finances were not in good shape threatened to resign if the government went ahead with its plans. Petitions came into the house of commons from dissenters and churchmen, supporting or opposing the government's bill. But church reaction was not strong enough to prevent Spring-Rice's bill from passing its first reading 273 to 250, with a slender majority of 23.[54] The debate on the second reading was, therefore, sharp and intense, with churchmen raising the 'Church in danger' cry, Liberal Party MPs arguing that church property was state property, and dissenters arguing that this bill provided a

---

[49] Ellens, *Religious Routes*, 54–6; *The Patriot*, 11 May 1836.

[50] Cowherd, *Politics of English Dissent*, 94; Ellens, 'Lord John Russell', 238.

[51] Cowherd, *Politics of English Dissent*, 94–5; Ellens, *Religious Routes*, 59–60; Ellens, 'Lord John Russell', 238–9.

[52] Hansard, *Parl. Debs*, xxxvi, col. 1207 (3 Mar. 1837).

[53] Hansard, *Parl. Debs*, xxxvi, cols 1224–5 (3 Mar. 1837); Chadwick, *Victorian Church*, 146–7. See also W. Metcalfe, *The Opinion of Sir John Campbell on the Law of Church-Rates, as Stated in His Letter to the Right Hon. Lord Stanley* (1837); J. Nicholl, *Church Rates: Observations on the Attorney General's Letter to Lord Stanley* (1837).

[54] Hansard, *Parl. Debs*, xxxvii, col. 549 (16 Mar. 1837). See also Rev. W.S. Bricknell, *The Grievance of Church Rates* (1837).

Table 6.2: *Division on Spring-Rice's 1837 Church Rate Abolition Bill, Second Reading*

Liberal Party groups	Ayes	Noes
Administration	14	0
Liberals	2	0
Radicals	33	0
Reformers	81	43
Repealers	27	0
Whigs	116	14
None listed	21	3
All Liberal Party	299	60
Conservative Party	1	235
Totals	300	295

Sources: Hansard, *Parl. Debs*, xxxviii, cols 1073–7 (23 May 1837); *The Times*, 24 May 1837; House of Commons, Division Lists, 16 Mar. 1837 (Division numbers were not added to the official Division Lists until 1839).

solution acceptable to them, and should be passed. But when the bill came up for its second reading, the government's majority had been reduced to five, with the division 300 to 295 (Table 6.2).[55]

This was a government bill and, as we saw in 1834, and will see in the following divisions, the Whigs voted overwhelmingly with the government, even though, by this time, the government had made a significant shift in opinion regarding the nature of church rate reform and abolition. Spring-Rice's bill went much further than Althorp's, abolishing church rates and replacing the revenue by improving the management of church finances. So, like the appropriation behaviour, we see here that Whig MPs followed the government. Further, the Liberal Party as a whole was much more cohesive in this division. More interesting, however, is the behaviour of the Reformers, and the surprising number of Reformers' Noes. They voted against the government more than any other Liberal Party group, just as they had done in 1834. The significance of this will become clearer as we analyse the rest of the divisions and discuss the Reformers as the 'centre' of the Liberal Party in the conclusion.[56]

Melbourne subsequently withdrew the bill, knowing it would never pass the Lords with such slender Commons support. It came as no surprise, therefore, that the election of 1837 saw dissenters requesting church rate pledges from candidates, and a weakened Whig–dissent relationship. After the Whig failures to abolish church rates in 1837, the political agitation of dissenters turned towards extracting specific promises from candidates regarding church reform, and to return Radicals rather than Whigs.[57] This election, Cowherd argues, weakened Whig–dissent relations, and led to 'the formation of a more Liberal Party under middle-class leadership'.[58] Church rate agitation lessened after the

[55] Hansard, *Parl. Debs*, xxxviii, col. 1073 (23 May 1837).

[56] The *Morning Chronicle*, 24 May 1832, ascribed the reduction in the government's majority as being due to increased conservative whipping and Liberal Party MPs being absent.

[57] Parkes (WEST): Parkes to Edward Ellice Sr, 24 Aug. 1837.

[58] Cowherd, *Politics of English Dissent*, 95–6.

Table 6.3: *Division on Duncombe's 1840 Church Rate Exemption Motion*

Liberal Party groups	Ayes	Noes
Administration	0	3
Liberals	6	1
Radicals	16	0
Reformers	24	12
Repealers	7	1
Whigs	7	17
None listed	4	5
All Liberal Party	64	39
Conservative Party	0	80
Totals	64	119

Sources: Hansard, *Parl. Debs*, lii, cols 116–17 (11 Feb. 1840); House of Commons, Division Lists, 11 Feb. 1840, No. 27.

1837 election. Russell told Melbourne that church rate reform would have to wait until parliamentary opinion was ripe.[59] The action now moved fully to the backbenches.

In 1839, T.S. Duncombe, Radical MP for Finsbury, moved, and had passed, a resolution on 30 July which said that, due to the case of some dissenters being jailed for non-payment of church rates, the house of commons should take up the question in the 1840 session. In a straight party vote, a poorly attended House passed his resolution 42 to 22.[60] The following year, on 11 February 1840, Duncombe brought in a church rate motion. His plan was that church rates should not be abolished, but that dissenters should be exempted from paying them, upon swearing the following oath:

> I, A.B., do solemnly and sincerely declare that I am not of the communion of the Church of England, as by law established, but I do dissent therefrom; and I do solemnly declare that on that account I object to the payment of Church-rates; and I do not do so from any pecuniary or interested motives, but for the sake of my conscience only.[61]

In addition to objecting to this motion on the grounds that the Church was a national institution and provided good for all, Russell argued for the government that the proposal was unworkable, and that people would claim to be dissenters when in fact they were not.[62] And after a short debate, the house of commons voted against Duncombe's motion 64 to 119, a majority of 55 against (Table 6.3).[63]

Compared with 1839, more MPs voted in this division, and the combination of Conservative, Reformer and Whig votes was enough to defeat the motion. Again, the Reformers proved to be the least coherent liberal group. Later in the session, on 7 July

[59] Ellens, *Religious Routes*, 67–8.
[60] Hansard, *Parl. Debs*, xlix, cols 1006–7 (30 July 1837).
[61] Hansard, *Parl. Debs*, lii, cols 88–92 (11 Feb. 1840).
[62] Hansard, *Parl. Debs*, lii, cols 96–7 (11 Feb. 1840).
[63] Hansard, *Parl. Debs*, lii, cols 116–17 (11 Feb. 1840).

1840, Sir John Easthope, Liberal MP for Leicester, brought in a simple motion to exempt dissenters from church rates along the same lines as Duncombe's plan. But he was forced to withdraw the motion when the Speaker reminded him that the house of commons could not entertain the same question twice in one session.[64] Easthope then brought in two church rate motions in 1841. The first was on behalf of William Baines, jailed in Leicester in November 1840 for not paying his church rate.[65] Although Easthope claimed that he was simply bringing in the petition on behalf of Baines, his motion ended with the words:

> and that thus to imprison William Baines for refusing to contribute towards the expenses attending the worship of the Established church, from which he conscientiously dissents, is to punish him for acting in accordance with what he regards as a religious duty, and is, a violation of the principles of religious freedom.[66]

Russell responded on behalf of the government that, while he supported religious freedom and freedom of conscience, he could not allow laws to be broken or allow those who broke laws to be given special treatment.[67] By 1841 church rate debates kept getting shorter and shorter, and the motion on behalf of Baines failed quickly, 40 to 45.[68] On 25 May, Easthope brought in his second church rate motion of 1841, this time moving that church rates be abolished and replaced with pew rents. His speech was a litany of the attempts to abolish church rates, and after another short debate, he was given leave to bring in a bill which, owing to the 1841 election and the pressure of parliamentary business, did not come to light until 1842.[69]

On 16 June 1842, during Peel's ministry, Easthope brought in his delayed church rate abolition motion, proposing, as he had in 1841, to replace church rates with pew rents and other financial reforms. He spoke again about dissenters' aggravation, and the lingering bitterness that failing to provide a solution had caused between dissenters and churchmen.[70] Again the debate was short, highlighted by Peel arguing that pew rents would have an adverse effect on the poor, and by Sharman Crawford, Radical MP for Rochdale, attacking Easthope for ignoring the issue of establishment.[71] The motion was defeated 164 to 82 (Table 6.4).[72]

This was also a more-or-less straight party vote, but the general absence of party leaders voting on each side ensured that the motion was never taken seriously enough, and was eventually withdrawn. Like appropriation, church rate agitation was both subverted by chartism and lost initiative through the increasingly frustrating failures within the house of commons. The 1840s saw few petitions presented to the Commons, and there were relatively few cases of refusal to pay rates resulting in imprisonment. In

---

[64] Hansard, *Parl. Debs*, lv, cols 545–6, 553 (7 July 1840).
[65] Cowherd, *Politics of English Dissent*, 155–6; Chadwick, *Victorian Church*, 150–1.
[66] Hansard, *Parl. Debs*, vii, cols 360–7 (18 Mar. 1841).
[67] Hansard, *Parl. Debs*, lvii, cols 390–1 (18 Mar. 1841).
[68] Hansard, *Parl. Debs*, lvii, cols 390–1 (18 Mar. 1841).
[69] Hansard, *Parl. Debs*, lviii, cols 765–82, 783–4 (18 Mar. 1841).
[70] Hansard, *Parl. Debs*, xiii, cols 1613–23 (16 June 1842).
[71] Hansard, *Parl. Debs*, lxiii, cols 1624–8 (16 June 1842).
[72] Hansard, *Parl. Debs*, lxiii, cols 1637–9 (16 June 1842).

Table 6.4: *Division on Easthope's 1842 Church Rate Abolition Motion*

Liberal Party groups	Ayes	Noes
Administration	0	0
Liberals	19	1
Radicals	6	0
Reformers	25	0
Repealers	2	0
Whigs	21	1
None listed	9	0
All Liberal Party	82	2
Conservative Party	0	162
Totals	82	164

Sources: Hansard, *Parl. Debs*, lxiii, cols 1637–9 (16 June 1842); *The Times*, 17 June 1842; House of Commons, Division Lists, 16 June 1842, No. 129.

fact, it was not until the next parliamentary generation that this question was revitalised by another Liberal Party backbencher, John Trelawny, Liberal MP for Tavistock. He introduced, and subsequently withdrew, a church rate abolition motion in 1849, headed a parliamentary committee that examined the question in 1851, and brought in church rate abolition motions from 1858 to 1863.[73] But the fruit of Trelawny's work lies outside the chronological scope of this book.

We see, therefore, in the behaviour of Liberal Party MPs on this issue, that party cohesion was problematic. Although many of the later debates and divisions were close to being straight party votes in terms of the different liberal groups present in each lobby, they were not divisions that displayed a great deal of party action. Frontbenchers and backbenchers rarely voted together, the Reformer 'centre' could not agree on church rates, and the inattention to whipping kept Liberal Party church rate motions from succeeding. The usual arguments that church rate abolition failed because of the fear of the house of lords and the Church are too simple, therefore, when we consider that the Liberal Party could not get any proposal passed.

Church Rates as a Defining Issue for Liberal Politics

Having seen how MPs voted, we must also examine why Liberal Party MPs acted the way they did and how it illuminates liberal politics in this period. Liberal Party MPs often moved in different division lobbies, depending on the nature of the church rate motion, but their differences often came from the same political base. There were three main areas in which we may examine the cohesiveness of Liberal Party ideology on church rates: the church of England as an establishment, the Church as a national institution, and support for religious liberty.

---

[73] See Ellens, *Religious Routes*, 101–271; Ellens, 'Lord John Russell', 242; *The Parliamentary Diaries of Sir John Trelawny, 1858–1865*, ed. T. Jenkins (Camden Society, 4th ser., xl, 1990), 10–14.

The majority of Liberal Party MPs supported the establishment of the church of England, even if they brought in a church rate abolition motion, backed by their dissenting constituents. If we look at a few examples, from high Whig to disestablishment Radical, we see the depth of Liberal Party feeling about church establishment. On the first night of the second reading debate on Spring-Rice's 1837 church rate abolition bill, Andrew Johnston, Whig MP for St Andrew's, moved an amendment hostile to the government's bill. Johnston wanted to show the depth of support for the idea that church rate revenue was anglican money, and only applicable to anglican ends. He said that he:

> was sorry he could not support the resolutions of his Majesty's Government, and that the task devolved on him of moving the amendment; he regretted it because he was a supporter of the general principles of the party of which [he] belonged . . . [but he moved that] . . . it is the opinion of this House that funds may be derived from an improved mode of management of Church lands, and that these funds should be applied to religious instruction within the Established Church, where the same may be found deficient in proportion in the existing population.[74]

This represented a strain of liberal argument closest to the Conservatives. Most Whigs, however, argued that the Church should be supported from, essentially, 'common good' grounds. Russell said in 1840: 'The principle on which alone they could maintain the established Church was, that it was for the common good, and that was a principle which entitled them to ask for that burden to be laid upon all'.[75]

Throughout the church rate debates, moderate Whigs argued that there must be a substitute for the revenue from church rates, if they were to be abolished. According to Brent, liberal anglican Whigs sought to liberalise the Church, but could not do so by threatening its existence.[76] Some Whigs took the argument a little further and said that the survival of the Church as an establishment depended upon the removal of such abuses as church rates.

> It must be allowed that experience has shown that these Church rates had long been the cause of great scandal to the Church . . . Parliament could in no way show itself friendly to the Church establishment, it could in no way secure to that establishment a more immediate and permanent benefit – than by removing the scandal inseparable from church rates.[77]

Edward Divett, the Whig backbencher who proposed church rate abolition before Althorp in 1834, said that 'He was anxious to do away with compulsory payment of Church rates; but he was equally anxious to preserve the property now held by the church, and to make it available for the promotion of sound religion'.[78]

---

[74] Hansard, *Parl. Debs*, xxxviii, cols 930–2 (22 May 1837). Johnston also opposed Russell's 1835 appropriation motion.

[75] Hansard, *Parl. Debs*, lii, col. 97 (11 Feb. 1840).

[76] Brent, 'Whigs and Protestant Dissent', 909.

[77] Sir Robert Rolfe, solicitor-general and Whig MP for Penryn, Hansard, *Parl. Debs*, xxxviii, col. 961 (22 May 1837).

[78] Hansard, *Parl. Debs*, xxii, col. 384 (18 Mar. 1834).

Reformers, even though they usually split in their voting, generally sought to retain the Church establishment. Charles Wynn, moderate Reformer MP for Montgomery-shire, who would drift to the Conservatives by 1837,[79] argued in 1834 that the very existence of an established church protected the general state of religion in the country.[80] John Wilks, Reformer MP for Boston, said that church rate abolition was essential, at the very least to remove the stain of churchmen being seen as tax collectors.[81] Edward Baines, the Reformer MP for Leeds who brought in a church rate abolition motion, even argued that the charge that dissenters wanted disestablishment was exaggerated.[82] In fact, disestablishment sentiments, as expressed by Sharman Crawford during the debate on Easthope's church rate abolition bill, were rare in the house of commons, no matter how common outside.

> The question, in his opinion, really at issue was the connexion of the church and the state. The question at issue was whether there should be a church establishment in England paid by the people or not . . . If there ought to be a church by law established it had a right to Church rates. If it had a right to tithes, it had a right to Church rates. It was his opinion that all such practices should be abolished, and no man compelled to pay in any shape for the religion of any other man.[83]

The second area where we may see differing strains of the same liberal politics during church rate debates was on the question of the Church as a national institution. In the church rate debates, we see the necessary modification of the classical liberal idea of the sanctity of private property. Although slightly different from other property in the sense that church rates were a fiscal entitlement, the liberal attitude towards church property is illuminating. Liberal Party MPs argued almost unanimously that the property of the Church was also the property of the state. Thomas Barrett-Leonard said: 'I look upon church property as national property, for what property is it otherwise?'[84] Spring-Rice said during a defence of his 1837 church rate abolition bill: 'the church property I view in the same light as I view the crown property'.[85] Russell had stated the government's view of the importance of the Church as a national institution when he said that ministers 'were of the opinion, that the church was conducive to the promotion of morality, to the maintenance of good order, and to the advancement of civilization: moreover, that the doctrine and discipline of the Church of England were consonant to the feelings of the people of this country'.[86] This provided another premise to the liberal

---

[79] Robert Stewart argues that Wynn had become a Conservative by 1832, but Wynn lists himself in *Dod* as a 'moderate Reformer' until 1838. See R. Stewart, *The Foundation of the Conservative Party 1830–1867* (1978), 374.

[80] Hansard, *Parl. Debs*, xxii, col. 1054 (21 Apr. 1834).

[81] Hansard, *Parl. Debs*, xxii, col. 1030 (21 Apr. 1834).

[82] Hansard, *Parl. Debs*, xxxviii, col. 932 (22 Mar. 1837).

[83] Hansard, *Parl. Debs*, lxiii, cols 1627–8 (16 June 1842).

[84] Essex RO, Barrett-Leonard Papers, D/DL, O24/4: response to appeal from Maldon dissenters, 24 June 1847.

[85] Hansard, *Parl. Debs*, xxxvi, col. 1238 (3 Mar. 1837).

[86] Hansard, *Parl. Debs*, xxix, col. 1049 (21 Apr. 1834).

argument that national institutions were answerable to the best interests of the populace, and that exclusively narrow control of established church property was no longer tenable in the reformed political world.

Constituent Pressure and Expectations

Now that we have seen how MPs reacted to church rate legislation from a base of liberal politics, we may look briefly at the pressure applied on them by constituents and pressure groups, before drawing conclusions about the meaning of the church rate debates for the early Liberal Party. The church rate issue in the constituencies has been examined in detail by Ellens. But it will be helpful to see briefly how certain important pressure groups and constituency experiences may have affected MPs' behaviour in the house of commons. The 1830s and 1840s witnessed a culmination of local agitation against church rates which began in 1818–19. In 1824 in Sheffield there was agitation against church rates, which continued through the 1830s in Manchester, with those areas in dissenting control refusing to levy them. And at Rochdale in 1840 there was a riot and the troops had to be called out.[87] In 1831, *The Patriot* was founded as a national journal for dissenting interests, and a specific pressure group, the Church Rate Abolition Society, was founded in London on 19 October 1836.[88] It was made up of respectable dissenting ministers, dissenting MPs and even some liberal churchmen. Its purpose was to consolidate dissenting opinion on the issue and to unite behind the demand that church rates be abolished totally.[89] Although it had a very auspicious start, including having the moderate Reformer MP for Ashburton, Charles Lushington, in the chair at its inaugural meeting, the Church Rate Abolition Society failed to 'seal the doom of church rates', in the *Morning Chronicle*'s overly optimistic phrase.[90] It was too moderate, and was prone to being talked out of agitation by government promises of church rate reform. By 11 December 1839, the Church Rate Abolition Society had petered out of existence.[91] Broader dissenting pressure groups, such as the Religious Freedom Society (founded in November 1838), and the Anti-State-Church Association (founded in April 1844) took dissenters' interests further, arguing for a whole package of reforms for dissenters, not just church rate abolition. But they failed as well.[92]

If we look briefly at some representative examples of constituents' correspondence to Liberal Party MPs, we may see a corresponding variance in opinion on the question of church rates and dissenting grievances to that we saw in the house of commons. Terry Jenkins has argued that there was a 'remarkable social gulf' between the Liberal Party in parliament and the people that the party was supposed to represent. This gulf would have been ruinous for the party if there had not existed 'genuine bonds of sympathy between the parliamentarians and the electors'. He also claims that nonconformity, and the

[87] Cowherd, *Politics of English Dissent*, 155; Brent, 'Whigs and Protestant Dissent', 891.

[88] *The Patriot*, 22 Feb. 1831; Ellens, *Religious Routes*, 32.

[89] *Morning Chronicle*, 20 Oct. 1836; Cowherd, *Politics of English Dissent*, 94; Ellens, 'Lord John Russell', 238; Ellens, *Religious Routes*, 56–7.

[90] *Morning Chronicle*, 20 Oct. 1836.

[91] Ellens, *Religious Routes*, 76–7.

[92] Cowherd, *Politics of English Dissent*, 154; Ellens, *Religious Routes*, 74–92.

support for the removal of nonconformist grievances, constituted that bond.[93] The strength of that bond, as well as the tension within it, may be seen in the attitudes of constituents, as reflected in constituency correspondence. The dissenting deputies sent out a 'Questions put by the Committee of Deputies of Protestant Dissenters to Candidates . . . with a view to ascertain their sentiments upon points affecting the civil and religious rights of Protestant Dissenters'.[94] This put candidates for parliamentary seats in the position of having to address church rates in election speeches. The dissenting Reverend Thomas Newman of Nailsworth wrote to W.H. Hyett, Whig MP for Stroud, that Althorp's 1834 church rate bill did not go far enough.

> [The] question is not *the amount exacted*, but the injustice of *any* compulsory contri-
> bution. In truth his Lordship's proposal is an insult to our understandings as well as
> a violation of our consciences . . . [and that] . . . the conviction is now forced on us,
> that as the ecclesiastical establishment of the country, is a perversion of Christianity,
> and a lure to the ambition of worldly men, so it must ever be oppressive in its
> influence and reproachful in its aspect towards the vast body of protestant
> Nonconformists.[95]

In a radical address to Henry Parnell, Whig MP for Dundee, the 'non-electors of Dundee' wrote: 'we will not with one consent contribute a single farthing to keep up "pampered prelacy" to oppress and instruct us, and our dissenting brethren of England'.[96] In a letter dated 30 November 1834, Thomas Pewtress, one of D'Eyncourt's constituents, wrote to him, saying that he trusted him to follow up on dissenters' claims.

> I am connected with the Dissenters & a Member of the United Committee seeking
> to obtain redress of their grievances, it is my duty to request on their behalf the
> avowal of your sentiments as to granting their claims. I felt assured from the liberal
> sentiments you have expressed it is scarcely necessary to trouble you for a reply but
> I wish to have it in my power to satisfy others at the present important crisis.[97]

D'Eyncourt replied on 2 December 1834, saying that he had always been a strong supporter of dissenters' rights, as civil rights: 'Every vote I have given in parliament, and every sentiment I have uttered there and else where, will justify the strongest assurance on your part that there exists no firmer or more ardent friend of religious liberty in its widest practical sense, than myself'.[98] On 7 March 1839, J.H. May, a dissenting minister in North Devon, wrote to James Buller, the Liberal candidate for that seat, saying that he would vote for Buller if he could guarantee to be sympathetic to dissenters' grievances. May said that he:

---

[93] T.A. Jenkins, *The Liberal Ascendancy, 1830–1886* (1994), 18.

[94] Lincolnshire Archives Office, D'Eyncourt Papers, H19/31: undated flyer.

[95] Gloucestershire RO, Hyett Papers, D6/F32/f. 71: Rev. Thomas Newman to W.H. Hyett, 1 May 1835.

[96] Southampton UL, Broadlands Archives Trust, Parnell Papers, bundle 15: address from the non-electors of Dundee to Henry Brooke Parnell, 12 Nov. 1836.

[97] Lambeth Archives Department, Minet Library, D'Eyncourt Papers, IV/3/15: Thomas Pewtress to Charles Tennyson D'Eyncourt, 30 Nov. 1834.

[98] Lambeth Archives Department, Minet Library, D'Eyncourt Papers, IV/3/21: Charles Tennyson D'Eyncourt to Thomas Pewtress, 2 Dec. 1834.

should like to know what your views are relative to what we call the just claims of dissenters, whether you are ready to place on an equal footing in every respect with the rest of her Majesty's subjects? . . . There are many grievances yet to be redressed before we as dissenters shall feel satisfied. Amongst these, the abolition of Church rates which is such a bone of contention in this Kingdom at this time.

Showing the multiple uses to which political correspondence could be put, he then asked Buller to pay his travelling expenses to the polling place.[99] William Aldam, Liberal MP for Leeds, responded to a request for a church rate pledge from Reverend Gild of the West Riding Baptist Associated Churches:

I have declared myself a friend of the total abolition of church rates, and may add that I would not support any measure which, put an end to church rates but throw the maintenance of the fabric of the church upon the national funds . . . disapproving of the jurisdiction of Ecclesiastical Courts in matter arising out of church rates, I should support a release of any person imprisoned under an order of these courts.[100]

But the reaction against church rate abolition and redress of dissenting grievances was also strong. Although hardly a conventional constituent, E.B. Pusey, regius professor of Hebrew at Oxford and a leader of the Oxford Movement, wrote to William Ewart, Radical MP for Liverpool, saying that he was very disappointed to see Ewart's name in the division lists among the supporters of the admission of dissenters into the universities, and support for other dissenting reforms shows the close examination that some electors paid to division lists on church issues.[101] One of Thomas Buxton's constituents wrote to say that Buxton's support for church rate reform showed that:

you are not an honest man, you were afraid of offending the dissenters of this place. Your conduct is a tissue of humbug and hypocrisy. You have shown the cloven foot, and you will find at the next election, I and my family have always voted for you, but shall do so no longer. Many others will do the same. I am an elector.[102]

These examples of constituents' expectations of Liberal Party MPs, and the pressure they placed on them to support or oppose church rate reform, show not only the ways in which they thought they could influence Liberal Party MPs (and, therefore, indicating their own sense of inclusion within liberal politics) but also the deeply symbolic nature of the church rate issue. The language used shows that church rates were indeed a 'giant-sore', as Chadwick has argued, and that they carried with them the hopes of a complete raft of reform of dissenting grievances.

---

[99] Devon RO, Buller Papers, 2065M/SS, 2/10: J.H. May to James Wentworth Buller, 7 Mar. 1839.

[100] Doncaster Archives Department, Aldam Papers, DD.WA/D/P/1, item 2: William Aldam to Rev. Gild, 26 June 1841. See also Essex RO, Barrett-Leonard Papers, D/DL, O24/4: Thomas Barrett-Leonard's response to Maldon dissenters, 24 June 1847.

[101] Liverpool RO, Ewart Papers, 920MD 293, ff. 6–7: E.B. Pusey to William Ewart, 25 Apr. 1834.

[102] Bodl., Buxton Papers, MSS Britain Emp. s444: Anon. to Thomas Fowell Buxton, 19 Feb. 1837.

Conclusion

This chapter has examined both parliamentary behaviour and the importance of symbolism in the church rate debates. These should not, however, be seen as two separate things. MPs spoke and voted the way they did both because of the nature of the issues themselves and because the church rate debates were symbolic of all dissenters' grievances. But, if we examine parliamentary behaviour and symbolism separately for a moment, we may then see how mutually dependent they were. In the division analyses, we saw that when there was a large government division, Liberal Party MPs were more or less evenly split on church rate abolition. Further, when the government proposed a very mild church rate reform in 1834, 162 backbenchers (53% of all backbenchers) voted against it. When the government then went further in 1837, 298 backbenchers (82%) voted for the change. Further, backbenchers led the action in parliament for church rate reform and abolition when the government would not take it up. But the most interesting aspect of the divisions in the Liberal Party is the differences between the party's constituent groups. Not surprisingly, Radicals voted overwhelmingly for church rate abolition. Repealers did the same, for the reasons mentioned earlier. But Whigs and Reformers were split between those who sought church reform that retained the basic structure of church finances (i.e., that all were to contribute to its upkeep), and those who thought that stricter church rate reform was necessary to preserve the Church against more radical attack. Reformers behaved much like the Whigs, although voting slightly more strongly in favour of church rate reform. If the Reformers formed the 'centre' of the party, then one of the major reasons that church rate abolition never received full Liberal Party support was the failure of this centre to act like a centre, that is, to act as a moderate ground between the Whigs and the Radicals. With a split centre, unlike the behaviour shown in the appropriation divisions in Chapter 2, the Liberal Party coalition could not solve a church issue because they had no base from which to withstand pressure from the house of lords and the bishops, as they had in 1832 over parliamentary reform.

If voting in divisions was the direct action that Liberal Party MPs displayed over church rates, then the way they spoke and the way they related to their constituents showed the symbolic aspects of the issue. This chapter has suggested how important it was for those MPs to introduce church rate reform motions, to speak in debates and to correspond positively with constituents who pestered them for action on the question. Further, as was shown in Chapter 2, church rates were central to the liberal politics presented in electioneering material and speeches. For the most part, however, Liberal Party MPs knew that the 'teacup squabbles' of church rates were mainly being solved locally, and that it was only in certain places, and with certain notable church rate refusal cases, that the issue was presented as a serious problem. But the patchy nature of the extent of church rate grievances did not prevent it becoming a national issue. For dissenters, and reform-minded people, church rates provided an easily understandable example of the second-class citizen status of nonconformists and catholics. Other significant dissenters' concerns, such as admission to the universities, did not have such broad appeal because they did not seem to affect the daily lives of people in parishes. It is for that reason that church rates became symbolic of the treatment of dissenters, and that is the way the subject was mainly discussed in parliament. But the idea of symbolism in the church rate debates goes much further than just the rates alone. This chapter has shown that a certain type of symbolism itself was central to liberal politics – the idea that parliament had the duty to discuss issues of national concern whether or not there was much hope of legislation to solve the problems. Liberal Party MPs looked to parliament as the centre of political life, defined in its broadest sense. If dissenters and others could not expect the house of commons to take their grievances seriously, the whole basis of the reformed parliament would be undermined.

We may now return to the questions raised earlier. The church rate issue did follow appropriation in the sense that the Whig government proposed a very mild reform in the early 1830s (1834), and then stricter reform in the mid 1830s (1837). This move also garnered more Liberal Party support than the 1834 proposal had, and it did it by the same means – the government moving 'left' and acquiring Radical and 'left-leaning' Reformer votes. But the church rates controversy, seen as an accommodation issue, reveals different things about the Liberal Party than the appropriation debates did. These conclusions speak to the Liberal Party's failed reaction to other civil rights movements in the 1840s and 1850s. In the appropriation debates, we saw the Liberal Party cohering around the idea that Ireland was a special case, that the church of Ireland's population was so small in relation to the overall religious population that appropriation was important for maintaining order and civility in that country. With church rates, however, we see Liberal Party MPs' failure to behave as a party because English church reforms were too difficult, too close to home, to treat as dispassionately as they thought they were treating Irish church issues. Further, while Liberal Party MPs recognized almost imme- diately the symbolic value of being seen to be sensitive to dissenters' grievances by at least addressing church rates, they failed to see that church rates were equally symbolic for Conservatives and high churchmen.

We shall see this behaviour repeated when we discuss the Maynooth controversy in 1845 in Chapter 7. In those debates, Conservative Party backbenchers lambasted Liberal Party MPs for supporting the idea that no one should pay for the religion of another in the church rate debates, but contradicted themselves when supporting the idea of a catholic seminary maintained from public money. And, as will be shown, Liberal Party MPs did not fail to see this inconsistency, but they argued, in essence, that Ireland was a special case, and that part of being liberal was recognizing the need for such flexibility.

Chapter 7. Irish Religion in British Politics:
The Maynooth Difficulties for Liberal Party MPs

If church rates showed the importance of symbolism and the idea that parliament had a duty to discuss issues of importance even if they were largely being solved locally, the Maynooth controversy of 1845 showed the significance that national institutions and their responsiveness had for most Liberal Party MPs, as well as the importance of acting 'liberally', that is, having a certain principle of governance, but varying its application in different circumstances. This chapter will analyse how Liberal Party MPs reacted in these ways to Peel's 1845 Maynooth proposals, how they dealt with opposition from many of their dissenting constituents, and how their seemingly inconsistent behaviour when compared with that on church rates was explained away using liberal political ideas and language. The Maynooth debate touched on liberal politics concerning national institutions and their responsibilities, government policy towards Ireland, voluntaryism, and religions and religious toleration. The question of whether liberal MPs acted as a 'party' in terms of speaking, voting and relating to their constituents will show that, although they came from different backgrounds, and may have supported the Maynooth bill for different, often contradictory reasons, their generally positive reaction to it displayed strong ideas of a Liberal Party and how attached MPs were to their sense of liberal politics.

Few parliamentary controversies in the 19th century could provide a better opportunity to examine the nature of parties in this period than the 1845 debate on Peel's Maynooth proposals. It raised questions on several important and controversial fronts in British politics in the first half of the 19th century, including religious establishments, accommodation of different religions by the state, government policy towards Ireland, and the behaviour of MPs in relation to their constituents' wishes. Questions of party were also thrown up in the air. The *British Quarterly Review*, an evangelical nonconformist quarterly, wrote in August of that year that 'the new grant to the college at Maynooth has disturbed nearly all the old landmarks of party. The men who have been accustomed to do battle side by side have been marshalled against each other'.[1]

Maynooth opponents attacked the bill from entirely different perspectives and with entirely different motives. Anglican high churchmen opposed the increased grant because it carried with it the potential of further supporting (or endowing) the catholic church in Ireland. Voluntaryist dissenters opposed it because they saw it as another example of state support for religion, and they fought this as strenuously as they did the establishment of the church of England.[2] *The Times*, in fact, 'praised' Peel for alienating so many different MPs and extra-parliamentary groups with one proposal.[3] Both sides of the

---

[1] *British Quarterly Review*, ii (1845), 104.
[2] *The Spectator*, 12 Apr. 1845.
[3] *The Times*, 17 Apr. 1845.

house of commons, therefore, were split internally. Some Conservatives supported the bill for the reasons that Peel proposed it (explained below); others opposed it on basically anti-catholic grounds. Some Liberal Party MPs supported the bill as a conciliation towards Ireland, while others (although relatively few, as we shall see) voted against it on voluntaryist grounds.

Peel brought Maynooth difficulties to the surface of British politics because he subjected the nature of the grant to full parliamentary scrutiny by proposing to increase its funding and make it permanent. This raised the spectre of endowing catholicism in Ireland, of further concessions to Irish catholics, and possibly similar proposals for England and Wales. Since 1808, St Patrick's College at Maynooth had received an annual grant of £9,250 from Westminster. The amount was small enough, and public distrust of catholic seminaries insignificant enough, that the grant was renewed every year with little difficulty and controversy in the first three decades of the 19th century. Anti-Maynooth agitation began to grow slowly during the 1830s, however, after catholic emancipation in 1829 drew attention to appeals for catholic rights.[4] What had been founded to provide native seminarial training for Irishmen who had previously been trained in France became a focus for anti-catholic (and anti-Irish) opinion in England. Having a seminary in Ireland had been attractive not least for the reasons that it might eliminate the possibility that Irish seminarians would inculcate revolutionary ideals in France; and because, once the revolution started (and throughout the Napoleonic wars), Irish seminarians could not travel legally to France, and so needed a domestic training institution. Whig attempts at reform in Ireland in the 1830s, including appropriation, had brought the status of Maynooth College further into question. In the 1840s, the English press became increasingly critical of the reasoning behind the original grant; and the Oxford tractarian movement frightened many English protestants into focusing their anti-catholicism on Ireland in general and on Maynooth in particular.[5] Had Peel not been convinced that the college was in genuine distress, he almost certainly would not have chosen 1845 as the time to increase government support for Maynooth. From the standpoint of retaining the strength of his government, any question as potentially divisive as Maynooth should have been delayed at least until a more favourable wind started to blow.[6]

After lengthy cabinet deliberations in 1844, Peel decided to propose a Maynooth bill early in the next parliamentary session. During the debate on the queen's speech on 4 February 1845, he announced that the government intended to increase the Maynooth grant and make it permanent.[7] This announcement was initially greeted with indifference. Informed protestant opinion was preoccupied with the tractarian crisis in Oxford.

---

[4] E.R. Norman, 'The Maynooth Question of 1845', *Irish Historical Studies*, xv (1967), 411.

[5] D.A. Kerr, *Peel, Priests, and Politics: Sir Robert Peel's Administration and the Roman Catholic Church in Ireland, 1841–1846* (Oxford, 1982), 224–89; Norman, 'Maynooth Question', 411.

[6] Kerr, *Peel, Priests, and Politics*, 249–59. Kerr provides a detailed analysis of whether the college needed the money it requested from the government. He concludes that it did, and that the college trustees were largely blameless for its poor financial condition (except for a brief experience with a lax bursar). Indirect corroborative evidence for this may be found in the fact that the cabinet did not question the need to any great extent. Further, all significant anti-Maynooth agitation was based on the principle of funding a catholic college, not on the question of whether it needed the money.

[7] Hansard, *Parl. Debs*, lxxvii, cols 83–4 (4 Feb. 1845).

But soon enough the ultra-protestant press let out a cry of protest. The evangelical anglican *Record* called for 'RESISTANCE' against popery, and wrote articles denying the government's commitment to Maynooth, and denouncing the nature of teaching there.[8] The first direct anti-Maynooth agitation came from Nottingham on 11 February 1845, where a meeting was held, a petition raised and 9,000 signatures obtained.[9] The main opposition to Peel's proposals from outside the house of commons came from the new Anti-Maynooth Committee, set up by the Protestant Association at two meetings in London's Exeter Hall on 25 February and 18 March 1845.[10] At its own first meeting on 20 March 1845, the Anti-Maynooth Committee urged protestant sects to suppress their differences temporarily and to unite behind the opposition to the Maynooth grant. It also called for a massive petitioning movement to individual MPs and local noblemen, and for electors to threaten wavering MPs that voting for the increased grant would lessen their chances of success at the next election.[11] The first voluntaryist note, and the first indication that the opposition to Maynooth would not unite all protestants, came from the Baptist Union which, on 26 March 1845, said it was absolutely opposed to 'the application of the resources of the State to ecclesiastical purposes'.[12] This was the background to the debate within the house of commons.

Parliamentary Action on Maynooth, 1845

The voluntaryist plea for petitions was certainly heeded. On 3 April 1845, just before Peel stood up to introduce his bill to the house of commons, the Speaker suggested that MPs having petitions relating to Maynooth should present them at that moment: 'A vast number of members, especially on the ministerial side of the House, instantly started up, rustling with parchments, which appeared to excite considerable sensation in the House'.[13] This commotion threw Peel off course momentarily, and he found himself having to begin his speech with reference to the state of opinion on Maynooth. He said he had expected a reaction such as the one he had just witnessed, but the cabinet had prepared the Maynooth bill with care, and with the concerns of potential opponents in mind. Through its proposals, the government wished to improve Maynooth College. That was the purpose of the bill, not to weaken protestantism in England and Ireland. He then proceeded to discuss the poor state of the college and its need for greater provision. Peel outlined three options for dealing with the Maynooth grant. The government could discontinue it altogether; it could do nothing, retaining the annual nature of the grant, and leaving the college to find any extra funding; or the government could extend the grant and make it permanent, 'in a friendly and liberal spirit'. Peel chose the last, and

---

[8] Norman, 'Maynooth Question', 410; Kerr, *Peel, Priests, and Politics*, 270–1; A.S. Thelwall, *Proceedings of the Anti-Maynooth Conference of 1845* (1845), vi; *Morning Chronicle*, 8 Feb. 1845; G. Cahill, 'The Protestant Association and the Anti-Maynooth Agitation of 1845', *Catholic Historical Review*, xliii (1957), 273–308.

[9] Thelwall, *Proceedings of the Anti-Maynooth Conference*, ix–x.

[10] Norman, 'Maynooth Question', 414; Thelwall, *Proceedings of the Anti-Maynooth Conference*, vii, xi–xv.

[11] Thelwall, *Proceedings of the Anti-Maynooth Conference*, xv, and esp. 'The Address to the Protestants in All Parts of the Kingdom', xvii; Norman, 'Maynooth Question', 415.

[12] *The Times*, 1 Apr. 1845; Kerr, *Peel, Priests, and Politics*, 271.

[13] Thelwall, *Proceedings of the Anti-Maynooth Conference*, xix; Norman, 'Maynooth Question', 415–16.

Table 7.1: *Division on the Maynooth Grant 1845, First Reading*

Liberal Party groups	Ayes	Noes
Administration	0	0
Liberals	32	0
Radicals	10	4
Reformers	2	0
Repealers	27	0
Whigs	23	4
None listed	12	2
All Liberal Party	110	10
Conservative Party	108	106
Totals	218	116

Sources: Hansard, *Parl. Debs*, lxxix, cols 109–11 (3 Apr. 1845); *The Times*, 5 Apr. 1845; House of Commons, Division Lists, 3 Apr. 1845, No. 35.

proposed increasing the annual grant from £9,250 to £26,000, to make it permanent, and to grant an additional £30,000 (non-recurrent) for immediate new building.[14]

The bill passed its first reading 218 to 116, with the party split as shown in Table 7.1.[15] The level of support among liberal MPs was quite high, with less than 10% opposing the bill. Even attendance at the first reading division was considered important for some Liberal Party MPs. John Abel Smith, Whig MP for Chichester, rose out of his sick bed just to vote in the division.[16] The liberal *Morning Chronicle* welcomed Peel's proposal, and was more pleased at the 'all but unanimous support of the liberal members who voted on the occasion'.[17]

The Anti-Maynooth Committee reacted swiftly to the bill's first reading. They were pleased with the overall level of opposition (116 MPs, 35% of the total; it was, they reported, 'an auspicious indication from divine providence'). They also said that it was clear from the sympathetic hearing that Peel's proposal had been given by the Liberal Party front bench (particularly from Russell) 'that leading statesmen contemplate endowing the whole Roman priesthood in Ireland'. They then urged further petitioning and putting direct pressure on MPs.[18] It was in this immediate aftermath of the bill's first reading that the larger provincial protest against Maynooth really began. In addition to the Anti-Maynooth Committee meetings in London, there were meetings in Liverpool, Hull, Finsbury, Nottingham and Stepney, all within a week of the bill's first reading.[19] Enthused by this general reaction to the bill, the Anti-Maynooth Committee sent a

[14] Hansard, *Parl. Debs*, lxxix, cols 18–19 (3 Apr. 1845); Norman, 'Maynooth Question', 416; Raymond Cowherd, *The Politics of English Dissent: The Religious Aspects of Liberal and Humanitarian Reform Movements from 1815–1848* (1959), 159.

[15] Hansard, *Parl. Debs*, lxxix, cols 109–11 (3 Apr. 1845); see also Thelwall, *Proceedings of the Anti-Maynooth Conference*, xiii–xxvi.

[16] West Sussex RO, John Abel Smith Papers: journal entry, 3 Apr. 1845.

[17] *Morning Chronicle*, 5 Apr. 1845.

[18] Thelwall, *Proceedings of the Anti-Maynooth Conference*, xxvii; Norman, 'Maynooth Question', 416.

[19] Thelwall, *Proceedings of the Anti-Maynooth Conference*, xxx.

Table 7.2: *Division on the Maynooth Grant 1845, Second Reading*

Liberal Party groups	Ayes	Noes
Administration	0	0
Liberals	40	11
Radicals	16	3
Reformers	3	2
Repealers	43	0
Whigs	36	10
None listed	18	5
All Liberal Party	165	31
Conservative Party	160	147
Totals	325	178

Sources: Hansard, *Parl. Debs*, lxxix, cols 1042–5 (18 Apr. 1845); *The Times*, 19 Apr. 1845; House of Commons, Division Lists, 18 Apr. 1845, No. 43; *The Spectator*, 26 Apr. 1845; Kerr, *Peel, Priests, and Politics*, 280; Machin, *Politics and the Churches*, 176–7.

deputation to Peel on 9 April 1845 to ask for a delay in the second reading, to give time for opinion to be further expressed in the country. He refused. Russell was approached on the same day, and asked to move for postponement, but was similarly disinclined.[20] Petitions flowed in from all parts of the country, 10,204 (with 1,284,296 signatures) opposing the bill, and only 90 (with 17,482 signatures) supporting it.[21] The Anti-Maynooth Committee appealed to Queen Victoria on 14 April 1845,[22] and *The Times* came out against the bill three days later.[23] The agitation also had a distinct impact on by-elections. Several pro-Maynooth candidates lost or withdrew from various contests.[24]

The second reading debate displayed the hardening of opinion among MPs on the question. But despite the anti-Maynooth agitation in the country, the bill passed this stage 325 to 178, with the party split as shown in Table 7.2. Even with nearly double the number of Liberal Party MPs voting, the percentage opposed to the bill rose from roughly 9% on its first reading to only 14% on its second. John Abel Smith, Whig MP for Chichester, provided private commentary on the nature of the anti-Maynooth agitations, and the division on the second reading. In his journal entry for 18 April 1845, he wrote:

> Division on Maynooth – question carried by the votes of the opposition – Peel having a majority of his own party against him. It is discouraging for those who would wish to hope that the world is improving in wisdom . . . [to see such] . . . intolerant bigotry . . . [displayed] . . . both in and out of the House of Commons.[25]

[20] Norman, 'Maynooth Question', 416; Thelwall, *Proceedings of the Anti-Maynooth Conference*, xxxi–xxxii.

[21] J. Wolffe, *The Protestant Crusade in Great Britain 1829–1860* (Oxford, 1991), 199. On 11 April alone, there were 2,400 petitions presented against the bill. See Thelwall, *Proceedings of the Anti-Maynooth Conference*, xxxiii.

[22] Norman, 'Maynooth Question', 427–8.

[23] *The Times*, 17 Apr. 1845; Wolffe, *Protestant Crusade*, 200; Kerr, *Peel, Priests, and Politics*, 277.

[24] G.I.T. Machin, *Politics and the Churches in Great Britain, 1832–1868* (Oxford, 1977), 171.

[25] West Sussex RO, John Abel Smith Papers: journal entry, 18 Apr. 1845.

Table 7.3: *Division on Ward's 1845 Maynooth Appropriation Motion*

Liberal Party groups	Ayes	Noes
Administration	0	0
Liberals	6	45
Radicals	1	21
Reformers	3	34
Repealers	0	5
Whigs	13	27
None listed	4	18
All Liberal Party	27	150
Conservative Party	297	0
Totals	324	150

Sources: Hansard, *Parl. Debs*, lxxix, cols 1311–14 (24 Apr. 1845); *The Times*, 25 Apr. 1845; House of Commons, Division Lists, 24 Apr. 1845, No. 45.

On 23 April 1845, H.G. Ward, Radical MP for Sheffield, proposed a motion that surplus funds from the revenue of the established church of Ireland be directed towards Maynooth.[26] This had the potential of splitting the liberal side of the House because so many of those MPs had been in favour of appropriating the same funds for general education in Ireland in the 1830s.[27] The *Morning Chronicle* supported Ward's motion, and called it 'unanswerable'. But it was defeated, with 150 Liberal Party MPs voting with Ward, and 27 against. The question on this division was whether the bill could stand without Ward's amendment. To vote for appropriation, therefore, was to vote 'No' in this instance (Table 7.3).[28]

This division showed the strength that the idea of appropriation had in liberal politics, and, perhaps more importantly, the degree to which Liberal Party MPs as a group (nearly 85% in this division) thought that the church of Ireland, as a national institution, had responsibilities to the population of Ireland as a whole. Only high church Whigs and Liberals voted against this idea, and even then they were few in number. Nearly all Liberal Party frontbenchers, Russell included, voted with Ward, which they certainly had not done during the appropriation debates of the 1830s. If there can be said to be anything resembling early Liberal Party policy in this period, appropriation was such a policy.

Ultimately, the anti-Maynooth agitation failed both inside and outside the house of commons. The bill was passed, and received the royal assent in August. As will be discussed below, the various Maynooth opponents started quickly to feud among themselves over how best to attack the bill, and over what their ultimate aims were.[29] The reaction of the Conservative Party, and of anglicans in general, to the Maynooth bill has

[26] Hansard, *Parl. Debs*, lxxix, cols 1244–52 (24 Apr. 1845).

[27] Norman, 'Maynooth Question', 429.

[28] See the debate in Hansard, *Parl. Debs*, lxxix, cols 1244–314 (24 Apr. 1845); *The Times*, 26 Apr. 1845; *The Spectator*, 26 Apr. 1845; Thelwall, *Proceedings of the Anti-Maynooth Conference*, lxxvi–lxxvii.

[29] G.I.T. Machin, 'The Maynooth Grant, the Dissenters and Disestablishment, 1845–1847', *EHR*, lxxxii (1967), 73–4.

been well discussed elsewhere. But a short summary of it will serve well for comparison with the more lengthy discussion of Liberal Party reaction below. Tory anglican opposition to the Maynooth grant was based on the perception that the government seemed willing to consider concurrent endowment of the catholic church. Their fears were further fed by a perception that the increased, permanent grant 'seemed to undermine the Protestant nature of church establishment'.[30] By its very nature (and by the assumptions implicit in Peel's proposal), it not only encouraged catholicism in Ireland, but tractarianism in England. These concerns were sometimes taken to quite hyperbolic levels. On behalf of the Anti-Maynooth Committee, J.P. Plumptre, Conservative MP for East Kent, sent out a public address in which he claimed that the great danger of the Maynooth grant was that it would 'endow popery once more in a land that has been rescued from its yoke'. It was, he continued, 'madness little short of high treason against heaven'.[31] Many Conservative MPs were, therefore, strong opponents of the bill, and willing conduits for petitions against it. The Maynooth bill was simply one in a series of measures that rent the conservative party from its leadership.

So much was happening on the Conservative side of the house of commons that the reaction within the Liberal Party has understandably been overlooked. This is probably due to the fact that Maynooth did not damage the Liberal Party to any degree in comparison with the Conservatives. The significance of Maynooth for the Liberal Party lies beneath the surface of contemporary events, and is to be found in questions of the nature of the party and its shared liberal politics. The most immediate impression Maynooth gives to these questions is that, despite the overwhelming liberal support shown in the divisions on the bill, the controversy shows how diverse and complex the party really was. The Maynooth debates displayed potential divisions among all groups in the Liberal Party, as well as the individual struggles of Liberal Party MPs who voted to conciliate Ireland while recognizing that they may have violated their own consciences in doing so.[32] The Whigs were generally in favour of the increased grant. Mainly anglican, and mostly supporting the idea of church establishment, they saw no reason why the state should not financially support the instruction of the clergy of the majority of the population. Ireland was overwhelmingly catholic, therefore Irish priests should be trained properly to meet the needs of that population. Further, having seen the difficulties that arose when they attempted Irish reforms in the 1830s, many leading Whigs saw the Maynooth bill as an easy way to placate the Irish. Showing religious and national toleration towards the Irish in this way would bring back benefits in goodwill manyfold. The Whigs, therefore, seemed both pragmatic and tolerant.[33] The Radicals, on the other hand, were split over Maynooth; their strong ideological commitments forced them to justify their actions beyond mere expediency. Many leading Radicals, including John Bright, opposed the bill on voluntaryist grounds. Others, including Cobden and Hume, agreed with the Whigs that the increased grant was necessary to placate the Irish. They got around the inconsistency with voluntaryism by arguing that Ireland was a special

[30] Machin, *Politics and the Churches*, 171.

[31] Wolffe, *Protestant Crusade*, vii.

[32] M.R. Watts, *The Dissenters: Vol. II, the Expansion of Evangelical Non-conformity* (Oxford, 1995), 549–50; T.A. Jenkins, *The Liberal Ascendancy 1830–1886* (1994), 61.

[33] Jenkins, *Liberal Ascendancy*, 61; A. Sykes, *The Rise and Fall of British Liberalism 1776–1988* (1997), 36–9.

case.[34] Reformers were also somewhat split, as the divisions analysed above show. But the majority were in favour of the grant. Repealers were universally in favour of Peel's bill.

It was outside the House, and with dissenters, that the Liberal Party found its greatest difficulty over the Maynooth controversy. There were two main divisions of opinion among dissenters regarding the bill. The first group were opposed to the grant on anti-catholic grounds. They saw it as concurrent endowment of catholicism. The second group were opposed to all connections between church and state, and Maynooth was just one of those connections.[35] But Maynooth presented a problem for voluntaryist dissenters. Being dissenters, most of them supported the idea of a liberalisation of attitude towards a non-anglican religion. Being voluntaryists, however, they opposed state money supporting a specific denomination. The endowment of catholicism in Ireland would only strengthen the idea of establishment generally. Liberal and radical newspapers, monthlies and quarterlies tried to reason with the voluntaryists not to join in with anti-catholic opposition to the bill. No matter how much they disliked it on voluntaryist grounds, *Tait's Edinburgh Magazine* urged dissenters not to oppose the bill because that would force them to join in with bigoted high churchmen, which was the greater evil.[36] After explaining that it too was opposed to much of what was contained or implied in the Maynooth bill, the *Morning Chronicle* urged its liberal dissenting readers not to join in the 'No Popery' cry over Maynooth. If dissenters (voluntaryists especially) were to close ranks with the Tories and high churchmen just to see the bill defeated, it would not be a victory for religious liberty, or of the voluntary principle, but of 'No Popery'. Further, if voluntaryists were to aid in getting the bill defeated, they would be disappointed to find that their anti-Maynooth allies were temporary, and would in no way aid the church rate abolition movement.[37]

But the voluntaryists were internally divided. Moderates thought it important to ally with the anglicans to see the bill itself defeated. The extremes thought Maynooth a perfect opportunity to attack all forms of state support for religious institutions.[38] The friction between the two groups did nothing to lessen the uneasy position voluntaryists held in the Anti-Maynooth Committee. Always an ad hoc group with nothing more in common than their opposition to Maynooth, the committee found it difficult to conduct business with some of the voluntaryists constantly clamouring for disestablishment.[39] Although they tried to emphasise the need for protestant unity, the leadership of the Anti-Maynooth Committee found it difficult to hold on to its rebellious section of voluntaryists. In mid May 1845, after the Maynooth bill's second reading, many voluntaryists in the Anti-Maynooth Committee withdrew from what they saw as simply an anti-catholic organisation.[40]

---

[34] J.P. Parry, *The Rise and Fall of Liberal Government in Victorian Britain* (New Haven, CT, 1993), 162–3; J.P. Ellens, *Religious Routes to Gladstonian Liberalism: The Church Rate Conflict in England and Wales, 1832–1868* (University Park, PA, 1994), 93–4; Jenkins, *Liberal Ascendancy*, 61–2.

[35] Norman, 'Maynooth Question', 424–6.

[36] *Tait's Edinburgh Magazine*, May 1845, p. 338. *Tait's* was a radical and Benthamite journal.

[37] *Morning Chronicle*, 15 Apr. 1845.

[38] Machin, 'Maynooth Grant', 68–9.

[39] Ellens, *Religious Routes*, 93.

[40] Machin, *Politics and the Churches*, 175; Norman, 'Maynooth Question', 433–4; Kerr, *Peel, Priests, and Politics*, 280.

Ultimately, of course, the voluntaryists did not succeed in helping to defeat the bill. But their impact was still to be felt. Many voluntaryists considered forming their own party after their defeat on Maynooth. Some electoral groups were formed to run candidates for parliament (the Anti-State Church Electoral Association in Bristol being an example of these). They tried to widen their appeal by championing free trade and universal suffrage, but they failed largely because these issues were not exclusively voluntaryist.[41] They had pinned hopes on the 1845 and 1846 by-elections, but were unable to return voluntaryist candidates because their message had limited appeal.[42] They were fortunate, however, in that Russell's 1846 education measures were dropped in their laps.[43] Opposition to state support for education, combined with opposition over Maynooth, allowed voluntaryist candidates to win seats in the 1847 election in Edinburgh, Bradford, Lambeth, Tower Hamlets and Finsbury.[44]

Maynooth as a Defining Issue for Liberal Politics

Although the struggle for the passage of Peel's bill has attracted much attention for historians of the Conservative Party, it provides at least as much material for the Liberal Party. We have seen how Liberal Party MPs voted in divisions, and have had some indication of the ways in which the new liberal politics made itself significant during the debates. But it is as a defining issue that Maynooth holds the most importance for the Liberal Party. It illuminates the difficulties the party had with maintaining the support of dissenters, the questions over the endowment of churches as national institutions, Maynooth as a civil rights issue and as a measure of goodwill towards Ireland and, most importantly, the willingness of Liberal Party MPs to vote against the wishes of their constituents (and sometimes against arguments they made during the church rates debates) in order to treat Maynooth (and Ireland) as a special case. This may neatly be termed 'considered inconsistency', the idea that liberal politics must make room for reflection and, when necessary, seemingly contradictory behaviour. In this sense, of course, Peel acted liberally on Maynooth, as he was to do over the corn laws. So, as stated in the Introduction, 'liberalism' was sometimes to be found outside the Liberal Party.

Maynooth presented difficulties for Liberal Party MPs for more reasons than just a simple disagreement with some of their most ardent supporters, the dissenters. In the first place, that disagreement displayed a fundamental problem in liberal politics during the reform period because that politics included elements which, on the surface at least, seemed contradictory. The liberal idea of inclusion clashed with the idea of equal treatment if, for whatever reason, all groups could not be included or at least not included at the same time. An easy and complete solution to this dilemma lay in adopting the idea of voluntaryism. But voluntaryism also ran up against liberal ideas about national institutions and the importance of maintaining them.[45] Further, Maynooth showed the division between nonconformists and catholics, who made up two important groups within the Liberal

---

[41] Machin, *Politics and the Churches*, 177.

[42] Machin, 'Maynooth Grant', 76–7.

[43] Watts, *The Dissenters*, 550.

[44] Ellens, *Religious Routes*, 93–4; Machin, 'Maynooth Grant', 76–7.

[45] Machin, *Politics and the Churches*, 174; Kerr, *Peel, Priests, and Politics*, 279; Machin, 'Maynooth Grant', 68–9.

Party.[46] As long as the liberal agenda at any one time did not bring up the divisions between these two groups, the ideas of Liberal Party unity and the completeness of liberal politics was enough to prevent any real damaging splits. But 1845 was not that time. Tractarianism and Maynooth illuminated this potential division and made it very difficult for Liberal Party MPs to support one course of action or another on Maynooth.

The two main strains of opinion opposed to the Maynooth grant, therefore, made difficulties for the Liberal Party, but it was the strict voluntaryists who caused the most problems. Thomas Duncombe, Radical MP for Finsbury, opposed Peel's bill on strict voluntaryist grounds. 'It was all nonsense', he argued during the debate on the first reading, 'for hon. Gentlemen to deceive themselves by supposing that this vote was intended for any other purpose than to endow another Church'. And, like some other Liberal Party MPs, he said that he could hardly support the Maynooth bill when he had voted against church rates in the 1830s.[47] But another Radical, John Roebuck, MP for Bath, said that objections to Maynooth based on the voluntary principle were misplaced, and that the purpose of the Maynooth bill was to further education in Ireland, not to endow another church. The important thing in the Maynooth issue, he argued, was not the question of upsetting the voluntaryist principle, an ideal with which he 'deeply sympathized', but the question of 'a contribution in the best form towards the teaching of the only teachers of the Irish people'.[48] And this contribution did not have to be accepted, according to Ralph Osborne, Liberal MP for Wycombe. Voluntaryists ought not to worry about the potential further step of establishing the catholic church in Ireland, he argued, because it was unlikely that that church would accept such a connection with the British government.[49] The *Morning Chronicle* summed up the argument that voluntaryism must be put on hold with regard to Maynooth: 'The Irish Catholics are very well disposed to the voluntary principle, but if they find its English advocates employ it to defeat a Maynooth grant, while they are unable to disturb the rich establishment of the Protestant minority, they will hardly give those advocates credit for . . . love of equal justice'.[50] Still, voluntaryist constituents appealed to Liberal Party MPs to oppose the measure, and castigated them when they had voted in favour of it. Samuel Gree of the Lambeth Anti-Maynooth Committee wrote to Charles D'Eyncourt, Radical MP for Lambeth, that Peel's bill produced 'a deep sense of . . . wrong, moral and political'.[51]

The voluntaryist principle might have appealed to Liberal Party MPs in theory, but they decided to make other issues paramount in the Maynooth debate. Joseph Hume, Radical MP for Montrose, outlined the liberal idea that a measure of civil rights was necessary for Ireland, and that support for Maynooth would be a partial step in that direction. He argued during the bill's second reading 'that no men could live satisfac-

[46] Jenkins, *Liberal Ascendancy*, 60–1.

[47] Hansard, *Parl. Debs*, lxxix, col. 108 (3 Apr. 1845). See also Norman, 'Maynooth Question', 424–6; *British Quarterly Review*, ii (1845) 104; Machin, *Politics and the Churches*, 174.

[48] Hansard, *Parl. Debs*, lxxix, cols 573–4 (11 Apr. 1845).

[49] Hansard, *Parl. Debs*, lxxix, col. 55 (3 Apr. 1845).

[50] *Morning Chronicle*, 16 Apr. 1845; Kerr, *Peel, Priests, and Politics*, 278.

[51] Lincolnshire Archives Office, D'Eyncourt Papers, 2TDE/H46.33: Samual Gree to Charles Tennyson D'Eyncourt, 14 May 1845.

torily with each other in the same country, unless there was an equality of civil rights'.[52] Russell had ended his speech on the introduction to the bill in similar terms.[53] Two years previously, he had written to Le Marchant on Peel and Ireland that he worried that there was 'no better hope for the future than the continuance of the past negligences & ignorance'.[54] But during the Maynooth debate, he argued firmly that conciliatory measures such as Maynooth would signal a new course in relations between Ireland and England, and that further such approaches might effectively counter the Repeal movement.[55]

> I . . . shall be most happy if the Roman Catholics of Ireland . . . shall feel that we, on our part, are ready to do them justice; that we are not led by any narrow prejudice, . . . but that the people of this country are not led by a spirit of religious bigotry to refuse that which is just to them; and that they may look at this measure, not as a final measure, but as one of a series of measures, by which we may hope to unite the two countries in an enduring bond.[56]

And John Abel Smith, Whig MP for Chichester, wrote in his journal after voting Aye on the first reading division:

> I have just finished the 'Past & Present Policy of England Towards Ireland' by Charles Greville & am delighted with it. It is a clear & most useful summary of the grievous misgovert of this country in Ireland. I trust the vote of this night gives promise of an early settlement of the Church question in Ireland & the restoration of the Roman Catholic Religion to some part of its lost rights.[57]

Further, the *Morning Chronicle*'s Dublin correspondent reported that, except for 'the Orange and Ultra-Tory party, . . . the result of the [first reading] division on the Maynooth grant . . . was received with great delight'.[58]

Even with these arguments being put forward, one of the most striking aspects of Liberal Party MPs' behaviour on Maynooth was that many of them found themselves forced to vote against the wishes of their constituents. This, in itself, would not have been so interesting but for the fact that they spoke directly about it during the debates. Many Liberal Party MPs opened their speeches by saying that, with regret, they would have to vote against their constituents' expressed desires, and then spent much time explaining why. On the night that Peel introduced his measure, Sir William Clay, Reformer MP for Tower Hamlets, even presented petitions against the bill from his constituents, and then went on to speak in favour of the bill, and vote for it in divisions.[59] During the second

---

[52] Hansard, *Parl. Debs*, lxxix, col. 707 (15 Apr. 1845).

[53] Hansard, *Parl. Debs*, lxxix, cols 96–7 (3 Apr. 1845).

[54] PA, Le Marchant Papers: Russell to Le Marchant, 26 Aug. 1843.

[55] Hansard, *Parl. Debs*, lxxix, cols 95–6 (3 Apr. 1845).

[56] Hansard, *Parl. Debs*, lxxix, cols 96–7 (3 Apr. 1845).

[57] West Sussex RO, John Abel Smith Papers: journal entry, 3 Apr. 1845.

[58] *Morning Chronicle*, 7 Apr. 1845.

[59] Hansard, *Parl. Debs*, lxxix, cols 80–106 (3 Apr. 1845). See also E.R. Rice, Reformer MP for Dover, Hansard, *Parl. Debs*, lxxix, col. 890 (17 Apr. 1845).

reading debate, Lord Worsley, Whig MP for Lincolnshire North, who had presented 136 petitions from his own constituents against the bill, outlined the difficulties of Liberal Party MPs when faced with this dilemma.

> I presented petitions . . . from all the Dissenting bodies in the division of the county which I represent; . . . on no previous occasion has there been so universal a sentiment of opposition to a Government measure. . . . I feel I should ill discharge my duty as a Member of this House, if I did not at once avow that my opinion on this question does not coincide with the views of my constituents. I have the satisfaction, however, of recollecting, that though I gave no pledges, my general opinions on this question were known to my constituents. During the period I have been in Parliament, I have invariably voted for the grant of 9,000*l.* to Maynooth, and I have been three or four times re-elected after having done so.[60]

This clearly shows the difficulties that the timing of the Maynooth bill presented for many MPs. Tractarianism and other religious controversies such as the simmering church rates issue had heightened sensitivity to religious questions. Charles D'Eyncourt, Radical MP for Lambeth, received many letters from constituents, asking him to vote against Maynooth. In a strong example of liberal 'no popery', J.B. Wilks from the Camberwell Anti-Maynooth Committee appealed to D'Eyncourt not to support Peel, but to fund Maynooth from the church of Ireland.

> I have for many years been of Liberal politics, and as such have cheerfully supported yourself and Mr Hawes.

> But considering Popery to be the great enemy to what every man considers *his birthright,* viz. *liberty to think, liberty to judge of right and wrong, liberty to conclude and to decide after mature* reflection as to what he considers the best *course to follow to bring him to happiness,* consider Popery I again repeat, as a system depriving of these unalienable, untransferrable rights, I am bound to consider it an enemy of God and Man.

> . . . Give what you think to the *Irish people,* and do it, if you please, out of that rich Ecclesiastical fund, that is so disproportionately great to the number of its members, but do not strengthen a religion which has ever been the greatest barrier to liberty of soul and I may say of body also.

> I had rather never exercise my vote again than give it to those Honorable [*sic*] Gentlemen, however talented, who betray us in this great struggle for liberty of conscience.[61]

D'Eyncourt replied, saying:

> I am very far from treating lightly the opinion of my constituents [and] it has pained me extremely to differ so widely from a portion of them, numerous and enlightened as that represented by the Committee in whose name you address me.

[60] Hansard, *Parl. Debs,* lxxix, cols 735–6 (15 Apr. 1845).

[61] Lincolnshire Archives Office, D'Eyncourt Papers, 2TDE/H46/35: J.B. Wilks to Charles Tennyson D'Eyncourt, 12 Apr. 1845.

Although my colleague and myself support the Bill, you will have seen that we voted
with Mr. T. Duncombe for limiting its operation to 3 years.[62]

He went on to say that even though this limitation was not in the bill, he voted for the
grant anyway because the college needed it, and because he hoped Maynooth could
survive until appropriation could be passed. Further, D'Eyncourt changed his mind
about pairing with W.E. Powell, Conservative MP for Cardiganshire, on the third reading
of the bill, so that his vote could be recorded. Powell agreed and, as he wrote to
D'Eyncourt, was also keen to get his name on the division list, 'anxious to gratify my
constituents by voting against it'.[63]

The *Morning Chronicle* summarized the Maynooth difficulties for Liberal Party MPs
when it wrote that they were 'dragged . . . in contrary directions by their conscience,
their party, their places, or their constituencies'.[64] Voting against the wishes of their
liberal constituents was part of what was termed above 'considered inconsistency'. This
required Liberal Party MPs to be as liberal as possible, to think carefully about the
support they had received from dissenters, consider their previous behaviour on political
religious issues (such as church rates), gauge the needs of Maynooth and the catholic
church in Ireland and, of course, consult their own consciences about the best way they
should act. In the end, those MPs who spoke and voted in favour of the increased grant,
who had also voted and spoken against other such funding of specific denominations,
displayed a basic tenet of liberal politics which demanded that Maynooth (and, in many
ways, Ireland as a whole) be regarded as a special case, and that the principles of
government may need to be varied in their application in specific circumstances. Richard
Sheil, Liberal MP for Dungarvon, warned MPs that they 'must take Ireland as it is; and
you must adopt your policy to the condition of the people'.[65] Although some Liberal
Party MPs ignored the question of inconsistency when speaking on Maynooth, many
addressed it directly. Sir George Grey, Liberal MP for Devonport, summarized it neatly
when he said during the second reading debate that his vote:

> would, in common he believed with those of many other hon. Gentlemen, be in
> opposition to the conscientious opposition and the strong remonstrances of the
> friends and supporters whose confidence he had enjoyed on public grounds, the loss
> of whose confidence, from the support of this measure, he should much regret; but
> from whom, consulting his own conscience, and having regard to his own consistency
> in considering a measure of so much importance to the good government of Ireland,
> the general welfare of these dominions, and the security of the British Crown, he was
> compelled to differ.[66]

---

[62] Lincolnshire Archives Office, D'Eyncourt Papers, 2TDE/H46/40: Charles Tennyson D'Eyncourt to J.B.
Wilks, 23 May 1845.

[63] Lincolnshire Archives Office, D'Eyncourt Papers, 2TDE/H46/27: W.E. Powell to Charles Tennyson
D'Eyncourt, 12 May 1845.

[64] *Morning Chronicle*, 1 Apr. 1845.

[65] Hansard, *Parl. Debs*, xxix, col. 106 (3 Apr. 1845). See also R.L. Sheil, *Sketches Legal and Political* (1855),
241–3, for Sheil's arguments about the Maynooth grant being the logical extension of catholic emancipation.

[66] Hansard, *Parl. Debs*, lxxix, cols 873–4 (17 Apr. 1845). For an example of an MP being unable to consider
any inconsistency in his behaviour, see Thomas Duncombe, Radical MP for Finsbury, Hansard, *Parl. Debs*, lxxix,
col. 108 (3 Apr. 1845), when he said he was opposed to Maynooth on the same basis that he opposed church
rates. He thought the Maynooth grant was simply another establishment of another church.

This inconsistency was not lost on the Anti-Maynooth Committee. The chairman, Sir Culling Eardly Smith, told them on 1 April 1845:

> I am not going to allude to the right or wrong of church rates. But I think it will be found, that all members of parliament, who were on the liberal side, laid down this principle, – that A should not be taxed for B's religion. Now every liberal, who, after having said that, does now tax us to maintain popery, is acting inconsistently.[67]

And during the fourth sitting of the Anti-Maynooth Committee on 2 May 1845, he said:

> I call on those who have hitherto styled themselves, par excellence, the Liberal Party, to act on their own principles . . . I appeal to them, if they do not mean to be inconsistent – if they do not mean that their conduct and professions in 1845 should contradict their conduct in 1832 [when they played the popular card in support of parliamentary reform] – I call on them to yield now, as with it they coincided then, to the unquestionably declared popular feeling of this country.[68]

The Reverend A. Ewing from Halifax said that if supporters of Maynooth claimed to base their actions on liberalism, he called it 'pseudo-liberalism', which was not what he considered to be the liberalism of 'Religious Liberty'.[69] The *British Quarterly Review* argued that 'liberalism and Romanism are opposites, and that the common cause now subsisting among us between these opposite systems, is wholly the result of circum-stances, the systems themselves being devoid, in their main tendencies, of all affinity and natural relationship'.[70] *The Times* agreed, saying that 'It is not Liberalism but Romanism which Peel is forcing on the nation'.[71] Yet William Cowper, Whig MP for Hertford, said that he 'rejoiced at the triumph of the truth of Whig principles, when the right hon. Baronet [Peel] was compelled by his sense of duty, as by his view of the necessities of the time, to adopt them'.[72] J.S. Trelawny, the Radical MP for Tavis-tock, who would later make a serious parliamentary challenge to church rates, had addressed that question earlier during the second reading debate. He admitted that, on the surface, it would appear that he should oppose the Maynooth bill. He was a strict voluntaryist and opposed to further endowments of religion. But he considered Ireland a 'peculiar' case, and that was the reason he was going to vote for Peel's bill. Even those who shared his voluntaryist views 'could not forget entirely the special circum-stances of [Ireland]; . . . Something conciliatory must be done, . . . immediately . . . It was a time when a liberal member ought to risk something for peace, to

---

[67] Thelwall, *Proceedings of the Anti-Maynooth Conference*, 88–9; Norman, 'Maynooth Question', 425.

[68] Thelwall, *Proceedings of the Anti-Maynooth Conference*, 85.

[69] Thelwall, *Proceedings of the Anti-Maynooth Conference*, 84.

[70] *British Quarterly Review*, ii (1845), 112–13.

[71] *The Times*, 17 Apr. 1845.

[72] Hansard, *Parl. Debs*, lxxix, cols 638–40 (14 Apr. 1845). See also Kerr, *Peel, Priests, and Politics*, 281 for Kerr's arguments about how Gladstone had come to the same conclusion.

sacrifice popularity, to render government possible . . . Something must be done for Ireland'.[73]

Macaulay, Liberal MP for Edinburgh, made a similar argument when he said: 'I do not conceive that it is open to me, however strong my general feeling might be on the voluntary principle, to meet the Irish, who ask for 17,000*l* more for the education of their priests, and to say to them, I am on principle opposed to such a grant'.[74] H.M. Tuite, Liberal MP for Westmeath, summed up this idea when he said during the second reading debate that liberals ought not to worry if they felt they were appearing inconsistent by voting for Maynooth: 'Men of liberal opinions not unfrequently saw reasons to change their minds on important subjects'.[75]

It is also as a question of the importance and significance of national institutions that Maynooth can help explain the strength of MPs' attachment to their ideas of liberal politics. *Tait's Edinburgh Magazine* brought up the subject of considered inconsistency, and the duty of the government to support national, and popular, institutions. It urged success for Peel's bill, but only reluctantly; and it pointed out that for each reason liberals should support it, there were equal reasons they should oppose it. It was an education bill, but the instruction at Maynooth was sectarian. It was an attack on the protestant ascendancy in Ireland, yet the attack was popish. It would conciliate one-third of the empire; however it did so by forcing protestants to pay for catholicism. It was restitution for Ireland, but that restitution would be paid by those who did not commit the crimes: 'And while we feel the difficulty of supporting a measure containing so much that every religious liberal must strenuously disapprove, and have all the respect for those liberals who deem themselves bound to oppose it, we deeply regret the success of the opposition'.[76]

Tait's, therefore, hinted at the liberal tenet that the government, as the supreme national institution, had a responsibility to ensure that differing groups and potentially hostile interests be integrated into the common weal by accepting 'an over-arching code of law which guaranteed each a wide variety of liberties'.[77] This emphasis on the responsibilities of national institutions was an increasingly important feature of liberal politics. *The Spectator*, another liberal periodical, made special reference to this aspect of support for Maynooth. It argued that the state should aid, indeed ensure, that religious ministers were well trained: 'The public-weal is much concerned that the ministers of all churches should be intelligent and well-informed'.[78] Even Radicals such as Richard Bellew, MP for Louth, submerged their voluntaryist tendencies in favour of the liberal belief in the responsibilities of national institutions. During the first reading of the bill, Bellew discussed the 'national' nature of the obligation of the state to provide training for priests in Ireland.

---

[73] Hansard, *Parl. Debs*, lxxix, col. 899 (17 Apr. 1845). See also *The Parliamentary Diaries of Sir John Trelawny, 1858–1865*, ed. T.A. Jenkins (Camden Society, 4th ser., xl, 1990), 38, in which Trelawny wrote about an 1858 motion to inquire into the Maynooth grant, saying that the hostility to Maynooth would 'come at last to be regarded as both ridiculous & impracticable'.

[74] Hansard, *Parl. Debs*, lxxix, col. 654 (14 Apr. 1845).

[75] Hansard, *Parl. Debs*, lxxix, col. 906 (17 Apr. 1845).

[76] *Tait's Edinburgh Magazine*, May 1845, p. 337.

[77] Parry, *Rise and Fall of Liberal Government*, 3.

[78] *The Spectator*, 12 Apr. 1845.

In a matter of such paramount importance, the state should be everything or nothing. The education of the religious instructors of the people should be made a great national object, or it should not, in any respect be interfered with. The scheme should be large and extensive, or there should be no scheme whatsoever.[79]

He then went on to argue at length and in detail why he preferred the state to be everything (rather than nothing) in this, and similar, matters. During the first reading debate, Russell was so bold as to argue: 'I am anxious to see the spiritual and religious instruction of that great majority of the people of Ireland endowed and maintained by the State'.[80]

Like the church rate debates, therefore, Maynooth shows how central the ideas of the responsibilities of national institutions were to liberal politics, as well as the strength of the idea that parliament itself, as the supreme national institution, had responsibilities to other such institutions. Liberal Party thinking on this was nearly universal, from utilitarian backbenchers to high church Whigs on the front bench.

Conclusion

It was difficult for Liberal Party MPs to speak and vote on Peel's Maynooth bill without angering someone. This was usually the case with their dissenting and high church constituents. Backbench manuscript collections are completely devoid of constituency correspondence praising MPs for their Maynooth stances. For most Liberal Party MPs, however, their ideas of liberal politics were strong enough to withstand temporary difficulties with certain sections of the anti-Maynooth community. As we have seen in this chapter, Liberal Party MPs displayed their ideas about national institutions and their responsibilities, the past governmental treatment of Ireland and how it must be taken as a special case, the question of voluntaryism (as had been the case with church rates), and religions and religious toleration. Perhaps most significantly, they dealt with the critiques of consistency by arguing that being a liberal politician meant that a certain degree of 'considered inconsistency' was necessary at times. This shows, more than anything else, the extent of liberal thinking on Irish affairs, and how Ireland could best be governed short of repeal of the Union. Practically no Liberal Party MPs, except, of course, Repealers, thought that repeal was the best way to ensure progress and conciliation in Ireland. Consequently, in the liberal mind, Irish problems required different solutions from those to English problems. This, in turn, sometimes forced Liberal Party MPs to propose or support ideas for Irish reform that they would have opposed for England, and to argue for these reforms based on a number of different arguments, as outlined above. These diverse liberal justifications for behaviour on Maynooth were similar to the initially diverse free trade agendas that we will encounter in Chapter 8. There, as with Maynooth, the strength of their attachment to liberal politics meant that, however difficult their specific actions on a parliamentary topic might have been, liberal MPs sought to remain under the broad umbrella of the Liberal Party.

[79] Hansard, *Parl. Debs*, lxxix, col. 80 (3 Apr. 1845).
[80] Hansard, *Parl. Debs*, lxxix, col. 94 (3 Apr. 1845).

Chapter 8. Free Trade Agendas: The Construction of an Article of Faith, 1837–50

The previous chapters in Part 2 have focused on Ireland and religion, and on the various ways those issues came to mean more for Liberal Party MPs than the individual topics themselves. Similarly, 'free trade', and the arguments used to advance it, reveal more about Liberal Party MPs than simply their ideas on economics. 'Free trade' in the first half of the 19th century represented a spectrum of economic and fiscal (as well as political and social) ideas rather than a single, fixed ideology of worldwide laissez-faire capitalism. It raised fundamental questions about government and sovereignty, as well as economy and trade. Further, free trade theory and ideology were themselves evolving, and contested, throughout the early 19th century. In terms of political actors in the house of commons, ideas about free trade were, not surprisingly, equally broad and fluid. 'Free traders' included moderate tariff reformers, fixed duty men and strict free traders, who brought with them all sorts of different justifications for trade reform, as well as diverse ideas about the effects of such reform. Liberal Party MPs were found on all points of this spectrum, as well as in protectionist circles. But these varying agendas came somewhat closer together as most Liberal Party MPs became more committed to free trade as the period progressed. The years 1837–41 were central to this experience, not so much because all Liberal Party MPs changed their minds about free trade (although many did), but because of their willingness to support free trade measures as part of a liberal political agenda with party overtones. By 1841, and certainly by 1852, most Liberal Party MPs accepted this party umbrella without radically changing their individual ideas about free trade and protectionism. Liberal Party frontbench policy, backbench opinion, language and rhetoric, and attendance and voting in the house of commons coalesced under this umbrella from 1837 to 1841, and continued and strengthened the broad Liberal Party free trade agenda so much that free trade might be termed a party article of faith by 1850.[1]

Given the importance of this episode in 19th-century history, it is somewhat surprising that there has been little examination of free trade and the liberals as a party in the house of commons, until recently. Obviously, the subjects of Peel, the Conservatives and corn law repeal have received the most attention,[2] but those historians

---

[1] This broad free trade agenda had become so synonymous with the phase 'free trade' that, by 1868, it was used in a way that would have seemed wildly loose in the early 1830s. J.E.T. Rogers, the liberal educationalist, said in an election speech that free trade was 'the liberation of your bread from the tax of the monopolist', and then a few moments later said: 'Now, what do we mean by free trade or free exchange? We mean the permission given to each individual to find the best market for what he has to sell, and the most advantageous for what he has to buy'. J.E.T. Rogers, *The Free Trade Policy of the Liberal Party* (Manchester, 1868), 3, 5.

[2] J.B. Conacher, *The Peelites and the Party System 1846–1852* (1972); N. Gash, *Politics in the Age of Peel: A Study in the Technique of Parliamentary Representation 1830–1850* (1953); N. Gash, *Reaction and Reconstruction in English Politics, 1832–1852* (Oxford, 1965); B. Hilton, *Corn, Cash, and Commerce: The Economic Policies of the Tory Governments 1815–1830* (Oxford, 1977); N. McCord, *Free Trade: Theory and Practice from Adam Smith to Keynes*

who have raised questions relating to the Liberal Party have traditionally concentrated either on the Whig cabinets and Russell's conversion to free trade, or on Radicals and Anti-Corn Law League supporters.[3] The historiography of the 1980s and 1990s cast light on the previously undervalued ideological influences on liberal politicians. The influence of religion, both in terms of intellectual development, as well its connections with commercial questions, pushed some of the economic and political science arguments about free trade in the 1830s and 1840s slightly into the background.[4] The most recent historiography, however, has gone in two new directions. The first is a new school of quantitative analysis, led by Cheryl Schonhardt-Bailey. It mostly concerns the Tories, but also considers Whigs, Liberals and Reformers, focusing particularly on the influence of the type of seat held by an MP on his corn law voting behaviour.[5] The second new trend in historiography, led by Anthony Howe, seeks not only to place free trade at the very heart of the rising tide of liberalism as an ideology during the 19th century, but also to re-emphasize the centrality of political economy as the ideological force behind free trade philosophy. Finally, Howe's work with the Cobden diaries and letters, and his important edited collection of Cobden studies, entitled *Re-thinking Nineteenth-Century Liberalism*, have shown how important Cobden was in helping to stage-manage corn law repeal motions and the presentations of petitions in the house of commons, even before he had been elected an MP, and the extent to which leading free traders looked to Cobden for advice and strategy

[2] (*continued*) (1970); D.P. O'Brien, *The Classical Economists* (Oxford, 1975); W.O. Aydelotte, 'Voting Patterns in the British House of Commons in the 1840s', *Comparative Studies in Society and History*, v (1962–3), 134–63; W.O. Aydelotte, 'Constituency Influences on the House of Commons, 1841–1847,' in *The History of Parliamentary Behavior*, ed. W.O. Aydelotte (Princeton, NJ, 1977); W.O. Aydelotte, 'The House of Commons in the 1840s', *American Historical Association Conference, July 1953* (Washington, DC, 1953); S. Fairlie, 'The Corn Laws and British Wheat Protection, 1829–76', *Economic History Review*, xxii (1969), 562–73; S. Fairlie, 'The Nineteenth-Century Corn Law Re-considered', *Economic History Review*, xviii (1965), 562–75. Anna Gambles' *Protection and Politics: Conservative Economic Discourse, 1815–1852* (Woodbridge, 1999) provides an important corrective to the traditional emphasis on the Peelites.

[3] A. Howe, *Free Trade and Liberal England* (Oxford, 1997), *passim*, esp. ch. 2; F.A. Dryer, 'The Whigs and the Political Crisis of 1845', *EHR*, lxxx (1965), 514–37; J.P. Parry, *The Rise and Fall of Liberal Government in Victorian Britain* (New Haven, CT, 1993), esp. 168–73; Lars Magnusson, *The Tradition of Free Trade* (2004); Gambles, *Protection and Politics*; A. Howe, 'Free Trade and the Victorians', in *Free Trade and Its Reception 1815–1960*, ed. Andrew Marrison (1998), 164–83; *From the Corn Laws to Free Trade: Interests, Ideas, and Institutions in Historical Perspective*, ed. C. Schonhardt-Bailey (Cambridge, MA, 2006).

[4] See J.P. Parry, *Democracy and Religion: Gladstone and the Liberal Party, 1867–1875* (Cambridge, 1986); R. Brent, *Liberal Anglican Politics: Whiggery, Religion, and Reform, 1830–1841* (Oxford, 1987); P. Mandler, *Aristocratic Government in the Age of Reform: Whigs and Liberals 1830–1852* (Oxford, 1990), esp. 170–99, 218–35; J.W. Burrow, *Whigs and Liberals: Continuity and Change in English Political Thought* (Oxford, 1988), introduction; R. Brent, 'God's Providence: Liberal Political Economy as Natural Theology at Oxford, 1825–60', in *Public and Private Doctrine: Essays in British History Presented to Maurice Cowling*, ed. M. Bentley (Cambridge, 1993), 85–107; B. Hilton, *The Age of Atonement: The Influence of Evangelicalism on Social and Economic Thought, 1785–1865* (Oxford, 1988); B. Hilton, 'Whiggery, Religion and Social Reform: The Case of Lord Morpeth', *HJ*, xxxvii (1994), 829–59. An important exception to this trend was Miles Taylor's *The Decline of British Radicalism, 1847–1860* (Oxford, 1995).

[5] *Free Trade: The Repeal of the Corn Laws*, ed. C. Schonhardt-Bailey (Bristol, 1996); *The Rise of Free Trade*, ed. C. Schonhardt-Bailey (4 vols, 1997); *From the Corn Laws to Free Trade*, ed. Schonhardt-Bailey; C. Schonhardt-Bailey, 'Linking Constituency Interests to Legislative Voting Behaviour: The Role of District Economic and Electoral Composition in the Repeal of the Corn Laws', in *Computing Parliamentary History, George III to Victoria*, ed. J.A. Phillips (Edinburgh, 1994), 86–118; C. Schonhardt-Bailey, 'Party and Interests in the British Parliament of 1841–47', *British Journal of Political Science*, xxxiii (2003), 581–605.

on the timing of such events to work best with the state of public opinion at any one time.[6]

This chapter aims to continue this process of bringing liberal MPs back into the free trade historiography. It will not be an analysis of free trade itself, or of political economy, but an examination of what various free trade measures introduced into the house of commons can tell us about the gradual formation of the Liberal Party, the divergent ideas about free trade among Liberal Party MPs, and the importance of free trade for showing how strong the language and symbolism of party were for the liberals. It will provide a narrative analysis of some of the major free trade motions and bills brought into the House: inquiries into the corn laws from 1837 to 1839, the 1841 sugar duty reduction debates, Peel's 1846 repeal of the corn laws, the repeal of the navigation acts in 1849 and the protectionist amendment to the 1850 queen's speech.[7] The debates on these motions and bills, bolstered by evidence from the manuscript collections of backbench MPs, reveal how diverse Liberal Party thinking was on free trade matters.

Liberal Party MPs who supported free trade thought it was consistent with what they saw as natural economic law.[8] Viscount Morpeth, Liberal MP for Yorkshire West Riding, stated in 1846 that free trade 'does follow the laws of nature, and bends to the rules that guide the seasons in their course';[9] just as Viscount Howick, Whig MP for Northumberland North, had urged in 1839 that trade had followed 'a natural course' with which it was unwise, and even dangerous, to interfere.[10] Two strong advocates of corn law repeal, Charles Villiers, Reformer MP for Wolverhampton, and Sir William Molesworth, Radical MP for Leeds, often spoke of the almost religious expectation that free trade would introduce an era of international co-operation and bring about the improvement of mankind, because it 'was the best possible security for contentment at home and permanent tranquillity abroad';[11] and that once free trade was adopted,

> Civilised nations, instead of being separated, as now, by commercial restrictions, would form one vast social system, cemented together by similar wants, by interests closely interwoven, and by mutual dependence upon one another. The extended intercourse thence arising, facilitated by daily improvements in the means of conveyance, would soon obliterate those noxious jealousies and hateful national antipathies, the fertile sources of wars and their attendant evils, to which may mainly be attributed the slow moral and social improvement of mankind.[12]

Free trade would also lead to national unity and peace, once the social evil of protection was eliminated. In fact, as Joseph Hume, while Radical MP for Kilkenny, argued, other

[6] Howe, *Free Trade and Liberal England*; Howe, 'Free Trade and the Victorians'; *Re-thinking Nineteenth-Century Liberalism: Richard Cobden Bicentenary Essays*, ed. A. Howe and S. Morgan (2006); *The Letters of Richard Cobden*, ed. A. Howe (2 vols, Oxford, 2007).

[7] Free trade as expressed through various Whig government budgets will not be examined. This has been well discussed in Howe, *Free Trade and Liberal England*, chs 1, 2; H.C.G. Matthew, 'Disraeli, Gladstone, and the Politics of Mid-Victorian Budgets', *HJ*, xxii (1979), 615–43.

[8] Parry, *Rise and Fall of Liberal Government*, 143–4.

[9] Hansard, *Parl. Debs*, lxxxiii, cols 803–17 (12 Feb. 1846).

[10] Hansard, *Parl. Debs*, xlvi, cols 546–50 (13 Mar. 1839).

[11] C.P. Villiers, Hansard, *Parl. Debs*, xlvi, col. 355 (12 Mar. 1839).

[12] Sir W. Molesworth, Hansard, *Parl. Debs*, xlvi, cols 460–3 (13 Mar. 1839).

government social intervention was useless until free trade had been secured: 'All attempts to relieve [labourers and other distressed persons] and give them continued prosperity would be useless, unless the Legislature went to the root of the evil which now weighed them to the earth'.[13] The broadest free trade agenda, mostly held by Radicals, blamed protectionism (and specifically import duties) for holding down demand by inflicting higher prices on the consumer, producing inadequate revenue for the treasury, and actually damaging the profit-making ability of most traders.[14] Corn law repeal activists even sealed their letters with yellow, diamond-shaped, 'free-trade wafers', one of which said: 'Thanks for cheap postage. May we soon get cheap bread. Free communication with all parts of the Empire is good, but free trade with all parts of the world will be better still'.[15] And many of them thought of free trade as an inextricable part of the overall liberal agenda, which also included parliamentary and church reform, and the ballot.[16]

Liberal protectionists, on the other hand, argued that free trade would be an abandonment of the English farmer and, specifically, that corn law repeal was the thin edge of a dangerous wedge which would damage other traditional economic interests.[17] 'Once begin innovation', said Gilbert Heathcote, Reformer MP for South Lincolnshire, 'and where would it end?'[18] Shipping protectionists on the liberal benches argued that repeal of the navigation laws would damage shipping unfairly, and that it was ill-timed.[19] As John Wawn, Liberal MP for South Shields, argued, 'The timber duties and marine duties must be abolished, and the pilotage and light-dues greatly modified, before they could repeal the navigation laws with safety'.[20]

Party played an equally important role in free trade debates among liberals. Some Liberal Party MPs opposed corn law inquiries in the late 1830s because they seemed tainted by party interest in courting the manufacturing vote,[21] while others were pleased at the idea that free trade had become a party question because they held it to be of deep ideological significance.[22] For instance, Thomas Thompson's *Catechism on the Corn Laws:*

---

[13] Hansard, *Parl. Debs*, xlvi, cols 716–17 (15 Mar. 1839); see also Lord Vaney, Liberal MP for Durham South, Hansard, *Parl. Debs*, xxxiii, cols 996–7 (16 Feb. 1846).

[14] *Report and Minutes of Evidence from the Select Committee on Import Duties*, Parliamentary Papers, 1840 (601), v, 103 (v). The first page number indicates the page within volume v; the second page number refers to the number within the select committee report itself.

[15] Manchester Central Library Archive, John Benjamin Smith Papers, MS 923.2 S333.3, iii, item 327: envelope of letter from Joseph Hume to John Benjamin Smith, 26 July 1841. There were other wafers as well, with different sayings, sold by J. Gadsby of Manchester, for 1s. per pack.

[16] See, for example, Manchester Central Library Archive, John Benjamin Smith Papers, MS 923.2 S330, volume of newspaper cuttings: J.B. Smith's address to the electors of Stockport, *Stockport Advertiser*, 15 Mar. 1852; see also Smith Papers, MS 923.2 S345, letter 3: Richard Cobden to J.B. Smith, 4 Mar. 1852.

[17] Essex RO, Barrett-Leonard Papers, D/DL/F193: Thomas Barrett-Leonard, Reformer MP for Maldon, journal entry, 10 May 1839.

[18] Lincolnshire Archives Office, Heathcote Papers: G.J. Heathcote, speech to his constituents, as reported in *The Globe*, 1 Mar. 1834.

[19] See, for example, James Clay, Reformer MP for Hull, Hansard, *Parl. Debs*, ciii, cols 574–6 (12 Mar. 1849).

[20] Hansard, *Parl. Debs*, ciii, cols 585–6 (12 Mar. 1849).

[21] For instance, Craven Berkeley, Reformer MP for Cheltenham, Hansard, *Parl. Debs*, xli, col. 935 (15 Mar. 1838).

[22] For example, Sir Benjamin Hawes, Reformer MP for Lambeth, Hansard, *Parl. Debs*, lviii, cols 76–7 (7 May 1841); H.G. Ward, Reformer MP for Sheffield, Hansard, *Parl. Debs*, lviii, col. 212 (11 May 1841); Thomas Macaulay, Whig MP for Edinburgh, Hansard, *Parl. Debs*, lviii, col. 195 (11 May 1841).

With a List of Fallacies and the Answers (1831) mixed free trade ideology and party language. This famous pamphlet is a series (365 – one for each day of the year) of answered objections to corn law abolition. It is mostly gainsaying, but displays a distinct ideology of strict free trade, even to the extent of arguing that any potential suffering under a free trade system would be natural, and those who might temporarily suffer would gain in the end. Party language is found in the following:

> [Question] 233. That the nation is dividing itself into two parts; the *conservative* and the *revolutionary*. *Blackwood's Ed. Mag.; A[nswer].* The *conservative* mean those who having got what does not belong to them, intend to keep it; and the *revolutionary*, mean those who would take it from them. All men who take what is not their own are conservative the next day.[23]

And some liberal protectionists deeply regretted that they had to differ from the rest of the party when opposing free trade measures.[24] It will be argued here, therefore, that the dramatic increase in voting for free trade among Liberal Party MPs between 1837 and 1850 was partly the result of party concerns, especially this acceptance of a free trade agenda, as well as partly the result of personal ideology on trade issues. Language, particularly the naturalistic language used to trumpet free trade measures, became more prominent and important between 1837 and 1850, especially between 1837 and 1841. In fact, it was the free trade rhetorical agenda that Liberal Party MPs became most strongly attached to by the end of the reform period. After a brief discussion of the general background to free trade issues as raised in the 1830s and 1840s, this chapter will analyse the debates on the motions and bills mentioned above, and draw conclusions on the meanings of free trade and free trade rhetoric for liberal politics.

Background to Free Trade Issues, 1837–50

Protection of British industries and agriculture had existed for centuries.[25] During the early 19th century, however, the corn laws had come to symbolise the debate over free trade and a continuation of protectionism. By 1815, some sections of public opinion, tired of the cost of 18th-century wars, called for retrenchment in government expenditure, and for greater economy in achieving political ends. The house of commons had ended the wartime income tax in 1816, which forced administrators to look elsewhere for revenue. Tariff reform was government policy in the liberal tory administrations of

---

[23] Thomas Perronet Thompson, *Catechism on the Corn Laws: With a List of Fallacies and the Answers* (1831), 45. Thompson became one of the most significant promoters of free trade. See Michael Turner, '"The Bonaparte of Free Trade" and the Anti-Corn Law League', *HJ*, xli (1998), 1011–34. John Bowring was equally important in trying to champion British-style free trade in Europe and further abroad. See David Todd, 'John Bowring and the Dissemination of Free Trade', *HJ*, li (2008), 373–97.

[24] Durham County RO, Bowes Papers, D/St/C1/16/279: John Bowes, Reformer MP for South Durham, printed address to his constituents, 8 June 1841.

[25] D.G. Barnes, *A History of English Corn Laws from 1660 to 1846* (1930), introduction and ch. 1.

the 1820s.[26] And after the passage of the Reform Act of 1832, many Liberal Party MPs sought to have the reforming spirit pushed further into government economics. As William Hyett, Whig MP for Stroud, addressed his constituents in a post-election speech on 15 December 1832,

> When the finances of the country shall come under the consideration of a reformed House of Commons, it will be the duty of every honest member to reduce the burdens of the country to the lowest possible amount, consistent with national faith and national safety. Let us have a repeal of our corn-laws. (Cheers). A repeal of the varying scale of duties, which are alike injurious to the agriculturalist, the manufacturer, and the merchant. If it should be necessary, substitute a low fixed duty; but, if possible, let there be free trade in corn as in everything else (Cheers).[27]

Whig party leaders had, however, generally been mostly interested in administrative and institutional reforms in the early 1830s, even though political economy had been infused into their ideology. As the 1830s progressed, the reform governments rebuffed the idea of abolishing the corn laws and other measures, for several reasons. They had genuine reservations about the effects of corn law repeal on farmers and landowners, but also because protectionism seemed like a valid and strong food policy. The corn laws were an attempt to secure a substantial agricultural base in the face of a grain surplus in Europe that did not end until 1838. Further, with the recurring depressions of the 1830s and 1840s, and the fear of food supplies being cut off in the event of war, protectionism was couched in terms of responsible government, given all the concerns just mentioned.[28] The government benches, consequently, preferred to push religious and social reform, which, as we shall see in the next section on 1837–47, left Liberal Party backbenchers to push for free trade, not only as an economic and fiscal question, but also as a political and social one. They did this initially through motions for inquiries into the corn laws.[29]

---

[26] Howe, *Free Trade and Liberal England*, 1–4; Parry, *Rise and Fall of Liberal Government*, 23; Hilton, *Corn, Cash, and Commerce*, 264–301, 306–7. For the history of the corn laws, see Barnes, *History of English Corn Laws*; R.L. Schuyler, *The Fall of the Old Colonial System* (Oxford, 1945); *Free Trade*, ed. Schonhardt-Bailey; McCord, *Free Trade*; *Rise of Free Trade*, ed. Schonhardt-Bailey: of particular interest in vol. iv are: G.M. Anderson and R.D. Tollison, 'Ideology, Interest Groups, and the Repeal of the Corn Laws', 38–52; D.A. Irwin, 'Political Economy and Peel's Repeal of the Corn Laws', 287–308; D. Verdier, 'Between Party and Faction: The Politics behind the Repeal of the Corn Laws', 309–38; Schonhardt-Bailey, 'Party and Interests', 581–605.

[27] Gloucestershire RO, Hyett Papers: speech of W.H. Hyett, *Gloucester Journal*, 15 Dec. 1832.

[28] Fairlie, 'Nineteenth-Century Corn Law Reconsidered', 562–73; Fairlie, 'Corn Laws and British Wheat Protection', 88–110; A. Gambles, 'The Boundaries of Political Economy: Tory Economic Argument, 1809–1847', Oxford University PhD, 1996, 81–135; A.D. Macintyre, 'Lord George Bentinck and the Protectionists: A Lost Cause?', *TRHS*, 5th ser., xxxix (1989), 141–65; D. Walker-Smith, *The Protectionist Case in the 1840s* (Oxford, 1933); T.L. Crosby, *English Farmers and the Politics of Protection 1815–1852* (Hassocks, 1977). See also A. Gambles, 'Rethinking the Politics of Protection: Conservatism and the Corn Laws, 1830–1852', *EHR*, cxiii (1998), 928–52.

[29] I. Newbould, *Whiggery and Reform, 1830–41: The Politics of Government* (1990), 104; Howe, *Free Trade and Liberal England*, 3–4; Parry, *Rise and Fall of Liberal Government*, 113–54, esp. 143–5; Mandler, *Aristocratic Government*, chs 6, 7.

There had been a few motions from liberal backbenchers to inquire into the state of the corn laws in the early 1830s, but it was not until 1837 that annual motions began in earnest. The debates on the motions in the late 1830s were generally technical, with heavy use of statistics and comparisons with other economic interests. The language was also very earthbound. MPs, especially Liberal Party MPs, seemed initially reluctant to resort to romantic appeals to the natural beauty of political economy, or to the solid traditions of agricultural protection. This changed by the end of the 1839 debate, signalling a trend for the 1840s.

On 16 March 1837, Sir William Clay, Reformer MP for Tower Hamlets, rose and moved for an inquiry into the corn laws, arguing that anything that worked so badly ought to be examined. They were an economic inconsistency when compared with other commodities, he argued, they affected the poor through higher bread prices, they failed to protect the farmer and the consumer, and were only a benefit to the landed classes. He only departed from this line of argument to display the liberal sense of progress, and the efficacy of free trade in improving the lot of common people.

> [I]t is asked, how should we employ our agricultural labourers if we eat cheap foreign corn instead of dear English corn? If their labour be at present wasted, we had better maintain them in absolute idleness than employ them in wasting capital as well as their own time; but in truth there would be employment for them in the thousand channels, which in a thriving community, and with rapidly increasing wealth, are open to industry.[30]

And, although his motion was simply for an inquiry into the operation of the corn laws, he told MPs that his solution would be to 'sweep wholly away' the corn law duty system, and replace it with a fixed duty 'of moderated amount . . . [which] should be in amount an exact equivalent for the burthens which the agricultural capitalist has to sustain', showing a recognition that the realistic limit which free trade arguments could be carried to the house of commons was to suggest a fixed duty on corn.[31] Charles Villiers, the Reformer MP for Wolverhampton who would take up the question annually from 1838, seconded the motion, making the utilitarian argument that the government should not enact legislation that protected one economic interest in the country at the expense of others.[32] In a relatively short debate, Liberal Party MPs stuck to two main themes: the effect of the corn laws on the poor and the labourers in manufacturing districts on one side, and on the other, that agricultural interests could not afford to be hurt at that particular moment. Joseph Hume, Radical MP for Middlesex, said:

> The Corn-laws ground the people down to misery . . . Parliament maintained a cruel, a grinding – he would say a famishing, Corn-law. The Poor-laws were grinding down able-bodied men with large families; while the Corn-laws were keeping up the

[30] Hansard, *Parl. Debs*, xxxvii, cols 562–87 (16 Mar. 1837) for the full text of his speech, quote at col. 570.
[31] Hansard, *Parl. Debs*, xxxvii, cols 583–4 (16 Mar. 1837).
[32] Hansard, *Parl. Debs*, xxxvii, cols 587–92 (16 Mar. 1837).

Table 8.1: *Division on Clay's 1837 Corn Law Inquiry Motion*

Liberal Party groups	Ayes	Noes
Administration	8	1
Liberals	2	2
Radicals	22	5
Reformers	35	25
Repealers	7	2
Whigs	13	26
None listed	4	3
All Liberal Party	91	64
Conservative Party	0	161
Totals	91	225

Source: Hansard, *Parl. Debs*, xxxvii, cols 615–16 (16 Mar. 1837); *The Times*, 17 Mar. 1837; House of Commons, Division Lists, 16 Mar. 1837, no division number.

price of their food. The labouring man was crushed and borne down, and all this was done for the benefit of the landed interest.[33]

On the protectionist side of the Liberal Party, Henry Handley, Radical MP for Lincoln-shire South, said that he would only support corn law repeal when it proved necessary, and was economically viable, for all monopolies and protection for specific industries to be eliminated.[34] Gilbert Heathcote represented the stronger liberal protectionist case when he argued that both agricultural labourers and landowners would be devastated by any major change in the corn laws, and that when they had petitioned parliament for help in previous years, 'they were told to relieve themselves'. He hoped Clay's motion would fail so that agriculturists could be left to solve their own problems.[35] Clay's motion failed 91 to 225, with many of the Liberal Party voting against him, especially Whigs. This is shown clearly in Table 8.1.

The next year, Charles Villiers, Reformer MP for Wolverhampton, began to introduce corn law inquiry motions on an annual basis. In February 1838, he consulted Richard Cobden, asking for extensive statistics and explanations of the idea of comparative natural advantage. Cobden sent a lengthy and detailed report.[36] Villiers introduced his first inquiry motion on 15 March 1838. In a long speech, he broadened the reasoning behind opposition to the corn laws beyond simple political economy to include social issues as well. This was the first major appearance in the house of commons of a liberal free trade argument that brought in other aspects of liberal politics and ideology. He said that he moved an inquiry into the corn laws for several reasons, and it is significant to note the

[33] Hansard, *Parl. Debs*, xxxvii, cols 612–13 (16 Mar. 1837).
[34] Hansard, *Parl. Debs*, xxxvii, cols 601–2 (16 Mar. 1837).
[35] Hansard, *Parl. Debs*, xxxvii, cols 602–3 (16 Mar. 1837).
[36] *Letters of Richard Cobden*, ed. Howe, i, 125–8: Richard Cobden to C.P. Villiers, 17 Feb. 1838. Villiers and Cobden had a close correspondence on the corn laws, and especially Villiers' annual motions. Villiers sought advice and information from Cobden on commercial and trading statistics, the work of the Anti-Corn Law League, the timing of introducing his inquiry motions and the possibility of forming a free trade party. See *Letters of Richard Cobden*, ed. Howe, i, 179, 181, 210, 223–4, 227, 228–9, 235–6, 244–5.

order in which he listed them. First, he argued, the corn laws should be looked into because those enfranchised by the Reform Act largely demanded it.

> Those to whom the elective franchise had been given by the Reform Bill, deemed the Corn-laws one of the greatest wrongs of the unreformed Parliament, and the reason why they had sought the franchise was, because it would enable them to test the disposition of the new Parliament on this subject.[37]

Popular support for parliament was ebbing away as long as the corn laws were not dealt with, he continued. The recently enfranchised might turn to violence, and the house of commons must listen to those they might have to repress eventually. Second, many MPs in the House had stood as champions of the poor, and now the poor needed cheap bread. It was their duty to respond by amending or eliminating the corn laws. Third, he compared the typical agricultural protectionist to a sort of county Luddite who opposed any advance in technology or economic thinking. Fourth, he argued at length against the idea that the agricultural classes needed special protection, and that they were already exempt from so many taxes that they did not have a claim to government protection. Fifth, some foreign markets were closing themselves to other British products in retaliation. And finally, he argued that, in the 20 years the corn laws had been in operation, they had done nothing to improve the lot of the agriculturalist or the agricultural labourer.[38] In seconding the motion, Sir William Molesworth, Radical MP for Leeds, continued this broad attack. In his opinion,

> the tendency of the Corn-laws was to create discontent, uneasiness, and an infinitude of moral evils, amongst the great bulk of the community; and it could . . . easily be proved, that the statute which [Villiers] proposed to repeal, materially impeded the advance of this country in a career of wealth, power, and social improvement, which might, and would, be without parallel in the universe.[39]

Molesworth concluded the rest of his speech in somewhat anthropological terms, arguing that the degree of civilization in a country depended on the proportion of the population producing food. More advanced societies had a relatively small percentage of their populations involved in agriculture. Where large proportions of populations were directly involved in food production, societies were basic and backward, with little time or manpower for the variety of occupations and industries that were to be found in advanced societies. Molesworth worried that the continuation of the corn laws would mean that England would prevent itself from attaining a higher degree of civilization. This was taken as far as arguing that social ills, such as prostitution, could be traced to the continued operation of the corn laws.[40]

     The debate proceeded much like the 1837 debate, except that it was slightly longer. Sir William Clay, the MP behind the 1837 motion, proposed that, if Villiers' motion

---

[37] Hansard, *Parl. Debs*, xli, col. 910 (15 Mar. 1838). For an overview of Villiers' career, see W.O. Henderson, 'Charles Pelham Villiers', *History*, xxxvii (1952), 25–39; see also a collection of his free trade speeches, C.P. Villiers, *Free Trade Speeches* (2 vols, 1883).

[38] Hansard, *Parl. Debs*, xli, cols 909–23 (15 Mar. 1838).

[39] Hansard, *Parl. Debs*, xli, col. 923 (15 Mar. 1838).

[40] Hansard, *Parl. Debs*, xli, cols 923–31 (15 Mar. 1838).

Table 8.2: *Division on Villiers' 1838 Corn Law Inquiry Motion*

Liberal Party groups	Ayes	Noes
Administration	7	2
Liberals	11	7
Radicals	23	4
Reformers	33	22
Repealers	3	4
Whigs	14	33
None listed	8	3
All Liberal Party	99	75
Conservative Party	0	229
Totals	99	304

Source: Hansard, *Parl. Debs*, xli, cols 946–9 (15 Mar. 1838); *The Times*, 16 Mar. 1838; House of Commons, Division Lists, 15 Mar. 1838, no division number.

passed, a fixed duty should be used as a stopgap measure before complete abolition of duties.[41] Some Liberal Party MPs, such as Sir Ronald Ferguson, Reformer MP for Nottingham, presented petitions from constituents urging corn law abolition and an extension of free trade.[42] The liberal protectionists, however, continued to join their conservative counterparts in opposing the motion. They contested the assertion that corn law repeal enjoyed wide public support, and argued that large sections of the country would be thrown out of work when it was found they could not compete with cheap foreign grain.[43] When pressed to a division, Villiers' motion lost 99 to 304. There was not much change in the proportion of liberal MP groups voting Aye or No, but there was a slight increase in the number of Liberal Party MPs voting. This was soon to change, however, as Liberal Party leaders sought to address the corn laws directly, as part of a party plan.

Although more Liberal Party leaders (generally the 'Administration' MPs listed in Tables 8.1 and 8.2) supported the corn law inquiry motions than opposed them, the cabinet was reluctant to propose a government bill because the majority of the Commons were opposed to it, and it would have brought unnecessary hostility down on the government. But both the economic situation in the country, and the Liberal Party's precarious majority in the House, pressed urgently upon the Whigs to take decisive action. Bad harvests in 1837 and 1838 had created an economic depression which would last until 1842, with high levels of unemployment. Working-class agitation gained important support from radical intellectuals who argued that traditional structures like the corn laws, which supported a political and landed elite, must be swept away. A raft of grievances was presented to parliament between 1839 and 1841, many of them dealing with economics and trade, but others to do with church and constitutional

[41] Hansard, *Parl. Debs*, xli, cols 939–40 (15 Mar. 1838).

[42] Hansard, *Parl. Debs*, xli, col. 944 (15 Mar. 1838).

[43] See, for example, Edward Cayley, Whig MP for the North Riding of Yorkshire, Hansard, *Parl. Debs*, xli, cols 941–3 (15 Mar. 1838).

questions heightened by the crisis. Anti-corn law petitions from the Manchester Chamber of Commerce, for example, had stopped between 1828 and 1838. After 1838, they came to parliament in force.[44] The Liberal Party majority in the house of commons had been reduced to almost nothing through by-election losses, and the government's legislative ability was weakened. Meanwhile, the continental grain glut had finally run out. Bad harvests in north-western Europe since 1836 had more or less eliminated the fear that Britain would be swamped by cheap continental grain.[45] With the price of wheat rising from 39s. 4d. per quarter in 1835 to 70s. 8d. in 1839, the cabinet realized that the corn laws must be addressed.[46] Further, Radicals had been grumbling about the danger of corn law repeal becoming stagnant in parliament. As J.B. Smith wrote to Joseph Brotherton, Radical MP for Salford 1832–57, 'are we to go on year after year & get nothing?' Further, he urged Brotherton to strengthen the case for corn law repeal by finding an MP of 'greater weight' than Villiers to introduce motions. By this stage Radicals saw some chance of gaining more division votes for repeal, and wanted each motion to be in the best of hands. 'Let me know your views by return [of post] if you can, for our friends are rather impatient on this point', he told Brotherton.[47] They wished to raise the profile of corn law repeal in the house of commons, but failed in this respect.

Early in the 1839 session, Villiers introduced his corn law inquiry motion. He further broadened his attack on the corn laws, and paid special attention to how much damage it was reportedly doing to other commercial interests. Rather than repeat his 1838 statements on the impact of the corn laws on social questions, he made the economic and commercial case for repeal. He argued against the claim that the corn laws were needed to support agricultural labourers because that idea had never been employed when it came to the invention of new farm machinery. Labourers of all classes had had to pay more for bread since 1828, which had a bad effect on wages. Manufacturers had to pay their employees more, and this impacted greatly on their ability to compete with other European countries. In almost Ricardian language, Villiers argued that:

> The Corn-laws might rob A to benefit B, but they did not create wealth; they did not benefit the public generally; and when it was borne in mind that, in order to afford the exclusive protection to one class, we were ruining the manufactures and contracting the commerce of the country, it was surely time for the Legislature to interpose, and to consider whether the danger and national loss that would accrue from the contraction of the commerce of the country would not be much greater than that could possibly arise out of a repeal of the Corn-laws.[48]

Molesworth, again, brought the two strands of the anti-corn law argument up during the 1839 debate.

[44] *Select Committee on Import Duties*, v, 270 (162), question 2062: Testimony of J.B. Smith, 27 July 1840.

[45] Fairlie, 'Nineteenth-Century Corn Laws Reconsidered', 562–3, 568, 572.

[46] Fairlie, 'Corn Laws and British Wheat Protection, 1829–76', 88–110; Parry, *Rise and Fall of Liberal Government*, 142–7; Howe, *Free Trade and Liberal England*, 24–5, 42; L. Brown, *The Board of Trade and the Free Trade Movement* (Oxford, 1958), 222–5; Brent, *Liberal Anglican Politics*, 292–8.

[47] Manchester Central Library Archive, John Benjamin Smith Papers, MS 923.2 S333, i, item 83: J.B. Smith to Joseph Brotherton, 28 Dec. 1838. This volume also contains a good account of the formation of the Anti-Corn Law League and Smith's role in it.

[48] Hansard, *Parl. Debs*, xlvi, col. 353 (12 Mar. 1839). His motion was in cols 334–61.

I desire freedom of trade on account of two very different classes of benefits – the one of an economical kind, affecting the production and distribution of wealth; the other of a moral and social kind, affecting the relations between members of this community, and the relations of this country with the nations of the globe.[49]

Viscount Howick, who had previously opposed a change in the corn laws in cabinet, spoke in favour of the motion in terms of the providential nature of free trade. Free trade was, he argued, 'the instrument obviously designed by Providence'. It was part of 'the natural order of things', and 'that beautiful mechanism of society, which seems to me to bear so clearly the impress of unerring wisdom and divine benevolence'.[50] Charles Thomson spoke about the damage that protection was doing to foreign trade in other goods.[51] Joseph Hume and Sir George Strickland, Reformer MP for Yorkshire West Riding, described the corn laws in moral terms. Protection had led, Hume argued, to increased distress, poverty, lawlessness and misery. This would continue 'unless the Legislature went to the root of the evil'.[52] And Strickland argued that any 'measure which is morally wrong can never be politically right'.[53]

The liberal protectionists brought up arguments similar to the ones they had used in 1837 and 1838,[54] except that Edward Cayley, Whig MP for Yorkshire North Riding, realized that Villiers' motions were getting more serious, and that the debates on them were lasting longer. He defended the corn laws on the traditional grounds of protecting agricultural labourers and landowners, but he went much further than he had in previous years, and attacked industrialists for what he saw as their assumptions that they were the engines driving England's economic power. In a purple passage, he vowed that he would rather the future of England rest on the land than industrial 'tenants of a day':

To hear the language which is spoken by some who advocate the repeal of the corn laws, one would almost imagine, that this isle of ours, in all its richness and beauty – the offspring of centuries of British liberty, energy, and industry, had sprung into existence but yesterday – the creature and spawn of Manchester; that history was a fiction, and the monuments of the dead forsworn. [Loud cries of hear, hear, hear!] . . . Sir, I will not consent to place the whole exertions and employment of my countrymen on so insecure and treacherous a base as that of a foreign trade, daily, we are told, slipping from under our feet, and hourly at the mercy, of the caprice, the tyranny, the necessity of other Powers. . . . No! give me the broad lands of England and Ireland on which to rest the solid and lasting fabric of our national greatness.

[49] Hansard, *Parl. Debs*, xlvi, col. 441 (13 Mar. 1839).

[50] Hansard, *Parl. Debs*, xlvi, cols 546, 550 (13 Mar. 1839). See also Howe, *Free Trade and Liberal England*, 24–5.

[51] Hansard, *Parl. Debs*, xlvi, cols 432–3 (12 Mar. 1839). See also Molesworth, Hansard, *Parl. Debs*, xlvi, cols 460–3 (13 Mar. 1839).

[52] Hansard, *Parl. Debs*, xlvi, cols 716–17 (15 Mar. 1839).

[53] Hansard, *Parl. Debs*, xlvi, cols 364–5 (12 Mar. 1839).

[54] See Lord Worsley, Whig MP for Lincolnshire North, Hansard, *Parl. Debs*, xlvi, cols 628–33 (14 Mar. 1839); William O'Brien, Reformer MP for Limerick County, Hansard, *Parl. Debs*, xlvi, cols 809–11 (18 Mar. 1839); Henry Handley, Reformer MP for Lincolnshire, Hansard, *Parl. Debs*, xlvi, col. 743 (15 Mar. 1839).

Hold we and abide we by them, who will hold and abide by us, rather than by those who boast of their power to fly from us – who are 'tenants of a day, and have no interest in the inheritance'.[55]

Perhaps the most significant speech during the 1839 debate, however, was Russell's of 14 March 1839. Although he had come out in favour of a moderate fixed duty in January, he spoke more generally about the effects of free trade on industries in England and other countries.[56] He used examples of the silk, glove, wool and earthenware industries to show that, whenever there was high protection, the domestic industry invariably produced inferior products. When the duty was removed, the industry became more competitive and produced better goods.

> With these facts before me, I must at once confess, that I think, that, if other articles – corn, for instance – were allowed to be regularly imported at a low fixed duty, the effect would be the same as in the instances of silk gloves, wool and earthenware, and, moreover, I am quite convinced, that the result would be the improvement of agriculture . . . I think if there were greater freedom, the farmers would pay more attention, and exercise greater skill, and I have the concurrent opinions of Lord Spencer and many others of the greatest weight and name in the agriculture of the country, that such would be the case.[57]

By the time of the debate on Villiers' 1839 motion, Whig leaders had become convinced of the importance of corn law reform, not just for commercial purposes, but for electoral and party purposes as well. Electoral support in the counties for liberal candidates had been slipping throughout the 1830s. Party leaders began to think that repeal of the corn laws might convince landowners that protection was a thing of the past, and that the reformed political world was also a free trade world. Further, liberal support in the boroughs, particularly in the north, would be solidified.[58] The danger of a corn glut, as well, and the arguments for protection as a hard-nosed food supply policy had lost much of their validity.[59] Finally, the broad appeal of a free trade agenda held the possibility for the liberals to present themselves as a disinterested party and government. It was important to show that parliament in general, and the cabinet in particular, was not beholden to one interest, that farming and manufacturing would both benefit from free trade, and that this appeal to all classes would show the Liberal Party to be the more natural party of government than the Conservatives.[60] With the cabinet now actively supporting this free trade motion, more Liberal Party MPs were persuaded to attend the House and vote in its favour. While the number of liberals opposed to Villiers' motion remained roughly the same as it had in 1837 and 1838, the number of Ayes increased by around 100, reflecting an increased perception of importance in this division, and more Liberal Party MPs attending. This may be seen more clearly in Table 8.3.

---

[55] Hansard, *Parl. Debs*, xlvi, cols 417–18 (12 Mar. 1839).

[56] *The Times*, 26 Jan. 1839; Parry, *Rise and Fall of Liberal Government*, 146.

[57] Lord John Russell, Hansard, *Parl. Debs*, xlvi, cols 701–2 (14 Mar. 1839).

[58] Parry, *Rise and Fall of Liberal Government*, 146.

[59] See Fairlie, 'Corn Laws and British Wheat Protection', 88–92, 109–10.

[60] Howe, *Free Trade and Liberal England*, 40–1; Mandler, *Aristocratic Government*, 218–35.

Table 8.3: *Division on Villiers' 1839 Corn Law Inquiry Motion*

Liberal Party groups	Ayes	Noes
Administration	20	0
Liberals	24	4
Radicals	28	3
Reformers	63	21
Repealers	8	6
Whigs	40	29
None listed	15	6
All Liberal Party	198	69
Conservative Party	0	275
Totals	198	344

Source: Hansard, *Parl. Debs*, lxxxiv, cols 353–4 (2 Mar. 1846); *The Times*, 20 May 1841; House of Commons, Division Lists, 18 Mar. 1839, No. 29.

Note: Parry writes that '33 ministerial MPs were absent' during this division (Parry, *Rise and Fall of Liberal Government*, 145, n. †). This may be a misreading of the Hansard 'Analysis of the Division', Hansard, *Parl. Debs*, xlvi, col. 864 (19 Mar. 1839), which lists 33 'Ministeria*lists*' absent (emphasis added). This more likely referred to the Liberal Party, rather than ministers only, because the only other group listed is 'Conservatives absent'. This is an interesting use of party labels by Hansard. Clearly, Hansard thought it better to list the liberals as 'Ministerialists' in 1839, yet by 1846, with the 'Analysis' of the third reading on Peel's Corn Importation Bill, the division is analysed using 'Liberal' and 'Conservative', the first such use of 'Liberal' and 'Conservative' in Hansard that I have found.

Even though this was not a government motion, this vote clearly set the stage for a shift in liberal politics as the 1840s began. Free trade issues had animated Liberal Party backbench behaviour, and the perception was that it was becoming more likely that some sort of government action would follow backbench pressure on corn law repeal. Close on the heels of the success in getting such an increase in voting in favour of an inquiry into the corn laws, the coalescing of the Liberal Party free trade agenda was enhanced by the report of the select committee on import duties. Set up on 5 May 1840, the select committee was chaired by Joseph Hume. It was to examine import duties and determine 'how far these Duties are for the protection to similar articles, the Produce or Manufacture of this Country, or of British possessions abroad, or whether the Duties are for the purposes of Revenue Alone'.[61]

In choosing and examining witnesses, Hume would expand this greatly into broader questions of free trade. Further, the membership of the committee left in no doubt the direction of the examination. It was made up of eight Liberal Party MPs (seven of whom were Radicals or Reformers) and six Conservative MPs.[62] The witnesses

[61] *Select Committee on Import Duties*, 100 (i), 5 May 1840.

[62] *Select Committee on Import Duties*, 100 (i), 8 May 1840. The committee consisted of Joseph Hume (Radical MP for Kilkenny), William Blake (Reformer MP for Newport), William Ewart (Radical MP for Wigan), Thomas Thornley (Reformer MP for Wolverhampton), William Williams (Radical MP for Coventry), C.P. Villiers (Reformer MP for Wolverhampton), Sir Henry Parnell (Whig MP for Dundee), Sir George Clerk (Conservative MP for Stamford), William Duncombe (Conservative MP for Yorkshire North), John Gore (Conservative MP for Carnavonshire), Sir George Sinclair (Conservative MP for Caithness), Sir Charles Douglas (Conservative MP for Warwick) and Aaron Chapman (Conservative MP for Whitby).

consisted of Sir John Guest (Reformer MP for Merthyr Tydvill), John Bowring (Radical MP for Kilmarnock 1835–7 and later for Bolton 1841–9), Matthew Forster (African trader and later Reformer MP for Berwick-upon-Tweed 1841–53), Alexander Johnston (Glasgow cotton trader and later Reformer MP for Kilmarnock 1841–4) and J.B. Smith (Manchester chamber of commerce president and later Radical MP for Stirling 1847–52). There were four witnesses from the board of trade, and 18 merchants, manufacturers and traders (not counting Foster, Johnston and Smith). No one from a protectionist background was called.[63] The witnesses were asked a mixture of technical questions regarding the amount of some of the duties placed on articles in their trade, as well as their opinions about what the effects of the duties were and their hopes for the future of the duties. Universally, they called either for a drastic reduction in the number of duties and in the amount of each (preferring a very low fixed duty in all cases), or for an abolition of all duties.[64] Sometimes, witnesses displayed the notion of natural commerce. According to Bowring, 'Manufactures will be found to be sound in the proportion in which they grow out of natural circumstances, and the natural tendencies of labour and capital, and have not been interfered with by legislation'.[65]

The (almost foregone) conclusions of the committee were that existing tariffs had 'neither congruity or unity of purpose; [and that] no general principles seem to have been applied'. Import duties were at times both protective and intended to increase revenue (hence, they were inconsistent) and, therefore, they were unproductive to the revenue. They imposed a consumer tax, and 'they diminish greatly the productive power of the country and limit our active trading relations'.[66] Further, the committee reported that it was clear that the specific natural advantages in different countries were the reason behind successful commerce in certain industries, not government protection, which they termed 'special favours'.[67] In its report, therefore, it recommended the reduction and simplification of duties, but significantly, not their abolition, at least not yet.[68] The committee voted on whether the report should be laid before the House, and Sir Charles Douglas, one of the Conservative committee members, tabled an amendment which said: 'The evidence, although partial and limited, is of so various and valuable a character, that [the Committee] do not feel they should be justified in expressing any opinion founded upon the impression it is calculated to create'. But Douglas could only get one other committee member (Chapman) to vote with him, and the report passed by four votes (H. Parnell, Thornely, Ewart and Villiers) to two (seven committee members were absent).[69]

---

[63] *Select Committee on Import Duties*, List of Witnesses, 108 (x), 6 July–6 Aug. 1840.

[64] See, for instance, Sir John Guest, 'I do not think the iron trade requires any protection at all', *Select Committee on Import Duties*, question 443, p. 144 (36), 13 July 1840; Matthew Forster, 'restrictions of every kind, and particularly high duties, . . . have an injurious effect on the African trade', question 1492, p. 236 (128), 23 July 1840.

[65] *Select Committee on Import Duties*, 162 (54), question 711, 15 July 1840.

[66] *Select Committee on Import Duties*, 101–3 (iii–v), 6 Aug. 1840.

[67] *Select Committee on Import Duties*, 104 (vi), 6 Aug. 1840.

[68] *Select Committee on Import Duties*, 104–5 (vi–vii), 6 Aug. 1840.

[69] *Select Committee on Import Duties*, 106–7 (viii–ix), 6 Aug. 1840. I take 'partial' in Douglas' motion to mean both incomplete and biased.

The select committee made it clear where Radicals and Reformers stood on most free trade issues and, more importantly, the directions in which they intended to push parliamentary action.

By 1841, therefore, it had become clear that the Whigs needed free trade as much as free trading Reformers and Radicals needed Whig cabinets to enact free trade legislation. Without some sort of action from the front benches, the Whigs were in danger of losing the support of the strict free traders in the Liberal Party, and possibly much of the middle class electorate in the boroughs.[70] Sir Stafford Northcote, legal assistant at the board of trade 1845–50 and Conservative MP for Dudley 1855–7 and Stamford 1858–66, wrote in 1862 that Whig leaders became convinced of free trade because they had to accept that the Radicals were an important part of their party, and had to curry favour with them.[71] This, in turn, as Anthony Howe has argued, raised the fear of losing office to the Conservatives if they were not successful. And further, as we shall see with the repeal of the navigation acts, bureaucratic advice from utilitarians and political economists at the board of trade pushed the free trade case even further.[72] On 30 April 1841, Russell gave notice that the government would move that the House go into committee for an inquiry on the corn laws. This proposal was to be considered alongside the 1841 budget, the main feature of which was a reduction of the duty on sugar and timber. And on 7 May, he tabled a motion for a fixed duty of 8s. per quarter on wheat, 5s. per quarter on barley and 3s. 4d. per quarter on oats. Although many Liberal Party MPs rejoiced that a liberal government had finally taken the lead in free trade matters,[73] debate on the corn law inquiry motion was to be postponed until June, after the division on the budget had taken place.[74]

The budget was an effort to increase the amount of foreign sugar and timber duty revenues by accepting higher quantities into the country, and to temporise the feeling among West Indian producers and Canadian timber barons (many of whom had been tory financed) that they had special privileges because they were colonials. The lowering of duties would also make colonial traders more competitive in free trade areas. So, although it is often referred to as the '1841 Whig free trade budget', in fact it retained some protection, and gave some imperial preference. But that was not the tone of most of the speeches during the debate. In rising to move that the House go into committee on the reduction of sugar duties, Russell said that if the question had simply been one of economics, he would have left it to the chancellor of the exchequer. But, he said, 'I consider it is a great national question', not only in terms of revenue, but to set the country on a more regular commercial course for a considerable period.[75] Radicals were generally pleased at the apparent free trade course the government was taking. William Ewart, Radical MP for Wigan, said:

[70] T.A. Jenkins, *The Liberal Ascendancy 1830–1886* (1994), 28–30, and esp. 34; Brent, *Liberal Anglican Politics*, 298; Gash, *Reaction and Reconstruction*, 184; Newbould, *Whiggery and Reform*, 319–21.

[71] Sir Stafford Northcote, *Twenty Years of Financial Policy: A Summary of the Chief Financial Measures Passed between 1842 and 1861, with a Table of Budgets* (1862), 10–12.

[72] Howe, *Free Trade and Liberal England*, 42–3; Brown, *Board of Trade, passim*.

[73] See, for example, Mark Philips, Whig MP for Poole, Hansard, *Parl. Debs*, lvii, cols 1349–51 (30 Apr. 1841).

[74] Lord John Russell, Hansard, *Parl. Debs*, lvii, cols 1294–5 (intention to bring in fixed duty motion) (30 Apr. 1841); Russell, Hansard, *Parl. Debs*, lvii, col. 16 (motion for fixed duty) (7 May 1841); Francis Baring, Hansard, *Parl. Debs*, lvii, cols 1295–407 (budget introduced) (30 Apr. 1841); see also Parry, *Rise and Fall of Liberal Government*, 146–7.

[75] Hansard, *Parl. Debs*, lviii, cols 16–42 (7 May 1841).

A great policy was involved in the change proposed. By a liberal reduction of duties, Great Britain would become the entrepôt of the sugar of the world. This was her natural position. This should be the general aim of our commercial policy. The ports of this country, not the ports of the continent, would, under a sound fiscal system, be the sugar markets for every other article, under the influence of our capital and commerce.[76]

George Grote, Radical MP for London, was more cautious (and nearer the mark), saying that he believed 'a nearer approximation to the principles of free trade' was at hand, and that he 'rejoiced that the proposition of the Government has opened to us the prospect of such considerable improvement, even though the realization is destined to be deferred'.[77]

The liberal protectionists who had opposed corn law repeal on the basis that it would hurt agriculture were largely silent. Only Henry Handley from Lincolnshire South spoke out against the budget, and then in terms of rejecting the modest protectionist tone of the measure as not strong enough.[78] Liberal opposition to the 1841 budget came mainly from a new source, those MPs who felt that free trade in sugar would increase the slave trade and that West Indian planters would not be able to compete with cheaper, slave-produced sugar from other countries in the New World. Stephen Lushington, Reformer MP for Tower Hamlets, sought exception to free trading principles when it came to this question:

I have ever been the friend of free trade, I have ever voted for an alteration in the Corn-laws, I maintain that opinion still. I have altered my sentiments with regard to the timber-duties; but I have always voted against every measure that tended to increase the slave-trade or give it fresh rigour.[79]

Generally the budget received strong support from Liberal Party backbenchers, and some of them particularly noted the importance of what they saw as a final connection between free trade and the Liberal Party. H.G. Ward, Radical MP for Sheffield, said that the budget identified 'a great principle with a great party'.[80] Sir Benjamin Hawes, Reformer MP for Lambeth, said that the electorate would now clearly see the differences between the Liberal Party and the Conservative Party.

With the increased enlightenment and information of the people, they would soon understand the principles which divided the two great parties. When they saw that one was the advocate of a liberal commercial policy, which would cheapen all the great necessaries of life, they would not be slow to rally round that party.[81]

[76] Hansard, *Parl. Debs*, lviii, col. 100 (10 May 1841).

[77] Hansard, *Parl. Debs*, lviii, col. 109 (10 May 1841). See also E.S. Cayley, *Letters to the Right Honourable Lord John Russell, MP, on the Corn Laws* (1849).

[78] Hansard, *Parl. Debs*, vliii, cols 77–8 (7 May 1841). See R.J. Olney, *Lincolnshire Politics 1832–1885* (Oxford, 1973) for the most comprehensive analysis of the importance of protectionism in Lincolnshire.

[79] Hansard, *Parl. Debs*, lviii, cols 80–1 (7 May 1841).

[80] Hansard, *Parl. Debs*, lviii, col 212 (11 May 1841).

[81] Hansard, *Parl. Debs*, lviii, cols 76–7 (7 May 1841).

Table 8.4: *Division on the 1841 Sugar Duties Motion*

Liberal Party groups	Ayes	Noes
Administration	14	0
Liberals	34	0
Radicals	33	0
Reformers	84	10
Repealers	17	0
Whigs	78	5
None listed	29	3
All Liberal Party	289	18
Conservative Party	12	319
Totals	301	337

Source: Hansard, *Parl. Debs*, lviii, cols 667–73 (18 May 1841); *The Times*, 20 May 1841; House of Commons, Division Lists, 18 May 1841, No. 86.

Party language continued after many Conservative MPs claimed that the Whigs were only bringing in a 'free trade' budget as a last-ditch party manoeuvre to regain some of their flagging support. Both Henry Labouchére, Reformer MP for Taunton, and T.B. Macaulay, Whig MP for Edinburgh, answered by saying that they thought the principles of free trade above party. Foreshadowing Peel's rationalisations in 1846, Labouchére said:

> although I am myself a strong party man, and though I wish to see the party to which I have the honour to belong maintained in power, yet so convinced am I of the necessity of introducing, with a view to the support of the commerce of the country, a thorough and searching reform into our commercial system, that I should think it the happiest day of my life on which I saw those to whom I have always been politically opposed acting on those principles if they come to be seated in power, and I trust that in such a case I should give them as cordial a support on these questions as I now give to those to whom I am attached by every political and personal tie.[82]

But the support Whig leaders gained by bringing in such a proposal was not enough to carry it. After five nights of debate, the sugar duties reduction measure failed 301 to 337, as seen in Table 8.4.

With this division, we may now see some of the more intriguing detail of the Liberal Party free trade spectrum. The MPs who voted against this measure were mainly concerned with the subject of sugar *specifically*, rather than free trade generally. But the slavery question proved overwhelming for three Reformers who had previously voted in favour of Villiers' 1839 corn law inquiry motion: Stephen Lushington (Reformer MP for Tower Hamlets), Sir Samuel Spry (Reformer MP for Bodmin) and Sir Thomas Style (Reformer MP for Scarborough).

[82] Hansard, *Parl. Debs*, lviii, col. 141 (10 May 1841). See also T.B. Macaulay, Hansard, *Parl. Debs*, lviii, col. 195 (11 May 1841).

After the government had lost this division, Peel introduced a confidence motion on 27 May 1841, which was carried 312 to 311 on 4 June.[83] Russell responded by forcing the free trade issue to the top of the ensuing election agenda. He said the corn laws 'imposed a greater restriction of trade and a greater evil on the community than any law since the time of Charles the 2nd'.[84] According to Parry, 'to place so directly before the electors a question of direct financial significance to them was a great constitutional innovation'.[85] And the 1841 election brought back some of the tone of the reform crisis. Liberal Party MPs tried to taint Conservatives with the charge of being bound by monopolists and beholden to outdated tradition.[86] The Reform Club distributed funds in various localities to aid free trade candidates, and received a good many contributions from landed liberals.[87] Even pressure from liberal electors could not change the minds of the few liberal protectionists, however. While he was in favour of a reduction in the sliding scale on corn duties, John Bowes, Reformer MP for Durham South, had disappointed a deputation of electors when he told them he could not support a fixed duty on corn.[88] Even though the free trade message generally resonated well with liberal electors, the Liberal Party still lost the election, mainly owing to increased Conservative support in small towns and counties.[89] By-elections throughout the late 1830s had indicated this might happen, but the loss of some seats still came as a surprise. The loss of the West Riding of Yorkshire was particularly upsetting.[90] The 'country' had returned Peel with a majority of 87, and repeal of the corn laws was eventually to come from a previously hostile Conservative front bench.[91]

The period 1837 to 1841 proved to be the crucial years for increased Liberal Party cohesion on trading questions. As we have seen, the important shifts in grain supplies in Europe between 1836 and 1838 changed the realities of questions of corn importation, frontbench pronouncements on corn questions led backbenchers at least to reconsider their attendance at corn law inquiry motions, the select committee on import duties' report hardened ideas about the purpose of duties, and the necessity of fighting the 1841 election on a free trade platform brought about much agreement that a Liberal Party free trade rhetoric was becoming central to the construction of a liberal politics. This was not lost on contemporaries, critics and supporters. The Tory *Quarterly Review* castigated the Whigs for changing tack on corn law questions, and blamed change of opinion on the front benches on desperate party bids for popularity. In order to court radical opinion in

[83] Hansard, *Parl. Debs*, lviii, cols 803–88 (Peel's speech), cols 892–963, 969–1044, 1049–111, 1121–246 (debate) (27 May 1841); cols 1241–6 (division) (4 June 1841).

[84] Hansard, *Parl. Debs*, lviii, col. 1262 (7 June 1841).

[85] Parry, *Rise and Fall of Liberal Government*, 147.

[86] For the 1841 election, see B. Kemp, 'The General Election of 1841', *History*, xxxvii (1952), 146–7, and esp. 150; Jenkins, *Liberal Ascendancy*, 36–8; Parry, *Rise and Fall of Liberal Government*, 147–9.

[87] Staffordshire RO, Littleton Papers, D260M/F/5/26/22: diary entry, E.J. Littleton (1st Baron Hatherton), 6 July 1841. Interestingly, in Birmingham, 'not one Manufacturer had given a shilling, a curious fact considering that it is on the question of cheapening Corn for the benefit of commerce that the Appeal to the Country has taken place'.

[88] Durham County RO, Bowes Papers, D/St/C1/16/293: response to deputation of electors, 15 June 1841.

[89] Parry, *Rise and Fall of Liberal Government*, 148–9.

[90] PA, Le Marchant Papers: Russell to Le Marchant, 10 July 1841.

[91] Kemp, 'General Election of 1841', 150.

the country, 'these drowning dwarfs with a compulsive grasp seized hold of the corn-law'.[92] For supporters, this period was the defining free trade moment for the Liberal Party. In 1868, J.E.T. Rogers would look back on this period and try to win back the heritage of free trade for the Liberal Party. By late 1840, he argued, 'so completely was Lord Melbourne converted – Liberal again, you see – to free trade principles, that he brought forward a budget in 1841, the purpose of which was their formal adoption in relation to three articles – corn, sugar, and timber'.[93]

Free Trade in Parliament 1846–50

The mid 1840s saw increased agitation for free trade, especially in terms of repeal of the corn laws. Petitions flowed into the House, and many Liberal Party MPs were urged by their constituents (electors and non-electors alike) to support Villiers' corn law inquiry motions, which had continued on an annual basis.[94] But there was difficulty at the top. Russell, and many other former cabinet members, were still publicly tied to the idea of fixed duties. A political journalist summed up the situation nicely when he wrote to Le Marchant:

> Lord John is naturally withheld by many considerations; . . . But assuredly if he could persuade the heads of the party that the question of Free Trade, being nothing but a question of time, was no longer worth opposing – that it would therefore be most prudent to adopt it at once – to reject discriminating duties altogether – to have no higher duty on anything than 10 percent – to have no duty on corn whatever – to convert the income tax into a property tax, &c &c, he would found the future industrial condition of England on a durable basis. And the question is almost entirely whether he & the whigs shall do this, or whether it shall, for the most part, be done without them – for done it will be in its chief features.[95]

Howick was pushing hard for a commitment to free trade on both a theoretical and practical basis. He argued the point with Whig leaders, including Russell, saying that it was 'our duty and our interest as a party to come forward very decidedly to demand free trade on the ground of justice to the working classes'.[96] And Russell finally came out in favour of free trade without fixed duties near the end of 1845. In the famous letter to his London constituents, dated 22 November 1845, he said that 'Observation and experience have convinced me that we ought to abstain from all interference with the

---

[92] 'Whig Tactics', *Quarterly Review*, lxxv (1845), 523–4. Typical of the reviews of this period, this article was ostensibly a review of *Vacher's Parliamentary Pocket Book* for 1845.

[93] Rogers, *Free Trade Policy*, 10.

[94] See, for example, Norfolk RO, Wilshere Papers, Y/L15/21: the massive (both in terms of numbers of signatures and size) petition from 'The Non-Electors of the Borough of Great Yarmouth' to William Wilshere, Liberal MP for Great Yarmouth, to support Villiers' motion of 1844, dated 'Feb. 1844'.

[95] PA, Le Marchant Papers: Mr Cowell to Le Marchant, 27 Oct. 1843. It appears that Cowell was a journalist for *The Times* because this letter is preserved in an envelope with the correspondence between Le Marchant and Thomas Barnes.

[96] Duke UL, Russell Papers: Howick (Grey) to Russell, 18 Jan. 1845, cited in Howe, *Free Trade and Liberal England*, 41.

supply of food. Neither a government nor a legislature can ever regulate the corn market with beneficial effects which the entire freedom of sale and purchase are sure of themselves to produce'.[97]

Reaction from the Liberal Party was immediate. F.A. Dryer has argued that 'the free-trade Radicals made their peace with the Whigs'.[98] The Radical MP H.G. Ward wrote to Russell: 'I cannot leave Town without thanking you for making us a *Party* again . . . We shall now act with you again frankly and heartily as we did upon the reform bill and in 1835'.[99] Charles Buller wrote to Howick: 'It is almost impossible to overestimate the importance of their once more rallying the whole Liberal party round the Whigs'.[100] Sir Francis Baring, Whig MP for Portsmouth, wrote to Le Marchant:

> Johnny's letter seems to have made a splash. So far as the thing itself I am very glad of it – he knows that for some time I have thought the day for the fixed duty gone by and it was principally to desire not to quit him that kept me from following Howick . . . As to the mode of announcing his change & the time . . . it is a clever move – it gets the party out of a very awkward position – places it at the head of the corn movement & cuts Peel out of the beautiful position which he might have taken. So far I quite agree – and if politics were a mere game of chess where you look to the intent of the move without reference to the player I should feel satisfied as to the result.[101]

It was not for the Whigs to repeal the corn laws, however. They failed to form a government during the crisis of 1845, Peel was called back, and on 27 January 1846, he introduced his Corn Importation Bill into the Commons.[102] Twelve nights in the House witnessed Conservatives speaking on both sides of the measure, and taking up the majority of debate time. Liberals, it seems, were content to let the Conservatives fight each other.[103] When Liberal Party MPs did speak, they repeated much of what they had said in previous corn law debates, except that they added their support for Peel and their belief that he had been converted by the merits of the free trade case. Morpeth argued that Peel was not overreacting to the Irish famine, but that he had realized that free trade was a natural system, and that the only way to avoid devastating drops in food supply was to repeal the corn laws.[104] Lord Vaney, Liberal MP for Durham South, repeated the idea that corn law repeal would lead to national unity, better relations with other countries,

[97] Letter reproduced in McCord, *Free Trade*, 89.
[98] Dryer, 'Whigs and the Political Crisis of 1845', 517.
[99] G.P. Gooch, *The Later Correspondence of Lord John Russell, 1840–1878* (vol. 1, 1925), 84, cited in Dryer, 'Whigs and the Political Crisis of 1845', 517–18.
[100] Grey Papers, III 79/11: Charles Buller to Howick (Grey), quoted in Dryer, 'Whigs and the Political Crisis of 1845', 518.
[101] PA, Le Marchant Papers: Sir Francis Baring to Le Marchant, 29 Nov. 1845; see also Charles Labouchére to Le Marchant, 10 Dec. 1845.
[102] Hansard, *Parl. Debs*, lxxxiii, cols 237–85, esp. 260–85 (27 Jan. 1846).
[103] There is little evidence that Liberal Party MPs thought that the Conservative Party was finished. As Russell wrote to Le Marchant, 'the tory party must be very strong if it bears such a shame as it is about to have. But English parties are immortal, though like the constitution, they are oft doomed to death'. PA, Le Marchant Papers: Russell to Le Marchant, 6 June 1846.
[104] Hansard, *Parl. Debs*, lxxxiii, col. 813 (12 Feb. 1846).

and peace.[105] And Richard Fitzgerald, Repealer MP for Tipperary, summarized his fellow party members' feelings on the necessity of repeal for Ireland, and that they were grateful for Peel's 'moral courage'.[106] On 5 February 1846, Villiers, who was now seeing all his work come to fruition, wrote a hasty note of cautious optimism to J.B. Smith, tinged with party machinations:

> There is an opinion among some of the Whigs that the measure is safe if Peel would be in a minority on the question of immediate [repeal] & go out. More[,] Tufnell [the Liberal Party whip] thinks the Whigs could carry it through if they were to come in. I am not so sure of that. Peel should be allowed to annilate [*sic*] the conservatives wch he will do if he stops in much longer.[107]

Some liberal protectionists stuck to their original positions. Lord Worsley, Whig MP for Lincolnshire North, complained that repeal was a permanent cure to a temporary problem. He thought it too dangerous to 'have a free trade in corn for ever, because they happened to have a scarcity of potatoes in the country right now'.[108] Gilbert Heathcote, Reformer MP for Rutlandshire (he had sat for Lincolnshire South 1832–41) and one of the strongest liberal protectionists, sought to 'maintain his own consistency' in opposing repeal. If he did not support Russell over repeal, he was certainly not going to support Peel.[109] But other liberal protectionists changed their stances in 1846. Lord Vaney had opposed corn law repeal in the past, but had become convinced that protection was no longer advantageous to the agricultural interest.[110] And Phillip Howard, Whig MP for Carlisle, was persuaded by the state of things in Ireland and the agitation for repeal in Britain that the corn laws must be repealed.[111]

Peel's bill passed its second reading on 2 March 1846, 351 to 254, with 222 Liberal Party MPs voting in favour and 14 against.[112] The Hansard division list for the third reading proves more helpful, however, for gauging opinion on Peel's bill because it lists MPs who were 'Absent – Aye' and 'Absent – No'. This reading division is analysed in Table 8.5.

After Peel's fall, and having reached one free trade object via the now divided Conservative Party, Russell and other Liberal Party leaders had to consider how best to retain the support of free traders, yet keep the liberal protectionists in the party. Some Liberal Party backbenchers, such as Henry Bulwer, formerly Radical MP for Marylebone and out of the House during this parliament, argued later in 1847 that 'as for Free Trade and Corn, the question is settled'.[113] For others, including Edward Horsman, Whig MP

---

[105] Hansard, *Parl. Debs*, lxxxiii, cols 996–8 (16 Feb. 1846).

[106] Hansard, *Parl. Debs*, lxxxiii, cols 1414–16 (23 Feb. 1846).

[107] Manchester Central Library Archive, John Benjamin Smith Papers, MS 923.2 S343, letter 5: C.P. Villiers to J.B. Smith, 5 Feb. 1846.

[108] Hansard, *Parl. Debs*, lxxxiii, cols 699–710 (10 Feb. 1846).

[109] Hansard, *Parl. Debs*, lxxxiii, cols 778–87 (12 Feb. 1846).

[110] Hansard, *Parl. Debs*, lxxxiii, cols 994–7 (16 Feb. 1846).

[111] Hansard, *Parl. Debs*, lxxxiii, col. 312 (27 Jan. 1846).

[112] Hansard, *Parl. Debs*, lxxxiv, cols 349–54 (2 Mar. 1846).

[113] Lincolnshire Archives Office, D'Eyncourt Papers, 2TDE/H/61/9: Henry Lytton Bulwer to Charles Tennyson D'Eyncourt, 18 May 1847.

Table 8.5: *Division on the Third Reading of Peel's 1846 Corn Law Repeal Bill*

Liberal Party groups	Ayes	Noes
Administration	0	0
Liberals	72	1
Radicals	24	2
Reformers	55	2
Repealers	15	0
Whigs	52	4
None listed	28	1
All Liberal Party	246	10
Conservative Party	133	271
Totals	379	281

Source: Hansard, *Parl. Debs*, lxxxvi, cols 721–6 (15 May 1846).
Note: This is not to be confused with 'Paired Off Aye' and 'Paired Off No'. 'Absent Aye' and 'Absent No' lists MPs who did not vote, and did not arrange a pair, but who were known to be strongly in favour of, or opposed to, the reading. *The Times*, 18 May 1840; House of Commons, Division Lists, 15 May 1846, No. 47. See also the following reports in *The Times*: 28 Feb. 1846, 2 Mar. 1846, 5 Mar. 1846, 30 Mar. 1846.

for Cockermouth, the question was not over, and the key to solving it was Cobden and his potential inclusion in the cabinet. Cobden was, of course, considered a leader of free trade Radicals on the liberal back benches, but, as Horsman argued, he was also considered a very able parliamentarian and potentially excellent cabinet minister. The difficulty facing Russell, Horsman warned, was to convince Cobden to cement his connection with the liberals before Peel courted him away.

> There are some of our friends, of high standing enough to make one ashamed to listen to them, bearing down everyone who doubts their assurances that Sir Robert Peel is sick of official life & will never resume it. Sick of official life he is, no doubt, but he has now an emancipated career before him, & we may depend upon it that his eye is at the moment on Cobden, & the manufacturers, he thinks will yet spin him the ladder by which he is to mount back to office.[114]

Clarendon argued along similar lines, saying that Cobden was 'an outlying deer to be stalked by Peel'.[115] While Russell did not offer Cobden a cabinet post in the end, Cobden's influence on free trade questions was significant. He urged Russell not to 'lose the *free trade* wind'. And, as we will see below with the repeal of the navigation acts, the Whig cabinet decided (with however much difficulty) to follow his advice.[116] Russell, for instance, urged Le Marchant to match liberal candidates' free trade opinions with the feelings of the constituency in the 1847 election.[117] And he also flatly rejected Robert

[114] Buckinghamshire RO, Horsman Papers, D/RA/A/3E/13: Edward Horsman to Russell, 22 June 1846.
[115] Quoted in Howe, *Free Trade and Liberal England*, 43.
[116] Howe, *Free Trade and Liberal England*, 43–4, 64–5. See also Mandler, *Aristocratic Government*, chs 6, 7.
[117] PA, Le Marchant Papers: Russell to Le Marchant, 24 Nov. 1846.

Slaney's request to consider reimposing a fixed duty.[118] The high politics of the period 1846 to 1849 proved difficult for Russell. A depression in manufacturing in 1847–8, the worsening famine in Ireland, and chartist activity provided a backdrop for the difficulties the government faced in parliament. Questions of taxation and finance were also troublesome. Without the revenue from protective duties, the government was forced to rely on the income tax, which had been unpopular with both Radicals and protectionists. 1848 proved the most difficult year, with the government having to present a budget no less than four times, and Liberal Party MPs proved very reluctant to follow cabinet dictates out of party loyalty. Russell partly solved this dilemma by attacking the 'old colonial system' of preferential duties. Russell announced in 1847 that the differential between foreign and colonial duties was to be eliminated by 1851 and, in 1848, with the Liberal Party following divergent paths in trade and parliamentary issues, the repeal of the navigation acts was broached.[119]

The navigation acts, which restricted much of the import trade (and all of the coastal and fishing trades) to British ships, and required that British-registered ships be British built, provided a legal monopoly for British shipbuilders. In 1826, Huskisson had succinctly stated the purposes of the navigation acts when he said to the house of commons:

> Our Navigation Laws have a two-fold object. First, to create and maintain in this country a great commercial Marine; and secondly, – (an object not less important in the eyes of statesmen) – to prevent any one nation from encroaching too large a portion of the Navigation of the rest of the World. Upon this system, our general policy has been to limit, as much as possible, the right of importing the production of foreign countries into this country, to ships of the producing country, or to British ships.[120]

But by 1847, Radicals had seen the navigation acts as the next target for trade reform. In early 1847, John Ricardo, Reformer MP for Stoke-upon-Trent and nephew of the famous economist, brought in a motion for a select committee on the acts, and it passed. Like the select committee on import duties, free traders were well represented on the committee, but there were also representatives of the shipping interest. It took evidence, in which 'existing prejudices on both sides were duly confirmed', but never formally reported due to a lack of time.[121] Ricardo then published his own 'report', his *Anatomy of the Navigation Laws*.[122] According to Ricardo, the navigation acts had failed because 'mercantile marine has flourished least where it is most protected; . . . monopoly has produced inferiority; . . . [through] restriction on the one part; and retaliation on the other, the field of enterprise is narrowed, the cost of transport is enhanced, and so fewer

[118] Birmingham UL, Slaney Correspondence: Russell to Robert Slaney, Whig MP for Shrewsbury, 31 Dec. 1849.

[119] Jenkins, *Liberal Ascendancy*, 57; Parry, *Rise and Fall of Liberal Government*, 171–3; Howe, *Free Trade and Liberal England*, ch. 2; Mandler, *Aristocratic Government*, chs 6, 7.

[120] W. Huskisson, *The Navigation Laws: Speech of the Right Hon. W. Huskisson in the House of Commons, Friday the 12th of May, 1826, on the Present State of the Shipping Interest* (1826), 4.

[121] S. Palmer, *Politics, Shipping, and the Repeal of the Navigation Laws* (Manchester, 1990), 104; see also J.L. Ricardo, *The Anatomy of the Navigation Laws* (1847), 1.

[122] Ricardo, *Anatomy of the Navigation Laws*.

ships are required altogether'.[123] And he concluded that the only group in the country that benefited from the navigation acts was the shipping interest. Again, this showed the idea of inclusion and cross-class appeal through free trade. Ricardo demanded that 'Every class of consumer' had a right to appeal to parliament for repeal of the Acts:

> The colonists must know why it is indispensable that they should be crippled in the competition which has been forced upon them . . . The merchants require the satisfactory justification for the contraction of their commerce, and the vexations and impediments of their trade . . . The manufacturers require proof of the urgency of a law which limits their markets, curtails the supply of their raw materials, and forces capital of other customers from barter into competition with them . . . The working classes must be told what real ground there is for denying to them the first possible import of the articles upon which their labour is expended . . . Finally, the whole community must be persuaded of the soundness of the policy which enhances to them the cost of every article for consumption or manufacture which is brought from beyond the seas.[124]

The cabinet realized that repeal of the navigation acts would provide the government with necessary support from Radicals, potentially attract Peelites to the liberal benches, and satisfy important colonial interests that monopolies and preference were equally doomed.[125] Some leading Whigs such as Palmerston and Brougham, however, had doubts about repealing the Acts unilaterally (without, that is, other countries doing something similar), and further thought that the navigation acts were something of a national institution and that to remove them so quickly after another national institution (the corn laws) had been swept away would bring about a backlash against free trade.[126] Still, the sentiment among the party generally was strong enough that the bill was brought in by the president of the board of trade, Henry Labouchére (Liberal MP for Taunton), on 16 February 1849. It was presented as a natural occurrence of the growing free trade atmosphere of the country. Free trade was couched as the solution to the depression, a necessity for increased international trade and, as always, an important element in promoting international peace.[127] During the second reading debate, James Wilson, Liberal MP for Westbury, used the occasion to follow this line of argument, hailing the achievements of free trade since 1842: 'It was impossible for [MPs] to hide from themselves the effect of the great free-trade measure which had been introduced into this country'.[128] Brodie Willcox, Liberal MP for Southampton, and a shipbuilder, used

---

[123] Ricardo, *Anatomy of the Navigation Laws*, 221.

[124] Ricardo, *Anatomy of the Navigation Laws*, 221–2. This prompted the anonymous reply, *Mr Ricardo's Anatomy of the Navigation Laws Dissected*, which was dedicated 'to the Committee of the General Shipping-owners Society', which critiqued Ricardo chapter by chapter. It was as gainsaying as Ricardo's was polemical. See [Anon.], *Mr Ricardo's Anatomy of the Navigation Laws, Dissected* (1848). See also J.H. Clapham, 'The Last Years of the Navigation Acts I', *EHR*, xxv (1910), 480–501; J.H. Clapham, 'The Last Years of the Navigation Acts II', *EHR*, xxv (1910), 687–707.

[125] On the navigation acts, see Palmer, *Politics, Shipping and Repeal of Navigation Laws*, 84–108; Howe, *Free Trade and Liberal England*, 56–60.

[126] Howe, 'Free Trade and the Victorians', 170–1.

[127] Henry Labouchére, Hansard, *Parl. Debs*, cii, col. 760 (16 Feb. 1849); see also Palmer, *Politics, Shipping and Repeal of Navigation Laws*, 147 and ch. 7; Parry, *Rise and Fall of Liberal Government*, 167–8.

[128] Hansard, *Parl. Debs*, ciii, cols 289–491 (9 Mar. 1849).

Table 8.6: *Division on the 1849 Repeal of the Navigation Acts, Second Reading*

Liberal Party groups	Ayes	Noes
Administration	3	0
Liberals	122	9
Radicals	12	0
Reformers	24	2
Repealers	11	1
Whigs	32	5
None listed	15	1
All Liberal Party	219	18
Conservative Party (including Peelites)	49	194
Totals	268	212

Source: Hansard, *Parl. Debs*, ciii, cols 625–9 (12 Mar. 1849); *The Times*, 14 Mar. 1849; House of Commons, Division Lists, 12 Mar. 1849, No. 44.

foreign examples to urge the case that the navigation laws hurt the maritime trade, arguing that American whalers had driven British ones out of the South Sea whale fisheries, and that Spain had lost a once mighty merchant marine when it enacted laws similar to Britain's navigation acts.[129]

Some leading Liberal Party MPs were concerned with some aspects of the bill. Edward Ellice Senior, Reformer MP for Coventry, had serious doubts about the bill in general, and the coastal trade part in particular, but thought party loyalty more important than the specific issue. As he said to Gladstone, 'if one does not vote with one's party when they are in the wrong, one might as well not vote with them at all'.[130] But instead of rallying the full Liberal Party to its side, the government found itself faced with over a dozen backbenchers who were either reluctant to agree with repeal, or reacted with outright hostility. John Wawn, Liberal MP for South Shields, argued that it was too soon to repeal the navigation acts before all the timber and marine duties had been finally abolished.[131] James Clay, Reformer MP for Tower Hamlets, argued a similar line,[132] and Labouchére's bill proved unpopular with the shipping interests in the City of London, as well as some provincial commercial interests, and the traditional protectionists.[133] And a hard core of 18 Liberal Party MPs voted against the measure, which was nearly twice as many as voted against the repeal of the corn laws in 1846, as may be seen in Table 8.6. On 12 March 1849, Labouchére's bill passed its second reading 268 to 212.

As with the 1841 sugar duties division, this represented another example of Liberal Party MPs voting different ways on different free trade measures. Of the 18 MPs who voted against Labouchére's bill and who had sat in parliament before 1847, six had voted

[129] Brodie Willcox, Hansard, *Parl. Debs*, cii, cols 589–90 (12 Mar. 1849).

[130] Apparently, Ellice said this to Gladstone while at a dinner at Lord Aberdeen's on the night of 14 March 1849. BL, Gladstone Papers, Add. MS 44,777, f. 285, quoted in Palmer, *Politics, Shipping and Repeal of Navigation Laws*, 150–1.

[131] Hansard, *Parl. Debs*, ciii, cols 585–6 (12 Mar. 1849).

[132] Hansard, *Parl. Debs*, ciii, cols 574–6 (12 Mar. 1849).

[133] Howe, *Free Trade and Liberal England*, 60–1.

in favour of repeal of the corn laws and/or the repeal of sugar duties. This is partly explained by the few Liberal Party MPs who had strong shipping interests. But, more importantly, it showed that liberal politics was broad enough to include those who disagreed on specific issues. Even so, the low number of Liberal Party MPs voting against the navigation acts shows how strong the coalescing of divergent free trade agendas had become by 1849, and hints at the acceptance of free trade as a party article of faith.

Of the liberal government's free trade measures, the repeal of the navigation acts was probably the most successful. Anthony Howe has described how it boosted the prosperity of the shipping trade but, more importantly, has shown the political benefits gained for the liberals by attaching themselves to the idea that free trade was in the best interests of the nation and freed the state from being pressured from individual commercial interests.[134]

But one further free trade division in the house of commons is worth a brief examination. On 31 January 1850, Villiers, the consistent proponent of corn law aboli-tion, moved the address to the queen on her speech opening the session. He used it as an opportunity to hail what he saw as the final accomplishment of free trade – the repeal of the navigation acts. He hoped to pre-empt a protectionist amendment by outlining the supposed benefits that free trade had brought for the country in the 1840s, 'notwithstanding the sneers sometimes cast upon the subject'.

> We are told that commerce and manufactures are thriving, and the condition of the people greatly improved from having fuller command of the necessaries of life . . . And my honest conviction at this moment is, that not a single thing that was feared by the opponents of free trade has come true, or has the slightest prospect of coming true; whilst the advantages expected by the free-traders have already been felt. The home trade has improved; the condition of the working classes has been ameliorated; not a sovereign has left the country; . . . [and] . . . the revenue is improving.[135]

Sir James Duke, Whig MP for London, seconded Villiers' motion, and warned protec-tionists that they were deceived if they thought that protectionist duties could be reimposed.[136] But Sir John Trollope, Conservative MP for Lincolnshire South, proposed an amendment to the address which said that agriculturalists and labourers were under severe distress from the abolition of free trade measures and local taxation.[137] A lengthy debate ensued, mainly made up of Conservative MPs decrying the state of agriculture in the country. Labouchére summarized the liberal position when he argued that the agricultural interest was simply not prepared to wait for the natural operation of a free trade system to reap benefits. As for agricultural distress, he said:

> as to the ultimate prosperity of the agricultural as well as other classes of the country, I, for one, entertain no doubt, provided this House perseveres in the course of policy they have deliberately adopted – provided we don't introduce doubt and hesitation into the minds of all classes, and paralyse industry by giving the country reason to

[134] Howe, *Free Trade and Liberal England*, 61.
[135] Hansard, *Parl. Debs*, cviii, cols 90–2 (31 Jan. 1850).
[136] Hansard, *Parl. Debs*, cviii, cols 109–13 (31 Jan. 1850).
[137] Hansard, *Parl. Debs*, cviii, cols 113–25 (31 Jan. 1850).

Table 8.7: *Division on the 1850 Protectionist Amendment*

Liberal Party groups	Ayes	Noes
Administration	0	3
Liberals	4	134
Radicals	0	15
Reformers	1	32
Repealers	2	5
Whigs	1	37
None listed	1	16
All Liberal Party	9	242
Conservative Party (including Peelites)	185	70
Totals	194	312

Source: Hansard, *Parl. Debs*, cviii, cols 253–7 (1 Feb. 1850).

Note: In this division, those who voted Aye voted in favour of the protectionist amendment. The 'free trade' vote, therefore, was the No vote. *The Times*, 4 Feb. 1850; House of Commons, Division Lists, 1 Feb. 1850, No. 2.

believe that we are wavering. Let us have courage to go on in the course we have adopted, and I, for one, see no reason to doubt that it will lead to the security and prosperity of all.[138]

The protectionist amendment was defeated on 1 February 1850, 194 to 312, with the lowest liberal protectionist vote of any free trade division in this period, as Table 8.7 shows. What this division symbolised was the culmination of the success of free trade measures in parliament since 1837. Among other things, this division established free trade as the orthodox position. Free trade now became canonical and a non-negotiable article of faith.

Conclusion

Liberal action, whether agitating for corn law repeal or showing support by voting for free trade in divisions, almost directly followed liberal thinking on trade and protection questions. Strict free traders supported corn law repeal and other free trade measures completely, and strict protectionists opposed them just as strongly and consistently. If we look at these two groups briefly, we may see the various strains of liberal opinion on free trade. And, if we examine those Liberal Party MPs who did change their opinions and voting behaviour on free trade measures, we may see the effect of a gradually strengthening 'party policy' and the making of the free trade party for the rest of the 19th century.

Two Liberal Party backbenchers, both strong free traders, wrote important works on trade and economic questions. Sir Henry Parnell's highly influential *On Financial Reform*

---

[138] Hansard, *Parl. Debs*, cviii, cols 217–18 (1 Feb. 1850).

was published in 1830, and dealt with questions of reducing taxation, reducing the civil list and implementing retrenchment. Foreshadowing the naturalistic language about free trade that other Liberal Party MPs would later use, Parnell wrote as if some sort of Darwinian selection had taken place, providing different countries with different means for economic prosperity, known as comparative natural advantage.

> The varieties of climate, situation, and soil, afford to every country some advantages in the employment of industry not possessed by others. By making use of such advantages, a country will contribute its greatest power in the production of wealth. All protection, therefore, by diverting the industry of the country from those branches of production for which it is best qualified, is mischievous; and, when once imposed, creates a mass of artificial interests, whose existence, depending on the system from which they sprung, forms a great obstacle in the way of getting rid of it.[139]

Parnell had a great impact with this volume, and his strong advocacy of parliamentary reform helped to create a situation which meant that free trade could potentially become a Liberal Party agenda issue, rather than being transformed through tariff-reform Huskissonianism to become a potential tory policy.[140] George Scrope, Reformer MP for Stroud, wrote in his important *Principles of Political Economy* in 1833 that when the 'restrictions' on agriculture, on manufacturing, on commerce, on exchange, on circulation of labour, as well as 'excessive and misdirected taxation', were removed,

> then will remunerative employment be secured to every British subject who is willing and able to work; then industry, being certified of its value and meet reward, will put forth its utmost energies; wealth will be created in greater abundance and in more wholesome proportion to the wants of consumers, among whom it will distribute itself more according to principles of natural justice.[141]

These two early appeals to natural forces and natural justice obviously influenced Liberal Party MPs greatly, because many of them brought up this idea of the natural and providential operation of free trade during the debates on various measures. In his evidence to the select committee on import duties, John Bowring, Radical MP for Bolton, said that 'Manufacturers will be found to be sound in the proportion in which they grow out of natural circumstances, and the natural tendencies of labour and capital, and have not been interfered with by legislation'.[142] Viscount Howick depicted protectionist tariffs and duties as 'complicated and artificial regulations', which would damage the natural mechanisms of free trade.[143] Such an unnatural system as protection had led to the production of many social evils, according to other Liberal Party MPs. Joseph Hume was convinced that the corn laws 'committed great injustice . . . [and that they

---

[139] Sir H.B. Parnell, *On Financial Reform* (1830), 74–6. Parnell was a Reformer MP for Dundee 1833–41.

[140] O'Brien, *Classical Economists*, 207–71.

[141] G.P. Scrope, *Principles of Political Economy, Deduced from the Natural Laws of Social Welfare, and Applied to the Present State of Britain* (1833), 453. See also O'Brien, *Classical Economists*, 272–92.

[142] *Select Committee on Import Duties*, 162–3 (54–5), question 711, 15 July 1840.

[143] Hansard, *Parl. Debs*, xlvi, col. 550 (13 Mar. 1839).

were] injurious to all classes, commercial and agricultural'.[144] The internationalist idea of greater peace and co-operation among nations was another point on the liberal free trade agenda. This had a naturalist aspect as well, as Sir William Molesworth argued. If free trade became the system which operated in Britain, he said,

> Then, by the gradual operation of those laws of human nature, in virtue of which men desire to buy at the cheapest and sell at the dearest market, each nation would take to itself that share in the general production, for which it is best adapted by the nature of its soil and the genius of its inhabitants. Civilised nations, instead of being separated, as now, by commercial restrictions, would form one vast social system, cemented together by similar wants, by interests closely interwoven, and by mutual dependence upon one another.[145]

Being a liberal protectionist was a little more difficult, however, as Thomas Barrett-Leonard, Reformer MP for Maldon, noted in his journal (which he often used to draft speeches): 'It is not denied that the course taken by the late government must be the cause of weakness to myself & others in agricultural counties who are looked upon as among their supporters'.[146] John Bowes, Reformer MP for South Durham, in a printed address to his constituents, regretted the necessity of voting against free trade because it caused him to differ 'from the great body of that Party with which I act, on a question brought forward as a main feature of its policy'.[147] Further, liberal protectionists opposed free trade measures on the grounds of the damage they thought it would do to the agricultural classes. Henry Handley, Reformer MP for Lincolnshire South, opposed repeal of the corn laws because 'in short, he was a farmer'.[148] Free trade would also unfairly benefit the commercial classes, and in the case of famines and other food supply problems, free trade was a permanent cure for a temporary problem. The ten liberal protectionists who maintained their protectionism in 1846 mainly sat for county seats, and were more or less equally distributed across the Liberal Party label spectrum (four were Whigs, three Reformers, one Radical – from an Irish county, one Liberal, and one with no label listed in *Dod*). The protectionist stronghold in Lincolnshire and the North Riding of Yorkshire was well represented, with five liberal protectionist MPs sitting for them or having represented them in the past.[149]

Still, some protectionists changed their minds between 1837 and 1850. Philip Howard, Whig MP for Carlisle, for instance, said during Peel's 1846 Corn Importation Bill that the conditions of the country had changed his views about free trade and protectionism.[150] And even Thomas Barrett-Leonard, who sat for an agricultural county, told his

---

[144] Hansard, *Parl. Debs*, xlvi, cols 716–17 (15 Mar. 1839); see also Hansard, *Parl. Debs*, xxxvii, cols 612–14 (16 Mar. 1837).

[145] Hansard, *Parl. Debs*, xlvi, cols 460–3 (13 Mar. 1839); see also C.P. Villiers, Hansard, *Parl. Debs*, xlvi, col. 355 (12 Mar. 1839).

[146] Essex RO, Barrett-Leonard Papers, D/DL/F193: Thomas Barrett-Leonard, journal entry, 10 May 1839.

[147] Durham County RO, Bowes Papers, D/St/C1/16/279: John Bowes, printed address to the electors of the Southern Division of the County of Durham, 8 June 1841.

[148] Hansard, *Parl. Debs*, xlvi, col. 743 (15 Mar. 1839).

[149] Gilbert Heathcote sat for South Lincolnshire 1832–41 and Rutland 1841–59; Edward Heneage sat for Great Grimsby 1835–52; Charles Pelham sat for Lincolnshire North 1832–46; Edward Cayley sat for Yorkshire North Riding 1832–62; and John Bell sat for Thirsk in Yorkshire North Riding 1841–51.

[150] Hansard, *Parl. Debs*, lxxxiii, col. 312 (27 Jan. 1846).

Table 8.8: *Liberal Party Votes on Free Trade Issues, 1837–50*

Year	Voted in favour of free trade measures	Voted against free trade measures
1837	91	64
1838	99	75
1839	198	69
1841	289	18
1846	246	10
1849	219	18
1850	242	9

constituents in Maldon in 1852 that, since Lord Derby was not determined to revive protection, then he must reluctantly give up the idea of reimposing any protective duties.[151] Of the 30 Liberal Party MPs who changed their votes on corn law repeal, 13 were Whigs, and ten of those were from county seats. None were from the wholly protectionist counties of Lincolnshire and Yorkshire North Riding, however. The MPs from those counties retained their protectionism throughout. Other Liberal Party MPs who changed their corn law votes were six Reformers, three of whom were from Irish county seats, and five Repealers, again mainly from Irish counties. The rest were three Liberals, and one with no label in *Dod*.

And, as shown by Table 8.8, and more graphically in Figure 8.1, liberal support for protection dropped dramatically in 1841, and dwindled to a handful by 1850. We can see, therefore, that there was a very clear swing towards free trade from 1839 onwards, and a subsequent decline in Liberal Party protectionist voting. Russell's statements on free trade issues from 1839 to 1845 clearly had an impact on Liberal Party MPs' voting behaviour, at the very least in terms of attendance at divisions. The 1839 announcement in particular was followed by a sharp increase in free trade attendance and voting. Once liberal leaders had set their governments on a free trade course, backbenchers followed. The free trade agendas came together after the 1837–41 period, and it is clear that the influences discussed in this chapter, not least of which were party influences, all played an important role in this process.

The historiography of free trade in this period has moved beyond explanations based on Peel's statesmanship and the outdoor agitation of pressure groups such as the Anti-Corn Law League.[152] More specifically, interpretations of the Liberal Party and free trade have been based on a reassessment of the free trade successes of the 1846–52 government,[153] free trade as part of a wider push for institutional reform to eliminate 'old

[151] Essex RO, Barrett-Leonard Papers, D/DL/O42/4: printed address to the electors of Maldon, 17 May 1852.

[152] In addition to Howe, *Free Trade and Liberal England,* 1–7, see Schonhardt-Bailey, 'Linking Constituency Interests', 86–118; *Rise of Free Trade,* ed. Schonhardt-Bailey, iv; Aydelotte, 'Constituency Influences', 225–46; Aydelotte, 'Voting Patterns', 134–63.

[153] Howe, *Free Trade and Liberal England,* 38–9, ch. 2 generally; Mandler, *Aristocratic Government,* 126, 187–99, 249–50, ch. 7 generally.

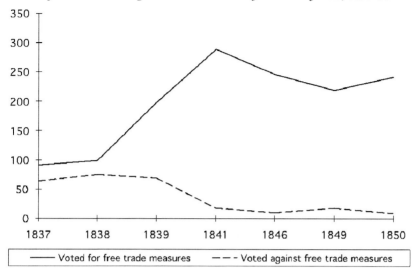

Figure 8.1: *Liberal Party Votes on Free Trade Issues 1837–50*
Note: There are, of course, fluctuations in the totals of MPs on this graph owing to the number of Liberal Party MPs in the house of commons at any one time, and the number voting on free trade motions and bills.

corruption',[154] the influence of liberal anglicans at Oxford and Cambridge on Whig economic thought,[155] the intertwining of religion and politics among dominant Whigs and Liberals[156] and the dominance of free trade rhetoric in the Liberal Party after 1846.[157] In this chapter I have tried to push the historiography a little further and suggest that there was an increasing liberal belief in the working of natural economic mechanisms, partly driven by the Irish famine and economic conditions in Britain in the middle years of the 1840s; that the language of liberal progress and free trade inevitability had an equally convincing effect on cautious Liberal Party MPs and wavering liberal protectionists; that party aspects played an important role in the movement of the Liberal Party to a free trade agenda; and, perhaps most importantly, that the symbolism and language of party have not been given due credit by most historians.

As we have seen, many Liberal Party MPs, especially Radicals and strong free traders, used naturalistic language when describing the operation of a free trade economic system. Although Hilton has stressed that much of the effective argument for free trade on natural grounds derived from evangelical ideas of morality and non-interference in God's providence,[158] and Mandler has argued for the influence of Scottish political economy and the

[154] P. Harling, *The Waning of 'Old Corruption': The Politics of Economical Reform in Britain, 1779–1846* (Oxford, 1996).

[155] Brent, 'God's Providence', 85–107.

[156] Parry, *Democracy and Religion*.

[157] Parry, *Rise and Fall of Liberal Government*, 168–73; Howe, 'Free Trade and the Victorians', 164–72; Gambles, *Protection and Politics*, 5–6.

[158] Hilton, *Age of Atonement, passim*.

Edinburgh Review,[159] it seems as if the combination of these two strains of influence into a belief in the workings of 'natural mechanisms' is more likely. As has been shown, Liberal Party MPs spoke of free trade as if it would unlock a great machine that had been straining against unnatural constraints. This was closely linked to the language of liberal progress and the belief that free trade was inevitable and that, once set in motion, the mechanism would run forever unaided. By the time of the navigation act debate in 1849 and the protectionist amendment debate in 1850, Liberal Party MPs were speaking of free trade as if it were the status quo and should not be tampered with.[160] And the election of 1852 was contested by many liberal candidates on the basis of 'protecting' free trade.[161] Perhaps most significant, however, is the direction that Liberal Party MPs seemed to drift towards throughout this period. Rather than fracture into smaller groups of liberal protectionists, tariff-only reformers and strict free traders, the diverse free trade agendas mirrored the broad language of liberal politics that had been under construction since 1832. Liberal protectionists stayed within the Liberal Party and did not join Derby and Disraeli. Further, 'official' party language from the front benches encouraged party tolerance over free trade. Spring-Rice wrote as early as 1840 that 'we rejoice that the Corn-Laws are not to be discussed upon the stern principles of party. The Liberal party ought to be tolerant, when they find that some of their most conscientious and honourable friends adhere to the principles of agricultural protection'.[162]

At the other end of the free trade agenda spectrum, the radical end, MPs and liberal candidates pushed for free trade to be an integral part of a further reforming agenda in the 1852 election. In a printed address to the electors of Stockport, J.B. Smith said:

> The results of [free trade] have exceeded the sanguine expectations of its warmest advocates; and it becomes FREE TRADERS to secure the benefits, on the enjoyment of which they have just entered. It appears to me, that these benefits can only be secured by a further reform in parliament – by an extension of the suffrage – a redistribution of the franchise – and above all, by giving voters the right of exercising their opinions consciously by means of the ballot.[163]

'Party' was equally important to Liberal Party action on free trade questions, as has been shown above. Not only did Whig cabinet members, especially Russell, choose appropriate party times to make announcements on trade and economics, but they realized they needed to move in a free trade direction for political survival.[164] If, as Mandler argues, 'party was in itself an absolute good [for Whig leaders] and party fidelity not to be disregarded', then Whig cabinet behaviour was consistent.[165] H.G. Ward, Radical MP

---

[159] Mandler, *Aristocratic Government*, 23–33.

[160] See esp. James Wilson, Liberal MP for Westbury, Hansard, *Parl. Debs*, cii, cols 489–91 (9 Mar. 1849); Henry Labouchère, Hansard, *Parl. Debs*, cviii, cols 217–18 (1 Feb. 1850).

[161] For instance, see Univ. of York, Borthwick Institute of Historical Research, Halifax Papers: Charles Wood to his electors in Halifax, 7 Apr. 1852; see also Halifax Papers: Frank Crossley to the electors of Halifax, 2 Apr. 1852.

[162] T. Spring-Rice, 'The Present State and Conduct of Parties', *Edinburgh Review*, cxliii (1840), 285–6.

[163] Manchester Central Library Archive, John Benjamin Smith Papers, MS 923.2 S330, *Stockport Advertiser*, 15 Mar. 1852.

[164] See Dryer, 'Whigs and the Political Crisis of 1845', *passim*; Howe, *Free Trade and Liberal England*, 64–5.

[165] Mandler, *Aristocratic Government*, 79.

for Sheffield, certainly saw this when he said that the government's 1841 budget linked 'a great principle with a great party'.[166] Sir Benjamin Hawes pushed the idea of natural progress towards party ends when he said that electors would gradually realize, through increased enlightenment, that the Liberal Party was the party of progress and prosperity.[167] Aligning Liberal Party language and symbolism with naturalistic arguments about the benefits of free trade, especially at a time when party consciousness was also increasing, may now been seen as a significant contributor to the adoption of free trade as one of the major political stances of the Liberal Party for the rest of the century.

---

[166] Hansard, *Parl. Debs*, lviii, col. 212 (11 May 1841).
[167] Hansard, *Parl. Debs*, lviii, cols 76–7 (7 May 1841).

Conclusion

Bagehot thought that moderation in opinion and in course of action was the only way of ensuring the permanence of government, and of party government.[1] Gladstone, similarly, set great store by the moral and political benefits of maintaining party affiliation. Although he allowed that party, to some degree, restricted 'liberty of thought and . . . the right of private judgment', he thought the advantages outweighed these circumscriptions. Politically, of course, party provided a structure for success in government, as well as in opposition; morally, it 'ennobled political life by the sense of mutual obligation'.[2] *Ideas of the Liberal Party* has shown the value of Bagehot's and Gladstone's assessments for the liberal coalition between 1832 and 1852. Part 1 was concerned with liberal MPs' ideas of their own political labelling and their own conceptions of liberal politics, showing how the construction and presentation of both of these aspects of politics in the 1832–52 period were part of growing ideas about the Liberal Party. Chapter 1 argued that MPs on the liberal side of the house of commons were increasingly willing to describe themselves as Liberals as the period progressed, in a sense giving up the liberty of using the more specific labels of self-description – Whig, Radical, Reformer and Repealer – and accepting the broader, and more moderating, Liberal. Chapter 2 showed how MPs subscribed to a liberal politics made up of a series of agenda points stressing institutional reform and free trade, both inside and outside the house of commons. Chapter 3 analysed the relatively extensive party structures that grew up in the mid 1830s, and laid bare how the mental attachment to the party can be shown through structural elements, particularly electioneering correspondence. Chapter 4 demonstrated that, even with the differing strains of opinion and ideas of political action among liberal MPs, ideas of co-operation among them were strong, and were couched strongly in liberal language. Part 2 dissected specific issues which help to show the various agendas that made up liberal politics during this period, and how Liberal Party MPs spoke and voted on these questions. Chapter 5 focused on ideas of national institutions and the governance of Ireland, specifically the right of the government to redistribute revenues from the church of Ireland to other worthy ends, and to what degree this might be the issue that formed the parliamentary party. Chapter 6 brought church reform to England, arguing that important significance can be drawn from the church rate issue in the ways in which Liberal Party MPs were eager to discuss the issue, even though it was mostly being solved at parish level. This showed the importance of symbolism in liberal politics. Chapter 7 used the Maynooth controversy to demonstrate how Liberal Party MPs explained the liberality of their actions when certain circumstances required it, and how a 'considered inconsistency' became a central idea of liberal politics. Finally, Chapter 8 showed how various free trade agendas gradually came together to form a party article of faith in this period, especially between 1837 and 1841.

[1] W. Bagehot, *The English Constitution* (1867), 128.

[2] BL, Gladstone Papers, Add. MS 44475: W.E. Gladstone, 'Party as It Was and Is', unpublished article, 1855.

In these ways, conceptions of the party are shown to have been extensively held, and powerful, especially considering the nature of early 19th-century politics. Liberal MPs labelled themselves as such in large numbers by 1847, adhered to a coherent set of political beliefs, and acted largely in line with them as well as moving together in the division lobbies. Throughout this period, it is now clear that there was a Liberal Party, which was discussed between MPs, and MPs and their constituents, publicly as well as privately. The evidence unearthed in the archives does not include strong denials of the existence of the party. Neither does it offer detailed descriptions of the party. This strongly implies that the existence, nature and purpose of that party were already well understood. This relatively indirect evidence has meant that 'ideas of the Liberal Party' have had to be found by reading between the lines in most of the standard political sources available to us, but those ideas have been shown in their different aspects in the various chapters. The simple fact that there was so much diverse evidence of this kind lends weight to the overall arguments presented here.

This study, therefore, brings together the historiographic arguments about the structures of politics in the reform period, and the arguments concerning the ideological bases of those structures. Both the 'old' generation of structural historians (Gash, Aspinall and Hanham) and the 'new' generation (O'Gorman, Phillips and Salmon) have provided important bases from which this book has drawn. Both schools have generally agreed that there was a party structure between 1832 and 1852, however loose compared with late 20th- and early 21st-century conceptions, and however well it survived during the 1850s. Further, Phillips and Salmon have shown how the effects of the Reform Act and its registration provisions prompted the necessity of banding together for party purposes, especially in the constituencies. This is undoubtedly true, but I have also been able to show how strong ideas of party were at the centre, regardless of how ineffective they might appear to modern eyes. The more ideological historiography has also found much acknowledgment here, especially the work of those historians who have focused on the liberals. Brent, Mandler and Parry will find agreement on various important points in this book. Church reform in Ireland and England obviously owed a good deal to the liberal anglicanism that Brent has analysed. This was particularly strong when one considers the very liberal ways in which the Church, as a national institution, was presented by Liberal Party MPs. Mandler's argument about the whiggish idea that parliament must become the centre of national political life, and not just a narrow, administrative talking shop, finds strong agreement here, especially when considering church rates. In fact, this thesis may have taken Mandler's ideas further than he wanted them to go. For, if the Whigs contributed anything to the new liberal politics, they moderated utilitarianism and made the strict liberals more whiggish as the 1832–52 period progressed. The reaction of Liberal Party MPs to the Maynooth controversy would have been quite different if this had not been the case. Parry's codification of a 'liberal value-system' has found a less extensive, although not less significant, parallel in the arguments for a new 'liberal politics' in this period. Liberal Party MPs put forward their ideas of institutional reform, civil and religious liberty, and free trade through a strongly political construction, presenting it not so much in intellectual journals as in election posters and hustings speeches. Further, in both public and private expression, they did not ruminate on the moral aspects of such a value system, but they discussed the political necessities of it, and the ways in which it had redefined the reformed political world.

John Vincent was right, therefore, to focus on the personal and ideological aspects of liberalism in his work on the post-1857 period. *Ideas of the Liberal Party* has shown, however, that both of these things were evident and strongly held in the previous generation of liberals, and among MPs, not just constituents. In the first study of its kind, it has shown how important the political 'middle rank' of MPs were to perceptions in the early to mid 19th century. Liberal backbenchers were far from the helots of politics. They constructed and presented political ideas that were at least partly instrumental in the formation of one of the most successful political parties in the modern period. Finally, this book has been able to show the value of neglected and overlooked sources. It has re-examined the mundane material of political life to argue that important and binding political ideals can be found at the most common level.

But if *Ideas of the Liberal Party* had only analysed the issues discussed above, it would have been of limited value, and would not have added much to our understanding of 19th-century politics as a whole, particularly after 1852. *Ideas of the Liberal Party* has gone further and shown a great deal about the political culture of the 1830s and 1840s, and with these things in mind, that culture must now been seen somewhat differently. Parts 1 and 2 described and analysed a complex process and dialogue between the structure, language, behaviour and presentation of that political culture. We have seen how political affiliations were communicated between Liberal Party MPs and constituents, and between backbench MPs themselves. Further, the changes in explanation and presentation of these affiliations were central to the argument that there were vital conceptions of a Liberal Party, and that there was a growing har- monisation of divergent political labels into the dominant one of 'Liberal' by 1847. There were also important changes in habits of political behaviour. On the one hand, these were forced, in such areas as whipping and increased party voting on the issues presented. On the other hand, unforced changes in attitudes toward liberal politics, and the willingness to accept an overarching agenda of that politics, loaded with various meanings and expectations, showed an important shift in conceptions of the political aspects of liberal ideology. Given these changes, the set of issues analysed in Part 2 shows Liberal Party behaviour as normative, rather than exceptional. Party formation was also embedded in what has been discussed here. But party, and especially the Liberal Party, was more than the sum of its parts. Backbenchers' concept of themselves ceased to be that of the independent member. By 1852, they thought of themselves as part of a party system which became the frontier of their political world. This is why the evidence presented here speaks to the post-1852 political world, and why it was not necessary to reinvent party structure and party ideas in the later 1850s. This is not to argue that everything was determined by 1852, however. If it had been, there would have been no need for the famous meeting in Willis's Rooms at the end of the decade. But the new structures, habits and expectations necessary for the more highly organised, professionally run and ideologically coherent parties of later decades were in place by the end of the 1832–52 period, as a result of the experiences analysed in this book. It was this which allowed the party of the 1860s and beyond to build its much-lauded dominance of Victorian politics.

Bibliography

This bibliography is divided into two main sections: primary sources and secondary sources, and is further subdivided into:

Primary Sources:
    Manuscript Collections
    Parliamentary Debates, Parliamentary Papers and Official Publications
    Newspapers and Reviews
    Contemporary Books, Pamphlets, Articles and Ephemera
  Secondary Sources:
    Books
    Journal Articles and Essays in Edited Books
    Theses

Depending on the context and the way in which the source was used, some sources published after 1852 (but before 1900) are listed under Primary Sources.

Primary Sources

Manuscript Collections

Berkshire Record Office
    Phillip Pusey Papers, Bouverie-Pusey Papers, D/EBp.
Birmingham University Library
    Correspondence of Robert Aglionby Slaney, Eyton Letters.
Bodleian Library, Oxford
    Clarendon Deposit MSS, John Barham Papers, b.33–8, c.357–91, c.428–32.
    Sir George Henry Dashwood Papers, MS DD Dashwood.
    Philip Pusey Papers, Dep.e.155.
    Rhodes House Library, Thomas Fowell Buxton Papers, MSS Britain Emp. s444.
Bristol University Library Special Collections Department
    William Pinney Papers.
British Library
    Gladstone Papers, Add. MS 44475, ff. 173–222, unpublished article, 'Party as It Was and as It Is', 1855.
British Library of Political and Economic Science, London
    Richard Potter Papers, Coll. Misc. 146.
    Thomas Thornley Letters (spelled Thornely at BLPES).
Buckinghamshire Record Office
    Acton Tindal Papers.
    Edward Horsman Papers, D/RA/A.

Cheshire Record Office
  Hugh Lupus Grosvenor Papers, Grosvenor Papers.
  Richard Grosvenor Papers, Grosvenor Papers.
  Robert Grosvenor Papers, Grosvenor Papers.
Christ Church, Oxford
  microfilm copies from the Brougham MSS, University College London; Ellice MSS,
    National Library of Scotland; Joseph Parkes Papers, transcribed by W.E.S. Thomas;
    Kent MSS, Library of Congress, Washington, DC; Lambton MSS, Lambton
    Estate Office; Melbourne MSS, Royal Archives, Windsor Castle; Pencarrow MSS,
    Pencarrow, Bodmin; Spencer MSS, Althorp House, Althorp.
Devon Record Office
  Sir Henry Seale Papers, D3889.
  James Wentworth Buller Papers, Buller of Crediton Collection, 2065 M.
Doncaster Archives Department
  Papers of William Aldam, Warde-Aldam Papers, DD WA.
Durham County Record Office
  John Bowes Papers, Strathmore Collection, D/St/C1/16.
Essex Record Office
  Thomas Barrett-Leonard Papers, Chelmsford, D/DL.
Gloucestershire Record Office
  William Henry Hyett Papers.
Hertfordshire Record Office
  Edward Bulwer Lytton Papers, D/EF/023.
  William Wilshere Papers, D/EX 14.
Lambeth Archives Department, Minet Library
  Charles Tennyson D'Eyncourt Papers, Lambeth, IV/3.
Lincolnshire Archives Office
  Charles Tennyson D'Eyncourt Papers, TDE, 2TDE, 4TDE.
  Gilbert John Heathcote Papers, ANC 12A/11, 12C/7.
Liverpool Record Office
  William Ewart Papers, 920 MD 293.
Manchester Central Library Archive
  John Benjamin Smith Papers, MS 923.2 S330-345.
The National Archives
  Lord John Russell Papers, 30/22.
National Library of Ireland
  Thomas Spring-Rice (1st Baron Monteagle) Papers, Monteagle Papers.
Norfolk Record Office
  Henry Lytton Earle Bulwer Papers, BUL 1.
  Sir William Browne Ffolkes Papers, NRS 7949, 7958, 8721, 8738, 8740–2, 8753,
    11781, MC 50/72–4.
  William Wilshere Papers, Y/L15.
North Yorkshire County Record Office
  Marmaduke Wyvill Papers, Wyvill MSS, ZFW.

Northumberland Record Office
  Sir Matthew White Ridley Papers, Ridley (Blagdon) MSS, ZRI.
  William Ord Papers, Blackett-Ord MSS, NRO 324/A.
Nottinghamshire Archives Office
  Edward Strutt Papers, DD.BK.
Nuffield College, Oxford
  Sir Joseph Whitwell Pease Papers, Gainford Papers.
Parliamentary Archives
  Sir Denis Le Marchant Papers.
Reform Club Archives, Pall Mall, London.
Sheffield City Archives
  William Thomas Spencer Wentworth-Fitzwilliam Papers, Wentworth-Fitzwilliam
    Collection, WWM/T1–50.
Shropshire Records and Research Centre
  Morris-Eyton Collection, Robert Aglionby Slaney Papers.
Somerset Record Office
  Edward Ayshford Sanford Papers, DD/SF.
Southampton University Library, Broadlands Archives Trust
  Henry Brooke Parnell (1st Baron Congleton) Papers, Congleton MSS.
  Palmerston Papers.
Staffordshire Record Office
George Anson Papers, D 615 P.
  George Granville Sutherland-Leveson-Gower (2nd duke of Sutherland) Papers,
    Sutherland MSS.
  Hatherton Collection, E.J. Littleton (1st Baron Hatherton) Papers, D260.
University College London Manuscripts Room
  James and Henry Brougham Papers.
  Joseph Parkes Papers.
University of Hull, Brynmore Jones Library
  Thomas Perronet Thompson Papers, DTH.
University of Manchester, John Rylands Library
  John Fielden Papers, FDN.
University of York, Borthwick Institute of Historical Research
  Correspondence of Sir Charles Wood (1st Viscount Halifax), Halifax Papers.
Wakefield Central Library, Local History Study Centre
  Papers of William Aldam, Aldam MSS, John Goodchild Collection.
West Sussex Record Office
  John Abel Smith Papers, Add. MSS 22338–568.
West Yorkshire Archive Service
  Edward Horsman Papers, Ramsden, box 72.
  William Battie-Wrightson Papers, Leeds, BW/C, BW/P.
Yale University, Beinecke Library
  Osborn Collection, Dod Papers, d 50 (3 vols).

Parliamentary Debates, Parliamentary Papers and Official Publications

Division Lists, House of Commons.
Hansard, *Parliamentary Debates* (3rd ser., 1832–52).
The Mirror of Parliament, 1828–41.
Northcroft's Parliamentary Chronicle, 1833–41.
Report and Minutes of Evidence from the Select Committee on Import Duties, Parliamentary
 Papers, 1840 (601), v, 99–473.
Report from the Select Committee on Bribery at Elections; Together with the Minutes of Evidence,
 Parliamentary Papers, 1835 (547), viii, 1–828.

Newspapers and Reviews

British Quarterly Review.
Eclectic Review.
Edinburgh Review.
Morning Chronicle.
The Patriot.
The Spectator.
Tait's Edinburgh Magazine.
The Times.

Contemporary Books, Pamphlets, Articles and Ephemera

Acland, J., *The Imperial Poll Book of All Elections from the Passing of the Reform Act in 1832
 to the end of 1864* (1869).
Adams, W.H.D., *English Party Leaders and English Parties: From Walpole to Peel; Including a
 Review of the Political History of the Last One Hundred and Fifty Years* (1878).
[Anon.], *Mr Ricardo's Anatomy of the Navigation Laws Dissected* (1848).
The Assembled Commons, 1837: An Account of Each Member of Parliament (1837).
Atkinson, W., *The Spirit of the Magna Carta: Or Universal Representation, the Genius of the
 British Constitution* (1841).
Bagehot, W., *The English Constitution* (1867).
A Biographical List of the House of Commons, Elected in October 1812 (1813).
Bricknell, Rev. W.S., *The Grievance of Church Rates* (1837).
Byrne, R., *The Parliamentary Vote-Book: Containing Such Divisions of the House of Commons
 in the Session of 1846* (1847).
Cayley, E.S., *Letters to the Right Honourable Lord John Russell, MP, on the Corn Laws* (1849).
Chambers, C.H., *Phases of Party* (1872).
Chambers, J.D., *The New Bills for the Registration of Electors Critically Examined* (1836).
_____ *A Complete Dictionary of the Law and Practice of Elections of Members of Parliament, and
 of Election Petitions and Committees for England, Scotland, and Ireland* (1837).
*Church Rates: A Letter to William Stratford Dugdale, Esq. Member of Parliament for the
 Northern Division of the County of Warwick, by a Birmingham Manufacturer, One of His
 Constituents* (Birmingham, 1837).
Clerk, J., *The Law and Practice of Election Committees* (1852).

Cockburn, A.E., *Questions on Election Law Arising from the Reform Act* (1834).

Cooke, G.W., *The History of Party from the Rise of the Whig and Tory Factions, in the Reign of Charles II, to the Passing of the Reform Bill* (1836).

Cooke, W.H., *Plain Instructions for Overseers and Electors in the Registration of Voters for Counties and Boroughs in England and Wales* (1835).

Coppock, J., *The Elector's Manual: Or Plain Directions by which Every Man may Know His Own Rights, and Preserve Them* (1835).

Cox, E.W., *Instructions to Committees and Agents of Candidates and to Returning Officers for the Management of an Election* (1847).

_____ *The Law and Practice of Registration and Elections* (1847).

Crosby, G., *Crosby's General Political Reference Book* (Leeds, 1838).

_____ *Crosby's Parliamentary Record* (Leeds, 1839).

Detrosier, R.R., *Lecture on the Utility of Political Unions* (1832).

Dod, C.R., *The Pocket Parliamentary Companion [and Parliamentary Companion]* (1833–52).

Election Budget, or an Appendage to the Poll Book Containing the Candidates' Addresses, with the Squibs, Songs, &c. of Both Parties, as Published During the Election at Great Yarmouth, 1830 (Yarmouth, 1830).

Election Day: A Sketch from Nature (1837).

The Elector's Scrap Book: Or, a Complete Collection of the Addresses, Speeches, and Squibs, during the Contested Election for the Borough of South Shields (South Shields, 1833).

Elliot, G.P., *A Practical Treatise on the Qualifications and Registration of Parliamentary Electors in England and Wales* (1839).

Facts Relative to the Employment of Children in Silk Mills (Manchester, 1833).

Fagan, L., *The Reform Club: Its Founders and Architect* (1887).

Ferguson, R.S., *Cumberland and Westmorland MPs from the Restoration to the Reform Bill of 1867* (1871).

Girdlestone, Rev. C., *Church Rates Lawful, but Not Always Expedient: A Sermon* (1833).

'Goodfellow, Gabriel', *The Book of Liberals: A Book for Liberals and Anti-Liberals; Being a Looking-Glass for the Former, and an Eye-Glass (or Spy-Glass) for the Latter* (1849).

Grant, J., *Random Recollections of the House of Commons from the Year 1830 to the Close of 1835, including Personal Sketches of the Leading Members of All Parties, by One of No Party* (1836).

_____ *The British Senate in 1838* (2 vols, 1838).

Grego, J., *A History of Parliamentary Elections and Electioneering in the Old Days* (1886).

Hannay, R., *History of the Representation of England* (1831).

The House of Commons Elected According to the Provisions of the Reform Act, to Serve in the Eleventh Imperial Parliament (1833).

Huskisson, W., *The Navigation Laws: Speech of the Right Hon. W. Huskisson in the House of Commons, Friday the 12th of May, 1826, on the Present State of the Shipping Interest* (1826).

Joseph Pease: A Memoir Reprinted from the 'Northern Echo' (1872).

A Key to Both Houses of Parliament: Consisting of Alphabetical Notices of the Lords and Commons of Great Britain and Ireland (1832).

Le Marchant, Sir D., *Memoir of John Charles, Viscount Althorp, Third Earl Spencer* (1876).

A Letter to Sir John Campbell on the Law of Church Rates (1837).

Lewis, C.E., *The Four Reformed Parliaments 1832–1842* (1842).

Lewis, Sir G.C., *Remarks on the Use and Abuse of Some Political Terms* (1832).

Liberal Registration Society, *Rules* (1860).

Lister, T.H., 'State of the Irish Church', *Edinburgh Review*, lxi (1835), 480–525.

Littleton, E.J., *Memoir and Correspondence Relating to Political Occurrences in June and July 1834* (1872).

A Manual of Queen Victoria's Second Parliament (1841).

McCullagh, W. Torrens, *Memoirs of the Right Honourable Richard Lalor Sheil* (2 vols, 1855).

Metcalfe, W., *The Opinion of Sir John Campbell on the Law of Church-Rates, as Stated in His Letter to the Right Hon. Lord Stanley* (1837).

Mosse, R.B., *The Parliamentary Guide: A Concise Biography of the Members of Both Houses of Parliament, Their Connexions, etc.* (1837).

Nicholl, J., *Church Rates: Observations on the Attorney General's Letter to Lord Stanley* (1837).

Northcote, Sir Stafford, *Twenty Years of Financial Policy: A Summary of the Chief Financial Measures Passed between 1842 and 1861, with a Table of Budgets* (1862).

O'Brien, T., *A Glance at Parties* (1844).

The Old and New Representation of the United Kingdom Contrasted (1833).

The Origins, Objects, and Advantages of Political Unions (1832).

Paget, J., *The Registration of Voters Act* (1843).

Parliamentary Agents Rules, Parliamentary Archives, Historical Collection 68 (1836).

Parliamentary Candidate Society, *Proceedings* (1831).

The Parliamentary Indicator: Containing a List of the Members Returned to the Commons' House of Parliament, at the General Election in January, 1835 and the Division on the Speakership (1835).

Parliamentary Manual for the Year 1838 (1838).

The Parliamentary Test Book, for 1835: A Political Guide to the Sentiments Individually Expressed, and the Pledges Given, at the Late General Election, by Each of the 658 Members of the Second Reformed House of Commons (1835).

Parnell, Sir H.B., *On Financial Reform* (1830).

Parties and Factions in England at the Accession of William IV (1830).

Past Performances and Present Promises of the Liberal and Tory Parties (1841).

The Politics of 1837 by an Old Reformer, Respectfully Addressed to Viscount Melbourne (1837).

The Popular Dod, ed. 'Tommy' (1884).

Price, G., *Complete Election Guide: The Reform Act* (1832).

Proceedings of the Parliamentary Candidate Society (1831).

Rae, W.F., 'Political Clubs and Party Organization', *Nineteenth-Century*, iii (1878), 919–20.

Raikes, T., *A Portion of the Journal Kept by Thomas Raikes, Esq., from 1831 to 1847* (1856).

The Real Character of the Provisions of the Bill for Abolishing Church Rates, Viewed Chiefly with Reference to the Coronation Oath (Durham, 1837).

Reflections on the O'Connell 'Alliance' or Lichfield House Conspiracy (1836).

The Reformed Parliament: Biographical Sketches of All the Members of the House of Commons; Their Political Principles; Places of Residence, &c., &c. (1833).

Ricardo, J.L., *The Anatomy of the Navigation Laws* (1847).

Rogers, J.E.T., *The Free Trade Policy of the Liberal Party* (Manchester, 1868).

———— *A Manual of Political Economy* (Oxford, 1868).

Saunders' Portraits and Memoirs of Eminent Living Political Reformers (1840).

Scrope, G.P., *Principles of Political Economy, Deduced from the Natural Laws of Social Welfare, and Applied to the Present State of Britain* (1833).

Sewell, R.C., *A Manual of the Law and Practice of Registration of Voters in England and Wales* (1849).

Sheil, R.L., *Sketches, Legal and Political* (1855).

Smith, H.S., *The Parliaments of England, from 1st George I, to the Present Time* (3 vols, 1844).

Spring-Rice, T., 'The Present State and Conduct of Parties', *Edinburgh Review*, cxliii (1840), 275–314.

Thelwall, A.S., *Proceedings of the Anti-Maynooth Conference of 1845* (1845).

Thompson, Thomas Perronet, *Catechism on the Corn Laws: With a List of Fallacies and the Answers* (1831).

Torrens, R., *Letters on Commercial Policy* (1833).

_____ *The Budget: A Series of Letters on Financial, Commercial, and Colonial Policy by a Member of the Political Economy Club* (1841).

_____ *Tracts on Finance and Trade: Submitted to the Electors of the United Kingdom* (1852).

Vacher's Parliamentary Companion: Containing Correct Lists of the House of Peers and House of Commons with the Town Residences of the Members, and Other Information (1833–).

Villiers, C.P., *Free Trade Speeches* (2 vols, 1883).

Wade, J., *The Black Book; or, Corruption Unmasked!* (1820).

_____ *Political Dictionary; or, Pocket Companion* (1821).

_____ *New Parliament: An Appendix to the Black Book* (1826).

_____ *The Extraordinary Black Book* (1831).

_____ *Appendix to the Black Book: An Exposition of the Principles and Practices of the Reform Ministry and Parliament* (1835).

Walpole, S., *The Life of Lord John Russell* (2 vols, 1889).

Walsh, Sir. J., *On the Present Balance of Parties in the State* (1832).

Warwick, W.A., *The House of Commons: As Elected to the Fourteenth Parliament of the United Kingdom, being the Second of Victoria* (1841).

Webb's List of the Members of the House of Commons Elected December 1832 (1833).

West, Sir A., *Recollections 1832–1886* (1899).

Westmacott, C.M., *A Guide to the Elections: Or, Four Years of the Whig Ministry* (1834).

What Next? Or the Peers and the Third Time of Asking (1837).

'Whig Tactics', *Quarterly Review*, lxxv (1845), 519–32.

Whyte, William, *The Inner Life of the House of Commons* (2 vols, 1897).

Wilson, Joshua, *A Biographical Index to the Present House of Commons* (1806–8).

Wordsworth, C., *The Registration of Voters Act* (1843).

Secondary Sources

Books

Adelman, P., *Victorian Radicalism: The Middle-Class Experience, 1830–1914* (1984).

Akenson, D.H., *The Church of Ireland: Ecclesiastical Reform and Revolution, 1800–1885* (New Haven, CT, 1971).

Alington, C., *Twenty Years: Being a Study in the Development of the Party System between 1815 & 1835* (Oxford, 1921).

Ashford, L.J., *The History of the Borough of High Wycombe from Its Origins to 1880* (1960).

Aspinall, A., *Three Nineteenth Century Diaries* (1949).

Barnes, D.G., *A History of English Corn Laws from 1660 to 1846* (1930).

Beales, D.E.D., *The Political Parties of Nineteenth-Century Britain* (1971).

Bentley, Michael, *Politics without Democracy 1815–1914* (Oxford, 1984).

Blease, W.L., *A Short History of English Liberalism* (1913).

Bourne, J., *British Politics 1832–1885* (Oxford, 1994).

Brent, R., *Liberal Anglican Politics: Whiggery, Religion, and Reform, 1830–1841* (Oxford, 1987).

British Parliamentary Election Results 1832–1885, ed. F.W.S. Craig (1977).

Brock, M., *The Great Reform Act* (1973).

Brown, L., *The Board of Trade and the Free Trade Movement* (Oxford, 1958).

Buckley, J.K., *Joseph Parkes of Birmingham and the Part which He Played in Radical Reform Movements from 1825–1845* (1926).

Bulmer-Thomas, I., *The Growth of the British Party System* (1967).

Burn, W.L., *The Age of Equipoise: A Study of the Mid-Victorian Generation* (1964).

Burrow, J.W., *Whigs and Liberals: Continuity and Change in English Political Thought* (Oxford, 1988).

Cannon, J., *Parliamentary Reform, 1640–1832* (Cambridge, 1973).

Chadwick, O., *The Victorian Church* (vol. 1, 1966).

Christie, I.R., *The Peelites and the Party System 1846–1852* (1972).

_____ *British 'Non-Elite' MPs 1715–1820* (Oxford, 1995).

Cook, C. and B. Keith, *British Historical Facts 1830–1900* (1975).

Cooke, A.B. and J.R. Vincent, *The Governing Passion: Cabinet Government and Party Politics in Britain 1885–86* (Brighton, 1974).

Cowherd, Raymond, *The Politics of English Dissent: The Religious Aspects of Liberal and Humanitarian Reform Movements from 1815–1848* (1959).

Cox, G.W., *The Efficient Secret: The Cabinet and the Development of Political Parties in Victorian England* (Cambridge, 1987).

Craig, F.W.S., *Chronology of British Parliamentary By-elections, 1833–1885* (Chichester, 1977).

Crosby, T.L., *English Farmers and the Politics of Protection 1815–1852* (Hassocks, 1977).

Cruikshank, R.J., *The Liberal Party* (1948).

Davis, R.W., *Dissent in Politics 1780–1830: The Political Life of William Smith MP* (1971).

_____ *Political Change and Continuity, 1760–1885: A Buckinghamshire Study* (1972).

Eccleshall, R., *British Liberalism: Liberal Thought from the 1640s to 1980s* (1986).

Ellens, J.P., *Religious Routes to Gladstonian Liberalism: The Church Rate Conflict in England and Wales, 1832–1868* (University Park, PA, 1994).

English Party Politics: 1600–1906, ed. A. Beattie (1970).

Escott, T.H.S., *Club Makers and Club Members* (1914).

Evans, E.J., *Political Parties in Britain, 1783–1867* (1985).

Fisher, D.R., 'Politics and Parties', in *The History of Parliament: The House of Commons 1820–32*, ed. D.R. Fisher (2009), 319–73.

Free Trade: The Repeal of the Corn Laws, ed. C. Schonhardt-Bailey (Bristol, 1996).

Free Trade and Its Reception 1815–1960: Freedom and Trade, Volume I, ed. A. Marrison (1998).

From the Corn Laws to Free Trade: Interests, Ideas, and Institutions in Historical Perspective, ed. C. Schonhardt-Bailey (Cambridge, MA, 2006).

Fyfe, H., *The British Liberal Party* (1928).

Gambles, Anna, *Protection and Politics: Conservative Economic Discourse, 1815–1852* (Woodbridge, 1999).

Gardiner, J. and N. Wenborn, *The History Today Companion to British History* (1995).

Gash, N., *Politics in the Age of Peel: A Study in the Technique of Parliamentary Representation 1830–1850* (1953).

____ *Reaction and Reconstruction in English Politics, 1832–1852* (Oxford, 1965).

Gilmartin, K., *Print Politics: The Press and Radical Opposition in Early Nineteenth-Century England* (Cambridge, 2005).

Gooch, G.P., *The Later Correspondence of Lord John Russell, 1840–1878* (1925).

Halévy, E., *A History of the English People in the Nineteenth Century: Vol. III, the Triumph of Reform 1830–1841* (1950).

____ *The Growth of Philosophic Radicalism* (1952).

Hanham, H.J., *The Reformed Electoral System in Great Britain, 1832–1914* (1968).

____ *Elections and Party Management: Politics in the Time of Disraeli and Gladstone* (Hassocks, 1978).

Harling, P., *The Waning of 'Old Corruption': The Politics of Economical Reform in Britain, 1779–1846* (Oxford, 1996).

Haury, D., *The Origins of the Liberal Party and Liberal Imperialism: The Career of Charles Buller, 1806–1848* (1987).

Hawkins, A., *Parliament, Party and the Art of Politics in Britain, 1855–1859* (1987).

____ *British Party Politics 1852–1886* (1998).

Hay, W.A., *The Whig Revival, 1808–1830* (2005).

Hill, B., *The Early Parties and Politics in Britain, 1688–1832* (1996).

Hilton, B., *Corn, Cash, and Commerce: The Economic Policies of the Tory Governments 1815–1830* (Oxford, 1977).

____ *The Age of Atonement: The Influence of Evangelicalism on Social and Economic Thought, 1785–1865* (Oxford, 1988).

The History of Parliamentary Behavior, ed. W.O. Aydelotte (Princeton, NJ, 1977).

The Holland House Diaries 1831–1840, ed. A.D. Kriegel (1977).

Howe, A., *Free Trade and Liberal England* (Oxford, 1997).

Huch, R.K., *Joseph Hume: The People's MP* (Philadelphia, PA, 1985).

Hyde, F.E., *Mr Gladstone at the Board of Trade* (1934).

Jaggard, E., *Cornwall Politics in the Age of Reform 1790–1885* (Woodbridge, 1999).

Jenkins, T.A., *Gladstone, Whiggery, and the Liberal Party, 1874–1886* (Oxford, 1988).

____ *The Liberal Ascendancy, 1830–1886* (1994).

____ *Parliament, Party and Politics in Victorian Britain* (Manchester, 1996).

Jennings, Sir I., *Party Politics: The Growth of Parties* (2 vols, Cambridge, 1961).

Johnson, L.G., *General T. Perronet Thompson 1783–1869: His Military, Literary and Political Campaigns* (1957).

Joyce, P., *Democratic Subjects: The Self and the Social in Nineteenth-Century England* (Cambridge, 1994).

Judd, G.P., *Members of Parliament 1734–1832* (New Haven, CT, 1955).

Jupp, P., *The Governing of Britain, 1688–1848: The Executive, Parliament, and the People* (2006).

Kerr, D.A., *Peel, Priests, and Politics: Sir Robert Peel's Administration and the Roman Catholic Church in Ireland, 1841–1846* (Oxford, 1982).

Koss, S.E., *Nonconformity in Modern British Politics* (Hamden, CT, 1975).

_____ *The Rise and Fall of the Political Press in Britain* (1984).

Language, Print and Electoral Politics 1790–1832: Newcastle-under-Lyme Broadsides, ed. H. Barker and D. Vincent (Woodbridge, 2001).

Le May, G.H., *The Victorian Constitution* (1979).

The Letters of Richard Cobden, ed. A. Howe (2 vols, Oxford, 2007–10).

The Literary Companion to Parliament, ed. Christopher Silvester (1996).

MacCalmont's Parliamentary Poll Book: British Election Results 1832–1918, ed. J.R. Vincent and M. Stenton (Brighton, 1971).

Maccoby, S., *English Radicalism 1832–1852* (1935).

MacDonagh, O., *Early Victorian Government, 1830–1870* (1977).

_____ *The Emancipist: Daniel O'Connell 1830–47* (New York, 1989).

Machin, G.I.T., *Politics and the Churches in Great Britain, 1832–1868* (Oxford, 1977).

Macintyre, Angus, *The Liberator: Daniel O'Connell and the Irish Party 1830–1847* (1965).

Magnusson, Lars, *The Tradition of Free Trade* (2004).

Mandler, P., *Aristocratic Government in the Age of Reform: Whigs and Liberals, 1830–1852* (Oxford, 1990).

McCallum, R.B., *The Liberal Party from Earl Grey to Asquith* (1963).

McCord, N., *Free Trade: Theory and Practice from Adam Smith to Keynes* (1970).

Mitchell, L.G., *Lord Melbourne, 1779–1848* (Oxford, 1997).

Moore, D.C., *The Politics of Deference: A Study of the Mid-Nineteenth Century English Political System* (Hassocks, 1976).

Munford, W.A., *William Ewart, MP 1798–1869: Portrait of a Radical* (1960).

Newbould, I., *Whiggery and Reform, 1830–41: The Politics of Government* (1990).

Nossiter, T.J., *Influence, Opinion, and Political Idioms in Reformed England: Case Studies from the North-East 1832–74* (Brighton, 1976).

O'Brien, D.P., *The Classical Economists* (Oxford, 1975).

O'Gorman, F., *The Emergence of the British Two-Party System, 1760–1832* (New York, 1982).

_____ *Voters, Patrons, and Parties: The Unreformed Electoral System of Hanoverian England 1734–1832* (Oxford, 1989).

Olney, R.J., *Lincolnshire Politics 1832–1885* (Oxford, 1973).

Ostrogorski, M.M. and F. Clarke, *Democracy and the Organization of Political Parties* (New York, 1902).

Palmer, S., *Politics, Shipping, and the Repeal of the Navigation Laws* (Manchester, 1990).

The Parliamentary Diaries of Sir John Trelawny, 1858–1865, ed. T.A. Jenkins (Camden Society, 4th ser., xl, 1990).

Parry, J.P., *Democracy and Religion: Gladstone and the Liberal Party, 1867–1875* (Cambridge, 1986).

_____ *The Rise and Fall of Liberal Government in Victorian Britain* (New Haven, CT, 1993).

_____ *The Politics of Patriotism: English Liberalism, National Identity, and Europe, 1830–1886* (Cambridge, 2006).

Pentland, G., *Radicalism, Reform, and National Identity in Scotland, 1820–1833* (Woodbridge, 2008).

Phillips, J.A., *Electoral Behaviour in Unreformed England: Plumpers, Splitters and Straights* (Princeton, NJ, 1982).

_____ *The Great Reform Bill in the Boroughs: English Electoral Behaviour, 1818–1841* (Oxford, 1987).

Prest, J., *Lord John Russell* (1972).

_____ *Politics in the Age of Cobden* (1977).

Public and Private Doctrine: Essays in British History Presented to Maurice Cowling, ed. M. Bentley (Cambridge, 1993).

Reid, S. J., *Life and Letters of the First Earl of Durham, 1792–1840* (2 vols, 1906).

Rethinking the Age of Reform: Britain 1780–1850, ed. A. Burns and J. Innes (Cambridge, 2007).

Re-thinking Nineteenth-Century Liberalism: Richard Cobden Bicentenary Essays, ed. A. Howe and S. Morgan (2006).

The Rise of Free Trade, ed. C. Schonhardt-Bailey (4 vols, 1997).

Robbins, L., *Robert Torrens and the Evolution of Classical Economics* (1958).

Russell, R., *Early Correspondence of Lord John Russell, 1805–1840* (1913).

Salmon, P.J., *Electoral Reform at Work: Local Politics and National Parties, 1832–1841* (Woodbridge, 1996).

Schuyler, R.L., *The Fall of the Old Colonial System* (Oxford, 1945).

Seymour, C., *Electoral Reform in England and Wales: The Development and Operation of the Parliamentary Franchise 1832–1885* (New Haven, CT, 1915).

Sharpe, Michael, *The Political Committee of the Reform Club* (1996).

A Short History of Parliament: England, Great Britain, the United Kingdom, Ireland & Scotland, ed. C. Jones (Woodbridge, 2009).

Smith, E.A., *Whig Principles and Party Politics: Earl Fitzwilliam and the Whig Party 1748–1833* (Manchester, 1975).

_____ *Lord Grey, 1764–1845* (Oxford, 1990).

Southgate, D., *The Passing of the Whigs 1832–1886* (1962).

Stewart, R., *The Foundation of the Conservative Party 1830–1867* (1978).

Sykes, A., *The Rise and Fall of British Liberalism 1776–1988* (1997).

Taylor, M., *The Decline of British Radicalism, 1847–1860* (Oxford, 1995).

Thomas, J.A., *The House of Commons 1832–1901: A Study of Its Economic and Functional Character* (Cardiff, 1939).

Thomas, W.E.S., *The Philosophical Radicals: Nine Studies in Theory and Practice, 1817–1841* (Oxford, 1979).

Trevelyan, G.M., *The Two-Party System in English Political History* (Oxford, 1926).

Trinder, B.S., *A Victorian MP and His Constituents* (Banbury, 1969).

Tyrrell, A., *Joseph Sturge and the Moral Radical Party in Early Victorian Britain* (1987).

Vernon, J., *Politics and the People: A Study in English Political Culture, c.1815–1867* (Cambridge, 1993).

Victorian Liberalism: Nineteenth-Century Political Thought and Practice, ed. R. Bellamy (1990).

Vincent, J.R., *The Formation of the Liberal Party, 1857–1868* (1966).

_____ *Pollbooks: How Victorians Voted* (Cambridge, 1967).

Walker-Smith, D., *The Protectionist Case in the 1840s* (Oxford, 1933).

Wasson, E.A., *Whig Renaissance: Lord Althorp and the Whig Party 1782–1845* (New York, 1987).

Watts, D., *Whigs, Radicals, and Liberals 1815–1914* (1995).

Watts, M.R., *The Dissenters: Vol. II, the Expansion of Evangelical Non-conformity* (Oxford, 1995).

Weaver, S.A.W., *John Fielden and the Politics of Popular Radicalism 1832–1847* (Oxford, 1987).

Webb, R.K., *Modern England from the 18th Century to the Present* (1980).

Who's Who of British Members of Parliament, ed. M. Stenton and S. Lee (4 vols, Hassocks, 1976).

Wolffe, J., *The Protestant Crusade in Great Britain 1829–1860* (Oxford, 1991).

Woodbridge, G., *The Reform Club, 1836–1978* (New York, 1978).

Wooton, G., *Pressure Groups in Britain 1720–1970* (1975).

Journal Articles and Essays in Edited Books

Anderson, G.M. and R.D. Tollison, 'Ideology, Interest Groups, and the Repeal of the Corn Laws', in *The Rise of Free Trade: Vol. 4, Free Trade Reappraised, the New Secondary Literature*, ed. C. Schonhardt-Bailey (1997), 38–58.

Arnstein, W., 'The Religious Issue in Mid-Victorian Politics: A Note on a Neglected Source', *Albion*, vi (1974), 134–43.

Aspinall, A., 'English Party Organization in the Early Nineteenth Century', *English Historical Review*, xli (1926), 389–411.

Aydelotte, W.O., 'The House of Commons in the 1840s', *American Historical Association Conference*, July 1953 (Washington, DC, 1953).

_____ 'Voting Patterns in the British House of Commons in the 1840s', *Comparative Studies in Society and History*, v (1962–3), 134–63.

_____ 'Constituency Influences on the House of Commons, 1841–1847', in *The History of Parliamentary Behavior*, ed. W.O. Aydelotte (Princeton, NJ, 1977).

Baer, Marc, 'Political Dinners in Whig, Radical, and Tory Westminster, 1780–1880,' in *Ideas and Institutions of Victorian Britain, Essays in Honour of George Kitson Clark*, ed. R. Robson (1967), 1–19.

Beales, D.E.D., 'Parliamentary Parties and the "Independent" Member, 1810–1860', in *Ideas and Institutions of Victorian Britain, Essays in Honour of George Kitson Clark*, ed. R. Robson (1967), 183–206.

_____ 'The Electorate Before and After 1832: The Right to Vote and the Opportunity', *Parliamentary History*, xi (1992), 79–98.

Beckett, J.V., 'A Back-Bench MP in the Eighteenth Century: Sir James Lowther of Whitehaven', *Parliamentary History*, i (1983), 79–98.

Bernstein, G.L., 'The Origins of Liberal Politics, 1830–1874', *Journal of British Studies*, xxviii (1989), 75–89.

Berrington, H., 'Partisanship and Dissidence in the Nineteenth Century House of Commons', *Parliamentary Affairs*, xxi (1968), 338–74.

_____ 'A Back-Bench MP in the Eighteenth-Century: Sir James Lowther of White-haven', *Parliamentary History*, i (1983), 79–83.

Best, G.F.A., 'The Whigs and the Church Establishment in the Age of Grey and Holland', *History*, xliv (1960), 103–18.

Brent, R., 'The Whigs and Protestant Dissent in the Decade of Reform: The Case of Church Rates, 1833–1841', *English Historical Review*, cii (1987), 887–910.

_____ 'God's Providence: Liberal Political Economy as Natural Theology at Oxford, 1825–60', in *Public and Private Doctrine: Essays in British History Presented to Maurice Cowling*, ed. M. Bentley (Cambridge, 1993), 85–107.

Brett, P., 'Political Dinners in Early Nineteenth-Century Britain', *History*, lxxxi (1996), 527–52.

Cahill, G., 'The Protestant Association and the Anti-Maynooth Agitation of 1845', *Catholic Historical Review*, xliii (1957), 273–308.

Clapham, J.H., 'The Last Years of the Navigation Acts I', *English Historical Review*, xxv (1910), 480–501.

_____ 'The Last Years of the Navigation Acts II', *English Historical Review*, xxv (1910), 687–707.

Close, D., 'The Formation of the Two-Party Alignment in the House of Commons between 1832 and 1840', *English Historical Review*, lxxxiv (1969), 257–77.

Condon, M., 'The Irish Church and the Reform Ministries', *Journal of British Studies*, iii (1964), 120–42.

Coohill, J., 'Parliamentary Guides, Political Identity, and the Presentation of Modern Politics, 1832–1846', *Parliamentary History*, xxii (2003), 263–84.

Cox, G.W., 'Development of a Party-Oriented Electorate', *British Journal of Political Science*, xvi (1986), 187–216.

Cromwell, V., 'The Losing of the Initiative by the House of Commons, 1780–1914', *Transactions of the Royal Historical Society*, 5th ser., xviii (1968), 1–17.

Davis, R.W., 'The Whigs and Religious Issues, 1830–5', in *Religion and Irreligion in Victorian Society: Essays in Honor of R.K. Webb*, ed. R.W. Davis and R.J. Helmstadter (1992), 29–50.

Dryer, F.A., 'The Whigs and the Political Crisis of 1845', *English Historical Review*, lxxx (1965), 514–37.

Eastwood, D., 'Robert Southey and the Meaning of Patriotism', *Journal of British Studies*, iii (1992), 205–87.

_____ 'The Age of Uncertainty: Britain in the Early-Nineteenth Century', *Transactions of the Royal Historical Society*, 6th ser., viii (1998), 91–115.

Ellens, J.P., 'Lord John Russell and the Church Rate Conflict: The Struggle for a Broad Church, 1834–1868', *Journal of British Studies*, xxvi (1987), 232–57.

Elvins, B., 'The Roots of the Liberal Party in Cornwall', *Parliamentary History*, xxiv (2005), 295–315.

Fairlie, S., 'The Nineteenth-Century Corn Law Re-considered', *Economic History Review*, xviii (1965), 562–75.

_____ 'The Corn Laws and British Wheat Protection, 1829–76', *Economic History Review*, xxii (1969), 562–73.

Finlayson, G.B.A.M., 'Joseph Parkes', *Bulletin of the Institute of Historical Research*, xlvi (1973), 186–201.

Fontana, B., 'Whigs and Liberals: The Edinburgh Review and the "Liberal Movement" in Nineteenth-Century Britain', in *Victorian Liberalism: Nineteenth-Century Political Thought and Practice*, ed. R. Bellamy (1990), 42–57.

Gambles, A., 'Rethinking the Politics of Protection: Conservatism and the Corn Laws, 1830–1852', *English Historical Review*, cxiii (1998), 928–52.

Gash, N., 'Peel and the Party System 1830–1850', *Transactions of the Royal Historical Society*, 5th ser., i (1951), 47–69.

_____ 'The Organization of the Conservative Party 1832–1846, Part I', *Parliamentary History*, i (1982), 137–59.

_____ 'The Organization of the Conservative Party 1832–1846, Part II', *Parliamentary History*, ii (1983), 131–52.

Graham, A.H., 'The Lichfield House Compact, 1835', *Irish Historical Studies*, xii (1961), 209–25.

Hawkins, A., ' "Parliamentary Government" and Victorian Political Parties, c.1830–1880', *English Historical Review*, civ (1989), 638–69.

Henderson, W.O., 'Charles Pelham Villiers', *History*, xxxvii (1952), 25–39.

Hilton, B., 'Peel: A Re-appraisal', *Historical Journal*, xxii (1979), 585–614.

_____ 'Whiggery, Religion and Social Reform: The Case of Lord Morpeth', *Historical Journal*, xxxvii (1994), 829–59.

Hoppen, K.T., 'The Franchise and Electoral Politics in England and Ireland 1832–1885', *History*, lxx (1985), 202–17.

Howe, A., 'Free Trade and the Victorians', in *The Rise of Free Trade: Vol. 4, Free Trade Reappraised, the New Secondary Literature*, ed. C. Schonhardt-Bailey (1997), 164–83.

_____ 'Free Trade and the Victorians,' in *Free Trade and Its Reception 1815–1960*, ed. Andrew Marrison (1998), 164–83.

Irwin, D.A., 'The Reciprocity Debate in Parliament, 1842–1846', in *Free Trade and Its Reception 1815–1960: Freedom and Trade, Volume I*, ed. A. Marrison (1998).

Jenkins, T.A., 'The Whips in the Early-Victorian House of Commons', *Parliamentary History*, xix (2000), 259–86.

Kemp, B., 'The General Election of 1841', *History*, xxxvii (1952), 146–57.

_____ 'Reflections on the Repeal of the Corn Laws', *Victorian Studies*, v (1962), 189–204.

Kitson Clark, G., 'The Repeal of the Corn Laws, and the Politics of the Forties', *Economic History Review* (2 vols, ser. 4, 1951), 1–13.

Kriegel, A.D., 'The Politics of the Whigs in Opposition, 1834–1835', *Journal of British Studies*, vii (1968), 65–91.

_____ 'Liberty and Whiggery in Early Nineteenth-Century England', *Journal of Modern History*, lii (1980), 253–78.

Ledger-Lomas, Michael, 'The Character of Pitt the Younger and Party Politics, 1830–1860,' *Historical Journal*, xlvii (2004), 641–61.

Lopatin, N., 'Political Unions and the Great Reform Act', *Parliamentary History*, x (1991), 105–23.

Lopatin-Lummis, N., ' "With All My Oldest and Native Friends". Joseph Parkes: Warwickshire Solicitor and Electoral Agent in the Age of Reform', *Parliamentary History*, xxvii (2008), 96–108.

Machin, G.I.T., 'The Maynooth Grant, the Dissenters and Disestablishment 1845–1847', *English Historical Review*, lxxxii (1967), 61–85.

Macintyre, A.D., 'Lord George Bentinck and the Protectionists: A Lost Cause?', *Transactions of the Royal Historical Society*, 5th ser., xxxix (1989), 141–65.

Maloney, J., 'Gladstone, Peel and the Corn Laws', in *Free Trade and Its Reception 1815–1960: Freedom and Trade, Volume I*, ed. A. Marrison (1998), 28–47.

Matthew, H.C.G., 'Disraeli, Gladstone, and the Politics of Mid-Victorian Budgets', *Historical Journal*, xxii (1979), 615–43.

McLean, I., 'Rational Choice and the Victorian Voter', *Political Studies*, xl (1992), 496–515.

Mermagen, R.P.H., 'The Established Church in England and Ireland: Principles of Church Reform', *Journal of British Studies*, iii (1964), 143–7.

Newbould, I., 'William IV and the Dismissal of the Whigs, 1834', *Canadian Journal of History*, xi (1976), 311–30.

_____ 'Whiggery and the Dilemma of Reform', *Bulletin of the Institute for Historical Research*, liii (1980), 229–41.

_____ 'The Emergence of a Two-Party System in England from 1830–1841: Roll Call and Reconsideration', *Parliaments, Estates, and Representation*, v (1985), 25–31.

_____ 'Whiggery and the Growth of Party 1830–1841: Organization and the Challenge of Reform', *Parliamentary History*, iv (1985), 137–56.

Nockles, P., 'Church or Protestant Sect? The Church of Ireland, High Churchmanship, and the Oxford Movement, 1822–1869', *Historical Journal*, xli (1998), 457–93.

Norman, E.R., 'The Maynooth Question of 1845', *Irish Historical Studies*, xv (1967), 407–37.

O'Boyle, L., 'The Image of the Journalist in France, Germany, and England, 1815–1848', *Comparative Studies in Society and History*, x (1967–8), 290–317.

O'Gorman, F., 'Electoral Deference in "Unreformed" England: 1760–1832', *Journal of Modern History*, lvi (1984), 391–429.

_____ 'Party Politics in the Early Nineteenth Century', *English Historical Review*, cii (1987), 63–84.

_____ 'Campaign Rituals and Ceremonies: The Social Meaning of Elections in England 1780–1860', *Past & Present*, no. 135 (1992), 79–115.

O'Neill, M., 'A Backbencher on Parliamentary Reform, 1831–1832', *Historical Journal*, xxiii (1980), 539–63.

Parks, S., 'The Osborn Collection: A Sixth Biennial Report', *Yale University Library Gazette*, liv (1980), 125.

Phillips, J.A., 'The Structure of Electoral Politics in Unreformed England', *Journal of British Studies*, xix (1979), 76–100.

_____ 'Popular Politics in Unreformed England', *Journal of Modern History*, lii (1980), 599–625.

_____ 'Parliamentary Parties and Municipal Politics: 1835 and the Party System', in *Computing Parliamentary History, George III to Victoria*, ed. J.A. Phillips (Edinburgh, 1994), 48–85.

_____ and C. Wetherell, 'The Great Reform Bill of 1832 and the Rise of Partisanship', *Journal of Modern History*, lxiii (1991), 621–46.

_____ 'The Great Reform Act and the Political Modernization of England', *American Historical Review*, c (1995), 411–36.

Ramm, A., 'The Parliamentary Context of Cabinet Government', *English Historical Review*, xcix (1984), 739–69.

Ransome, M., 'Some Recent Studies in the Composition of the House of Commons', *University of Birmingham Historical Journal*, vi (1957–8), 132–48.

Rivers, I., 'Biographical Dictionaries and Their Uses from Bayle to Chalmers', in *Books and Their Readers in Eighteenth-Century England: New Essays*, ed. I. Rivers (2001), 135–69.

Sainty, J. and G.W. Cox, 'The Identification of Government Whips in the House of Commons 1830–1905', *Parliamentary History*, xvi (1997), 339–58.

Salmon, P., 'The English Reform Legislation, 1831–32', in *The History of Parliament: The House of Commons 1820–32*, ed. D.R. Fisher (2009), 374–412.

_____ 'The House of Commons, 1801–1911', in *A Short History of Parliament*, ed. C. Jones (2009), 249–70.

Schonhardt-Bailey, C., 'Linking Constituency Interests to Legislative Voting Behaviour: The Role of District Economic and Electoral Composition in the Repeal of the Corn Laws', in *Computing Parliamentary History, George III to Victoria*, ed. J.A. Phillips (Edinburgh, 1994), 86–118.

_____ 'Party and Interests in the British Parliament of 1841–47,' *British Journal of Political Science*, xxxiii (2003), 581–605.

Smith, E.A., 'The Election Agent in English Politics, 1734–1832', *English Historical Review*, lxxxiv (1969), 12–35.

Thomas, J.A., 'The System of Registration and the Development of Party Organization, 1832–1870', *History*, xxxv (1950), 81–98.

Thompson, A.F., 'Gladstone's Whips and the General Election of 1868', *English Historical Review*, lxiii (1948), 189–200.

Thompson, F.M.L., 'Whigs and Liberals in the West Riding, 1830–1860', *English Historical Review*, lxxiv (1959), 214–39.

Todd, David, 'John Bowring and the Dissemination of Free Trade,' *Historical Journal*, li (2008), 373–97.

Turner, Michael, ' "The Bonaparte of Free Trade" and the Anti-Corn Law League,' *Historical Journal*, xli (1998), 1011–34.

Verdier, D., 'Between Party and Faction: The Politics behind the Repeal of the Corn Laws', in *The Rise of Free Trade: Vol. 4, Free Trade Reappraised, the New Secondary Literature*, ed. C. Schonhardt-Bailey (1997), 309–38.

Wasson, E.A., 'The House of Commons, 1660–1945: Parliamentary Families and the Political Elite', *English Historical Review*, cvi (1991), 635–51.

_____ 'The Whigs and the Press, 1800–50', *Parliamentary History*, xxv (2006), 66–87.

Woolley, S.F., 'The Personnel of the Parliament of 1833', *English Historical Review*, liii (1938), 240–62.

Theses

Clarke, J.C., 'The Fortunes of the Ellice Family: From Business to Politics 1760–1860', University of Oxford PhD, 1973.

Close, D., 'The General Elections of 1835 and 1837 in England and Wales', University of Oxford PhD, 1967.

Coohill, J., 'Ideas of the Liberal Party: Perceptions, Agendas, and Liberal Politics in the House of Commons, 1832–1852', University of Oxford PhD, 1998.

Eastwood, D., 'Governing Rural England: Authority and Social Order in Oxfordshire, 1780–1840', University of Oxford PhD, 1985.

Gambles, A., 'The Boundaries of Political Economy: Tory Economic Argument, 1809–1847', University of Oxford PhD, 1996.

Glynn, J.K., 'The Private Member of Parliament 1833–1868', University of London PhD, 1949.

Gurowich, P.M., 'Party and Independence in the Early and Mid-Victorian House of Commons: Aspects of Political Theory and Practice 1832–68, Considered with Special Reference to the Period 1852–68', University of Cambridge PhD, 1986.

Pflaum, A.M., 'The Parliamentary Career of Thomas S. Duncombe, 1826–1861', University of Minnesota PhD, 1975.

Salmon, P.J., 'Electoral Reform at Work: Local Politics and National Parties, 1832–1841', University of Oxford PhD, 1997.

Index

Please refer to the Notes on the Text (p. ix) for an explanation of how party and political terms are used in this index.

Ireland (cont.)
  jury bill for 68
  landlords 68
  leases 68
  manufactures 68
  national education 68, 113, 115
  poor laws 68
  religious affiliation 115
  religious census 114
  tenant right 68
  Tithe Bill 80
  union with Great Britain *see* Union, Great
    Britain and Ireland
Irish Church Temporalities Bill 116

jacobin/jacobite 1, 17
Jenkins, Richard 54
Jenkins, Terry 82, 149
Jervis, John 36
Jewish disabilities 23, 65, 70, 133
Jocelyn, Viscount 52
Johnston, Alexander 108, 184
Johnston, Andrew 147
Johnston, Priscilla 108
Johnstone, Sir John Jervis Bempde 36
juries and the jury system 71
justice system 71
juvenile offenders 71

Keane, Richard 126
Kemp, Thomas 35, 37
Kendal 15, 60, 83
Kendal and Westmorland Freeholders 60
Kennedy, James 35, 37
Kent, East 160
Kerry, County 23
Kiernan, J. 57
Kilkenny 172
Kilmarnock 31, 184
King, Lord 96
Kingdom, James 57
King's Lynn 34

Labouchère, Henry 187, 194–6
Labour Party 4
laissez-faire 170
Lambeth 57, 85, 91, 97, 103, 162, 163, 165, 186
Larpent, George 87
Le Marchant, Sir Denis 17, 56, 78, 83–9, 164, 189, 190, 192
Leader, J. Temple 33
Leeds 52, 56, 148, 151, 172, 178
Leeds Parliamentary Reform Association 60
Leicester 75, 145
Leicestershire South 39
Leigh, Rev. W. 108
Lennox, Lord William 34
Leominster 25, 61
Lester, Benjamin 39
Lethbridge, Sir Thomas 19
liberal (as general political term) 1, 14, 71

liberal anglicanism/liberal anglicans 3, 5, 141, 147
Liberal Brigade 99–102
Liberal-Conservative 39
Liberal Party
  constituent political groups 2, 13–45
  contemporaries' conceptions of 1–16, 204–7
  control 77–98
  definition of 2, 6, 13–45, 204–7
  development of 1, 4, 13–45
  Finance Committee 86
  Gladstonian 2, 74
  historiography 1–9, 204–7
  management 82–96
  organisation 77–109, 204–7
  pre-Gladstonian 6, 114
  'union of' 61, 99–109
Liberal Registration Association 91
liberal toryism 17
liberal value system (Parry) 2, 5, 46, 75, 205
liberalism 1–10, 204–7
Liberals (as Liberal Party subgroup) 2, 13, 14, 17, 19–45, 64–74, 107, 115, 119–20, 122, 128, 140, 143–4, 146, 157–9, 177, 179, 183, 187, 192, 195, 200
Lichfield House 99, 102–9
Lichfield, Lord 102
Lincoln 89
Lincolnshire 200
Lincolnshire North 165, 191
Lincolnshire South 173, 177, 186, 191, 196
Littleton, E.J. 50, 55, 84, 102, 108
Littleton, Edward 55
Liverpool 151, 157
local courts 71
local government 52
London 6, 79, 83–5, 87, 88, 90–1, 96, 149, 186, 195–6
Louth 30, 43, 168
Luddism/Luddites 178
Lushington, Charles 149
Lushington, Steven 186–7
Lynn Regis 34
Lytton, Edward 89

Macauley, T.B. 168, 187
Machin, G.I.T. 133
Macintyre, Angus 108
magistrates 71
Maldon 139, 199, 200
Manchester 85, 100, 139, 149, 181
Manchester Chamber of Commerce 48, 180, 184
Mandler, Peter 2, 3, 5, 83, 84, 201, 202, 205
Mangles, Captain 87
Manners-Sutton, Charles 57, 103–9
Manual of Queen Victoria's Second Parliament 24
manufacturing interest 173
Marlow 38
Marshall, William 25, 61, 96
Marylebone 52, 60, 191
Marylebone Reform Electoral Sub-committee 60
Matheson, James 88